VIAPOLITICS

VIAPOLITICS

Borders, Migration, and the

Power of Locomotion

- - - - - - - - - - - - - -

Edited by

WILLIAM WALTERS, CHARLES HELLER,

AND LORENZO PEZZANI

DUKE UNIVERSITY PRESS · *Durham and London* · 2022

© 2022 Duke University Press

Designed by Matthew Tauch
Typeset in Huronia Latin and Alegreya Sans by
Westchester Book Group

Library of Congress Cataloging-in-Publication Data
Names: Walters, William, [date] editor. | Heller, Charles, [date]
editor. | Pezzani, Lorenzo, [date] editor.
Title: Viapolitics : borders, migration, and the power of locomotion /
edited by William Walters, Charles Heller, and Lorenzo Pezzani.
Description: Durham : Duke University Press, 2021. | Includes
bibliographical references and index.
Identifiers: LCCN 2021012717 (print) | LCCN 2021012718 (ebook)
ISBN 9781478013372 (hardcover)
ISBN 9781478014287 (paperback)
ISBN 9781478021599 (ebook)
Subjects: LCSH: Immigrants—Transportation. | Border security—
Social aspects. | Human smuggling. | Refugees—Legal status, laws,
etc. | BISAC: SOCIAL SCIENCE / Human Geography | SOCIAL
SCIENCE / Emigration & Immigration
Classification: LCC JV6201 .V53 2021 (print) | LCC JV6201 (ebook) |
DDC 388/.04208691—dc23
LC recordavailableathttps:// lccn.loc.gov/2021012717
LC ebook recordavailableathttps:// lccn.loc.gov/2021012718

Cover art: Djordje Balmazovic (Škart collective) in
collaboration with asylum seekers in Banja Koviljača camp
in Serbia, NN, *Damascus, Syria*, 2015. Courtesy of the artist.

CONTENTS

Part III: The Geophysics of Migration

ACKNOWLEDGMENTS

The road to *Viapolitics* has been long and winding, and we have incurred many debts along the way. William Walters began reflecting on the absence of vehicles and routes in migration and border studies, and forging the concept of viapolitics to draw attention to them, in a series of lectures and articles starting in 2011. Charles Heller and Lorenzo Pezzani first encountered this concept in 2013, which helped them capture the ambivalent role of boats both as the means illegalized migrants use to contest exclusionary border policies by crossing the sea and as the object of border control. From then on, we began a dialogue around viapolitics and embarked on a voyage through which we expanded our understanding of this concept and its dimensions in different directions. Mat Coleman was engaged in early discussions about this book idea. We thank him for his insights and encouragement.

Because we felt viapolitics offered us a lens that allowed us to see new things in the world, we decided to invite a group of scholars we admire—and whose work already exemplified the attention to vehicles and routes we sought to foster—to travel with us and try this approach out collectively. We are profoundly grateful to all our contributors for their enthusiasm and readiness to explore this viapolitical gaze with us, which has led to inspiring chapters. We thank them for the commitment and patience they have shown throughout this book project.

We are grateful also to Courtney Berger, our editor at Duke University Press, and her assistant, Sandra Korn. Their support for this book on its journey has been unwavering. Three anonymous referees provided incredibly careful feedback and supportive criticism on earlier versions of the manuscript. We feel the book has been considerably enriched by their engagement. Our editorial work on this book has been facilitated in part by funding from the Faculty of Public Affairs, Carleton University, for which we are grateful. We thank Elena Gwynne for skillfully producing an index for this book at short notice. We also thank Rhys Steckle for his work as a research assistant formatting our chapters. It is a happy coincidence that his excellent doctoral work on the colonization roads of Upper Canada has come to completion at the same time as *Viapolitics*.

As editors working in three different countries and on two continents, we have done most of our work via digital platforms but occasionally in person at conferences and workshops. We are grateful for the opportunities that the 2014 Borders in Globalization opening conference in Ottawa and the 2016 conference on new materialities in migration and border studies at Ludwig-Maximilians Universität in Munich offered us to present our work as a team.

We developed many of the ideas that fed into this book project and in particular our introductory essay in various formats and settings. William Walters was fortunate to give presentations at the Heyman Center for the Humanities, Columbia University, a workshop on ethnographies of control at University of Stockholm, a workshop on migration routes at Brown University, the new borderlands conference at Carl von Ossietzky University, Oldenburg, the Flying University of Transnational Humanities summer school, Hanyang University, Seoul, and public lectures at the University of Zürich, University of Neuchâtel, and the Zolberg Institute of Migration and Mobility at the New School, New York. He thanks colleagues for those kind invitations and all who offered comments and suggestions that have helped to sharpen his thinking about vehicles and politics. He has also benefited greatly from working with some excellent graduate students who have shared his enthusiasm for this topic. In particular he thanks Leslie Muñoz, Amaha Senu, Victoria Simmons, Rhys Steckle, and Ugur Yildiz. Finally, he acknowledges the debt he owes to Christina Gabriel and Zoë Walters for their unfailing love and patience while he worked on *Viapolitics*. He also thanks Christina for being an indispensable interlocutor on migration topics over the years.

Charles Heller and Lorenzo Pezzani have presented their research on viapolitics as it emerged out of their collaborative Forensic Oceanography project on numerous occasions. They are grateful for each of these invitations, all of which cannot be acknowledged here. In particular, the Kosmos Workshop titled "Cataloging Logistics: Migration, Humanitarianism, Borders" that was held in May 2016 at Humboldt University in Berlin brought together several colleagues—in particular Manuela Bojadzijev, Sandro Mezzadra, and Giorgio Grappi—whose critical logistical gaze has contributed to their understanding of viapolitics. They also had the pleasure of discussing many of the ideas central to this volume, especially those concerning the way migrant routes and trajectories are represented, with Thomas Keenan and Sorhab Mohebbi in the frame of events associated with their traveling exhibition *It's Obvious from the Map* at the Istanbul Design Biennale, at Redcat in Los Angeles, and at the European Graduate School in Malta.

Charles Heller would like to thank several friends and colleagues with whom he has shared thoughts on vehicles, routes, and infrastructures and the geophysics of power over the years. In particular, he thanks Cristina Del Biaggio for sharing her knowledge of the Alpine frontier; Olivier Clochard, Philippe Rekacewicz, Lucie Bacon, and Davide Lagarde for their exchanges on the cartography of migrants' trajectories during the 2019 International Festival of Geography in Saint-Dié; Joris Schapendonk and Mehdi Aliouar for their thinking of and in movement; Emmanuel Mbolela (whom he met at a conference at the University of Geneva), and Mamadou Bah (whom he met during the KFDA festival in Brussels), for exemplifying the way the narration of trajectories allows us to cut through the boundaries of time and space and weave new political connections. He is grateful for the support of the Swiss National Science Foundation, which has supported several of his research projects during the time of writing.

Lorenzo Pezzani would also like to thank the organizers and participants of the April 2019 "Imaginative Mobilities" seminar at the New School in New York, where he presented a draft of the introduction to this volume. Some of the ideas that have informed this project have been developed in the frame of his "Hostile Environments" project, which has been supported by a Small Grant of the British Academy and has been presented at the Royal College of Art and at Birkbeck Law School in London; at Bard College and at Columbia University Graduate School of Architecture, Planning and Preservation in New York; at the Oxford Migration Studies Society Conference; and at ar/ge Kunst in Bozen/Bolzano, Italy, and z33 in Hasselt, Belgium, as an exhibition and a series of events. He would also like to thank his colleagues and students at Goldsmiths, University of London, whose insights have greatly enriched this project.

Our thinking has been deeply inspired by the political imagination of those who are constantly forging new infrastructures of movement in the face of restrictive migration policies and violent borders. Their obstinacy and inventiveness, often exercised at the cost of their own lives, has shown us that viapolitics is not only an analytical category: for many, it is a daily practice of making and remaking the world, of drawing new connections where there only appeared to be walls.

Viapolitics: An Introduction | William Walters, Charles Heller, and Lorenzo Pezzani

A Tale of Two Ships

What is a vehicle? What is a route? This book accords the vehicle, its infrastructure, and the material geographies it navigates a central place in the study of contemporary migration and borders. We argue that these elements afford us a privileged vantage point from which to interrogate today's highly contentious migration politics, while at the same time cutting through some of the conceptual boundaries that have come to structure migration studies. Scholars, activists, and publics have come to recognize that the border and the camp are not just elements in the infrastructure of controlling (mobile) populations but key concepts, symbols, and points of view. We argue it is time to grant the vehicle a similar status and recognize it as a key site of knowledge and struggle in migratory processes. We call this the moment of *viapolitics*. This book assembles a remarkable, transdisciplinary group of scholars with whom we explore this concept, developing it through empirically rich and diverse cases and in connection with a range of methods that includes archival research, critical cartography, ethnography, and forensic architecture. But we think concepts are better approached in context and from the ground up. So, we begin this book with a tale of two ships.

On February 21, 2011, Canada's then prime minister, Stephen Harper, was photographed alongside his minister for citizenship and immigration, Jason Kenney, standing on board a rusty freighter, the MV *Ocean Lady* (see figure 1.1). The

FIGURE I.1 · Prime Minister Stephen Harper (center), Minister of Citizenship and Immigration Jason Kenney (right), and Canadian Border Services Agency official Ivan Peterson (left) stand on board the MV *Ocean Lady* for a photo opportunity in Delta, British Columbia, February 21, 2011. Source: Canadian Press/Jonathan Hayward.

photograph is somewhat peculiar for the fact that the two politicians are positioned at the stern of the ship, looking backward, and not at its bow. After all, ancient political thought gave us the political metaphor of the ruler as helmsman of the ship of state (Winner 1980, 129; Foucault 2007): we are accustomed to thinking of our leaders as navigating a forward path. Why are Harper and Kenney gazing backward, as though transfixed by the wake of the ship?

Their unusual positioning only makes sense once we learn that this was a carefully staged photo opportunity. In fact, it was only the first of several occasions in which the *Ocean Lady* would be used by government ministers as a backdrop for migration-related media events. The ship is not at sea but firmly anchored in port. In all probability the two politicians were standing at the stern so that the frame could include the name *Ocean Lady*, which is emblazoned across its rusty hull. The *Ocean Lady* had come to prominence in Canadian and international media two years earlier, in October 2009, when it arrived off the coast of Victoria, British Columbia, carrying seventy-six Sri Lankan refugees seeking asylum in Canada. The passengers had fled renewed violent conflict between the Sri Lankan state and the Tamil Tigers, and decided to attempt to seek refuge in Canada, where there is a large ethnic Tamil Sri Lankan population (*National Post* 2012). However, because such travel has been made increasingly difficult by unattainable visa requirements and carrier sanctions that bar the majority of the populations of the Global South from accessing safe means of transport to and legally entering states of the Global North, they had to rely on a smuggling network to which, according to the testimony of journalist Maran Nagarasa (who was among the travelers), each paid $40,000 (Brosnahan 2014). The rusty cargo ship allowed the passengers to cross thousands of kilometers of the ocean's liquid expanse, blending in with global maritime traffic that connects the world map. In this way, the *Ocean Lady* reminds us of the capacity of shipping to effectively transform the world's oceans into a global border line, through which all coastal states are potentially in contact with each other. It also reminds us of the capacity of the cramped and often difficult conditions on board a ship to transform people: Nagarasa reports that on some days he felt such despair that he considered jumping overboard, yet he took strength from helping fellow travelers, and that over time a bond developed among the travelers (*Toronto Star* 2014). After journeying forty-five days in often stormy weather, the passengers saw a plane with a Canadian maple leaf flying overhead. Many waved with joy, taking this as a sign they were heading to Canada and safe haven (*Toronto Star* 2014). "That night we all slept peacefully" reported Nagarasa, despite the grim conditions on board. The aircraft, however, signaled less the safe arrival the passengers longed for than the opening act in a state-crafted process of violent reception that starkly materialized the following morning: "When we opened our eyes the next morning, there were people boarding the ship and pointing guns at us." It transpired that Canadian authorities had been tipped off by foreign intelligence services and had tracked the ship for three days. On October 17, the *Ocean Lady* was stopped by the Canadian Navy and boarded by an RCMP emergency response team off the west coast of Vancouver Island (*National Post* 2012). While claiming asylum following a highly militarized disembarkation, the migrants were subjected to a lengthy detention process and a heightened level of scrutiny that seemed purposefully designed to send a deterrent message with regard to any future ship arrivals (*National Post* 2012).

Media coverage of the ship incident in Canada was intense and was typically framed in terms of themes of illegality and the suspect identities and motives of the migrants. In the hands of many in the press, the rust on the hull of the *Ocean Lady* was not innocent but conferred a stain on the motives and identity of its passengers (Mountz 2010). The fact that the original ship's name had been painted over and hidden only heightened its mystery (Bradimore and Bauder 2011, 653). Speculation about connections to terrorism was rife. The negative tone of the coverage was strengthened by government ministers who repeated claims about the abuse of Canada's asylum process and sought to frame the incident in terms of a problem of human smuggling and organized crime (Bradimore and Bauder 2011). After having enabled its passengers to cross the oceans, the *Ocean Lady* served as both stage and prop in the political theater in terms of which the Conservative government had moved to dramatize questions of migration and asylum in recent years. The images, like the ship they portray, traveled far and wide, accompanying stories about the incident but also the wider field of policies and laws to which the incident was quickly attached. As Stephanie Silverman (2014) explains, this and other similar ship incidents provided fuel for the government to boost its campaign to make the deterrence of unwanted migrants a key political issue and to formalize its use of mandatory immigration detention for a one-year period.

Yet as prominent as it became, this incident was far from being the only way in which boats and migrants were appearing before the Canadian public. Less than three years before the arrival of the *Ocean Lady* on the Pacific coast, by a twist of fate, a not dissimilar boat incident was being commemorated by the very same prime minister who stood on its deck. In this case, however, it was a story of nonarrival. The ship in question, the *Komagata Maru*, was a Japanese steamship that had been chartered in 1914 by Gurdit Singh, a Sikh of Punjabi origins and a sympathizer of the anticolonial Ghadar Party. Renisa Mawani discusses the ship's trajectory at length in her chapter as well as her book, *Across Oceans of Law*. We evoke it here briefly to illustrate the very different ways in which vessels can become vehicles of politics within the migration field.

The *Komagata Maru* left Hong Kong with 376 passengers on board, mostly Sikhs, and after stops in China and Japan finally reached the port of Vancouver. There, its passengers were denied entry on the basis of the "continuous journey regulation," which prohibited immigration to those who had not reached Canadian shores with a direct trip. This was one of many legal tools forged by white colonies—particularly within the British Empire—to impose a differential access to mobility for racialized populations at the turn of the nineteenth century (McKeown 2008). Since steamship companies, under pressure from the Canadian government, did not operate a direct transit from India to Canada (Johnston 1989), this regulation de facto banned legal entry to Indians, who at the time were British subjects as much as Canadians. It was precisely this differential access to mobility with which the British Empire was endowing its subjects that Gurdit Singh and his fellow passengers had set out to challenge with their trip, but without success (Mongia 1999). Eventually the ship was forced to return to Calcutta where, following a violent struggle with the British colonial administration, nineteen passengers were killed and 210 were imprisoned

(Balachandran 2016, 190–91; Mawani 2016). The experience of the journey was transformative for those who survived, and many subsequently became radical anticolonial and left-wing activists (Balachandran 2016, 194–95).

Almost a century afterward, in August 2008, Harper offered an apology "on behalf of the Government of Canada" for the "hardship" caused to its passengers by the "detention and turning away of the *Komagata Maru*," and six years later his ministers unveiled a commemorative stamp on the occasion of the centennial anniversary of the event (see figure I.2), which has been since remembered as a black mark on Canadian history. It is truly remarkable that the same government could seek to commemorate and even atone for a wrong committed in 1914 while taking steps that appeared to be repeating that wrong once again—it is remarkable as well that media coverage rarely managed to connect these two worlds. It would seem that a particular conceptual border was being reinforced, one that allowed the exclusionary racism in operation against the *Komagata Maru* and its passengers to be relegated to an aberrant past with no connection to present-day events. Partha Chatterjee (1993) has called this tactic

FIGURE I.2 · At an event in Toronto on May 6, 2014, a stamp is unveiled commemorating the one hundredth anniversary of the *Komagata Maru* incident. Minister of Citizenship and Immigration Jason Kenney is second from the right, accompanied by other cabinet ministers, politicians, and the CEO of Canada Post, Deepak Chopra (far left).

the "rule of colonial difference," an expression with which he refers to how colonial modes of governance are often conveniently consigned to the museum of past horrors, and simply thought of as a temporary aberration from the universally valid—and now supposedly fully realized—principle of the modern state.

Will some future Canadian government offer official apologies for the treatment accorded to the passengers of the *Ocean Lady*? Will their case and that vessel also appear on stamps and in museums of immigration? Will their stories serve as salutary lessons in tolerance and atonement? We can't say. What we can say with some confidence is that in both these cases, past and present, there existed an antiship of state: the ship as political danger, the ship as disorder, and even as the signifier of a sovereignty under threat, while eventually becoming, after many decades, neutralized and reappropriated within official narratives as a symbol of atonement. What we can also say is that placing *Ocean Lady* and *Komagata Maru* on the same timeline, one on which these vessels appear conceptually side by side despite the temporal distance and different historical context that separates them, allows us to interrogate these cases in a different light.

Viapolitics

We introduce this collection of essays with this tale of two ships because it illustrates in microcosm the three dimensions we seek to bring into conversation when we speak of viapolitics. As we use it, "via" has a threefold field of reference.

First, "via" foregrounds vehicles of migration ("I am traveling via ship"). These ships are first of all vehicles, adapted for locomotion across the liquid territory of the ocean, which their passengers use to reach a distant land. Access to these vehicles, however, is distributed unequally and contested—policing access to means of transportation is one of the privileged ways in which countries of the Global North seek to bar access to their territories to populations of the Global South. At sea, the ships become the moving location of a collective experience, where new bonds and identities are forged, as Mawani shows for the *Komagata Maru*, but where land-based social hierarchies might also have been in part reproduced or even intensified. The vehicle and its journey is a space-time of hope and fear, a compression chamber for the transformation of self, but in which the self that will come out on the other shore is undetermined. Note also that once these ships get caught in the spotlight of media attention, they become sites of political controversy and dissensus, public forums that often crystallize wider tensions and disputes concerning migration (Latour 2005a, 2005b; Callon, Lascoumes, and Barthe 2009; Weizman 2010; Venturini 2010).

Second, "via" highlights routes and the infrastructures that underpin them ("We are traveling to Vancouver via Shanghai"). Indeed, we note that the etymology of "via" comes from the Latin word for road or way. As Elisabeth Povinelli (2011) aptly puts it, routes "are the condition of previous circulatory matrixes and become part of the matrix that decides which other kinds of things can pass through and be made sense of within this figured space." The case of the *Komagata Maru* demonstrates how routes can become sites of politics in their own right: the "continuous journey" regulation made the route into a tool of exclusion in the hands of the Canadian state, which the Indian passengers sought to contest. Vehicles and routes, however, do not exist in isolation but are inseparable from broader "mobility systems" within which they are embedded (Urry 2007). They are dependent, in other words, on networked infrastructures of migration (Xiang and Lindquist 2014). In the case of our two ships, these infrastructures include ports, logistical standards, and administrative procedures that allowed (or hindered) their navigation, but also the smuggling networks and the migrants' collective knowledge of circulation that is forged en route.

Third, "via" speaks to the geophysical environments ("They arrived via sea") across which vehicles, routes, and infrastructures extend, and which, despite easily fading into the background of our attention, profoundly shape viapolitics. The ship stories described above epitomize the ambivalent role of oceans, which at once connect and divide (McKeown 2011). Ships, like all means of locomotion, involve a taming and mobilizing of the earth's forces to enable movement (Law 1984), in this case the "mobile forces in the air and water" (Semple 1911, 292). But states also seek to harness the "geopower" (Grosz 2012) of the oceans to turn them into an extensive border zone. The form of power states exercise over this liquid terrain (Elden 2010) is both constrained and enabled by the element of water.

These ship stories, then, exemplify the lively and at times violent interaction between people on the move and the vehicles, networked infrastructures, and geophysical environments across which they travel. To this contested entanglement we give the name *viapolitics*. Foucault (1990) famously invented the concept of biopolitics to identify the historical threshold when vital life comes to be constituted as an object of power/knowledge and a site of political calculation and intervention. By a similar logic, we propose viapolitics to name those situations when the space-time of travel and the vehicles enabling it become objects of contention and transformation, simultaneously a means through which people seek to move and a means through which their movement is governed. Viapolitics, then, for us is by definition located in a field of tension and conflict involving states and migrants but also many other actors, such as transport companies, who play an ambivalent role. Through viapolitics, it is precisely these conflictual encounters and the friction (Tsing 2005) they generate that we seek to bring to the fore.

To be sure, we are not the first to observe that vehicles, infrastructures and routes, and geophysical environments matter for the study of struggles over borders and migration, or that human movement is never unassisted but always mediated by particular body/machine interactions that affect culture and politics. Rather than claim absolute novelty, we envisage viapolitics as a concept and approach that may serve as a point of convergence for critical and innovative research in the fields of migration and border studies and enhance dialogue with many others. Among the many strands of research that have explored these issues and have shaped our thinking, the interdisciplinary field of mobilities studies is the one we are probably most indebted to (Sheller and Urry 2006; Cresswell 2006; Urry 2007; Adey 2017).[1] This approach has been crucial in challenging the sedentarist assumptions embedded in much social thought, interrogating mobility as an accomplishment that is always contextual, embodied, and enacted by means of specific assemblages of systems, devices, and practices. While the concept of mobility is at times employed in a neutral and descriptive way that risks homogenizing the many different conditions and statuses under which people move (McNevin 2019), we have been drawn to the work of scholars who have foregrounded inequality and unevenness in how people move, and who moves, where and when (Cresswell 2010; Sheller 2018; Merriman 2019). It is therefore fair to say that a great deal of our thinking in framing this book has been inspired by this mobilities turn, which has generated important work also within migration studies.[2]

Yet there are at least two reasons why we have not framed this intervention as a study of mobilities, but insist on the specificity of viapolitics. First, a question of language and normativity. Few terms are more laden with positive connotations today than "mobility" (Walters 2015a; McNevin 2019). While scholars have criticized liberal ideologies that simplistically equate mobility with freedom and liberty (Adey 2017, 112), there can be no doubting that, like "flexibility" or "resilience," mobility has become a keyword of what Pierre Bourdieu and Loïc Wacquant (2001) call neoliberalism's "planetary vulgate." In proposing the concept of viapolitics, we want to induce a stutter; we want a term that moves critical thought "to the outside" (Foucault 2007, 116–18). Second, in speaking of viapolitics we emphasize not migratory mobilities per se, but something more specific: all those situations where movement and its mediations are called into question and become a focus of struggle and politics. This "contentious mobility" (Sodero and Scott 2016) is what via-*politics* is made of. Methodologically, this means that while we share with mobility studies an interest in "what happens on the move" (Cresswell and Merriman 2011), viapolitics is further drawn to events, ruptures, and controversies where the black box of migration is opened up.[3]

If we are both inspired by and distinct from mobility studies, we do not locate viapolitics comfortably within the existing boundaries of migration and border studies. Quite the contrary. We use the term "locomotion" in our title, a term that—as far as we are aware—has no theoretical status within either migration or mobility studies. The etymology of locomotion derives from "loco," meaning place, and "motion." The *Oxford English Dictionary* clarifies that it applies equally to the "action or *power* of movement" between places of humans and animals as much as vehicles. Locomotion then, like mobility, connotes a movement between places without carrying the baggage associated rightly or wrongly with migration (e.g., that occurs between countries). At the same time, more than terms like mobility or migration, it suggests an intimate connection between moving and the physical mechanisms—including bodily practices—that sustain movement. In some uses, a locomotive is, after all, another word for a railway train.[4]

Our claim is that many aspects of the politics of migration will look quite different when we enter the migration assemblage along the gangplank or through the cabin door. Our hope is that by attending to spaces, experiences, and machineries that have been at once vital but at the same time relegated to scenery or backdrops or entirely neglected in the study of human migration, some of the limits of migration and border studies will be challenged. One of the challenges we have in mind concerns the regulation of knowledge about migration. We are certainly not alone if we note that in recent years, with the burgeoning rise of studies and analyses dedicated to human mobility, migration and borders have become institutionalized objects of study, with constantly expanding but clearly defined boundaries. While this "becoming discipline" of migration and border studies has allowed for the proliferation of research dedicated to those topics, it has also had a "disciplining effect" (Garelli and Tazzioli 2013) on our way of understanding all the phenomena we now designate as migration, instituting and naturalizing a number of conceptual boundaries. Oppositions like free versus forced, internal versus international, and citizen versus alien have come to structure our thinking in the same way as disciplinary demarcations, geographical frames of analysis, and historical compartmentalizations have. As a result, forms of human mobility that have occurred in different temporal and geographical contexts (such as the slave trade across the Black Atlantic, Indian and Chinese indentured migration, transatlantic migration from Europe to the "New World," post–World War II boat-people "crises") are treated as distinct and rarely connecting fields of inquiry, as the myopia of the Canadian discourse that allowed politicians and journalists to compartmentalize two boat arrivals with eerie similarities reveals in our opening ship stories. Viapolitics prompts the contributions in this book to trace paths across these conceptual walls, debordering the study of migration and borders from that of the wider world, and offering thick cuts through time and space as we follow means of transport and the way they have been used, perceived, and governed.

Two crucial boundaries that we seek to transgress through viapolitics and in assembling the chapters in this volume are precisely those of time and space. Temporally, viapolitics is a powerful antidote to the divide that marks research on migration and borders between, on the one hand, various social sciences focusing on the present and, on the other, historiographies focusing on the distant past. This split makes it extremely difficult to connect the present to broader trajectories of change in terms of human mobility and its government. By starting from the vehicles used for movement, instead, our contributors—who range across the historian/social science divide—are able to offer genealogies of movement and its control that connect these different temporalities and challenge the presentism of much migration, border, and mobility studies. Spatially, and building very much on the mobilities as well as transnationalism turns in the social sciences, we seek to challenge the methodological nationalism that still characterizes certain areas of migration studies and that takes for granted the historical political technology of territorial borders while retaining an excessive Euro-American focus. While Europe and North America figure prominently in this book as well, the focus of several contributions outside of Europe—Indonesia, for example, in chapter 5—on migratory processes between continents (chapters 2, 3, and 4), within countries (chapter 1), or across several states located along particular migration routes (chapters 6 and 7) begins to trouble the map of migration and border studies in important ways. While a prevalent focus on South-North migrations betrays some of the limits of our own endeavor, Ranabir Samaddar's afterword to the volume starts sketching potential scenarios of what a viapolitical lens might offer when applied to forms of mobility that are more firmly centered in the Global South.

By cutting across different temporalities and geographical scales, viapolitics allows us to demonstrate that if immigration as a category and object of power only emerged with the consolidation of the territorial nation-state, the control of the movement of some bodies and vehicles—always determined along the conflictual lines of class, race, and gender—long predates it (chapters 1 and 2). Furthermore, while as Darshan Vigneswaran (2019) has demonstrated, the dominant narrative in the fields of migration and border studies is a linear one that focuses on the progressive consolidation of the nation-state in Europe and the concomitant passage from the policing of mobility from the local scale to the external rim of national borders and more recently to a tendentially global level (for examples of such as narrative, see Torpey 1999; Cresswell 2006, 2010), viapolitics allows our contributors to explore the emergence of forms of policing of mobility in many different places and underline the way they have operated across varying scales that have not followed a linear evolution. Following the fragmented developments and shifts of what, inspired by Saskia Sassen (2008), we might call "mobility control capabilities" across land, air, and sea, the chapters in this book chart a story of multidirectional transformation and constant reassemblage that often connects with the history and tensions of empire (Cooper 2005). In all these different ways, viapolitics operates as an epistemic device that allows one to question and unravel the whole edifice of scholarly analyses, governmental practices, and policy discourses that has been built around the phenomenon that we call migration and borders.

Once we begin to think about the history of human movement and the constraints imposed on it not in linear or epochal terms nor in geographical compartments such as the nation-state but in terms of events, setups, and constellations, it becomes apparent that the place that the movement of bodies and vehicles across space occupies in those different setups is actually quite variable. While it is a truism to say that migration involves journeys (even if, as the famous slogan "We didn't cross the border, the border crossed us" indicates, it is sometimes borders themselves that do the journeying, and a mere change in legal status is sufficient to turn certain people into migrants without any physical movement needed), not all such movements are equal in the way they are made visible, memorable, grievable, or governable. Viapolitics marks the point at which these practices, questions, and mediations of movement move into and out of the foreground of governmental, public, and scholarly attention according to what Jacques Rancière (2006) has called a "partition of the sensible"; it signals the threshold at which the mobility of peoples becomes a stake in social and political struggles, and a field of power/knowledge. Some of these

vehicles, routes, and infrastructures have grown to occupy a spectacular prominence in contemporary struggles surrounding migration, in policy discourse, and
in media representations, as was the case during the so-called migrant crisis that
reached its peak in summer 2015 in Europe. From the trucks inside which the
dead bodies of migrants seeking to reach northern Europe were found along
an Austrian highway in August 2015 (*New York Times* 2015); to the trains alter-
nately prevented from traveling and greeted by local populations as they arrived
in German train stations; to the Macedonian train tracks and motorways along
which migrants have often been forced to bike or walk (chapter 7, this volume); to the overcrowded wooden and rubber boats used by illegalized migrants
(chapter 8, this volume; Ellebrecht 2020), these vehicles, routes, infrastructures,
and the terrains across which they extend have once again reached center stage.
And yet insufficient effort has been made to attend to them seriously, and as a
result they remain all but hidden in plain sight.

The task we undertake here is to bring these aspects to the foreground. In the
remainder of this introduction, we discuss further the three main dimensions of
viapolitics we have alluded to above—vehicles, routes and infrastructures, and
geophysical environments—which structure the three main parts of this book
and outline the way our chapters contribute to their understanding. However,
we should note at the outset that these three themes do not form a rigid analytical triangle with equal weight across all the studies that follow. Instead, chapters
are organized in terms of which of these themes they tend to emphasize.

Vehicles of Migration

Part I of this book focuses on the vehicles of migration. Our call for a reckoning
with the vehicular might provoke a degree of unease in some readers. Migration
is about humans, not ships or planes. Is it not a form of detached aestheticism
or dispassionate scholasticism to train one's focus on vehicles at the very time
when people are drowning while crossing borders, while the rise of xenophobic
social movements is generating enhanced risk, and predatory employers creating ever greater precarity for migrants in so many countries? Let us be quite
clear. We are not interested in fetishizing vehicles or a narrowly technological
view of the sort that is quite common in some versions of transportation history.
If we call for research to engage migration from the angle of vehicles and their
infrastructures, it is precisely because of the complex ways in which the vehicular

mediates and illuminates very human struggles over borders and belongings, life and death, security and insecurity, here and there, and much else.

How do vehicles come to participate in these broader sociopolitical controversies? Let's take ships again. One of the things that interests us is the way in which ships represent simultaneously a space of alterity and a microcosm of existing social hierarchies. On the one hand, Foucault's (1986) oft-quoted vision of ships as "heterotopic spaces" emphasizes key ways in which the ship has long summoned a different world, set apart from the land. At the same time, we take the view that in many respects the vessel does not so much diverge from as operate as an index and spatial diagram of wider power relations, reproducing and reinforcing "existing land-based social hierarchies" (Cusack 2014). For instance, during the "age of mass migration," the different traveling classes of the transatlantic liners reproduced and entrenched class divisions. In the context of today's Mediterranean crossings (see, e.g., Squire et al. 2017), a macabre political economy in which race, gender, and class intersect determines the position of the different people on board the unseaworthy boats that leave Libya, with the poorer migrants able to afford only a place in the boat's hold and thus exposed to the greatest risk of dying en route. As these examples show, reading the spatial micropolitics of these vessels can reveal class and racial hierarchies. In chapter 1, Ethan Blue shows how analyzing the contested design of the deportation trains that in the 1920s channeled migrants toward the ports from which they were to be expelled from the United States can reveal contradictory rationales concerning economy, hygiene, space, and criminality, as well as racialized and gendered identities.

And yet vehicles are not only a locus of (re)production of oppressive categories and violence but also the place where new solidarities and bonds were and continue to be created in the least likely circumstances. In Markus Rediker, Cassandra Pybus, and Emma Christopher's (2007, 4) account of the eighteenth-century slave ship, they underline that: "Amid all the violence, suffering, and death on the lower deck of the *Brookes* and on countless other slavers, new means of communication and new solidarities were being formed among the enslaved, through the language of resistance in action (hunger strikes, leaps overboard, and insurrection) and through new patterns of speech." Drawing on insights from studies of transatlantic slavery, Renisa Mawani's essay (chapter 2) explores the archive of testimonies of passengers who traveled on board the *Komagata Maru* to "take a closer look at the decks of the ship; the tensions, solidarities, and identities that passengers formed with one another, especially across religious lines," and shows how important these ties were in forging forms of resistance to empire, both during the transgressive voyage itself and later in Indian independence movements. In the process, she reminds us that "racial and colonial histories were not produced on terra firma" alone but were also "shaped by forced and transgressive voyages" that changed conceptions of freedom and coercion.

While certainly not lying outside of the grasp of power, ships, as well as planes, have historically been a locus of distinctive and unique authority systems. Captains, for instance, are vested with a particular power grounded in the problems of governing microsocieties that float or fly at great remove from systems of terrestrial rule; they exercise a "necessity of authority" that even an avowed communist like Engels affirmed (Winner 1980, 128–29). Chapter 3 focuses on stowaways who embark on cargo ships off the coasts of Africa and the way they are governed. Amaha Senu underlines the complex and competing rationales between captains and their crews at sea, and insurance companies and their many representatives dispersed across many ports. While he demonstrates that thanks to digital technologies, cargo ships remain far more connected to firm land than in the past, he underlines the considerable autonomy that captains retain on board in managing the presence of stowaways. Facing the knowledge and practices deployed to mitigate the risk that stowaways constitute for shipping companies and which effectively enlist cargo ships into a mobile and privatized management of borders, Senu also underlines the "rival knowledge" forged by stowaways to navigate the multiple risks that they encounter during their travel. While migrants' use of overcrowded boats to cross fault lines such as the Mediterranean is a widely studied phenomenon, and one that is spectacularized in the media (chapter 8, this volume), Senu offers a rare glimpse into these much less covered fringes of the maritime world.

Although we focus on the materiality of the vehicles themselves, the socialities and forms of governance they come to be embedded in and generate, we hesitate at the prospect of casting the vehicle as merely one more material object to be added to the growing encyclopedia of new materialist studies (Salter 2015; Braun and Whatmore 2010; Latour and Weibel 2005), as we also highlight the role of vehicles in discourses, representations, and imaginaries. Vehicles, as well as roads and journeys for that matter, have a very special and distinctive place in the cultural imaginary of many societies. Consider, again, the repeated ways in which political thought and public imagination have mobilized the ship as an image for governance (Foucault 2007; Walters 2015b). Likewise, from Odysseus to the *Wizard of Oz*, we are struck by the extraordinarily different yet recurrent ways in which the journey features in fiction, poetry, religion, and song as a figure of life, chance, change, discovery, and so on. There is, in short, an entire mythopoetics of the road (Lehari 2000). In this book we bring both a material and an aesthetic sensitivity to the vehicle's place in migration struggles, asking how the vehicle becomes mobilized not only on land, sea, and air but in the imagination, and in the mobilization of publics toward various political aims. Chapter 4 builds on Julie Y. Chu's anthropological fieldwork with Chinese transmigrants to North America, made infamous in international media as victims as well as perpetrators of particular human smuggling disasters. Chu explores the way in which a specific sociotechnics of "dis/comfort" have come to mediate our ideas of in/civility and racialized identity, and how the cramped environs of a long line of vehicles—from the slave ship to the container ship to the budget airline—have served as the objects and public forums where these struggles have played out. Charles Heller and Lorenzo Pezzani (chapter 8) seek to contest the spectacularization of migrants' overcrowded boats crossing the Mediterranean by foregrounding instead all the other boats they interact with—or precisely don't, because the latter decide to stay away. They underline the contested logistics of border control and rescue at sea that have been at the center of the shifting policies and practices of different actors at the EU's maritime frontier, and have shaped in decisive ways what they call "liquid violence." Heller and Pezzani also remind us that in addition to sharpening its focus on the vehicles of migration, scholarship needs to attend to all the other vehicles that populate the securitized borders and routes of today's migration world.

Trajectories, Routes, and Infrastructures

Were we to confine our attention to vehicles only, we would risk reifying an array of objects much in the way that media coverage did when it fixated on the *Ocean Lady* as a "mystery ship." For the fact is that ships, trains, planes, and other vessels achieve their functions only when they operate in connection with wider networks and infrastructures of other people and things. Bruno Latour puts it well when he insists that it is misleading to think that a plane or a pilot flies. "Flying is a property of the whole association of entities that includes airports and planes, launch pads and ticket counters. B-52s do not fly, the US Air Force flies" (Latour 1999, 182; cited in Chu 2010, 109). Chapters in part II of this collection embrace the invitation of mobilities scholars to consider mobilities "in their fluid interdependence and not in their separate spheres" (Sheller and

Urry 2006, 212), and focus more specifically on situations in which routes and infrastructures become entangled in politics.

Calling for migration studies to move beyond a rather fetishizing gaze at the behavior of migrants, Biao Xiang and Johan Lindquist argue that scholars should shift their attention from migration understood as the movement of people across borders to migration infrastructures—"the systematically inter-linked technologies, institutions, and actors that facilitate and condition mobil-ity" (2014, S124; see also Hui 2016, 74–76). It is a point we share in this book. Johan Lindquist's contribution to this volume (chapter 5), in which he focuses on the power relations that invest low-skilled, documented migration from rural Indonesia to various other Asian countries and the Middle East, is exemplary of the insights afforded by such a move. By focusing on processes of recruitment, documentation, transport, temporary housing, reception, and "physical encap-sulation centered on the 'protection' (*perlindungan*) of the migrant," Lindquist foregrounds how normal it is for migrant workers to be escorted, sometimes to their most rural villages. Through vivid descriptions of the minivans employed by these escorts, Lindquist shows they are used to create channeled forms of mobility that he likens to corridors. In the process, the chapter challenges our assumptions that migration under modernity can be modeled as the movement of free individuals.

Our approach to the infrastructural dimension of viapolitics is informed by critical discussions of logistics (Cowen 2014; Grappi 2015; Chua et al. 2018) and the way they have recently been brought to bear on migration and borders (Martin 2012; Mezzadra 2016). This logistical gaze is essential in several ways. First, it allows us to examine how different modalities of transport are con-nected to one another, not only in terms of what could be called in logistic jargon "intermodality"—the seamless passage from one transport infrastruc-ture to another—but also in terms of their historical and conceptual entangle-ments. These connections are apparent, to start with, at the level of migrants' biographies. Studies of migrant journeys reveal their stop/start, discontinuous character, and the fact that a given migrant's trajectory might include crossing mountains on a donkey and oceans on a passenger jet (Mainwaring and Brigden 2016; Yildiz 2019), or by train and on foot, as chapter 9 (Garelli and Tazzioli) describes, focusing on the Alpine border between Italy and France, underscores this. But it is not only at the level of personal experience that these entangle-ments between and across different mobility systems are evident. They are equally significant at the level of whole territories and in shaping entire trajectories of migration history. This point can be briefly illustrated if we consider how aviation transformed the temporality and the landscape of migration in the second half of the twentieth century (chapter 10, this volume). It is almost a staple of commentary on globalization and migration to observe that aviation, much like digital technologies, has shrunk the world. It has brought people and places much closer together, compressing long journey times of ocean crossing into a matter of hours. One might have imagined that the rise of commercial aviation would have consigned migration by sea to history, and together with it the whole iconography of ships, ports of embarkation and disembarkation, and journeys of hope and despair. Yet in the aftermath of the tightening of visa regimes, the sanctions preventing airlines from embarking passengers without authorization and ever more sophisticated practices of airport security have combined to make access to aviation extremely difficult for many—particularly citizens of the Global South. As a result, just when a technological determinism might have predicted that the sea was no longer a space of migration, the very opposite has happened: oceanic crossings by boat have returned with a spectacular and tragic vengeance (chapter 8, this volume). This exemplifies the way the procedures and technologies of logistics that have been designed to enable the smooth flow of people and goods across global transportation systems also generate a form of antilogistics—the production of discontinuities for specific categories of people who are barred from accessing certain transport infrastructures. In turn, we might say that migrants engage in a form of alter-logistics—the forging of alternative transport infrastructures that are inextricably made of actual vehicles as much as of their shared knowledge of circulation (what Papadopoulos and Tsianos [2013] call "mobile commons") and professional smugglers' networks. These tensions surrounding transport infrastructures and competing logistical perspectives are foregrounded in several chapters (see in particular chapter 3).

Finally, a strong focus of several chapters is on the ways these networked infrastructures of movement have become objects of governance, and on the politics of knowledge involved in naming and analyzing these infrastructures so as to make them governable. "Trajectories" is the term that, we suggest, might most accurately designate illegalized migrants' precarious connections: difficult to plan in advance as a travel route, trajectories are the embodied paths of movement traced in space that emerge from the clash between migrants' movement and the friction they encounter (see Schapendonk 2011). "Routes" instead is the term widely used within policy fields to objectify migrants' bifurcated paths and turn them into a space of governance. Maribel Casas-Cortes and Sebastian Cobarrubias (chapter 6), as well as Sabine Hess and Bernd Kasparek (chapter 7) offer different genealogies of "routes thinking" and management, the first largely centered on Spain in relation to Africa, the second focused on the Balkans. Both demonstrate how the route has become a key mediator in the way in which states seek to apprehend—we use the term in its double sense—the turbulence of migratory movements. Crucially, these chapters reveal how the concept and object of the route bind together in new ways a multiplicity of actors across a transnational space and are thus generative of new governmental practices. Casas-Cortes and Cobarrubias seek to denaturalize what they call "routes thinking" by describing the way a collective of *sans papiers* in Spain returned the gaze onto one of the maps of "migrant routes," resubjectifying with their own embodied experiences the lines that had been abstracted from the friction of the real world. Hess and Kasparek further draw our attention to other spatial concepts, such as the corridor as a form of channeling movement, this time in connection with humanitarian and security logics that intensified in Europe during the so-called summer of migration of 2015. In a different context, Renisa Mawani (chapter 2) foregrounds the idea of passage, which, following Rediker, Pybus, and Christopher (2007, 2), she suggests is more than one part of an oceanic voyage; it is also a concept that can map distributions of violence and expropriation over time and space. In sum, variable geometries are at stake and nothing is straightforward about routes. Different ways of conceptualizing pathways and movements merit our attention. Routes, passages, corridors, and trajectories are just some of the ways this book grapples with these geometries and their power effects.

In addition to vehicles, then, transport and migration infrastructures, migrants' actual trajectories and their solidification into routes by those who seek to govern them are themes that figure prominently across this book and are central to our approach. Viapolitics allows us to bring together and push further different perspectives outlined above, which, in their emphasis on movement, transversal connections, and networks, have challenged classical migration studies' focus on the conditions that drive migration in countries of origin or the experiences and the dynamics of immigrants when they settle in cities and countries of destination. Here, rather than beginning and end points in a migration journey—which have become ever more elusive—what is foregrounded is the space-time of passage, the policies, transport, and human infrastructures that shape it, and the way it has become an object of government and public discourse in its own right. In the process, our very understanding of borders— too often predicated on a neat division of inside/outside marked by a territorial boundary—is challenged by an attention to multiple bordering practices that cut across space and operate at multiple scales in the aim of shaping migrants' entire trajectories.

The Geophysics of Migration and Borders

In part III of this book, we turn to the geophysical characteristics of the spaces across which both vehicles of migration and their infrastructures operate. In this final part, we seek to foster a much deeper connection between mobility and the earth, to reconnect migration and borders with the world in all its elemental, geological, atmospheric, tempestuous force. In this endeavor, we draw on and contribute to a recent "environmental turn" in the field of (political) geography and the humanities more generally (Usher 2019, 16; Braun 2008). Some of the most inspiring work here has crystalized around the concept of "geopower" and the specific inflection Elisabeth Grosz (2012) has given to it.[5] Geopower refers to "forces contained in matter that precede, enable, facilitate, provoke and restrict 'life'" (Depledge 2013, 1). Geopower shapes human and state practices, and in turn political practices shape the way this geopower operates, namely, who is empowered or restricted by it. The concept of geopower is useful in reconnecting the geophysical and the social in nondeterministic and nonbinary ways (Yusoff 2018), and in rethinking the environment not simply as the "environs of humans" (that which is around and outside of us) but rather as a "relational practice" embedded in social and political matrixes of power/knowledge (Braun 2008; Youatt 2016). This concept helps attune us to the way the geophysical characteristics of environments such as arid deserts, choppy seas, or rugged mountain chains are perceived, experienced, and strategized by migrants and state actors alike, shaping the vehicles and infrastructures migrants resort to, and the legislations and bordering practices they encounter. There are at least three interrelated ways in which the geophysics of migration and borders are analyzed in this book: the harnessing of geopower toward and against border control; migrants' embodied experience of environments that are made hostile to them; and the volume of the terrains across which migration and borders operate.

The role of the geophysical in relation to border enforcement has been perhaps most fully theorized in the frame of the Mexico-US border, where the notion of "prevention through deterrence" was adopted by US border guards as early as 1993 (De Leon 2015; Boyce, Chambers, and Launius 2019). This enforcement strategy calls for the deployment of massive numbers of agents along the sections of the border that are easiest to cross, usually around urban areas. These concentrations, in turn, lead migrants to attempt to cross in areas such as the Sonoran Desert that are much more inhospitable and, therefore, more difficult to traverse, often leading to death (Squire 2015). In this strategy, we can clearly see the way the geophysical environment becomes embedded in strategies of migration deterrence, to the extent that Juanita Sundberg (2011) argues that "nonhuman actors—plants, animals, and biophysical processes—are *constitutive of* boundary making" in the same ways in which border guards, national and international institutions, legal frameworks, and surveillance systems are.[6] Bringing these actants to the fore offers a powerful antidote against what Sundberg (2014) calls the "methodological humanism" of borders research. Heller and Pezzani continue this strand of thought in their chapter on the Mediterranean frontier, where, they argue, most migrants die not only at but also through the sea, victims of ever-changing forms of "liquid violence." The shifting modalities of this violence are shaped by the design of operational zones and the strategic mobilization of legal geographies and surveillance technologies, as well as by the changing practices of state and nonstate actors. Glenda Garelli and Martina Tazzioli similarly contest the image of environments such as the Alps as naturally deadly, demonstrating instead that it is state intervention that turns them into deathscapes by making the harsh geophysical conditions of the mountains all the more dangerous and unpredictable (chapter 9). In all of these cases, the inhospitable and hazardous areas migrants are funneled into can be understood as terrains, a term that, according to Stuart Elden (2010, 804), describes "a relation of power, with a heritage in geology and the military, the control of which allows the establishment and maintenance of order." It is the imposition of complex legal norms and technologies of power onto these terrains, adapting to and harnessing their geopower, that turn them into territories. In our understanding of terrains and territories, we are also inspired by feminist research (Jackman et al. 2020) that has highlighted the Eurocentric and statist bias of much theorization on these topics, emphasizing instead the multiple perspectives, understandings, and embodied experiences beyond the calculative grasp of the state. Contributions to this volume follow this perspective by emphasizing the ambivalence of geopower and underlining that states have no monopoly over strategizing the geophysical (see also Gordillo 2018; Boyce 2016). For instance, earlier in this introduction we already alluded to the role of the oceans in shaping not only practices of power and control, but also the capacity of migrants to connect distant continents by "appropriating the mobile forces in the air and water to increase [their] powers of locomotion" (Semple 1911, 292).

Several of our contributors also emphasize migrants' embodied experience of environments that have been made hostile to them as a result of state policies and practices. In their contribution on the crossing of the Alpine borders between Italy and France, Garelli and Tazzioli show how as a result of increasing state control of roads and rail transport, illegalized migrants have resorted to trying to cross mountainous areas on foot. Their discussion of "the migrant walker" challenges the "romantic ambulatory culture that has dominated different disciplinary conversations surrounding walking." Rather than a free and adventurous hero or flaneur, migrants are forced to walk, on rocky paths, at times covered in snow, and surrounded by thick forests in which one may lose one's orientation. Likewise, in his genealogy of "the coercive racial viapolitics" of US settler colonialism, Blue emphasizes the embodied encounter of slaves and Indigenous peoples with the harsh elements during their forced treks on foot across the United States (chapter 1). The "coffles" formed by groups of slaves, whose movement "was powered by slaves' muscle and whatever food the drivers allowed them," as Blue writes, had to march regardless of heat or freezing cold. The forced removal of Indigenous peoples on the Trail of Tears "involved trudging across muddy roads and paths westward, through cold and rain, pain and suffering, deprivation, sickness and death." These contributions bring into sharp relief the ways in which, for those excluded from privileged mobility regimes that aim to offer seamless travel, the body violently rubs up against the material world (Pallister-Wilkins 2019).[7]

Finally, while geographic thought has tended to focus on the world of solid surface (*terra*) in its flat two dimensionality, we follow recent research in seeking to understand terrains and territories "as voluminous, elemental, fluid, and indeterminate" (Peters, Steinberg, and Stratford 2018, 5), attending as well to the territorialities of the oceans and the skies.[8] There is now growing attention to questions of volume (Weizman 2007; Elden 2013; Billé 2020), airspace (Neocleous 2013), and aeriality (Adey 2010) with regard to space and power. In chapter 10, Clara Lecadet and Walters bring these emerging 3D geographies of power into a productive conversation with the study of deportation by air. They focus on the network of airports that contributes to making the skies navigable. Specifically, they explore some of the diverse ways airports interact with deportation practices, whether as zones of departure, transit, or arrival, whether used by states to produce politically useful deportation spectacle or by migrants and activists, for whom airports can become zones of interruption. Lecadet and Walters pay special attention to Bamako-Sénou airport in Mali, where ex-deportees have managed, through organized efforts, to make the airport a site of struggle, solidarity, civic identity, and political voice regarding those who experienced forcible return. In this way, their chapter sketches fragments of an aerial geography of deportation whose existence has been largely overlooked by state-centric approaches to expulsion.

The epic stories of exile and exodus told by poets and religious books feature peoples crossing seas or, like Icarus and Daedalus, taking flight from island imprisonment. In an age when masses of people once again have to negotiate mountain ranges, deserts, oceans, and skies, as well as highways, railways, towns, and villages, it is high time we took the geophysics of migration and borders more seriously.

Viapolitics: The Road Ahead

Without a doubt, the essays gathered in this volume cannot—nor, for that matter, intend to—exhaust the various facets and analytical angles that a viapolitical gaze might afford. Rather, they should be read as a primer, gathering preliminary explorations that we see developing in the areas of research that are closer to us, while at the same inviting future research that will necessarily need to enlarge and diversify its spatial and temporal focus beyond what we have managed to do here.

Each of the chapters in this book cuts across the three dimensions of viapolitics (vehicles, infrastructures, and geophysics) that we have just discussed here in isolation from each other, even as they may bring a sharper focus on one dimension or another. Each chapter focuses in fact on a particular type of vehicle that, thanks to a certain infrastructure, enables travel across a corresponding terrain—land, air, and sea. After all, one of the most powerful advantages of the lens of viapolitics is precisely that it cuts through scalar divisions so as to keep in play the specificity of the analysis of practices of power and their inscription within broader political and economic transformations, past and present. It is only if one understands the jurisdictional distributions of the airspace that one can fully grasp, for example, the significance and politics of the minute gesture of passengers standing up to prevent a deportation flight from taking off. This articulation between politics on the scale of global space and at that of the "microphysical" is precisely one of the analytical moves that the concept of viapolitics allows.

Most importantly, however, we hope that after having explored viapolitics' manifold facets, it will become hardly possible to keep holding the two ship stories with which we have opened this book in separation from each other. For many years, the work of scholars, artists, and activists has denounced and attempted to expose the "imperial durabilities" (Stoler 2016) that link the events of the *Komagata Maru* to more recent stories of exclusion, such as those involving the MV *Ocean Lady*. Think of Ali Kazimi's documentary *Continuous Journey*, which traces the connection between the policies that led to the interdiction of the *Komagata Maru* and the 2014 Canada-US Safe Third Country Agreement; or Ken Lum's sculptural installation *Four Boats Stranded: Red and Yellow, Black and White* (2001), which "connects the historical legacy of the *Komagata Maru* and the colonization of First Nations to contemporary practices of racialized exclusion in Canadian immigration" through the miniaturized replicas of four boats that relate in different ways to the history of empire (Hameed and Vukov 2007, 93).[9] All these projects seek to confront the violence of what Ariella Aïcha Azoulay (2019, 2) has called the "imperial shutter": all of the ways in which, like a camera shutter separating a photograph from the context in which it was produced, the imperial enterprise has "distanced, bracketed, removed, forgotten, suppressed, ignored, overcome, and made irrelevant" different histories. We would like our contribution to sit in continuity with these attempts. While we certainly cannot claim that it will be our intervention that will change the perception of the two ship stories in the public debate, we do hope that it will provide fresh tools to "actualis[e] their... suppressed legacies and continuities" (Hameed and Vukov 2007, 93) and to think practices of mobility and systems of control in their deeper history and wider geographical connections.

Notes

1 Many examples could be offered, but we can mention in particular transport sociologies and histories (Mom 2003; Schivelbusch 1986; Gigliotti 2009), postcolonial cultural studies and radical histories of the Atlantic and other mobile worlds (Gilroy 1993; Linebaugh and Rediker 2000; Bhimull 2017); geographies of humanitarianism and refugees (Hyndman 2000; Mountz 2010); communication studies that take transport seriously (Morley 2011; Carey 2009); geographies and cultural histories of landscape, highway, and route (Lehari 2000; Hvattum et al. 2016); and philosophically attuned studies of everyday travel and spatiality (Thrift 2004; de Certeau 1984). Further research that has been important for our thinking of the different dimensions of viapolitics is mentioned in the following sections of this introduction.

2 There has been a lively and generative dialogue between mobilities and migration scholars, particularly in such areas as forced or clandestine migration (Gill, Caletrío, and Mason 2011; Mainwaring and Brigden 2016; Martin 2012; Schapendonk et al. 2018) and border crossing and immigration enforcement (Stuesse and Coleman 2014;

Mountz 2010; Loyd and Mountz 2018; Dijstelbloem, van Reekum, and Schinkel 2017). Nevertheless, and to echo one recent survey of these interdisciplinary fields (Hui 2016, 70), this traffic has been somewhat uneven and asymmetrical. The sharper focus mobilities approaches have brought onto how migratory movement is actually practiced, experienced, and mediated is still far from being the norm in migration and border studies.

3 Put differently, viapolitics starts in the midst of things. Here we have in mind the provocation that Deleuze and Guattari (1987, 25) directed toward social thought nearly forty years ago when they called for a philosophy that begins "in the middle, between things, . . . *intermezzo*." As mediators of movement, vehicles, routes, terrains, oceans, and skies are very much in the middle.

4 We also invoke locomotion because it offers some intriguing connections between movement and power. These have recently been explored by Hagar Kotef (2015, 80–83) in her important genealogy of the liberal governance of mobility (but see also Cresswell 2010; Adey 2017, esp. ch. 5; Sheller 2018). Kotef highlights in particular how the jurist William Blackstone saw a "clear bond between liberty and movement," such that liberty could, in his words, be understood as "the power of locomotion, of changing situation or removing one's person to whatsoever place one's own inclina-tion may direct; without imprisonment or restraint, unless by due course of law" (2015, 81, emphasis added). While we do not subscribe to this particular image of liberty, in *Viapolitics* we examine various ways in which the power of movement intersects with the distribution of freedoms and unfreedoms.

5 For a more extensive genealogy of the concept, see Luisetti (2019).

6 Here we see clearly how insufficient is the common understanding of the "envi-ronment" as that which is around, the background to, and clearly differentiated from the actions of humans (Youatt 2016), and what becomes apparent instead is a form of environmentality—a notion that builds upon Foucault's (2008) late work on biopolitics and governmentality, in which he described the then-budding forms of neoliberalism as "an environmental type of intervention," rather than a subject-based or population-based distribution of governance. The term was mostly taken up in the context of environmental studies (Luisetti 2018) but has then been use-fully reconceptualized by Jennifer Gabrys (2016, 191) as the multiple ways in which "environments, technologies, and ways of life [are] governed through . . . particular environmental distributions." As a result of what one may call border environmen-tality, borderscapes are turned into "hostile environments" for migrants (Pezzani and Heller 2019; Pezzani 2020).

7 This "politics of exhaustion" (Welander and Ansems de Vries 2016) operates by sub-tracting life-sustaining resources such as water, food, and health care provisions, and exposing people on the move to harsh socio-natural conditions along—and often also after—the journey: extreme heat or cold, as well as chronic sleep deprivation. Here the violence of borders expresses itself also as access to radically unequal levels of energy consumption and the ensuing differential speed of travel they produce: on

the one hand, the slow-paced walking across rugged terrains fueled by metabolic processes and, on the other, the high-consuming, fossil fuel–powered policing apparatus that unauthorized migrants have to confront (Nevins 2018, 2019).

8 Important research has also highlighted how, in an age of intensifying climate change and environmental crisis, the earth itself cannot be assumed to be the immutable backdrop over which perennially stable borders are drawn but needs to be understood as being in constant motion at speeds not usually associated with geophysical and geological processes. See, for instance, Ferrari, Pasqual, and Bagnato (2019) and Nyers (2012).

9 Lum's installation includes small replicas of a First Nations longboat, the first of four unnamed cargo ships that brought a total of 599 Fujian Chinese migrants to the shores of British Columbia in the summer of 1999, the *Komagata Maru*, and British colonial explorer Captain Vancouver's ship.

References

Adey, Peter. 2010. *Aerial Life: Spaces, Mobilities, Affects.* Malden, MA: Wiley-Blackwell.

Adey, Peter. 2017. *Mobility.* 2nd ed. New York: Routledge.

Azoulay, Ariella. 2019. *Potential History: Unlearning Imperialism.* London: Verso.

Balachandran, Gopalan. 2016. "Indefinite Transits: Mobility and Confinement in the Age of Steam." *Journal of Global History* 11: 187–208.

Bhimull, Chandra. 2017. *Empire in the Air: Airline Travel and the African Diaspora.* New York: NYU Press.

Billé, Franck, ed. 2020. *Voluminous States: Sovereignty, Materiality, and the Territorial Imagination.* Durham, NC: Duke University Press.

Bourdieu, Pierre, and Loïc Wacquant. 2001. "NewLiberalSpeak: Notes on the New Planetary Vulgate." *Radical Philosophy* 105 (January/February).

Boyce, Geoffrey A. 2016. "The Rugged Border: Surveillance, Policing and the Dynamic Materiality of the US/Mexico Frontier." *Environment and Planning D: Society and Space* 34 (2): 245–62.

Boyce, Geoffrey Alan, Samuel N. Chambers, and Sarah Launius. 2019. "Bodily Inertia and the Weaponization of the Sonoran Desert in US Boundary Enforcement: A GIS Modeling of Migration Routes through Arizona's Altar Valley." *Journal on Migration and Human Security* 7 (1): 23–35.

Bradimore, Ashley, and Harold Bauder. 2011. "Mystery Ships and Risky Boat People: Tamil Refugee Migration in the Newsprint Media." *Canadian Journal of Communication* 36: 637–61.

Braun, Bruce. 2008. "Environmental Issues: Inventive Life." *Progress in Human Geography* 32 (5): 667–79.

Braun, Bruce, and Sarah Whatmore, eds. 2010. *Political Matter: Technoscience, Democracy, and Public Life.* Minneapolis: University of Minnesota Press.

Brosnahan, Maureen. 2014. "Ocean Lady Migrants from Sri Lanka Still Struggling 5 Years Later." CBC News, October 18. http://www.cbc.ca/news/politics/ocean -lady-migrants-from-sri-lanka-still-struggling-5-years-later-1.2804118.

Callon, Michel, Pierre Lascoumes, and Yannick Barthe. 2009. *Acting in an Uncertain World: An Essay on Technical Democracy*. Cambridge, MA: MIT Press.

Carey, James. 2009. *Communication as Culture: Essays on Media and Society*. Rev. ed. New York: Routledge.

Chatterjee, Partha. 1993. *The Nation and Its Fragments: Colonial and Postcolonial Histories.* Princeton, NJ: Princeton University Press.

Chu, Julie. 2010. *Cosmologies of Credit: Transnational Mobility and the Politics of Destination in China*. Durham, NC: Duke University Press.

Chua, Charmaine, Martin Danyluk, Deborah Cowen, and Laleh Khalili. 2018. "Introduction: Turbulent Circulation: Building a Critical Engagement with Logistics." *Environment and Planning D: Society and Space* 36 (4): 617–29.

Cooper, Frederick. 2005. *Colonialism in Question: Theory, Knowledge, History*. Berkeley: University of California Press.

Cowen, Deborah. 2014. *The Deadly Life of Logistics: Mapping Violence in Global Trade*. London: University of Minnesota Press.

Cresswell, Timothy. 2006. *On the Move: Mobility in the Modern Western World*. London: Routledge.

Cresswell, Timothy. 2010. "Towards a Politics of Mobility." *Environment and Planning D: Society and Space* 28 (1): 17–31.

Cresswell, Timothy. 2011. "Mobilities I: Catching Up." *Progress in Human Geography* 35 (4): 550–58.

Cresswell, Timothy, and Merriman, Peter. 2011. "Introduction: Geographies of Mobilities—Practices, Spaces, Subjects." In *Geographies of Mobilities: Practices, Spaces, Subjects*, edited by Timothy Cresswell and Peter Merriman, 1–15. Farnham, UK: Ashgate.

Cusack, Tricia, ed. 2014. *Framing the Ocean, 1700 to the Present: Envisaging the Sea as Social Space*. Aldershot, UK: Ashgate.

de Certeau, Michel. 1984. *The Practice of Everyday Life*. Translated by Steven Rendall. Berkeley: University of California Press.

De Leon, Jason. 2015. *The Land of Open Graves: Living and Dying on the Migrant Trail*. Oakland: University of California Press.

Deleuze, Gilles, and Félix Guattari. 1987. *A Thousand Plateaus: Capitalism and Schizophrenia*. London: Athlone.

Depledge, Duncan. 2013. "Geopolitical Material: Assemblages of Geopower and the Constitution of the Geopolitical Stage." *Political Geography*, 45: 1–2.

Dijstelbloem, Huub, Rogier van Reekum, and Willem Schinkel. 2017. "Surveillance at Sea: The Transactional Politics of Border Control in the Aegean." *Security Dialogue* 48 (3): 224–40.

Elden, Stuart. 2010. "Land, Terrain, Territory." *Progress in Human Geography* 34 (6): 799–817.

Elden, Stuart. 2013. "Secure the Volume: Vertical Geopolitics and the Depth of Power." *Political Geography* 34: 35–51.

Elden, Stuart. 2017. "Legal Terrain—the Political Materiality of Territory." *London Review of International Law* 5 (2): 199–224.

Ellebrecht, Sabrina. 2020. *Mediated Bordering: Eurosur, the Refugee Boat, and the Construction of an External EU Border.* Bielefeld: Transcript Verlag.

Ferrari, Marco, Elisa Pasqual, and Andrea Bagnato. 2019. *A Moving Border: Alpine Cartographies of Climate Change.* New York: Columbia Books on Architecture and the City.

Foucault, Michel. 1986. "Of Other Spaces." *Diacritics* 16: 22–27.

Foucault, Michel. 1990. *The History of Sexuality. Volume One.* New York: Vintage.

Foucault, Michel. 2007. *Security, Territory, Population: Lectures at the Collège de France 1977–78.* New York: Palgrave Macmillan.

Foucault, Michel. 2008. *The Birth of Biopolitics. Lectures at the Collège de France, 1978–1979.* New York: Palgrave Macmillan.

Gabrys, Jennifer. 2016. *Program Earth: Environmental Sensing Technology and the Making of a Computational Planet.* Minneapolis: University of Minnesota Press.

Garelli, Glenda, and Martina Tazzioli. 2013. "Challenging the Discipline of Migration: Militant Research in Migration Studies, an Introduction." *Postcolonial Studies* 16: 245–49.

Gigliotti, Simone. 2009. *The Train Journey: Transit, Captivity, and Witnessing in the Holocaust.* New York: Berghahn.

Gill, Nick, Javier Caletrío, and Victoria Mason. 2011. "Introduction: Mobilities and Forced Migration." *Mobilities* 6 (3): 301–16.

Gilroy, Paul. 1993. *The Black Atlantic: Modernity and Double Consciousness.* Cambridge, MA: Harvard University Press.

Gordillo, Gastón. 2018. "Terrain as Insurgent Weapon: An Affective Geometry of Warfare in the Mountains of Afghanistan." *Political Geography* 64: 53–62.

Grappi, Giorgio. 2015. "Logistics, Infrastructures and Governance after Piraeus: Notes on Logistical Worlds." *Logistical Worlds,* August 4. http://logisticalworlds.org/blogs/logistics-infrastructures-and-governance-after-piraeus-notes-on-logistical-worlds.

Gregory, Derek. 2014. "Corpographies: Making Sense of Modern War." *Funambulist Papers* 59: 30–39.

Gregory, Derek. 2016. "The Natures of War." *Antipode* 48 (1): 3–56.

Grosz, Elizabeth. 2012. "Geopower." *Environment and Planning D: Society and Space* 30: 971–88.

Hameed, Ayesha, and Tamara Vukov. 2007. "Animating Exclusions: Ali Kazimi's Continuous Journey and the Virtualities of Racialized Exclusion." *TOPIA: Canadian Journal of Cultural Studies* 17: 87–109.

Hui, Allison. 2016. "The Boundaries of Interdisciplinary Fields: Temporalities Shaping the Past and Future of Dialogue between Migration and Mobilities Research." *Mobilities* 11 (1): 66–82.

Hvatum, Mari, Janike Kampevold Larsen, Britte Brenna, and Beata Elvebakk, eds. 2016. *Routes, Roads and Landscapes.* New York: Routledge.

Hyndman, Jennifer. 2000. *Managing Displacement: Refugees and the Politics of Humanitarianism.* Minneapolis: University of Minnesota Press.

Jackman, Anna, Rachael Squire, Johanne Bruun, and Pip Thornton. 2020. "Unearthing Feminist Territories and Terrains." *Political Geography* 80 (June).

Johnston, Hugh J. M. 1989. *The Voyage of the Komagata Maru: The Sikh Challenge to Canada's Colour Bar.* Vancouver: University of British Columbia Press.

Kotef, Hagar. 2015. *Movement and the Ordering of Freedom: On Liberal Governances of Mobility.* Durham, NC: Duke University Press.

Latour, Bruno. 1999. *Politics of Nature: How to Bring the Sciences into Nature.* Harvard, MA: Harvard University Press.

Latour, Bruno. 2005a. "From Realpolitik to Dingpolitik, or How to Make Things Public." In *Making Things Public: Atmospheres of Democracy,* edited by Bruno Latour and Peter Weibel, 14–41. Cambridge, MA: MIT Press.

Latour, Bruno. 2005b. *Reassembling the Social: An Introduction to Actor-Network-Theory.* Oxford: Oxford University Press.

Latour, Bruno, and Peter Weibel. 2005. *Making Things Public: Atmospheres of Democracy.* Cambridge, MA: MIT Press.

Law, John. 1984. "On the Methods of Long-Distance Control: Vessels, Navigation, and the Portuguese Route to India." *Sociological Review* 32 (Suppl. 1): 234–63.

Lehari, Kaia. 2000. "The Road That Takes and Points." *Place and Location* 1: 53–62.

Linebaugh, Peter, and Marcus Rediker. 2000. *The Many-Headed Hydra: Sailors, Slaves, Commoners, and the Hidden History of the Revolutionary Atlantic.* Boston: Beacon.

Loyd, Jenna, and Alison Mountz. 2018. *Boats, Borders, and Bases: Race, the Cold War, and the Rise of Migration Detention in the United States.* Oakland: University of California Press.

Luisetti, Federico. 2019. "Geopower: On the States of Nature of Late Capitalism." *European Journal of Social Theory* 22 (3): 342–63.

Mainwaring, Cetta, and Noelle Brigden. 2016. "Beyond the Border: Clandestine Migration Journeys." *Geopolitics* 21: 243–62.

Martin, Craig. 2012. "Desperate Mobilities : Logistics, Security and the Extra-logistical Knowledge of 'Appropriation.'" *Geopolitics* 17 (2) : 355–76.

Mawani, Renisa. 2016. "The Legacy of the Komagata Maru." *Globe and Mail,* May 18. https://www.theglobeandmail.com/opinion/the-legacy-of-the-komagata-maru/article30066572/.

Mawani, Renisa. 2018. *Across Oceans of Law: The Komagata Maru and Jurisdiction in Time of Empire.* Durham, NC: Duke University Press.

McKeown, Adam. 2008. *Melancholy Order: Asian Migration and the Globalization of Borders*. New York: Columbia University Press.

McKeown, Adam. 2011. "A World Made Many: Integration and Segregation in Global Migration, 1840–1940." In *Connecting Seas and Connected Ocean Rims*, edited by Donna Gabaccia and Dirk Hoerder, 42–64. Boston: Brill.

McNevin, Anne. 2019. "Mobility and Its Discontents: Seeing Beyond International Space and Progressive Time." *Environment and Planning C: Politics and Space*, August 29: 1–18.

Merriman, Peter. 2019. "Molar and Molecular Mobilities: The Politics of Perceptible and Imperceptible Movements." *Environment and Planning D: Society and Space* 37 (1): 65–82.

Mezzadra, Sandro. 2016. "MLC 2015 Keynote: What's at Stake in the Mobility of Labour? Borders, Migration, Contemporary Capitalism." *Migration, Mobility, and Displacement* 2 (1): 30–43.

Mom, Gijs. 2003. "What Kind of Transport History Did We Get? Half a Century of JTH and the Future of the Field." *Journal of Transport History* 24 (2): 121–38.

Mongia, Radhika. 1999. "Race, Nationality, Mobility: The History of the Passport." *Public Culture* 11: 527–56.

Morley, David. 2011. "Communications and Transport: The Mobility of People, Information and Commodities." *Media, Culture and Society* 33 (5): 743–59.

Mountz, Alison. 2010. *Seeking Asylum: Human Smuggling and Bureaucracy at the Border*. Minneapolis: University of Minnesota Press.

National Post. 2012. "I Fear My Homeland: Ocean Lady Claimant Tells IRB." January 24.

Neocleous, Mark. 2013. "Air Power as Police Power." *Environment and Planning D: Society and Space* 31: 578–93.

Nevins, Joseph. 2018. "The Speed of Life and Death: Migrant Fatalities, Territorial Boundaries, and Energy Consumption." *Mobilities* 13 (1): 29–44.

Nevins, Joseph. 2019. "Nature, Energy, and Violence on the U.S.-Mexico Border: The Exclusion Apparatus on the U.S.-Mexico Border and beyond Relies on Massive Energy and Fossil Fuel Consumption—and Embodies the Unequal Distribution of Environmental Resources and Life Chances between Origin and Destination Countries." *NACLA Report on the Americas* 51 (1): 95–100.

New York Times. 2015. "A Day after 71 Migrants Died, 81 Escaped the Back of a Truck in Austria." September 4. http://www.nytimes.com/2015/09/05/world/europe/71-migrants-found-dead-in-truck-likely-suffocated-austrian-official-says.html.

Nyers, Peter. 2012. "Moving Borders." *Radical Philosophy* 174 (August). https://www.radicalphilosophy.com/commentary/moving-borders.

Pallister-Wilkins, Polly. 2019. "Walking, Not Flowing: The Migrant Caravan and the Geoinfrastructuring of Unequal Mobility." *Society and Space*, February 21. https://www.societyandspace.org/articles/walking-not-flowing-the-migrant-caravan-and-the-geoinfrastructuring-of-unequal-mobility.

Papadopoulos, Dimitris, and Vassilis Tsianos. 2013. "After Citizenship: Autonomy of Migration, Organisational Ontology and Mobile Commons." *Citizenship Studies* 17 (2):178–96.

Peters, Kimberley, Philip Steinberg, and Elaine Stratford. 2018. "Introduction." In *Territory beyond Terra*, edited by Kimberley Peters, Philip Steinberg, and Elaine Stratford. Lanham, MD: Rowman and Littlefield International.

Pezzani, Lorenzo. 2020. "Hostile Environments." *E-Flux Architecture*, May 15. https://www.e-flux.com/architecture/at-the-border/325761/hostile-environments/.

Pezzani, Lorenzo, and Charles Heller. 2019. "'Hostile Environment'(s)—Sensing Migration across Weaponized Terrains." In *Ways of Knowing Cities*, edited by Laura Kurgan and Brawley Dare. New York: Columbia Books on Architecture and the City.

Povinelli, Elisabeth A. 2011. "Routes/Worlds." *E-Flux Journal*, no. 27 (September). https://www.e-flux.com/journal/27/67991/routes-worlds/.

Rancière, Jacques. 2006. *The Politics of Aesthetics: The Distribution of the Sensible.* New York: Continuum.

Rao, Vyjayanthi. 2011. "Speculative Seas." In *The Sea-Image: Visual Manifestations of Port Cities and Global Waters*, edited by Güven Incirlioglu and Hakan Topal, 119–64. New York: Newgray.

Rediker, Markus, Cassandra Pybus, and Emma Christopher, eds. 2007. *Many Middle Passages: Forced Migration and the Making of the Modern World.* Berkeley: University of California Press.

Salter, Mark, ed. 2015. *Making Things International 1: Circuits and Motion.* Minneapolis: University of Minnesota Press.

Sassen, Saskia. 2008. *Territory, Authority, Rights: From Medieval to Global Assemblages.* Updated ed. Princeton, NJ: Princeton University Press.

Schapendonk, Joris. 2011. "Turbulent Trajectories: Sub-Saharan African Migrants Heading North." PhD diss., Radboud University Nijmegen.

Schapendonk, Joris, Ilse van Liempt, Inga Schwarz, and Griet Steel. 2018. "Re-routing Migration Geographies: Migrants, Trajectories and Mobility Regimes." *Geoforum* 116 (November): 211–16. https://doi.org/10.1016/j.geoforum.2018.06.007.

Schivelbusch, Wolfgang. 1986. *The Railway Journey: The Industrialization of Time and Space in the Nineteenth Century.* Berkeley: University of California Press.

Semple, Ellen Churchill. 1911. *Influences of Geographic Environment: On the Basis of Ratzel's System of Anthropo-geography.* New York: Henry Holt.

Sheller, Mimi. 2018. *Mobility Justice: The Politics of Movement in an Age of Extremes.* London: Verso.

Sheller, Mimi, and John Urry. 2006. "The New Mobilities Paradigm." *Environment and Planning A: Economy and Space* 38 (2): 207–26.

Silverman, Stephanie. 2014. "In the Wake of Irregular Arrivals: Changes to the Canadian Immigration Detention System." *Refuge* 30: 27–34.

Sodero, Stephanie, and Nicholas Scott. 2016. "Special Issue: Canadian Mobilities, Contentious Mobilities." *Canadian Journal of Sociology* 41 (3): 257–76.

Squire, Vicki. 2015. "Acts of Desertion: Abandonment and Renouncement at the Sonoran Borderzone." *Antipode* 47 (2): 500–516.

Squire, Vicki, Angeliki Dimitriadi, Nina Perkowski, Maria Pisani, Dallal Stevens, and Nick Vaughn-Williams. 2017. "Crossing the Mediterranean Sea by Boat: Mapping and Documenting Migratory Journeys and Experiences." Final Project Report. University of Warwick. https://www.warwick.ac.uk/fac/soc/pais/research/researchcentres/irs/crossingthemed.

Stoler, Ann Laura. 2016. *Duress: Imperial Durabilities in Our Times*. Durham, NC: Duke University Press.

Stuesse, Angela, and Mathew Coleman. 2014. "Automobility, Immobility, Altermobility: Surviving and Resisting the Intensification of Immigrant Policing." *City and Society* 26 (1): 51–72.

Sundberg, Juanita. 2011. "Diabolic Caminos in the Desert and Cat Fights on the Río: A Posthumanist Political Ecology of Boundary Enforcement in the United States–Mexico Borderlands." *Annals of the Association of American Geographers* 101 (2): 318–36.

Sundberg, Juanita. 2014. "Animating United States–Mexico Border Studies." *Public Political Ecology Lab*, May 14. http://ppel.arizona.edu/?p=633.

Thrift, Nigel. 2004. "Driving in the City." *Theory, Culture and Society* 21 (4–5): 41–59.

Toronto Star. 2014. "Sri Lankan Journalist Aboard the Ocean Lady Jailed before Given Refugee Status." September 20.

Torpey, John. 1999. *The Invention of the Passport: Surveillance, Citizenship and the State*. New York: Cambridge University Press.

Tsing, Anna L. 2005. *Friction: An Ethnography of Global Connection*. Princeton, NJ: Princeton University Press.

Urry, John. 2007. *Mobilities*. Cambridge: Polity.

Usher, Mark. 2019. "Territory Incognita." *Progress in Human Geography* 33 (6): 789–806.

Venturini, Tommaso. 2010. "Diving in Magma: How to Explore Controversies with Actor-Network Theory." *Public Understanding of Science* 19: 258–73.

Vigneswaran, Darshan. 2019. "Europe Has Never Been Modern: Recasting Historical Narratives of Migration Control." *International Political Sociology* 14 (1): 1–20.

Virilio, Paul. 1986. *Speed and Politics*. New York: Semiotext(e).

Walters, William. 2015a. "Migration, Vehicles, and Politics: Three Theses on Viapolitics." *European Journal of Social Theory* 18 (4): 469–88.

Walters, William. 2015b. "On the Road with Michel Foucault: Migration, Deportation, and Viapolitics." In *Foucault and the History of Our Present*, edited by Sophie Fuggle, Yari Lanci, and Martina Tazzioli, 94–110. Houndmills, UK: Palgrave Macmillan.

Weizman, Eyal. 2007. *Hollow Land: Israel's Architecture of Occupation*. London: Verso.

Weizman, Eyal. 2010. "Forensic Architecture: Only the Criminal Can Solve the Crime." *Radical Philosophy* 164: 9–24.

Welander, Marta, and Leonie Ansems de Vries. 2016. "Refugees, Displacement, and the European 'Politics of Exhaustion.'" *OpenDemocracy*, September 30. https://www.opendemocracy.net/en/mediterranean-journeys-in-hope /refugees-displacement-and-europ/.

Winner, Langdon. 1980. "Do Artifacts Have Politics?" *Daedalus* 109 (1): 121–36.

Xiang, Biao, and Johan Lindquist. 2014. "Migration Infrastructure." *International Migration Review* 48: S122–S148.

Yildiz, Ugur. 2019. *Tracing Asylum Journeys: Transnational Mobility of Non-European Refugees to Canada via Turkey*. New York: Routledge.

Youatt, Rafi. 2016. "Interspecies." In *The Oxford Handbook of Environmental Political Theory*, vol. 1, edited by Teena Gabrielson, Cheryl Hall, John M. Meyer, and David Schlosberg. Oxford: Oxford University Press.

Yusoff, Kathryn. 2018. "The Anthropocene and Geographies of Geopower." In *Handbook on the Geographies of Power*, edited by Mat Coleman and John Agnew. Cheltenham: Edward Elgar.

Vehicles of Migration

Capillary Power, Rail Vessels, and the Carceral Viapolitics of Early Twentieth-Century American Deportation | Ethan Blue

Through much of his work, Michel Foucault sought to uncover what he called capillary forms of power. Foucault intended the capillary—miniscule circulatory blood vessels—as a metaphor for minute, corporeal, quotidian circulations and spatially diffuse struggles, distant from (and perhaps more important than) the traditionally recognized centers of political control. Despite the concept's generative potential, in his major works Foucault did not much use the concept of the capillary, or the *vessel*, to assess the significance of spatial travel, save for a brief passage at the end of *Discipline and Punish*. There, he noted that in the early nineteenth century, French prisoners, whose neck chains he said recalled those worn by galley slaves, had marched great distances. In 1837, the grim parade was replaced with "a carriage conceived as a moving prison, a mobile equivalent of the Panopticon" (Foucault 1979, 257–63).

The vehicle held six cells on each side of a central walkway in which two rows of prisoners sat, chained, facing each other. Sheet iron covered the walls; small holes allowed air to move. A door opened to the central corridor with a hatch for food and a covered grill. Guards might peer into each compartment, but inmates could not, he said, communicate with each other. Its designers lauded that women and children could be in the same carriage as criminals and the mad without risking contamination (Foucault 1979, 263).

From 1914 through the Second World War, the United States, then in the process of refining its immigrant control and deportation apparatus, experimented with similarly configured vehicles. Indeed, special train cars made constant deportation circuits throughout the country. They traveled across the land to gather a host of people who had been imprisoned within its proliferating carceral apparatus, thereby linking its prisons, hospitals, jails, asylums, workhouses, and immigrant detention centers into a coherent transcontinental carceral network, before conveying so-called undesirable peoples to borders and ports for exile. Though designed for noncitizens, US citizens, and especially children, were readily drawn within its net (Molina 2018).

This chapter assesses the deportation train cars that cycled through the United States and the spatio-political assemblage of which they were a part as objects that materialized—but also extended—Foucault's notion of capillary power. The train and its network were vessels in a dual sense: vehicles that moved through space as well as part of an enclosed (though never perfectly) circulatory/eliminatory system. Foucault's concern for French experience in punishment allowed him to misapprehend the constitutive relationship between colonial domains and metropolitan worlds, but analysis of coercive viapolitics in the United States—a settler colonial nation—demands understanding the connections among its forms.

Perhaps the most important viapolitical elements of US history are the forced removal of Indigenous peoples from the land, the importation of enslaved and unfree laborers to wrest profit from the earth, and the expulsion of so-called undesirable aliens from the settler-citizen population. They were, collectively and individually, racializing assemblages, spatially producing the conditions of white settler profit and reproduction, and effecting the elimination and/or radical exploitation of the citizen's many subordinated others. It is more than coincidental that deportation trains traveled on the transcontinental railroad, which is arguably the central infrastructure of nineteenth-century US imperial racial capitalism, dispossessing Indigenous peoples of their sovereignty and land, delivering exploitable labor, concentrating untold riches in capitalist firms, and consolidating the US state (Wehilye 2014, esp. chs. 12, 13; Karuka 2019).

Migrants who did not adhere to the eugenic contours of settler citizenship—in terms of race, sexual morality, political sensibility, physical and cognitive ability, or economic self-sufficiency—risked capture, arrest, and expulsion. In this chapter, deportation trains provide a material history and conceptual link between

US assertions of sovereign control over territory and population through the viapolitics of carceral circulation, a circulation that is, as Foucault (2007, 18) suggests, crucial to sovereignty. As technologies of mobile incarceration—the material infrastructure of spatial control and political power—these vessels have their own stories. And while most studies of deportation trains focus, understandably, on the Shoah, which analysts may or may not link to German imperialism, we can see here the racial and colonial contexts from which US versions emerged (Gigliotti 2009; Pressner 2007).[1]

I have examined the micropolitics of peoples' experiences of US train-board deportation journeys elsewhere, but in this chapter, I concentrate on the materiality and lineage of its vessels (Blue 2015, 2019). I briefly trace histories of the slave trade, Indian removal, and the so-called coolie traffic. Space prevents comprehensive accounts, but we can nevertheless identify practices that will help locate the deportation train as a third branch in a racializing assemblage to control land, labor, and populations. Next, I offer a detailed history of US deportation train carriages. Coupled with—and inextricable from—the murderousness of slave transport and Indian removal, modern US deportation revealed the settler project's biopolitical tendencies, sorting desirable, assimilable, productive (and reproductive) migrants from unwelcome arrivals (Mbembe 2003; see also Day 2015, 2016; Byrd 2011; Veracini 2015). The deportation assemblage was unforgiving and cruel, but it was not intended to be deadly. US deportation trains partially recapitulated the topological organization of slave traffic, but because their purpose was selective spatial elimination, the US deportation train planners' intent edged closer, conceptually, to Indian removal. Across the histories of US coercive viapolitics, debates over costs, gendered ideologies, perceptions of unfree passengers' danger or pathos, and new locomotive technologies affected the material design and spatial topology of circulation, contest, and control.

Genealogies of Forced Mobility

In the age of sail and wooden ships, seaborne vessels transported some 12.4 million Africans across the Atlantic to the Americas; 50,000 British convicts from early modern England to the Americas and, after revolution, still more to Australia; and some 580,000 so-called coolies from South and East Asia, brought from across the British Empire to the Americas and the Caribbean.[2] These many Middle Passages, as a recent collection of essays identified them, united multiple segments of the early modern world economic system and forced highly racialized and hyperexploited peoples into brutal systems of domination and labor control (Christopher, Pybus, and Rediker 2007). At the same time, the ships and their unfree passengers furthered the imperial aim of displacing Indigenous peoples and pulling profit from colonized lands. The vessels were among the era's most technologically sophisticated machines, and the physical transfers of wealth and human cargo they allowed drove world racial capitalism (Rediker 2007, 41–44; see also Robinson 2000).

The horrors of the Atlantic slave trade were shaped by the brutal human arithmetic by which traders calculated how many bodies might be packed into a ship's hold (see chapter 4, this volume), constrained only by how the death or illness of their cargo might cut into profits, drive up insurance costs, or be affected by the meager regulations that determined the number of slaves per ship's tonnage (Smallwood 2007). Vessels were designed for economy, speed, and security. In 1801, John Riland described how enslaved women and men were separated on the ship *Liberty*. The 140 men were packed immediately below the deck, chained by the wrist and ankle. Women were unchained and had somewhat more room to move. Children were also kept apart. Chillingly, given what we know of sexual abuse in slavery, young girls slept on the floor in the captain's cabin, and boys on the surgeon and first mate's cabin floor (Rediker 2007, 68–69). Ships' hulls were hydrodynamic enough to make good enough time across the Atlantic—speeding travel and having fewer deaths en route— with their sides still wide enough "for the more commodious stowing of Negroes" (50–51). Ships commonly included a movable wall on the deck, known as a barricado, which the slavers could erect in case of uprising.

The end of the Atlantic slave trade in 1807 scarcely diminished its US incarnation. As cotton culture depleted soil nearer the Eastern Seaboard, nearly one million slaves were driven deeper into North America via a second Middle Passage (Berlin 2004, 14–15).[3] The largest numbers were forced south and west on foot in groups known as coffles. Smaller coffles might involve just a few people; others included dozens. Major traders might move what they called "droves" of hundreds, chained to each other or to horses, through heat or freezing cold (Johnson 1999, 49–50).[4] No steam or sail fueled this travel. It was powered by enslaved peoples' muscle and whatever food the drivers allowed them, balance again struck between the slavers' stinginess and their desire for a lucrative sale.

The coffle's coercive viapolitics reiterated themes from the slave ship: sexual division and segregation by perceived risk, as well as the different technologies of control. Seen as the most dangerous, men bore the most surveillance and the greatest capital investment in the material of their coercion—iron chains and collars were common (Johnson 1999, 68). Women and children trailed the men. As aboard slave ships, women had marginally more ability to move. They were bound by ropes or, if physically unbound, watched by guards. Mothers and children were also tethered by the kin relations—mother to child, child to mother—at the center of their worlds (Johnson 1999).[5]

The coffle's topography differed from the slave ship's in important ways. Space in a ship's hold was ultimately finite, its volume constrained by a vessel's structural hydrodynamics. But in the coffle, in theory at least, new lengths of chain might forever be joined to one end or the other; a seemingly limitless number of people might be added. When traders forced their chattel to new regions to clear more ground or grow more cotton, thereby extending the circuits of capital and labor, the viapolitics of enslavement intersected with effort to force Indigenous peoples from their lands.

The phases of Indian removal lasted decades and endure, in Patrick Wolfe's (1999, 2) formulation, as a structure rather than an event. Still, in the 1830s, armed American invaders used war, treaties, cash, trickery, and trade to attempt total population transfer of Floridian Seminoles, Creek peoples from Georgia and Alabama, Chickasaws and Choctaws and Cherokee from their homes. Indigenous peoples attempted to survive the slow-or-faster apocalypse of settler invasion.[6]

US invaders dislocated the Cherokee from their homelands in the southern Appalachian mountains across the late eighteenth and early nineteenth centuries. Many migrated into Texas, Mexico, Arkansas, and elsewhere, overwhelming or joining with the Indigenous peoples already there. The pressure and pace accelerated radically when the federal government and the state of Georgia demanded access to Cherokee lands east of the Mississippi. Between 1830 and 1838, Cherokee who departed chose survival over confrontation with rapacious whites. They were profoundly reluctant to leave but feared worse if they stayed (Smithers 2015, 110–11). Most commonly, displaced Indian communities were driven from their homelands on foot. Rather than being segregated by sex or perceived dangerousness, as slaves were in a coffle, they more or less self-organized by family and by community.

After 1838, the Cherokee who refused to voluntarily relocate were driven into military stockades, which served as staging areas for forced removal (Smithers 2015, 93). Their Trail of Tears involved trudging down muddy roads and paths westward, through cold and rain, pain and suffering, deprivation, sickness, and death. When wagons were available, they were jammed in "like cattle or sheep" (113). Army rations were totally inadequate, and hunger physically, spiritually, and psychologically brutalized the Cherokee. Exposure to the elements, illness and malnourishment, and soldiers' unpredictable violence compounded the horror.

Slave traders driving coffles had a capital investment in their chattel as commodities and as labor power, but the US Army had neither material nor empathetic investment in Indian peoples' well-being. Death rates reached 50 percent for many nations (Dunbar-Ortiz 2014, 113; Trafzer 2000, 159). Because the actual energy necessary for the Cherokees' travel was caloric intake from food—which the army scarcely provided—physical movement led to deadly hunger. Without necessary sustenance, the energy Cherokees spent in placing one foot in front of the next consumed their very bodies. This was at the heart of the astounding mortality rates. Indian removal was a mode of quasi-genocidal elimination that drove out whole communities, families, towns, and villages.

As American Indian groups were facing brutal removal, by the 1830s, Britain was bowing to political pressure to abolish slavery. Undaunted, planters across the Caribbean basin soon developed a contract labor system in which Chinese and South Asian "coolies" became the new supply of hyperexploitable workers (Hoerder 2011, 16). More than 400,000 South Asian and more than 180,000 indentured Chinese workers came to the Caribbean (Putnam 2011, 99). Bound by contract rather than chains or permanent racial servitude, Chinese in Cuba nevertheless labored in conditions akin to the plantation-based racial slavery that preceded it, updated for a new political-economic regime (Hu-DeHart 1994, 48–51).

Many of the same ships and captains that traded enslaved Africans now transported Chinese workers. Mortality rates on these could reach 30 percent. The coolie trade ended officially in 1874, but patterns of servitude persisted (Hu-DeHart 1994, 45–46). Even after the 1875 Page Act and 1882 Chinese Exclusion Act federalized US immigrant restriction, businesses—particularly extractive industries, timber, and rail infrastructure—continued to seek exploitable workers from the periphery of the global economy. Shipboard conditions generally improved with the transition from sail to steam, but Asian travelers were still denigrated in the white press. Their structural position—particularly en route to labor sites rather than on plantations—approached, though did not match, that of European migrant laborers driven by structural compulsions (and who also bore considerably circumscribed freedoms). Their Pacific voyages reflected circumscribed voluntarism, rather than the radical unfreedom of slave ships (Barde 2008; McKeown 2008).

Deportation Train Cars: Topographies of Cost, Design, Control

The passages above suggest the coercive racial viapolitics of US land seizure and labor hyperexploitation as two fundamental components of US settler colonialism within a global racial capitalist system. The following delves in finer detail into the early twentieth-century politics of immigration control and deportation. This, I argue, is a key third component of US imperial viapolitics—the regulation through expulsion of who does, and does not, get to be a settler.

Deportation in the late nineteenth century was regionally based and relatively ad hoc (Blue 2017). In the early twentieth century, when the US Department of Labor began using deportation trains to expel those unwelcomed as settlers, federal immigration services did not own or maintain their own fleet of vehicles. Much like air deportation in many regions today, which utilizes and repurposes commercial routes and carriers (chapter 10, this volume), they used cars provided by major railroad and private transport firms. The first sets of eastbound European deportees were typically conveyed in Pullman tourist cars, updated versions of the mid-nineteenth-century vessels meant for working-class and middle-class customers. Even ordinary Pullman tourist cars, however, were part of a system that thrilled with traces of the sublime. A 1930 essayist mused, "Is not a steam locomotive a thing of the most stupendous beauty? It is the very materialization of power" (Wilson 1930, 303; cited in Stilgoe 1985, xii). An otherwise reserved historian fairly gushed that the passenger train was "a triumph of American technology," replete with "lighting, heating, air conditioning, food services, toilets, washrooms, a water supply, and sleeping, seating and lounging facilities.... All these systems must be fitted into the cramped spaces available between the side panels, under the floor, and in utility closets.... Dependability, weight, and cost are also crucial factors" (White 1978, xii). By 1917, Pullman cars of all classes had "innumerable hidden mechanisms" designed to make travel more comfortable. An individual car contained "nearly a mile of laminated copper wire, over a half mile of pipes," as well as innumerable switches, circuit boards, dynamos, motors, ventilators, push buttons, "and other apparatuses" (Welsh, Howes, and Holland 2010, 9). Even more impressive was the domestic opulence that wealthier travelers found in the suites of Pullman's sleepers, parlor cars, libraries, and dining cars (Richter 2005, 81–83). Well-to-do passengers, regardless of where they were in the nation, enjoyed a panoply of consumer delights (Stilgoe 1985, 66).

The Pullman cars that Southern Pacific leased were well suited to help the company profit from deportation traffic. According to Immigration Bureau agents, Southern Pacific had refined their own "prison cars" thanks to their role in the so-called coolie trade.[7] Indeed, Southern Pacific began carrying contract Chinese laborers aboard these cars from San Francisco to New Orleans, and then by sea to Cuba, to work on sugar plantations (Corbitt 1942; Hu-DeHart 1994; Jung 2006). Despite the prohibitions against the Chinese and others from the so-called Asiatic Barred Zone after the 1917 immigration act, the law required that people otherwise denied entry would still be permitted the "privilege of transit" through US territory—which many used to evade immigration law (Geiger 2010). Southern Pacific put steel mesh across car windows and paid a force of armed guards to prevent escapes.[8] Still, some immigration officials reported that Southern Pacific's cars were "not entirely satisfactory."[9]

The Open-Plan System and Liberal Social Hygiene

The means of coercive viapolitics aboard Southern Pacific's Chinese cars focused on maintaining the vehicles as closed containers that would "encapsulate" (chapter 5, this volume) their passengers. Because immigration agents and Southern Pacific guards considered all Chinese workers to be equally dangerous to the nation-state, they saw no need for internal train-board segregation, and sought only to keep Chinese travelers from escaping. Moreover, because Chinese migrants were predominantly male (largely due to the 1875 Page Act, which equated virtually all Chinese women with prostitution and thus radically restricted their entry), there would have been little concern with gendered segregation. To this end, the means of control were among coercive mobility's oldest—physical restraint in the form of screens across doors and windows, coupled with the threat of guard violence. Because they traveled more or less willingly under the structural compulsions of poverty and labor contract, manacles were unnecessary. Guards posted at each end of the train would prevent escape. Such mechanisms also mimicked an open plan of penal architecture and reflected the spatio-political priorities prior to the advent of disciplinary segregation. As means of control, they were cheap and relatively effective, though transit passengers probed for weaknesses and developed—and circulated—plans for how to escape (Geiger 2010; Young 2014).

This open-plan sensibility guided early deportation car design. On eastbound journeys between 1914 and 1916, in which people of European descent were conveyed from across the country to Ellis Island for removal across the Atlantic,

Southern Pacific provided tourist cars to the Immigration Bureau. Southern Pacific's profits would be highest, and the Department of Labor achieved greater efficiencies, when the trains were full. Agents in 1916 estimated saving $20,000 each year.[10]

Westbound parties contained more explicitly racialized peoples from Mexico and across the Pacific world and, consequently, used the more securitized "prison cars."[11] Once more, the oldest foundations of coercive mobility provided security: the screens and bars across the windows and armed guards at each door, with open-plan architecture within.

Yet some deportation agents espoused more refined sensibilities. As agents of a biopolitical, liberal democratic capitalist system, they were influenced by the Progressive Era's priorities of spatial and political segregation as a means of modern social planning and racial order. It bears remembering that *Plessy v. Ferguson*, the 1896 legal basis for Jim Crow segregation, was concerned with rail accommodation. Moreover, the ascendant ideals of what has been referred to as New Penology brought ideas of spatial segregation into America's prisons to categorize inmates by race, sex, and anticipated degrees of dangerousness or reformability (McLennan 2009; Perkinson 2010; Blue 2012).

Early Immigration Bureau correspondence reflected a struggle over cost and conditions aboard the trains. Budget-conscious managers advocated for packing as many people as possible into a single car to avoid hiring additional staff.[12] In contrast, more liberal guards and managers called for greater train-board differentiation, segregation, space, and supervision. Their interests were less in mollycoddling deportees than in maintaining control.

San Francisco Immigration Commissioner Samuel Backus was unhappy with the cars. A train left Seattle with four attendants and one deportation officer overseeing sixteen unfree passengers. Thirteen more would be added in San Francisco, two in Los Angeles, and seven in Denver. The group Backus described included "men, women, and children, black and white, in same [sic], immoral, convicts, diseased and respectable public charges." Yet the car contained "only thirteen sections, twenty six berth [sic] available for our use." Backus supported these putatively unfit people's removal—population control was his life's work—but told his superiors that cramming forty-three people into a single car was poor practice.[13] A month later and after another overloaded train, he repeated his point. Two different cars would permit better possibilities for oversight and partitioning.[14] Again, Backus's superiors told him to "use but one car and reduce number of attendants accordingly."[15] Chicago Immigration Commissioner Prentis tended to agree with Backus but suggested that "in addition to the question of economy," which he took as a given, "the question of safety should also be taken into consideration."[16]

Indeed, over the next few years, train-board agents and managers tried to balance the dimensions of safety and economy and turned more often to the prison-style cars. The racial differentiation in the early cars' architecture—prison cars for Asians and tourist cars for Europeans—had counterposed the Yellow Peril of Asian menace with the pathos of European unfortunates, and, for a time, replicated a fundamental structuring between the dangerous and the merely pathetic—all of whom should be excluded, but in more or less punitive or securitized ways. Yet as hysteria over European saboteurs, anarchists, and communists grew through the First World War, Red Scare, and Palmer Raids, the lines between the dangerous and the pathetic blurred. It was simpler and safer, most managers reasoned, to always use the prison cars. They never knew when the pathetic might rise to become a threat. Still, the prison cars left unresolved how, or if, deportation agents should keep different classes of people apart, leading to innovation in wagon design that revealed conflicting imperatives in the management of deportation by train.

The *Lorenzo* Debates: Cellular Systems versus the Open Plan

Much as elegant Pullman cars for wealthy passengers conveyed the delights of urbane consumption through space, deportation cars contained within them the multiple coercions of the US carceral state: the prison, the asylum, the hospital, and the jail. If, as historian John Stilgoe (1985, 66) has suggested, boarding a prestige car allowed passengers to "never leave the city" and permitted their entry into "the life of urban dreams," unfree travelers stepping into the deportation car would find the familiar nightmares of the workhouses, prisons, and asylums they had just left.

Four years into the transcontinental deportation rail system, officials remained discontented with their vehicles. One officer remarked that the bureau remained "dependent upon the goodwill of the railroad authorities in furnishing suitable and properly equipped cars," and the firms' goodwill often fell short. They had been providing cars that had a generally open plan, which permitted, many felt, too much intermingling among the deportees. Commissioner-General Anthony Caminetti wanted more partitioning. "The necessity of segregating the various classes, as well as separating the sexes, in a way to forestall criticism, is a troublesome proposition, viewed in light of our former car conditions."[17] It was telling that Caminetti's concern was as much about bureau image maintenance as it was about spatially ordered social hygiene.

Anticipating that deportation traffic would increase with the Great War's end, in December 1918 Caminetti recommended that the bureau acquire two purpose-modified "special cars." He proposed that they have movable partitions to facilitate deportees' segregation and to adjust to the changing numbers of each on a journey. The cars should also have accommodation for officers to oversee deportees while at work and space to rest while off duty.[18]

Throughout it all, however, were debates over cost. If the bureau came to control its own cars, Caminetti thought it would "produce satisfactory results at the minimum of cost."[19] Others thought it would be better if the Pullman Company were to "rebuild two of its tourist sleepers to meet our needs, leasing them to the government at a rate which would include up-keep, linen, porter-age, etc."[20]

Leo Russell, who became chief deportation agent in 1916, was somewhat less concerned about leasing or purchase, but lobbied for largely self-sufficient vehicles. He thought a kitchen tourist car with fourteen seating sections, a large kitchen and pantry, an icebox, and hot and cold water would be adequate. It should be staffed by a chief cook and an assistant, along with a commissary man and a porter. He hoped for a steel car rather than a wooden one, lit by electricity, not gas. Guards should have their own glassed-in compartment and their own restroom. There would be bars across the windows, of course.[21]

Russell believed in spatial segregation and social hygiene. Obviously unwell deportees should be given the upper berths whenever possible, and their food, utensils, bedding, and towels kept separate. The attending physician and deportation officer should minimize contact between the ill and the rest for fear of contagion. Echoing Caminetti's call for movable partitions, Russell recommended using a "collapsible glass partition" to help in segregation, too.[22]

After canvassing relevant staff, Caminetti recommended an experiment in leasing the Pullman car *Lorenzo*. The crew at the Pullman shop in Wilmington, Delaware, modified the car to meet the bureau's carceral specifications.[23] When it did, it invoked what contemporary prison planners understood as a cellular system, closer to the Benthamite ideal, whose spatial partitioning allowed for distinction by classificatory categories, and was seen by most reformers as an improvement on the open-plan system (see figure 1.1).

The *Lorenzo* had nine rooms—two parlors and seven staterooms, all lit by electricity—and one toilet. Each stateroom likely accommodated up to four

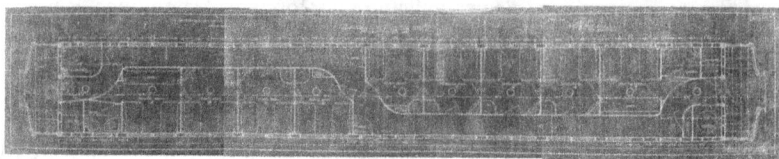

FIGURE 1.1 · Plan for the Pullman car *Lorenzo*. Staterooms were intended to provide a cellular structure for internal segregation. Source: RG 85, entry 9, file 54645/325, National Archives and Records Administration, Washington, DC.

people. A two-foot, two-inch-wide aisle ran the car's length, on the port side for half, crossing over, and along the starboard side for the other.[24]

Pullman would make the car available for charter at $15 per day, the cost of which included maintenance, light, linen, porterage, cleaning, storage, and more. Once a believer in a government-owned car, Caminetti now thought leasing was better, "as we secure the benefit of the regular service of the Pullman company, and avoid all expense bills for repairs, overhauling, etc."[25] The lease did not account for the costs of actually moving the car, however. Instead, the US Railroad Administration's Traffic Division provided rates for hauling the car.[26] Though this appeared costlier than the open-plan cars, Caminetti believed "this special car for segregating the various classes of deportees ... fully justified" the additional expense.[27] The lease was approved.[28] The *Lorenzo* made its first journey in a May–June 1919 circuit.

Looking back at the end of that trip, Leo Russell expressed his concerns. He noted that staterooms could be used to separate prisoners by class, hygiene, ailment, or potential for disruption; indeed, the "compartments are the ideal things for this purpose." Nevertheless, Russell thought the vessel needed to be hardened. It was a process in which planning for the state's worst-case scenario became the norm and set a template for the universal criminalization of so-called undesirable aliens. "When it comes to putting anarchists and criminals in these places, the compartment must be so secure that it will be practically impossible for one of these men to get out." Still, he complained that the windows on compartment doors were "entirely too small" and "limited surveillance." When the bunks were down, it was "practically impossible to see a man in the lower berth next to the window." Russell recommended the viewing port be enlarged, along with a host of other modifications.[29]

Russell appreciated that the *Lorenzo* had heavy wire screens and steel bars inside the windows that made it less visually obtrusive. "I know it is the Bureau's desire to have the car look as little like a prison car as possible," he wrote. Russell did not specify why the bureau wanted to be secretive, but it was possibly because, in the context of 1919's radical protests, the Palmer Raids, and anti-radical expulsions, officials feared that the leftists' allies might spot the cars and disrupt removal (Cannato 2009; Zimmer 2018). In any case, Russell pointed out that Southern Pacific's prison cars had steel bars outside the windows, and Pullman should do the same with the *Lorenzo*. Pullman's locks were made of soft bronze and "could be sawed through with a penknife." He had them replaced with case-hardened locks. Moreover, all the fittings should be attached with rivets rather than screws; the windows needed to be modified to open only six inches; and Pullman would need to install steel bars across the transoms.[30] Russell oversaw these changes to the *Lorenzo*'s material structure, according to much more carceral specifications. The *Lorenzo* thus came closer to realizing what Russell saw as a more perfect and economical state apparatus for territorial cleansing by rail, which conjoined a liberal desire for internal segregation with hardened securitization.

Surprisingly, given the efforts involved, the bureau ended its lease of *Lorenzo* on September 30, 1919.[31] Budgetary concerns, driven by an anticipated appropriations shortfall, were more pressing than new principles of carceral segregation. Liberal precepts of classification and spatial segregation were too costly; planners thought that the cheaper, open-plan version, without internal division, was good enough.

As a result, guards' labor rather than material partitioning would enforce differentiation among unfree passengers. It provided for a looser spatial order aboard the trains. According to the diaries kept by Leo Stanley, the chief surgeon at California's San Quentin state penitentiary and an occasional volunteer on the trains, agents still tried to distinguish between the dangerous and the pathetic, and reiterated spatial distinctions concerning notions of security, sex, and gender (Blue 2009, 2019). When Stanley boarded the eastbound deportation special in San Francisco in 1920, however, two cars were in use. One was a barred prison car, the other a tourist sleeper. The barred car was filled with men just released from state prisons and the so-called violently insane, presumably posing heightened threats of uprising or escape. Some wore shackles. Women and children, along with men taken to pose little danger, would travel aboard the tourist sleeper, which might not have bars but certainly still had guards.[32] Even the less-secure cars set women and children in one half and men in the other (Irwin 1935, 11). As with the slave ship and the slave coffle, the deportation train remained spatially oriented around political, criminal, and gendered differences. For all of the state efforts, however, deportees (save for those in manacles) could move within and across the spaces of the open-plan cars. Nevertheless, the trains cycled relentlessly from the interior of the nation toward the international border (Blue 2015).

By 1920, then, the Immigration Bureau seemed to have given up on the idea of owning or leasing its own deportation fleet, and relied on Southern Pacific or other private transport firms for their deportation cars. In 1934, the Lehigh Valley Railroad Company submitted a bid to provide cars to the deportation services and promised a reduced rate.[33] The Depression weakened the Pullman Company's grip on the sleeping car market, and Lehigh made a move into the field. A blueprint gave their proposed car's dimensions. Sleeping car 1099 was "Equipped for Chinese Service"—indicating that it had been used for transit Chinese and would do well for deportation traffic. (See figure 1.2.) The car had been built in 1910, and improved upon with a steel underframe, vestibule, and sheathing in 1925. It was some eighty feet long and ten feet wide; the roof reached fourteen feet above the tracks. The overall interior compartment was seventy-two and one-half feet long and ten feet wide. But space claimed by the male and female bathrooms, vestibules, annex, and a smoking room left around forty-five by nine and two-thirds feet of horizontal space in the main compartment. It was divided into twelve seating sections, each with two benches facing each other. Benches were about three feet wide, and with six feet, two inches from the back of one to the next. If two passengers sat on each bench, they had

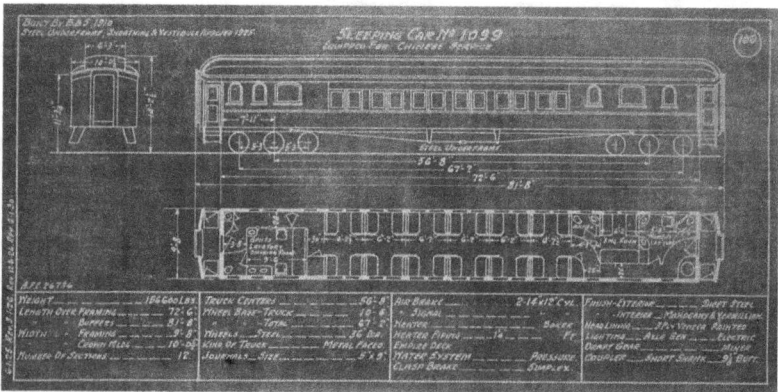

FIGURE 1.2 · A proposed open-plan deportation car, based on a model that was, according to blueprints, "Equipped for Chinese Service." Source: RG 85, entry 9, file 56193/283, National Archives and Records Administration, Washington, DC.

about three and a half square feet of horizontal area (plus whatever portion of the aisle they might claim) to sit and store their luggage. The compartment's interior height was not recorded, but vertical space was put to use, too—sleeping berths above the benches held bags by day, and people at night.[34]

Lehigh submitted other blueprints, marked up with yellow grease pencil to highlight modifications (see figures 1.3 and 1.4). The Lehigh agent noted that there were twenty-four seats with backs and room for twelve beds in this reconfigured and more highly securitized car. Additional space would hold extra cushions and convert seats into beds. A shower-bath would be replaced with wash basins, acknowledging a liberal sensibility for cleanliness—but nothing indulgent. The door to the toilet would have a glass window, in case a guard wanted to look inside.[35]

The violation of deportees' privacy was just one element of the train's additional securitization. An elevated platform near one door promised guards unencumbered vision. A screened door near the guard's seat could open and close, partitioning further between the deportees and the carriage door—something of a soft barricado from the days of the slave ship—and potentially providing the guard, but not the deportees, relative privacy during the journey. Moreover, new bars were placed across all doors and windows.[36]

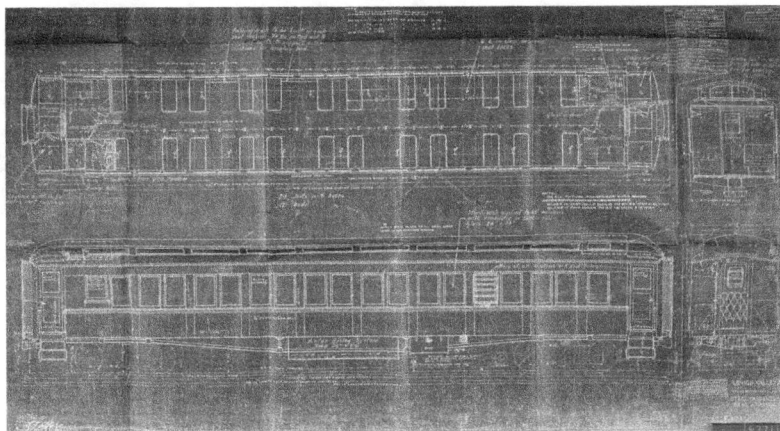

FIGURE 1.3 · Proposed modifications for train car securitization. An elevated guard's seat would allow better surveillance, and screen partitions and bars across the windows made for a more fully carceral vessel. Source: RG 85, entry 9, file 56193/283, National Archives and Records Administration, Washington, DC.

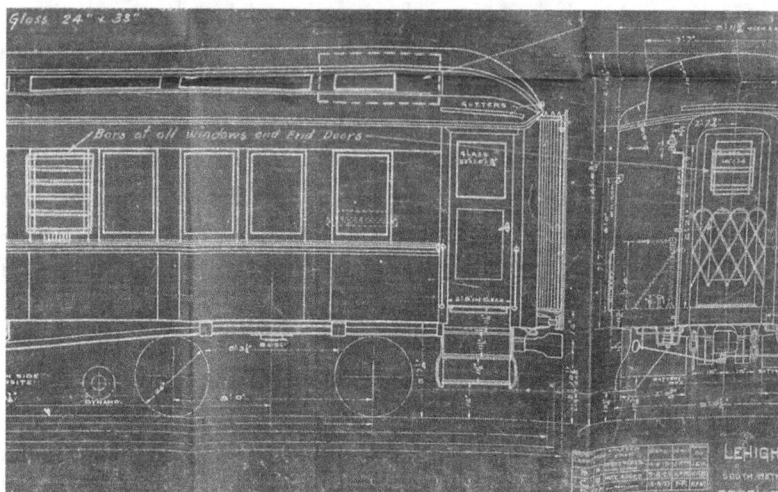

FIGURE 1.4 · Detail of figure 1.3.

Despite Lehigh's lobbying, it is unclear if the bureau ever chose their cars. At the very least, the blueprints suggest the open-plan design of the Depression-era vessels. Lehigh's soliciting agent would have been familiar with existing models, if only to make a viable bid. The blueprints indicated a regime that was a far cry from the murderous spatial arrangement of the slave ship *Brookes* or Nazi deportation and cattle cars, which allowed mere inches or less for each person. But the arrangement of bodies in mobile, carceral space—the viapolitics of this unfree travel—reflected the history and priorities of the US deportation regime and its economic efficiencies and inflictions of who could, or could not, be a settler.

Economies and Topologies of Settler Racializing Assemblages

The early twentieth-century US deportation train was a racializing assemblage of settler colonial population management that combined elements of both the coffle and the slave ship, even as it served the ends of spatially eliminating the supposedly unfit. Deportation agents, and particularly managers most concerned with costs rather than with train-board discipline, concentrated on how many people they might force into a single train car before creating either internal havoc, public scandal, or protest from their own guards. This number was limited in an absolute sense—only so many people might be packed into a finite and bound space. More fully necropolitical systems, as attempted by Nazi deportations or by slave traders seeking to maximize the number of bodies transported at lowest cost, would experiment with nightmarish degrees of density in mobile confinement. Indian removal was unbounded beyond the weapons soldiers wielded or the threat of death, but the lack of sustenance made for deadly travel—necropolitical, too, but of a different sort.

US deportation trains were founded upon and inextricable from these murderous systems but were more biopolitical elements in the racializing assemblages of settler state making and population control. Deportation agents imposed limits on train car capacities based on their sense of what was possible, up to the point of prompting rebellion—and those facing removal did sometimes rebel or refuse—thus bringing friction or, worse still, bad publicity into the system (Blue 2019, 105–13). Another limit came from agents' self-image as officers of a liberal democratic nation, who would not impose undue suffering on those they deemed either dangerous or pathetic, and while certainly unwelcome, did not merit killing. It was, nevertheless, a dominating means of coercion backed by violence.

Still, as officers experimented with these limits, the train's linear topology—like a coffle of chained slaves—could, in theory, be expanded indefinitely. The capacity of a ship's hold or a train car was limited (by varying definitions), but just as another length of chain could be hammered to the end of the coffle, another train car could always be added to the last. It was linear, segmented, and infinitely scalable, and it appealed tremendously to planners, even as cost-conscious managers clamored at every added expense. It suggests, too, the potential examination of logistical systems and tribology—the sciences of friction—in either conjoined linear systems (as in the coffle or train) or individual vessels within a network (slave ships, deportation buses and flights, or containerized shipping) as they develop or restrict flow and enable opportunities for those facing removal to challenge their expulsion. Each is embedded within historical contexts, forces, and infrastructures. Political movements compel or constrain deporting states and firms; unfree passengers push back. And administrative, labor, and fuel costs all contribute to smooth or chaotic systems (Netz 2004; Cowen 2014).[37]

The US deportation regime's experiment with the *Lorenzo* also suggests a bit about the brevity of Foucault's foray into coercive mobility and this literal example of capillary power and circulatory vessels. Foucault's carriages reiterated the themes of *Discipline and Punish*, a tale of progression (not progress) from the symbolically racialized ancien régime of galley slavery to a deracinated

metropolitan modernity enabled by technological advances. Yet despite its inge-
niousness, the "panoptic carriage had only a short history" (Foucault 1979, 264).
Foucault does not tell us why these meticulously designed carriages fell from
use. One suspects that simpler wagons were cheaper.

The typologies (and topologies) of forced travel speak to different viapolitical
forms in the US settler state. Slave transport facilitated a murderously necropolitical system, yet the property value invested in enslaved people's prices, and
the future profits of their labor, meant that traders sought to somewhat limit
deaths in transit. Indian removal was differently necropolitical: population removal to clear land for invaders and profit. Deportation traffic entailed a process of selective expulsion, bent on national population management and social
reproduction. By spatially eliminating the supposedly eugenically undesirable
from national territory, it sought to manage and regulate the lives of those who
remained. These deportation trains would not lead to the killing of the so-called
unfit, but neither would they permit them to live within the nation. Still, in their
material architecture and design, the trains operated around gendered principles
of internal differentiation among the dangerous, the contagious, and the merely
pathetic—in the name of political economy, national protection, and racialized
population control—matters that concern us today, now more than ever.

Notes

1 On train-based deportation in Belgium, see Feys (2019).
2 According to Marcus Rediker (2007, 5), 1.8 million Africans died crossing the Atlantic,
   and another 1.8 million likely died walking to the coast before boarding ships. See
   also Ekirch (1985) and Putnam (2011).
3 On ships in the internal trade, see Wesley (1942, 169–73).
4 See Ben Simpson narrative, "Interview with Ben Simpson," in *Texas Narratives*, vol.
   16, part 4, *Born in Slavery: Slave Narratives from the Federal Writers' Project, 1936–
   1938* (Library of Congress, Manuscript Division), https://www.loc.gov/resource/
   mesn.164/?sp=33.
5 The Domestic Slave Trade, "Modes of Transportation," n.d., http://www.inmotionaame
   .org/migrations/topic.cfm?migration=3&topic=3&tab=image.
6 On population transfer as a typology of removal, see Walters (2010, 78–80).
7 Assistant Commissioner-General, "Memorandum for the Acting Secretary," February 16, 1916, RG 85, entry 9, file 53775-202d, National Archives and Records Administration, Washington, DC (hereafter, NARA 1).

8 The Immigration Bureau conducted earlier experiments: see "Pullman Prison Car for Alien Criminals," *New York Times*, June 6, 1913.

9 Memorandum, February 16, 1916, RG 85, entry 9, file 53775-202d, NARA 1.

10 Memorandum, February 16, 1916, RG 85, entry 9, file 53775-202d, NARA 1.

11 Memorandum, February 16, 1916, RG 85, entry 9, file 53775-202d, NARA 1.

12 Taylor, Los Angeles, to Commissioner of Immigration, Seattle, February 1914, 52903/60-A, RG 85, entry 9, NARA 1.

13 Backus telegram to Washington, DC, office, February 20, 1914, 52903/60-A, RG 85, entry 9, NARA 1.

14 Backus to Commissioner of Immigration, Seattle, March 24, 1914, 52903/60-B, RG 85, entry 9, NARA 1.

15 Larned to Immigration Service, San Francisco, March 31, 1914, 52903/60-B, RG 85, entry 9, NARA 1.

16 Prentis to Commissioner General of Immigration, Washington, DC, April 18, 1914, 52903/60-B, RG 85, entry 9, NARA 1.

17 Caminetti to Oscar A. Price, Assistant Director General of Railroads, Washington, DC, December 6, 1918, 54645-325, RG 85, entry 9, NARA 1.

18 Caminetti to Price, December 6, 1918, 54645-325, RG 85, entry 9, NARA 1

19 Caminetti to Price, December 6, 1918, 54645-325, RG 85, entry 9, NARA 1.

20 Memorandum, January 2, 1919, 54645-325, RG 85, entry 9, NARA 1.

21 Russell, "Memorandum with Regard to Deportation Parties," January 6, 1919, 54645-325, RG 85, entry 9, NARA 1.

22 Russell, "Memorandum with Regard to Deportation Parties," January 6, 1919, 54645-325, RG 85, entry 9, NARA 1.

23 J. T. Ransom to Caminetti, March 10, 1919, 54645-325, RG 85, entry 9, NARA 1.

24 J. T. Ransom to Caminetti, March 10, 1919, 54645-325, RG 85, entry 9, NARA 1. The Immigration Bureau's contract to lease the *Lorenzo* for deportation traffic was modeled on the "analogous condition" and arrangements made for wartime "movements of United States hospital cars used for the transportation of wounded men." Pullman provided six attendants with the car, for the special wartime rate of $15 per day. Gerris Fort to Commissioner General of Immigration, ATTN Roger O'Donnell, March 28, 1919, 54645-325, RG 85, entry 9, NARA 1.

25 Memorandum for the Acting Secretary, April 5, 1919, 54645-325, RG 85, entry 9, NARA 1.

26 The US Railroad Administration would charge the Department of Labor 30 cents per mile dead-head—empty of deportees, but with necessary staff. The same rate would apply when there were between seven and twenty deportees. When there were more than twenty deportees, they no longer needed to pay the 30 cent per mile charge. Memorandum for the Acting Secretary, April 5, 1919, 54645-325, RG 85, entry 9, NARA 1.

27 Memorandum for the Acting Secretary, April 5, 1919, 54645-325, RG 85, entry 9, NARA 1.

28 Caminetti to Ransom, May 2, 1919, 54645-325, RG 85, entry 9, NARA 1.

29 Russell to Commissioner General of Immigration, June 24, 1919, 54645-325, RG 85, entry 9, NARA 1.

30 Russell to Commissioner General of Immigration, June 24, 1919, 54645-325, RG 85, entry 9, NARA 1.

31 Comissioner General to Ransom, September 29, 1919, 54645-325, RG 85, entry 9, NARA 1.

32 Leo Stanley, "Five Weeks Leave," Leo L. Stanley diaries, box 1, vol. 4, SC 070, Stanford University Archives, Stanford, CA.

33 J. N. Haynes to P. S. Millspaugh, "Reconditioning Cars for Deportation Parties," April 23, 1934, 56193/283, RG 85, entry 9, NARA 1.

34 Sleeping Car No. 1099 Blueprint, "Reconditioning Cars for Deportation Parties," 56193/283, RG 85, entry 9, NARA 1.

35 Blueprint 6771 and 6771 Revised, "Reconditioning Cars for Deportation Parties," 56193/283, RG 85, entry 9, NARA 1.

36 Blueprint 6771 and 6771 Revised, "Reconditioning Cars for Deportation Parties," 56193/283, RG 85, entry 9, NARA 1.

37 On order and chaos in US deportation, see Guariglia (2018), Hiemstra (2019), and Pope-Obeda (2018).

References

Barde, Robert Eric. 2008. *Immigration at the Golden Gate: Passenger Ships, Exclusion, and Angel Island.* Westport, CT: Praeger.

Berlin, Ira. 2004. *Generations of Captivity: A History of African-American Slaves.* Cambridge, MA: Harvard University Press.

Blue, Ethan. 2009. "The Strange Career of Leo Stanley: Remaking Manhood and Medicine at San Quentin State Penitentiary, 1913–1951." *Pacific Historical Review* 78 (2): 210–41.

Blue, Ethan. 2012. *Doing Time in the Depression: Everyday Life in Texas and California Prisons.* New York: New York University Press.

Blue, Ethan. 2015. "Strange Passages: Carceral Mobility and the Liminal in the Catastrophic History of American Deportation." *National Identities* 17 (2): 175–94.

Blue, Ethan. 2017. "From Lynch Mobs to the Deportation State." *Law, Culture, and the Humanities,* October 12. https://doi.org/10.1177/1743872117734168.

Blue, Ethan. 2019. "The Means and Meanings of Carceral Mobility: US Deportation Trains and the Early Twentieth-Century Deportation Assemblage." In *Caging Borders and Carceral States: Incarcerations, Immigration Detentions, and Resistance,* edited by Robert T. Chase, 93–124. Chapel Hill: University of North Carolina Press.

Byrd, Jodi A. 2011. *The Transit of Empire: Indigenous Critiques of Colonialism*. Minneapolis: University of Minnesota Press.

Cannato, Vincent J. 2009. *American Passage: The History of Ellis Island*. New York: Harper Perennial.

Christopher, Emma, Cassandra Pybus, and Marcus Rediker, eds. 2007. *Many Middle Passages: Forced Migration and the Making of the Modern World*. Berkeley: University of California Press.

Corbitt, Duvon C. 1942. "Chinese Immigrants in Cuba." *Far Eastern Survey* 13: 130–32.

Cowen, Deborah. 2014. *The Deadly Life of Logistics: Mapping Violence in Global Trade*. Minneapolis: University of Minnesota Press.

Day, Iyko. 2015. "Being or Nothingness: Indigeneity, Antiblackness, and Settler Colonial Critique." *Critical Ethnic Studies* 1: 102–21.

Day, Iyko. 2016. *Alien Capital: Asian Racialization and the Logic of Settler Colonial Capitalism*. Durham, NC: Duke University Press.

Dunbar-Ortiz, Roxanne. 2014. *An Indigenous Peoples' History of the United States*. Boston: Beacon.

Ekirch, Roger A. 1985. "Bound for America: A Profile of British Convicts Transported to the Colonies, 1718–1775." *William and Mary Quarterly* 42 (2): 184–200.

Feys, Torsten. 2019. "Riding the Rails of Removal: The Impact of Railways on Border Controls and Expulsion Practices." *Journal of Transport History*, March 9. https://doi.org/10.1177/0022526619832195.

Foucault, Michel. 1979. *Discipline and Punish: The Birth of the Prison*. Translated by Alan Sheridan. New York: Vintage.

Foucault, Michel. 2007. *Security, Territory, Population: Lectures at the Collège de France, 1977–1978*. New York: Picador.

Geiger, Andrea. 2010. "Caught in the Gap: The Transit Privilege and North America's Ambiguous Borders." In *Bridging National Borders in North America: Transnational and Comparative Histories*, edited by Benjamin H. Johnson and Andrew R. Graybill, 199–222. Durham, NC: Duke University Press.

Gigliotti, Simone. 2009. *The Train Journey: Transit, Captivity, and Witnessing in the Holocaust*. New York: Berghahn.

Guariglia, Matthew. 2018. "Wrench in the Deportation Machine: Louis F. Post's Objection to Mechanized Red Scare Bureaucracy." *Journal of American Ethnic History* 30 (1): 62–77.

Hiemstra, Nancy. 2019. *Detain and Deport: The Chaotic U.S. Immigration Enforcement Regime*. Athens: University of Georgia Press.

Hoerder, Dirk. 2011. "Migration, People's Lives, Shifting and Permeable Borders: The North American and Caribbean Societies in the Atlantic World." In *Migrants and Migration in Modern North America: Cross-Border Lives, Labor Markets, and Politics*, edited by Dirk Hoerder and Nora Faires, 1–48. Durham, NC: Duke University Press.

Hu-DeHart, Evelyn. 1994. "Chinese Coolie Labor in Cuba in the Nineteenth Century: Free Labor or Neoslavery." *Contributions in Black Studies* 12 (1): 38–54.

Irwin, Theodore. 1935. *Strange Passage*. New York: Harrison Smith and Robert Haas.

Johnson, Walter. 1999. *Soul by Soul: Life Inside the Antebellum Slave Market*. Cambridge, MA: Harvard University Press.

Jung, Moon-Ho. 2006. *Coolies and Cane: Race, Labor, and Sugar in the Age of Emancipation*. Baltimore, MD: Johns Hopkins University Press.

Karuka, Manu. 2019. *Empire's Tracks: Indigenous Nations, Chinese Workers, and the Transcontinental Railroad*. Oakland: University of California Press.

Mbembe, Achille. 2003. "Necropolitics." Translated by Libby Mentijes. *Public Culture* 15 (1): 11–40.

McKeown, Adam M. 2008. *Melancholy Order: Asian Migration and the Globalization of Borders*. New York: Columbia University Press.

McLennan, Rebecca M. 2009. *The Crisis of Imprisonment: Protest, Politics, and the Making of the American Penal State, 1776–1941*. Cambridge: Cambridge University Press.

Molina, Natalia. 2018. "Deportable Citizens: The Decoupling of Race and Citizenship in the Construction of the 'Anchor Baby.'" In *Deportation in the Americas: Histories of Exclusion and Resistance*, edited by Kenyon Zimmer and Cristina Salinas, 164–91. College Station: Texas A&M University Press.

Netz, Revel. 2004. *Barbed Wire: An Ecology of Modernity*. Middletown, CT: Wesleyan University Press.

Perkinson, Robert. 2010. *Texas Tough: The Rise of America's Prison Empire*. New York: Metropolitan.

Pope-Obeda, Emily. 2018. "National Expulsions in a Transnational World: The Global Dimensions of American Deportation Practice, 1920–1935." In *Deportation in the Americas: Histories of Exclusion and Resistance*, edited by Kenyon Zimmer and Cristina Salinas, 18–49. College Station: Texas A&M University Press.

Pressner, Todd. 2007. *Mobile Modernity: Germans, Jews, Trains*. New York: Columbia University Press.

Putnam, Lara. 2011. "The Making and Unmaking of the Circum-Caribbean Migratory Sphere: Mobility, Sex across Boundaries, and Collective Destinies, 1840–1940." In *Migrants and Migration in Modern North America: Cross-Border Lives, Labor Markets and Politics*, edited by Dirk Hoerder and Nora Faires, 99–128. Durham, NC: Duke University Press.

Rediker, Marcus. 2007. *The Slave Ship: A Human History*. New York: Viking.

Richter, Amy G. 2005. *Home on the Rails: Women, the Railroad, and the Rise of Public Domesticity*. Chapel Hill: University of North Carolina Press.

Robinson, Cedric J. 2000. *Black Marxism: The Making of the Black Radical Tradition*. Chapel Hill: University of North Carolina Press.

Smallwood, Stephanie E. 2007. *Saltwater Slavery: A Middle Passage from Africa to the American Diaspora*. Cambridge, MA: Harvard University Press.

Smithers, Gregory. 2015. *The Cherokee Diaspora: An Indigenous History of Migration, Resettlement, and Identity*. New Haven, CT: Yale University Press.

Stilgoe, John R. 1985. *Metropolitan Corridor: Railroads and the American Scene*. New Haven, CT: Yale University Press.

Trafzer, Clifford E. 2000. *As Long as the Grass Shall Grow and Rivers Flow: A History of Native Americans*. Belmont, CA: Thomson Wadsworth.

Veracini, Lorenzo. 2015. *The Settler Colonial Present*. London: Palgrave Macmillan.

Walters, William. 2010. "Deportation, Expulsion, and the International Police of Aliens." In *The Deportation Regime: Sovereignty, Space, and the Freedom of Movement*, edited by Nicholas De Genova and Nathalie Peutz, 69–100. Durham, NC: Duke University Press.

Wehilye, Alexander G. 2014. *Habeas Viscus: Racializing Assemblages, Biopolitics, and Black Feminist Theories of the Human*. Durham, NC: Duke University Press.

Welsh, Joe, Bill Howes, and Kevin J. Holland. 2010. *The Cars of Pullman*. Minneapolis: Voyageur.

Wesley, Charles H. 1942. "Manifests of Slave Shipments along the Waterways, 1808–1864." *Journal of Negro History* 27 (2): 155–74.

White, John H., Jr. 1978. *The American Railroad Passenger Car*. Baltimore, MD: Johns Hopkins University Press.

Wilson, Edward D. 1930. "Beauty in Ugliness." *Photo-Era* 64: 303.

Wolfe, Patrick. 1999. *Settler Colonialism and the Transformation of Anthropology: The Politics and Poetics of an Ethnographic Event*. London: Cassel.

Young, Elliot. 2014. *Alien Nation: Chinese Migration in the Americas from the Coolie Era through World War II*. Chapel Hill: University of North Carolina Press.

Zimmer, Kenyon. 2018. "The Voyage of the Buford: Political Deportations and the Making and Unmaking of America's First Red Scare." In *Deportation in the Americas: Histories of Exclusion and Resistance*, edited by Kenyon Zimmer and Cristina Salinas, 132–63. College Station: Texas A&M University Press.

TWO

From Migrants to Revolutionaries:

The *Komagata Maru*'s 1914 "Middle

Passage" | Renisa Mawani

On March 28, 1914, Indar Singh from Thalwandi, Lahore, boarded the *Komagata Maru* in Hong Kong alongside 164 Punjabi passengers.[1] He and others heard rumors that Gurdit Singh—a man they did not yet know—had successfully chartered a Japanese-owned steamship that would take them across the Pacific to Vancouver. When Gurdit Singh had visited the Hong Kong Gurdwara, a Sikh place of worship, the previous year, he met 150 men who were awaiting passage to North America. Now, those who could pay the twenty-pound fare accompanied Indar Singh on the voyage; many traded their life savings for dreams of a future on Canada's west coast.[2] On April fourth, after several delays by Hong Kong authorities, the *Komagata Maru* finally departed. The ship stopped in Shanghai, Moji, and Yokohama, picking up additional passengers before commencing its transpacific route to British Columbia. The 376 people aboard included 12 Hindus, 25 Muslims, and 339 Sikhs. All were adult men, save for two women and two children, including Gurdit Singh's six-year-old son, Balwant. On May 21, after six weeks at sea, the vessel arrived in Victoria, where the passengers were subjected to medical examinations. Two days later, the ship dropped anchor in Vancouver Harbour, where it was detained for two months, only to become a racial, political, and legal spectacle for those on shore. Figure 2.1 shows the passengers on the upper deck wearing their best clothes and looking to the shore awaiting their fate and future. In figure 2.2 we see leisure boats and

FIGURE 2.1 · *Komagata Maru*, 1914. Photographer/Studio: Canadian Photo Company. Vancouver Public Library, accession number 127.

FIGURE 2.2 · *Komagata Maru* with HMCS *Rainbow* in Vancouver Harbour surrounded by leisure boats, 1914. Photographer: Frank Leonard. Vancouver Public Library, accession number 6229.

rowboats filled with white men who were trying to get a closer glimpse of the ship, with the HMCS *Rainbow*, a Royal Canadian Navy vessel in the background.

As one of 376 passengers, and as one of twelve men with the same name, Indar Singh was in good company. He was listed on the ship's manifest as passenger 328. William Hopkinson, the immigration agent at Vancouver, and Daljit Singh, Gurdit Singh's personal secretary, drafted the manifest a day after the steamer arrived in the harbor. Under maritime law, all shipmasters were required to submit manifests when their vessels entered ports of call. As declarations of who and what was on board, manifests were early forms of legal writing that designated persons and cargoes as legal or illegal (Mawani 2018, 128). Against the backdrop of three recently enacted orders-in-council, the most egregious of which required travelers to make a continuous journey from their place of birth or naturalization, nearly all those aboard the *Komagata Maru* were deemed to be unlawful entrants (Macklin 2011).[3] Only twenty passengers, those who could prove previous domicile in Canada, were permitted to disembark.[4] The others, including Indar Singh, were confined to the ship amid deplorable conditions and eventually deported to Calcutta.

Like his fellow travelers, Indar Singh had been residing in Hong Kong and awaiting a steamer that would take him to North America. Many of the men who joined the ship were former Sepoys in the British Army, later employed as security guards, police officers, jailers, and night watchmen in Shanghai and Hong Kong. Some sought passage to Canada and the United States to pursue further education; others, including Indar Singh, were searching for steady employment and better wages (Jackson 2012). By the first decade of the twentieth century, and in efforts to enforce the continuous journey regulation, Canadian authorities instructed shipping companies not to carry Indians from the subcontinent or from ports in the "far east." Maritime regulation was part of a much larger nationalizing movement initiated by the white Dominions and aimed at restricting the mobility of Indian migrants. As Indians were British subjects, literacy tests in Australia and the continuous journey provision in Canada were written in ways that did not appear to be explicitly racial (Huttenback 1976; MacLean 2015; Reynolds and Lake 2012). Efforts to fortify the borders of white settler colonies against the perceived influx of Indians and other "Asiatics" reinforced and extended divisions between so-called free and unfree mobility. These distinctions, as Adam McKeown (2012, 22) points out, emerged and developed out of transatlantic slavery and shaped the regulation of other movements, including indentured labor. By the early twentieth century, the increased migration of nonindentured Indians and so-called voluntary migrants to Canada and other white Dominions created calls to expand control over various forms of movement (Mongia 2018, 2).

The voyage of the *Komagata Maru* has received considerable scholarly attention (see Chattopadhyay 2018; Dhamoon et al. 2018; Johnston 2014; Mawani 2018; Roy 2017; Sohi 2014). Yet the steamer's 1914 journey has largely been narrated through the coordinates of arrival, departure, nationalism, and territoriality, themes that center histories of migration as histories of landfall (see Mawani 2018, 1–13). On its inbound and outbound passage, the ship crossed the Pacific and Indian Oceans. Passengers spent six months confined to a vessel that was overcrowded and under-provisioned. Yet the materiality of the ship, its transoceanic routes, and the colonial and racial histories its seaborne movements engendered are not often discussed (Mawani 2018; Anim-Addo, Hasty, and Peters 2014; introduction, this volume). The *Komagata Maru* is unexceptional in this regard. As several scholars have noted, "mobilities 'at sea' are a vastly underexplored area" (Anim-Addo, Hasty, and Peters 2014, 337). Yet modes of travel mattered. Long passages by ship opened spaces for violence and coercion but also for intimacy, collaboration, and transgression.[5] As William Walters, Charles Heller, and Lorenzo Pezzani argue in the introduction to this volume, ships at sea were "the moving location of a collective experience," a place where new identities and alliances were forged but where "land-based social hierarchies" (6) could also intensify. Gurdit Singh and several other passengers viewed their voyage as a challenge to the regulations that Canada had imposed on Indian migrants. Colonial authorities on shore characterized those aboard as endangering Dominion, colonial, and ultimately, imperial rule. By September 1914, even before the *Komagata Maru* arrived on the Hooghly River outside of Calcutta, the Indian colonial state recast passengers from migrants to revolutionaries. These newly imposed identities, which were shaped by speculations on what had happened aboard the ship, authorized an unprecedented and repressive legal apparatus. In anticipation of the ship's arrival, the Indian colonial government introduced the Ingress into India Ordinance, which granted authorities sweeping powers to search incoming ships and to arrest and detain men returning from abroad (Mawani 2018). Operating in different regions, as new forms of border regulation, the continuous journey provision and the Ingress into India Ordinance were aimed at prohibiting the seaborne itineraries of Indian men, thereby curtailing the perceived radicalism thought to ensue from maritime travel.

This chapter builds on my book, *Across Oceans of Law: The Komagata Maru and Jurisdiction in the Time of Empire*. Whereas the book follows the *Komagata Maru* through time and space by tracing the circulations of law, radicalism, and racial violence the voyage engendered, this chapter takes a closer look at the decks of the ship. Specifically, I examine the tensions and solidarities that emerged, especially across religious lines, as well as the relations between Gurdit Singh and the Japanese crew. To pursue this line of inquiry, I draw inspiration from the literature on transatlantic slavery. Scholars of slavery have foregrounded the ship, the Middle Passage, and racial terror and rebellion at sea. In the absence of historical records, some have employed creative methods of reading archives and writing history, exploring gaps and silences through critical imaginaries (Hartman 2008, 2020; Philip 2008; Sharpe 2016). The conceptualizations produced by scholars of slavery are also generative. In *Many Middle Passages*, Marcus Rediker, Cassandra Pybus, and Emma Christopher (2007, 2) argue that the transatlantic slave trade offers useful analytic approaches "to explore other social and cultural transformations." The Middle Passage, for example, "is not merely a maritime phrase to describe one part of an oceanic voyage. It can, rather, be utilized as a concept—the structuring link between expropriation in one geographic setting and exploitation in another" (2). Approaching the *Komagata Maru*'s voyage through the methods and orientations developed by scholars of transatlantic slavery, I suggest, may invite new ways to connect the ship's 1914 voyage to other histories of racial and colonial violence, fugitive resistance, and solidarity that seek to trouble distinctions between free and unfree migration.

In this chapter, I draw on passenger testimonies to explore what happened at sea. Following the ship's arrival in September 1914, the Indian colonial government established the Komagata Maru Committee of Enquiry, which interviewed many of the returning passengers about their experiences aboard the ship. Most gave their evidence in confinement. Some were imprisoned in the Alipore Central Jail (Calcutta). Others, including Indar Singh, recalled the voyage from the Medical College Hospital, and still others gave evidence from their villages in Punjab. These testimonies, I argue, do not suggest intention or motivation. Rather, they give us a glimpse of what happened at sea. Reflecting on the archive of transatlantic slavery, David Kazanjian (2015, 82) terms this "speculative work." Traces of the archive, he argues, "might not be the expression of a subject's will, desire, intention, or voice but might still be readable by us, today, as a powerful political text." Some of the most generative forms of speculative work have come from scholars of slavery. The limits of the archive have demanded modes and methods of creative imagining, what Saidiya Hartman (2008, 11) has termed "critical fabulation." Speculation, I suggest here, poses different questions about the orienting terms and trajectories of mobility, especially the histories they enable and foreclose, including connections between the Atlantic and Pacific, transatlantic slavery and Indian migration, and forced and free movements. But speculation also informed the anxieties and operation of the colonial Indian state. What happened on the decks of the ship informed allegations of antico- lonial radicalism that introduced additional ways to police the peregrinations of Indian men.

The Middle Passage

The literature on transatlantic slavery provides a generative set of methods for thinking about movement, mobility, violence, and insurgency. Scholars have in- creasingly turned their attention to oceans and riverine regions, and to the racial terrors and rebellions that unfolded on slave ships as they passed through salt and fresh water (Grandin 2014; Johnson 2013; Rediker 2007; Smallwood 2008). Ships feature prominently as discursive objects, material technologies, and as sites and sources of history. In his field-defining book, *The Black Atlantic*, Paul Gilroy (1995, 4) describes the conceptual role of the ship as follows: "Ships immediately focus attention on the middle passage, on the various projects for redemptive return to an African homeland, on the circulation of ideas and activists as well as the movement of key cultural and political artefacts: tracts, books, gramo- phone records, and choirs." For Marcus Rediker (2007, 10), the ship operates as a material agent of history: "The slave ship and its social relations have shaped the modern world." If European vessels were central to conquest, long-distance trade, and the rise and expansion of global capitalism, he writes, "the Guinea- man was the linchpin of the system" (13). In its triangular passage from Eu- rope to West Africa, the Americas, and back to Europe, the slave ship produced modern forms of sovereignty and terror (Rediker 2010). Thus, ships were never modes of transport alone. They were moving spaces of terror, confinement, and freedom that dramatically altered the pathways of history.

The literature on the transatlantic slave trade is useful for thinking about migration and movement, both methodologically and analytically. What is of particular interest to me here is how scholars of slavery have foregrounded slave ships and Atlantic voyages to explore the subjection, subjectification, and violent transformation through which African captives were transformed into property. In a famous passage, Hortense Spillers (1987, 72) describes this pro- cess accordingly: "Those African persons in the 'Middle Passage' were literally suspended in the 'oceanic.'... Removed from the indigenous land and culture, and not-yet 'American' either, these captive persons, without names that their captors would recognize, were in movement across the Atlantic, but they were also *nowhere* at all." Africans were "culturally 'unmade,'" Spillers continues, "thrown in the midst of a figurative darkness that 'exposed' their destinies to an unknown course." This "unknown course," others have argued, was spatial, temporal, metaphysical, and always violent (Philip 2008; Smallwood 2008).

As a time-space of multiple forms and changing intensities of racial terror, the Middle Passage was a transition zone in which identities were imposed, contested, and disputed. At sea, captains and crews reconstituted Africans from persons to property and from humans to abstract value (Philip 2008, 196). "The human manufacturing process," Sowande' Mustakeem (2016, 7) writes, "and, more importantly, the interior holds of merchant ships served as vital sites of power sailors used to dehumanize captives, enforce dependency, inflict pain, establish authority, and prohibit any sense of control over one's personal life in the near and far future." The whip and the ledger worked in complementary ways, as forms of abstraction, commodification, and dehumanization (Rupprecht 2007). Regimes of violence unfolded on the littoral, at sea, and on land (Smallwood, 2008, 35–36). Efforts to transform Africans into property were initiated through racial violence that would eventually connect the shore, ship, and plantation. Africans may have been commodified in the Middle Passage, but for Stephanie Smallwood (2008, 153), it was on the block and in the marketplace "that human commodities became American slaves."

The slave ship, Rediker (2007, 204) reminds us, was "full of roiling, explosive social tensions," which authorized the limitless sovereignty of captains (on the unique authority systems onboard ships, see the introduction and chapter 3, this volume). Despite the brutality of the captain's decree, the decks and the hold opened new opportunities for kinship, resistance, and rebellion. Notwithstanding differences in birthplace, culture, and language, African men, women, and children forged intimate relations and solidarities. The Black Atlantic, Omise'eke Natasha Tinsley (2008, 199) argues, has always been the queer Atlantic. "Queer not in the sense of a 'gay' or same-sex loving identity waiting to be excavated from the ocean floor," she clarifies, "but as a praxis of resistance . . . forging interpersonal connections that counteract imperial desires for Africans' living deaths." Pleasure, desire, and camaraderie among African captives were modes of survival at sea, ways of life in the unbearable presence of bodily, cultural, and social death (see Patterson 1985).

To be clear, the Japanese-owned *Komagata Maru* was not a slave ship but a merchant vessel. Built by Connell and Company in 1890, and long after Britain formally abolished slavery, the steamer was commissioned by the German Hansa Line as a passenger-cargo ship (Mawani 2018, 88). By March 1914, the midsized ship had been sold twice and fully refurbished. Though it was equipped with fifteen cabins and a portable coal stove, it no longer carried passengers, only cargo. After signing the Charter Party with the ship's owners, Gurdit Singh had the lower decks cleaned, latrines installed, and wooden benches fitted to maximize the spaces where passengers could eat and sleep (Johnston 2014, 27). Unlike the slave ship that was rigidly organized by race, the Komagata Maru was arranged not by caste, region, or religion, but by a multifaith shipboard hierarchy that was loosely organized in spatial terms. As the commander of the ship, Gurdit Singh designated one cabin as his private quarters and another as his office. He assigned a third as the ship's Gurdwara where passengers—irrespective of religion—were invited to pray, congregate, and partake in religious lectures and sermons.[6] His close associates—including Daljit Singh, Amir Muhammed Khan, Bir Singh, and Harnam Singh—were also given cabins. The remaining Hindu, Sikh, and Muslim passengers lived in close quarters on the upper and lower decks. Indian colonial authorities on shore feared that these shipboard living arrangements, which undermined religious and caste distinctions, would encourage solidarities and shared ideas of revolution that might potentially extend from the decks of the ship, through port cities and further inland, as passengers reached their final destinations. Speculations of sedition and insurgency at sea provided one impetus for the Ingress into India Ordinance.

During its 1914 journey, the Komagata Maru did not carry forced or unfree laborers. One year earlier, the ship was licensed to transport Chinese indentured workers to Java. However, these plans never materialized (Mawani 2018). Instead, the steamer carried Punjabi migrants, who by all accounts chose to take passage from Hong Kong, Shanghai, Moji, and Yokohama to Vancouver. The ship was under the jurisdiction and authority not of a European or British captain but a Japanese one. According to the Charter Party, the forty-person crew was to follow Gurdit Singh's orders. When the vessel reached Vancouver, conditions aboard the ship were described as filthy and overcrowded. Although many passengers complained of the lack of fresh food and clean water, there were no reported illnesses or deaths at sea. Twenty passengers were allowed to disembark at Vancouver. Those detained on board were not confined to specific decks. Given the stark differences between the slaver and the merchant vessel, how might the Middle Passage, with its recollections of racial terror, trauma, and insurgency, be useful in analyzing the Komagata Maru's 1914 voyage?

One of the most significant aspects of the literature on transatlantic slavery, as I note above, is the emphasis that scholars have placed on the ship. Drawing on ocean metaphors and critical imaginaries, some have sketched out the struggles, solidarities, and transformations that characterized the Atlantic passage and beyond (Hartman 2008; Tinsley 2008). Africans were forced onto slave ships as captives. By the time they landed in the Americas, captives were transformed into commodities that could be bought, sold, and owned by others. The horrors of the Middle Passage and the devaluation of human life were resisted through love and companionship, mutiny and suicide (Mustakeem 2016; Tinsley 2008). If Smallwood (2008) identifies the voyage as a time-space in which African captives were violently remade "into Atlantic commodities," Rediker (2007) points to another dynamic in which African captives became shipmates. These competing identities were asserted through collective struggle against racial terror in the hold, at sea, and eventually on the plantation. Although the slave ship cannot be uncritically extended to seaborne passages in other times and places, the speculative methods of writing history that the scholarship on transatlantic slavery has produced highlights the ship as a space where racial and colonial violence was enacted, and where anticolonial histories and solidarities were imagined and cultivated.

Situating the *Komagata Maru*'s 1914 voyage alongside histories of transatlantic slavery may also trouble the presumed distinctions between free and forced mobility. "The greatest legacy of the early modern era," Adam McKeown (2012, 28) observes, "was the transatlantic slave trade from Africa, and its abolition. It was easily the most quantitatively significant long distance migration before the 1830s, and the migration that received the greatest public attention at the turn of the nineteenth century." Captains, sailors, abolitionists, and colonial authorities imposed racial distinctions between free (white) and unfree (black) labor that continue to inform discussions of migration today. Aboard the *Komagata Maru*, these characterizations of freedom and unfreedom were contested and ultimately defied by Gurdit Singh and the other passengers. For Singh, the 1914 voyage was a business venture that challenged Britain's claims to the free sea and Canada's immigration laws. Following their detention in Vancouver Harbour, several passengers referred to themselves as prisoners and "slaves" (Mawani 2018, 73). In recalling slavery, Gurdit Singh and his comrades placed the *Komagata Maru*'s journey into a much longer racial and colonial history of violent displacement and forced confinement under British imperial control (Mawani 2018, 224–25).

Indar Singh from Thalwandi left Lahore in 1907, traveling first to the Malay Peninsula and then to Hong Kong. The landlocked province of Punjab, the area from which he came, was the last to be colonized by British rule. In 1849, following the East India Company's annexation, British authorities sought to integrate the region's Hindus, Muslims, and Sikhs into an expanding empire (Ballantyne 2006; Grewal 1998). Recruited as Sepoys for the British Army, Punjabi men, mostly farmers, found new opportunities to travel overseas. After completing their service, many journeyed westward and eastward to port cities in East Africa, the Straits Settlements, and China and were employed as police officers, night watchmen, merchants, and laborers in plantations, mines, and factories (Aiyar 2015; Amrith 2015). In 1907, Indar Singh left Punjab to follow the overland and sea routes opened by British imperial rule. Between 1912 and 1914, and before boarding the *Komagata Maru*, he worked as a police officer in Hong Kong.[7]

In spring 1914, Indar Singh heard news from several Punjabi men that Gurdit Singh had secured the charter for a vessel that would take Indians to Canada. The previous year, the *Komagata Maru* had been employed as a cargo ship, carrying Japanese coal to port cities in the South China Sea. By early 1914, the ship's owners sent their broker, Mr. Odagiri, to Hong Kong, where they hoped he would secure a "coolie license" so they could transport Chinese indentured labor to Java. It was there that Odagiri met Gurdit Singh. The two reached an agreement by which Gurdit Singh would charter the ship for six months. In the meantime, the firm's application for an indenture license was successful. White contract tickets that legitimized the transport of Chinese indentured laborers, and which were aboard the steamer, would be the subject of controversy on the ship and on shore. Gurdit Singh "gave us [white] passes on which there was a Government seal," Indar Singh would later tell authorities. Other passengers noted that he allegedly acquired these tickets from the *Lat Sahib* at Hong Kong.[8] News of the voyage and the white tickets traveled quickly to nearby ports. "Those who had embarked at Hong Kong told us that the bara sahib at Hong Kong had given the order that we would be allowed to land," recalled Hazara Singh, who boarded in Shanghai.[9] Passengers believed that Hong Kong authorities had distributed the white tickets and thus sanctioned the *Komagata Maru's* transpacific journey.

In Calcutta, Indian officials asked why passengers like Indar Singh, Hazara Singh, and others willfully boarded a ship that might not be permitted to land in Vancouver. Many laid blame on Gurdit Singh, claiming that he deliberately misled them by fraudulently distributing white Chinese contract tickets as "government passes." After the ship arrived in Calcutta, Indian authorities observed that the "certificate clause is not signed by any Government officer in any of the tickets we have seen." Thus, they concluded that "the passengers were deceived by Gurdit Singh" to believe that the white tickets "contained a permit from the Government of Hong Kong authorizing them to land at Vancouver."[10] However, Gurdit Singh and his confidantes had been listening closely for changing legal developments on Canada's west coast. Ships bound for Hong Kong and other Asian port cities brought news and updates from afar that proved crucial to the *Komagata Maru*'s voyage.

Bhan Singh, a student from Jullundur, also boarded the steamer in Hong Kong. Like many others, he too had been searching for a ship that would take him to North America.[11] Given the changing legal restrictions directed against Indian travelers, Bhan Singh had been corresponding with "Thomas Cooke and Sons," who "assured him" that as a student, he would be allowed to enter the United States. He eventually found a steamship company that would issue him passage. Before boarding the ship, he heard rumors that "two or three students had been refused admission."[12] In the meantime, Bhan Singh received a letter from his friend, Mr. Udan Singh, inviting him to Vancouver. But after making several inquiries with steamship companies, Bhan Singh could not find a vessel. "One company, the Osaka Kishen Kaisha," responded that "the Immigration authorities had issued a strict order saying that if they brought any Indian passengers, the Immigration authorities would fine them 500 dollars in gold per head," he recalled.[13] Shortly thereafter, Bhan Singh met Gurdit Singh. Given his ability to speak English, Gurdit Singh hired him as an interpreter. He promised him passage to Vancouver and offered him a cabin in lieu of salary.

According to Bhan Singh, Gurdit Singh did not tell the passengers they would be allowed to disembark at Vancouver. He and his associates were well aware that a law prohibited the entry of Indian travelers who did not make a continuous journey. But while the ship was in Hong Kong, the men received news that the regulation had recently been struck down by the court. "The continuous journey clause," as Bhan Singh understood it, "was altogether cancelled by Chief Justice Hunter's judgment in Victoria." The case to which he referred was *Re Thirty Nine Hindus*, which was initiated by Husain Rahim, an alleged revolutionary and a member of the *Komagata Maru* shore committee who fought on behalf of the passengers in Vancouver. In November 1913, when the British Columbia Court of Appeal heard the case, Chief Justice Ian Hunter disallowed the continuous journey regulation. The Khalsa Diwan Society, Vancouver, immediately wrote to "the Temple Committee at Hong Kong saying 'let the passengers come over to Vancouver, they will be allowed to land now that the clause has been cancelled,'" Bhan Singh explained.[14] He received similar letters from "friends and also . . . from friends of other passengers at Hong Kong." Those "100 people of who[m] I have spoken, who were allowed to land," he continued, "had not 200 dollars in their pockets and they did not go by continuous journey ticket."[15] News of Hunter's decision was met with excitement and traveled in different directions. The clandestine knowledge that travelers carried to ports of call, and to Hong Kong in particular, shaped the seaborne itineraries and imaginaries of Punjabi men. Given these latest legal developments, Bhan Singh and Gurdit Singh believed that passengers would be allowed to disembark when the ship reached Vancouver. What they did not anticipate was that the continuous journey regulation would be revised and reissued by the Dominion government while the *Komagata Maru* was at sea.

With the alleged approval of the governor of Hong Kong, the white tickets issued to passengers, and news of recent legal developments in Vancouver, the ship commenced its passage under Gurdit Singh's command. The outbound voyage was relatively uneventful. The weather cooperated, save for one storm, and relations among the 376 passengers and the Japanese captain and crew were cordial and even amicable. A multifaith committee was appointed to oversee the distribution of food and water. The group of eleven was composed mainly of Sikhs, including Amar Singh and Bhan Singh, but it also included one Hindu, Pohlo Ram, and a Muslim, Amir Muhammed Khan. On the way to Vancouver, several passengers talked regularly with members of the Japanese crew, and on at least one occasion the Punjabi men invited them to share a meal (Mizukami 2019, 174–75).

The scholarship on the *Komagata Maru* has focused almost exclusively on the Sikh passengers at the expense of its Hindu and Muslim ones (see Johnston 2014). Yet the cramped shipboard conditions encouraged friendships, alliances, and solidarities across religious and caste lines. Karam Dad was one of twenty-five Muslims from the Shahpur District in what is now Pakistan. He left Punjab in 1908, one year after Indar Singh, and in the same year that the Dominion of Canada passed the continuous journey regulation. Karam Dad worked in Hong Kong, first as a night watchman and then as a police officer.[16] Like many others aboard the ship, he also heard rumors that a steamer would transport Indians to Canada. Although he did not know for certain whether the ship would be allowed to land, Karam Dad told the Komagata Maru Committee of Enquiry, "Other people were going, so also I went." Baru, another Muslim, heard similar accounts. "A ship had gone there before," he explained, "and sixty men in that ship were landed in Vancouver."[17]

In his testimony, Karam Dad recalled that he lived on the lower deck with eight or nine Muslim men. "There were other Mussalmans [approximately seventeen or eighteen of them] who used to live on the top deck of the ship," another passenger told authorities.[18] But Karam Dad's immediate shipmates included Pir Baksh, who joined at Hong Kong, where he was unemployed and awaiting passage to North America; Baru from Ludhiana, who boarded at Shanghai; Karam Ali from Dhaner, Ambala, who also joined at Hong Kong; and Amir Muhammed Khan, who was known as *munshi* (teacher) and was a close associate of Gurdit Singh. The Muslims said prayers and ate together on the lower deck. Given that Sikhs and Hindus were mainly vegetarians, the "food of the Mussalmans was cooked separately and the food of the Sikhs was cooked separately," Amir Muhammed Khan explained.[19] But several passengers reported that Muslims and Sikhs shared a common living space. "I was with the Sikhs," Khan recollected "I lived in a corner of the deck where the Sikhs were." Five "Muhammadans [were] also with me." Though Amir Muhammed Khan ate with Karam Dad and the other Muslims, he also had a cabin close to Gurdit Singh's quarters. When asked about the cabin, Khan retorted, "the room was simply *nam ka wasteh*," only because he was a munshi.[20] Although the Muslim passengers were a clear minority among the Sikhs, they told Indian authorities that Gurdit Singh treated them amicably, with courtesy and respect.

From Hong Kong to Vancouver, relations between the Japanese crew and the passengers were cordial and, in some cases, convivial. The chief engineer, Yokichi Shiozaki, who described himself as "a relation of one of the part-owners of the ship," socialized regularly with Gurdit Singh (Mizukami 2019).[21] Although Shiozaki was twenty years younger, Captain Cardew of the Royal Engineers described him as having a "more intimate" relationship with Gurdit Singh "than [did] the other Japanese officers."[22] The two allegedly discussed Japanese imperialism and Indian politics while sharing whiskey. Gurdit Singh drank daily, Shiozaki told officials. He drank beer and almost finished a full bottle of whiskey every three days.[23] He described his friend as "a very religious man." Although the chief officer said little more about their personal interactions, the two men were clearly on friendly terms. As tensions escalated on shore, Shiozaki told authorities that Gurdit Singh gave him "a dozen bottles of whiskey to keep for him at Vancouver."[24]

According to Bhan Singh, problems began when the steamer dropped anchor in Vancouver Harbour and passengers were unexpectedly detained. Supplies

FIGURE 2.3 · The ship's co-owner, Yokichi Shiozaki (far left), Chief Engineer Masayoshi Kajiyama (second from left), Captain Yamamoto (third from left), and Gurdit Singh (right side), July 1914. Vancouver Public Library, accession number 13162.

were running low and conditions were quickly deteriorating. "Enmity arose when the people were starving and there was no food at all," Bhan Singh explained. "I told Gurdit Singh, 'It is you who have to supply the provisions, not the Immigration Authorities nor the local committee of the Hindus at Vancouver. You have taken twenty pounds from each of the passengers; you must supply them with food. Do not let the passengers die of hunger, as you have got some money with you.' So he quarreled with me and made many people quarrel with me," Bhan Singh continued.[25] Under the Charter Party, Gurdit Singh was given the responsibility for supplying food, water, and provisions to the passengers. But when the ship reached Vancouver, and despite his legal obligations, authorities did not allow him to disembark. According to Pohlo Ram, a member of the rations committee and the ship's accountant, problems at Vancouver were about supplies and much more.[26] "The passengers had deposited money with Gurdit Singh," Pohlo Ram told officials. "They demanded it, and he said he would give it when they landed." The "Immigration officers were prepared to allow Bhan Singh to land," because he was a student, Pohlo Ram continued, "but Gurdit Singh prevented him." Thus, Ram and several others reached the conclusion that "Gurdit Singh was not a good man."[27]

Pohlo Ram told authorities that the "passengers had formed a clique owing to the bad food and bad treatment accorded them" by Gurdit Singh. But after being detained at Vancouver, "this clique dissolved, and a party was formed to enforce Gurdit Singh's authority and to act against the immigration authorities."[28] Rising tensions around food, water, and resources deepened the growing animosity between Gurdit Singh and Bhan Singh and further divided the passengers. "The men at Hoshiarpur and Jullunder were Bhan Singh's followers," Hazara Singh recalled. There were "about forty or fifty" of them.[29] Most of the remaining passengers supported Gurdit Singh. "The Muhammadans were on Gurdit Singh's side," Hazara Singh continued. "One of them [Amir Muhammed Khan] was a Munshi and all of them followed the Munshi."[30] The growing divide between Gurdit Singh and Bhan Singh would have serious repercussions for all those aboard. The animosity between them created hostilities and also engendered new solidarities aboard the ship. These developments fueled anxieties about sedition and revolution among colonial authorities in India. The *Komagata Maru*'s anticipated arrival in Calcutta inaugurated a new security regime—the Ingress into India Ordinance—that was to be in place for six-months but which remained in effect until February 1922, three months after Gurdit Singh surrendered to Punjab police (Mawani 2018, 192).

Becoming Revolutionaries

By the first decade of the twentieth century, Indian colonial officials expressed increased concerns about Indian men—especially from Punjab—traveling abroad via ship. Their fears were informed by the growing influence of Punjabi diasporic revolutionary organizations including Ghadr, which were expanding their reach from North America to Asian and African port cities (Aiyar 2015; Ramnath 2011). Their transgressive potential and expanding persuasion was partly the result of a circulating print culture, which allegedly traveled with Indian men aboard ships. The Ghadr newspaper, also known as the *Hindustan Ghadar* was first published in Urdu and then Gurmukhi, sought to educate its readers on the brutalities committed by the British in India. The party's politics were clear: they called for violent rebellion and an overthrow of imperial rule (Puri 1993; Elam 2014; Gill 2014; Ramnath 2011; Sohi 2014). The Indian colonial government aspired to prevent the circulation of the paper and its anticolonial agenda in two ways: first, by limiting the seaborne movements of Punjabi men, and second, by marshaling the Sea Customs Act to intercept all periodicals deemed to be seditious. Both strategies proved ineffective. In August 1914, following the outbreak of World War I, many Ghadarites traveled to India to fight against British imperial rule (Gill 2014). In November 1914, when Mr. Isemonger of the Punjab Police testified before the Komagata Maru Committee of Enquiry, he could not confirm the exact number of men who "returned to India . . . from America," though he was sure that the figures were "considerably greater" than they were in previous years. Sundar Singh, the deputy superintendent of Punjab Police, estimated that in 1914, between fifteen hundred and two thousand men arrived from abroad.[31] Speculations about what happened on the *Komagata Maru* fueled fears of anticolonial revolution that were already circulating through Ghadr channels and among Calcutta's working classes (Chattopadhyay 2018).

Scholars of transatlantic slavery have argued that mutiny and insurgency were common in the Atlantic world (see Rediker 2007). The Middle Passage was a period of racial violence and terror, but it did not diminish the defiance and struggles of African captives. Mutinous slave ships have inspired novellas, films, and academic writing. Although slave revolts at sea were common, some were effective and others failed (Taylor 2009). African women and men waited for opportunities to rise up against their European captains and crews. Some were inspired by religious observances, such as Layl-tul-Khadr or the night of power, marked by Muslims in the last ten days of Ramadan; others awaited bad weather (Grandin 2014).

Indian colonial authorities alleged that long seaborne voyages, on which passengers shared cramped quarters and were often idle, spawned insurgent views and rebellious plots. What was especially concerning about the maritime passage, as I have pointed out in the previous section, was that caste and religious distinctions that were vital to colonial governance on land were blurred and even diminished on the overcrowded decks of merchant ships. Food preparation, for example, did not often follow the purity rituals of caste observances. Thus, crossing the *Kala Pani* (or black water) was terrifying for several reasons. For Hindus, it resulted in a loss of caste (Anderson 2012, 25). For colonial authorities, the close proximities of shipboard experiences potentially encouraged dangerous solidarities, affinities, and insurgencies against British imperial power and control.

In India, fears of sedition and radicalism at sea held significant consequences on land. As colonial officials speculated as to what happened aboard ships and during long voyages, their fears informed calls for repressive legislation that targeted foreigners and nationals alike. In September 1914, while anticipating the *Komagata Maru*'s arrival, the Indian colonial government passed the Ingress into India Ordinance. Enacted one week after the Foreigners Ordinance, this provision—and the suspicions of sedition and insurgency that informed it—granted colonial administrators unprecedented power to arrest, detain, and imprison men returning to India from abroad (Mawani 2018, 204–5). When the *Komagata Maru* reached Calcutta, the district magistrate, Mr. Donald, boarded the ship with a coterie of British officials. Standing on the deck, he read out the ordinance, warning passengers that they would be arrested and imprisoned if they did not immediately follow the directions given by authorities (Mawani 2018, 201). Police officers from Bengal and Punjab searched the passengers for firearms and seditious materials but found nothing. Nonetheless, returnees were directed to board the special trains to Punjab. Nearly sixty men, including many of the Shahpur Muslims, complied. The others stayed with Gurdit Singh, as he promised to refund their tickets for the failed journey and to return monies that he had borrowed from them to buy coal in Moji. In what was described by authorities as the Budge Budge "riot," and by critics as the Budge Budge "massacre," forty people were killed, including twenty passengers. Many more were injured, and more than two hundred men were imprisoned in the Alipore Central Jail (Mawani 2018, 204).

Indian colonial authorities worried that a shipload of discontented men, who were supposedly under the seditious influences of Gurdit Singh and disaffected by their unsuccessful voyage, would only incite trouble on their arrival to Calcutta. Many feared that they would join forces with radicals in the city (Chattopadhyay 2018). Officials in Canada, India, and Hong Kong accused Gurdit Singh of wielding a dangerous influence over the passengers, particularly on the ship's forced return. According to Lieutenant-Colonel D. C. Phillot, Gurdit Singh was swayed by several "Japanese gentlemen, notables," who entertained him "at a hotel in Shamunusaki, specially selected for certain historical associations." Speeches were made "and the Japanese stated they hoped India would wake up and become free; that the Japanese would help them" so that "Japan, India, and China would form a powerful combination sufficient to 'down' the countries of Europe."[32] Gurdit Singh brought these messages back to the ship, authorities claimed. He discussed Japanese imperialism with Shiozaki and "preached sedition" to the other passengers.[33] The lectures that he allegedly delivered on board remained a point of dispute. Although Captain Yamamoto did not speak English and could not understand Punjabi, Urdu, or Hindi, he told authorities, through an interpreter, that passengers congregated for prayers twice and sometimes four times a day. After being questioned by the Committee of Enquiry, Yamomoto conceded that he could not fully distinguish between seditious lectures and prayers. What he could confirm was that "the lectures were given at the same place where the books were," presumably in the ship's Gurdwara.[34] These speeches, Yamamoto claimed, were intended to provoke passengers on "their return to India to instigate trouble." Gurdit Singh used the ship's failed voyage and his time at sea to encourage an "armed revolution," he recalled.[35] But Shiozaki offered a more sympathetic view of his friend: "Gurdit Singh seems to have looked upon himself as a deliverer of the oppressed in India."[36]

Anxious and apprehensive about what happened aboard the ship, Indian colonial officials, both in their questions to passengers and in their final report, strategically exploited the tensions between Gurdit Singh, Bhan Singh, and the Japanese crew. Drawing from the testimony of select passengers and crew, the commissioners reached the conclusion that Gurdit Singh and his associates were indisputably ill-intentioned. The *Komagata Maru*'s voyage was a deliberate attempt to defy Canada's immigration prohibitions, they claimed. Singh and the other passengers quarreled with the crew and interfered with the vessel's itinerary. According to Chief Officer Miaji, "Entries relating to . . . [these disturbances] were made in the log."[37] Punjab and Bengal authorities insisted that dangerous ideas were circulated to the passengers through the Ghadr newspaper, the *Hindustanee*, and other seditious periodicals. Drawing from Yamamoto's testimony, the commissioners claimed that the Ghadr newspaper was "received on board at Shanghai, Moji and Yokohama," as new passengers joined the steamer. "This [Ghadr] paper, specimen copies of which we have seen and had translated," one official continued, "is published by a revolutionary organization in America and openly advocates mutiny against the British Government in India." The paper "circulates freely in the Far East and in America, and we think that it was introduced into the *Komagata Maru* through the agency of these revolutionary societies in order to promote disloyalty and disaffection among those on board."[38] Although Gurdit Singh was adamant that he did not follow the Ghadrs, other passengers were believed to be Ghadr sympathizers (Johnston 2013).

The Ghadr paper was not the only revolutionary influence aboard the ship, the ship's captain, crew, and several passengers claimed. According to Yamamoto, Husain Rahim gave him "copies of the *Hindustanee* paper," of which he was the founder and editor, while the vessel was detained in Vancouver.[39] Hazara Singh confirmed that the passengers "received a bundle of newspapers in Gurmukhi at Vancouver," but since he did not read Gurmukhi, he did not know what these papers were.[40] When authorities asked Badan Singh whether he saw any "Gurmukhi newspapers put on board at Vancouver," he retorted, "I am illiterate, I do not know."[41] Mr. Hori, the third officer, claimed that he saw "the passengers reading newspapers written in Indian characters." Some men "were always lecturing on the subject of a revolutionary movement," he added. But the most dangerous influence was Gurdit Singh.[42] What Yamamoto and his crew called "revolutionary lectures," others described as religious sermons. When the ship was docked in Shanghai and to commemorate Baisakhi, Nanak Singh explained, Gurdit Singh "delivered a lecture on the life of the tenth Guru."[43]

It was on their outbound journey from Vancouver, Captain Yamamoto told authorities, that Gurdit Singh and his associates made "systematic efforts ... to excite the passengers against the authorities and to promote a rising against Government."[44] Gurdit Singh "posed as a revolutionary leader on board the steamer," officials concluded. His speeches and lectures "tended to bring many of the passengers to his side."[45] Other men also gave lectures. According to several witnesses, two Sindhi brothers—Jawahir Mal and Narain Das—who boarded the ship at Kobe, as it was en route to Calcutta, were thought to be troublemakers. Aged twenty-five and seventeen respectively, the two brothers supposedly delivered lectures every four to five days. According to Pal Singh, the brothers "used to say that the Government oppresses us very much and they do not allow us to land; they do not give us food and they are doing *zulum*."[46] But Jawahir Mal denied these allegations as he claimed to speak only "broken Hindustani."[47] After the ship anchored on the Hooghly River, Inspector Halden from the customs office insisted that the brothers' seditious influences were clearly visible. "There were two boys" who "were about twenty-one years of age. I never spoke to them, but I could see that they were not very good boys. *Sedition was stamped on their faces*."[48] The men expressed a "quiet insolence," the health officer added. One was wearing "blue pyjamas and the other [was dressed] in a pink kimona [sic]." They were well-educated "Poona Brahmins" and fluent in Japanese.[49] With their eclectic clothing, kimonos, pajamas, and Panama hats, and their many boxes of books, the brothers clearly stood out. Indian authorities described them as "malcontents."[50]

The Committee of Enquiry concluded that "the Government officers, who had expected to find a large number of destitute passengers on board [the ship], the majority of whom were violently hostile to Gurdit Singh, found instead that ... [most of the passengers were] completely under his control." During the voyage, many "had been excited to a state of serious disaffection towards the Government ... [and] a considerable number of them were armed and prepared to go to almost any length in their opposition to the authorities."[51] When the commissioners questioned Miaji as to why the captain and crew did not report the troubling temperament of the passengers, he replied accordingly: "The reason why I did not take it seriously was that these three or four hundred men were very few compared to the whole population of India, and there was not anyone among them of any influence or importance," not even Gurdit Singh.[52]

Despite Miaji's claims regarding the passengers' supposed insignificance, the *Komagata Maru's* arrival dramatically reshaped India's security regime. Through speculations over what happened at sea, Indian authorities transformed the returning passengers from migrants to revolutionaries who were supposedly intent on overthrowing British rule. Under the Ingress, Indar Singh was sent to the Medical College Hospital. Karam Dad was captured at Budge Budge and detained without charge in the Alipore Central Jail. On October 29, almost six weeks following the *Komagata Maru's* arrival and the Budge Budge massacre, Karam Dad and two hundred of his fellow travelers remained imprisoned without charge. Indian authorities were anxious about the solidarities and alliances that formed aboard the ship. Their response to speculations of what was happening on board was the Ingress, which expanded surveillance and detention from sea to shore, and further inland. Between 1914 and 1922, the Ingress was used to arrest and imprison thousands of Punjabi men suspected of sedition and insurgency at home and abroad. The new restrictions on mobility that the Ingress put into effect disrupted the ability of these men to travel, work, and ultimately, to earn a livelihood.

Conclusion

Writing against the archives of slavery with its many gaps and silences, and using innovative methods, including speculative work, scholars of transatlantic slavery have redirected attention to the ship, the sea, and the Middle Passage (Hartman 2008; Kazanjian 2015, 82; Philip 2008; Tinsley 2008). Voyages from West Africa to the Americas engendered forms of violence and terror as well as expressions of creativity, intimacy, and resistance that have required critical imaginaries to return them to history (Tinsley, 2008). This chapter draws inspiration from this scholarship and from the forms of speculation it invites us to consider. In the case of the *Komagata Maru*, centering the ship and its 1914 journey—as a viapolitical lens invites us to do—foregrounds the significance of the ship's passage as a period of transition, transformation, and transgression. The six months that the *Komagata Maru* was at sea and detained in Vancouver produced tensions, animosities, and alliances between the Sikh, Muslim, and Hindu passengers and their Japanese captain and crew. For many of the passengers, the voyage was a "politically transformative experience." Some became anticolonials and radicals, others political activists, and still others—including Gurdit Singh—became both (Balachandran 2016).

On November 5, 1914, the Komagata Maru Committee of Enquiry visited the Medical College Hospital to reexamine a number of men regarding the supposed disquietude and discontent that emerged among the passengers while the ship was at sea. Authorities questioned Indar Singh once again. "When you were not allowed to land at Vancouver," the commissioner asked, "you were very dissatisfied?" Yes, Indar Singh replied, "we felt very sorry. We lost so much money and I lost my employment." Has "the Government ill-treated you in this matter," the commissioner queried. "Without any reason," Indar Singh responded, the "Government has injured us innocent ones and looted us. . . . I left my home seven years ago and I left my service and lost so much money." However, the commissioner could not understand why Indar Singh was blaming government authorities. When pressed further, he replied, "Because Government allowed the ship to start we thought we should be allowed to land at Vancouver. Government could have told the man who chartered the ship [Gurdit Singh] that we would not be allowed to land." But they did not do so. The immigration prohibitions were revealed only after the ship arrived in Vancouver.[53]

At first glance, the passengers aboard the *Komagata Maru*, including Indar Singh, Karam Dad, and others, appear to be voluntary migrants. After all, they traveled from Punjab to Hong Kong, taking up employment as police officers and night watchmen, and then sought passage to North America in search of a better life. But as many of the passengers conveyed to authorities, their travels within the British Empire were constrained by the imperial and Dominion governments and also by the Indian colonial state. Freedom in this context was highly circumscribed through maritime regulations and racial exclusions. It opened the possibility for Indian men to travel to some jurisdictions in service of the British Empire (as Sepoys and security guards), while prohibited from others, including the white Dominions. Placing the *Komagata Maru*'s 1914 voyage alongside the literature on transatlantic slavery invites novel ways to problematize prevailing themes of choice, consent, and freedom that continue to shape discussions of mobility and migration (Mongia 2018). The British Empire enforced the movements of enslaved Africans, Chinese, Indian indentured labor, and so-called free migrants, opening certain routes, itineraries, and diasporas, while foreclosing others. In the case of the *Komagata Maru*, these foreclosures were facilitated by a series of repressive laws, the continuous journey regulation, and the Ingress into India Ordinance, which responded in different ways to speculations about radicalism at sea. According to Canadian and Indian colonial authorities, the *Komagata Maru* was transporting mutineers, seditionists, and revolutionaries who were inciting passengers to overthrow British rule.

After the ship's arrival in Calcutta, at least one traveler drew connections between regimes of shipboard violence inaugurated by transatlantic slavery and their collective experiences of coercion and confinement aboard the *Komagata Maru*. As one unidentified passenger described it, authorities "have made us beggars, slaves, close prisoners in solitary confinement for an indefinite period in a steamship."[54] These remarks gesture to transatlantic slavery, indenture, and voluntary migration from India as interconnected histories of racial coercion and violence while highlighting the tenuousness of freedom under British imperial rule (Mawani 2018). These intersecting histories of violence, and resistance vividly emerge when we center the ship and the sea.

Notes

Many thanks to William Walters, Charles Heller, and Lorenzo Pezzani for inviting me to contribute and for comments on earlier versions of this chapter. I would like to express my gratitude to Hardeep Dhillon and the participants of the "Mobilities and Immobilities" workshop at Harvard, especially Robert Diaz, who helped me to see what I was writing, as well as Ryan Edwards and Catie Peters.

1 Passenger testimony discussed here comes from *Proceedings of the Komagata Maru Committee of "Enquiry,"* vol. 2 (October 23–December 4, 1914) [hereinafter *Proceedings*]. IOR/L/PJ/6/1338. India Office Records, British Library, London.

2 Not all the passengers paid their fares. Many of the Muslim passengers, for example, did not pay for passage.

3 In 1908, the Dominion of Canada passed the continuous journey regulation, which was struck down and reenacted several times. Although the regulation did not make reference to race or nationality, it was directed explicitly at migrants from India. The other two orders-in-council prohibited laborers from entering British Columbia and required migrants to have $200 in their possession. For a discussion, see Macklin (2011, 40–67).

4 The numbers of those allowed to disembark range from twenty to twenty-two.

5 I am drawing from a capacious definition of intimacy presented by Lowe (2015).

6 The subject of these lectures, as I discuss below, was a point of contention. Some described them as religious, others as political and revolutionary.

7 *Proceedings*, Indar Singh, 331.

8 *Proceedings*, Indar Singh, 331.

9 *Proceedings*, Indar Singh, 333.

10 William Vincent and Members of the Komagata Maru Committee of Enquiry to the Secretary, *Draft Report* [hereinafter *Report*], no. 132, December 3, 1914, 8, National Archives of India, Delhi [hereinafter NAI]. Home Department—Political, January 13, 1915.

11 *Proceedings*, Bhan Singh, 477.

12 *Proceedings*, Bhan Singh, 477.

13 *Proceedings*, Bhan Singh, 477.

14 *Proceedings*, Bhan Singh, 478.

15 *Proceedings*, Bhan Singh, 479.

16 *Proceedings*, Karam Dad, 139.

17 *Proceedings*, Baru, 135.

18 *Proceedings*, Baru, 136; Karam Elahi, 139.

19 *Proceedings*, Amir Muhammed Khan, 112.

20 *Proceedings*, Amir Muhammed Khan, 144. "Nam ka wasteh" means "in name only."

21 *Proceedings*, Shiozaki, 20. On Shiozaki as an owner, see Mizukami (2019).

22 *Proceedings*, Captain Cardew, 50.

23 *Proceedings*, Shiozaki, 21.

24 *Proceedings*, Shiozaki, 37.

25 *Proceedings*, Bhan Singh, 479.

26 *Proceedings*, Bhan Singh, 475.

27 *Proceedings*, Pohlo Ram, 469–70.

28 *Proceedings*, Pohlo Ram, 468.

29 *Proceedings*, Hazara Singh, 334.

30 *Proceedings*, Hazara Singh, 335.

31 *Proceedings*, Isemonger, 492; Sundar Singh, 491.

32 NAI, Notes Political-A, nos. 211–24, September 1914. Hopkinson to Cory, June 30, 1914.

33 NAI, Notes Political-A, nos. 211–24, September 1914. Hopkinson to Cory, June 30, 1914.

34 *Proceedings*, Captain Yamamoto, 14.

35 *Proceedings*, Yamamoto, 13.

36 *Proceedings*, Shiozaki, 51.

37 *Proceedings*, Miaji, 34.

38 NAI, *Report*, 11–12.

39 *Proceedings*, Yamamoto, 37.

40 *Proceedings*, Hazara Singh, 334. Note that the *Hindustanee* was published in English and not Gurmukhi.

41 *Proceedings*, Badan Singh, 335.

42 *Proceedings*, Mr. Hori, 35.

43 *Proceedings*, Nanak Singh, 128.

44 NAI, *Report*, 15.

45 NAI, *Report*, 15.

46 *Proceedings*, Pal Singh, 220.

47 *Proceedings*, Jawahir Mal, 95.

48 *Proceedings*, Inspector Halden, 159, emphasis added.

49 *Proceedings*, Dr. W. C. Hossack, 179.

50 *Proceedings*, Inspector Halden, 159.

51 NAI, *Report*, 25.

52 *Proceedings*, Miaji, 32.

53 *Proceedings*, Indar Singh, 331–32.

54 *Proceedings of the Komagata Maru Committee of "Enquiry,"* vol. 3 (October 23–December 4, 1914), Exhibit 49. "An account in English of the tyranny over 'Komagata Maru' Passengers in Kobe." BL L/PJ/6 1338, 98. India Office Records, British Library, London.

References

Aiyar, Sana. 2015. *Indians in Kenya: The Politics of Diaspora.* Cambridge, MA: Harvard University Press.

Amrith, Sunil. 2015. *Crossing the Bay of Bengal: The Furies of Nature and the Fortunes of Migrants.* Cambridge, MA: Harvard University Press.

Anderson, Clare. 2012. *Subaltern Lives: Biographies of Colonialism in the Indian Ocean World, 1790–1920.* Cambridge: Cambridge University Press.

Anim-Addo, Anya, William Hasty, and Kimberley Peters. 2014. "The Mobilities of Ships and Shipped Mobilities." *Mobilities* 9 (3): 337–49.

Balachandran, G. 2016. "Indefinite Transits: Mobility and Confinement in the Age of Steam." *Journal of Global History* 11 (2): 187–208.

Ballantyne, Tony. 2006. *Between Colonialism and Diaspora: Sikh Cultural Formations in an Imperial World.* Durham, NC: Duke University Press.

Chattopadhyay, Suchetana. 2018. *Voices of Komagata Maru: Imperial Surveillance and Punjabi Workers in Bengal.* New York: Columbia University Press.

Dhamoon, Rita Kaur, Davina Bhandar, Renisa Mawani, and Satwinder Bains, eds. 2019. *Unmooring the Komagata Maru: Charting Colonial Trajectories.* Vancouver: University of British Columbia Press.

Elam, Daniel. 2014. "Echoes of Ghadr: Lala Har Dayal and the Time of Anticolonialism." *Comparative Studies of South Asia, Africa and the Middle East* 34 (1): 9–23.

Gill, Parmbir Singh. 2014. "A Different Kind of Dissidence: The Ghadar Party, Sikh History and the Politics of Anticolonial Mobilization." *Sikh Formations: Religion, Culture, Theory* 10 (1): 23–41.

Gilroy, Paul. 1995. *The Black Atlantic: Modernity and Double Consciousness*. Cambridge, MA: Harvard University Press.

Grandin, Greg. 2014. *The Empire of Necessity: Slavery, Freedom, and Deception in the New World*. New York: Metropolitan.

Grewal, J. S. 1998. *The Sikhs of the Punjab*. Rev. ed. Cambridge: Cambridge University Press.

Hartman, Saidiya. 2008. "Venus in Two Acts." *Small Axe* 12 (2): 1–14.

Hartman, Saidiya. 2020. *Wayward Lives, Beautiful Experiments: Intimate Histories of Riotous Black Girls, Troublesome Women, and Queer Radicals*. New York: Penguin Random House.

Huttenback, Robert. 1976. *Racism and Empire: White Settlers and Colored Immigrants in the British Self-Governing Colonies, 1830–1910*. Ithaca, NY: Cornell University Press.

Jackson, Isabella. 2012. "The Raj on Nanjing Road: Sikh Policemen in Treaty-Port Shanghai." *Modern Asian Studies* 46 (6): 1672–1704.

Johnson, Walter. 2013. *River of Dark Dreams: Slavery and Empire in the Cotton Kingdom*. Cambridge, MA: Harvard University Press.

Johnston, Hugh. 2013. "The Komagata Maru and the Ghadr Party: Past and Present Aspects of a Historic Challenge to Canada's Exclusion of Immigrants from India. *BC Studies* 178: 9–31.

Johnston, Hugh. 2014. *The Voyage of the Komagata Maru: The Sikh Challenge to Canada's Colour Bar*. Vancouver: University of British Columbia Press.

Kazanjian, David. 2015. "Scenes of Speculation." *Social Text* 33 (4): 77–84.

Lowe, Lisa. 2015. *The Intimacies of Four Continents*. Durham, NC: Duke University Press.

Macklin, Audrey. 2011. "Historicizing Narratives of Arrival: The Other Indian Other." In *Narratives of Contact and Arrival in Constituting Political Community*, edited by Hester Lessard, Rebecca Johnson, and Jeremy Webber, 40–67. Vancouver: University of British Columbia Press.

MacLean, Kama. 2015. "Examinations, Access, and Inequity within the Empire: Britain, Australia, and India, 1890–1910." *Postcolonial Studies* 18 (2): 115–32.

Mawani, Renisa. 2018. *Across Oceans of Law: The Komagata Maru and Jurisdiction in the Time of Empire*. Durham, NC: Duke University Press.

McKeown, Adam. 2008. *Melancholy Order: Asian Migration and the Globalization of Borders*. New York: Columbia University Press.

McKeown, Adam. 2012. "How the Box Became Black: Brokers and the Creation of the Free Migrant." *Pacific Affairs* 85 (1): 21–45.

Mizukami, Kaori. 2019. "The Komagata Maru Incident as Described in Two Japanese Works." In *Unmooring the Komagata Maru: Charting Colonial Trajectories*, edited by Rita Dhamoon, Davina Bhandar, Resina Mawani, and Satwinder Bains, 163–78. Vancouver: University of British Columbia Press.

Mongia, Radhika. 2018. *Indian Migration and Empire: A Colonial Genealogy of the Modern State*. Durham, NC: Duke University Press.

Mustakeem, Sowande'. 2016. *Slavery at Sea: Terror, Sex, and Sickness in the Middle Passage*. Chicago: University of Illinois Press.

Patterson, Orlando. 1985. *Slavery and Social Death: A Comparative Study*. Cambridge, MA: Cambridge University Press.

Philip, M. NourbeSe. 2008. *Zong!* Middletown, CT: Wesleyan University Press.

Puri, Harish. 1993. *Ghadar Movement: Ideology, Organization and Strategy*. Amritsar: Guru Nanak Dev University Press.

Ramnath, Maia. 2011. *From Haj to Utopia: How the Ghadr Movement Charted Global Radicalism and Attempted to Overthrow the British Empire*. Berkeley: University of California Press.

Rediker, Marcus. 2007. *The Slave Ship: A Human History*. London: Viking.

Rediker, Marcus. 2010. "Colloquy with Marcus Rediker on *The Slave Ship: A Human History*." *Atlantic Studies* 7 (1): 5–45.

Rediker, Marcus, Cassandra Pybus, and Emma Christopher. 2007. "Introduction." In *Many Middle Passages: Forced Migration and the Making of the Modern World*, edited by Emma Christopher, Cassandra Pybus, and Marcus Rediker, 1–19. Berkeley: University of California Press.

Reynolds, Henry, and Marilyn Lake. 2012. *Drawing the Global Colour Line: White Men's Countries and the Question of Racial Equality*. Cambridge: Cambridge University Press.

Roy, Anjali Gera. 2017. *Imperialism and Sikh Migration: The Komagata Maru Incident*. London: Routledge.

Rupprecht, Anita. 2007. "Excessive Memories: Slavery, Insurance, and Resistance." *History Workshop Journal* 64 (1): 6–28.

Sharpe, Christina. 2016. *In the Wake: On Blackness and Being*. Durham, NC: Duke University Press.

Smallwood, Stephanie. 2008. *Saltwater Slavery: A Middle Passage from Africa to American Diaspora*. Cambridge, MA: Harvard University Press.

Sohi, Seema. 2014. *Echoes of Mutiny: Race, Surveillance, and Indian Anticolonialism in North America*. Oxford, UK: Oxford University Press.

Spillers, Hortense. 1987. "Mama's Baby, Papa's Maybe: An American Grammar Book." *Diacritics* 17 (2): 64–81.

Taylor, Eric Robert. 2009. *If We Must Die: Shipboard Insurrections in the Era of the Atlantic Slave Trade*. Baton Rouge: Louisiana State University Press.

Tinsley, Omise'eke Natasha. 2008. "Black Atlantic, Queer Atlantic: Queer Imaginings of the Middle Passage." *GLQ: A Journal of Lesbian and Gay Studies* 14 (2–3). 191–215.

THREE

Stowing Away via the Cargo Ship: Tracing Governance, Rival Knowledges, and Violence en Route | Amaha Senu

It's often been said that you can look at dealing with stowaway cases a bit like conducting an orchestra.... One of the first things we [P&I clubs] would do is, we would appoint a local correspondent. So, if the ship's still in port and a stowaway has been found, then we would contact the local correspondent and we would ask them to liaise both with local authorities, the master, and the members [shipowners], the shipowner's local agent. Together, they will then try and arrange for the stowaway to be taken off.... The difficulty comes obviously when the ship departs. That is probably one of our other biggest challenges. If a ship's coming into port and she's going to be there for a day, it could be that what we then have to do is do as much as we can. If the ship's then going from Germany to Belgium, we need to kind of piece it all together and this is again where I come into conducting the orchestra. So, I'm making sure the people in Germany are doing what I want them to do. I got the people in Belgium on standby. I've got my guys in Tanzania on standby and I'm pulling them all together and making sure that the right information is being passed on to the relevant parties.
—NICK, senior claims executive, P&I club A

The above quote is taken from one of my interviews with officials from protection and indemnity insurance clubs (P&I clubs). These P&I clubs are nonprofit mutual insurance associations that provide cover against third-party liabilities for their members, who will typically be shipowners, charterers, and ship operators. Besides insuring against liabilities such as crew injuries, pollution, and damage to or loss of cargo, they provide insurance cover against the cost of stowaways and have developed a significant expertise on the issue. The clubs also have local P&I correspondents in various parts of the world who carry out a number of responsibilities on their behalf, including processing stowaway cases. While the activities of the clubs and their correspondents in relation to stowaways are discussed later in the chapter, the quote captures the essence of the coordination among geographically dispersed actors who come together in governing what these maritime authorities regard as the problem of stowaways in contemporary global shipping. The quote depicts a typical scenario of attempting to remove a stowaway found on board a single ship—a process that, nonetheless, involves the arduous task of orchestrating various actors across countries, continents, and maritime spaces, as my respondent aptly put it.

Accordingly, the itinerant figure of the stowaway who embarks on illegalized mobilities aboard contemporary cargo ships is a subject of keen interest in the global shipping industry, which has always been haunted by the economically costly but also safety- and security-related implications of finding stowaways on board. This has necessitated the drawing up and wide circulation of international regulations, guidelines, and procedures aimed at preventing stowaways from boarding ships and minimizing their disruptive effects on maritime traffic. The attention stowaways are accorded in the shipping industry sits in a stark contrast to their near-complete absence in border and migration studies as well as the mobilities research agenda. These literatures have maintained a vibrant research interest in the topic of boat migration but, with a few exceptions, not in stowaways.[1]

The marginality of stowaways within migration and border studies relates to what is often understood as the increasing invisibility of commercial shipping as a whole over the past decades, despite still being the backbone of global trade (Grey 2003; Sekula 2002, 54). Scholars have started to draw attention to the "seablindness" (Bueger and Edmunds 2017), "forgetfulness" (Birtchnell, Savitzky, and Urry 2015), and "terra-centric" tendencies (Anim-Addo, Hasty, and Peters 2014) besetting different disciplines in the social sciences today. However, such declarations also risk making exaggerated claims about the extent of the invisibility of shipping and the maritime space in contemporary social sciences, just to mention a few themes: the proliferation of research into maritime security and crimes (Bueger and Edmunds 2017); the ever-growing publications on the topic of boat migration across the Mediterranean, including the role of merchant shipping in saving lives (Basaran 2015; Senu 2020; chapter 8, this volume); the traction the maritime has been gaining in mobilities research by way of "cargo-mobilities" (Birtchnell, Savitzky, and Urry 2015) and the "mobilities of ships and shipped mobilities" (Anim-Addo, Hasty, and Peters 2014); as well as the various sociological works on the lives of seafarers (Alderton et al. 2004; Sampson 2013).

Nonetheless, despite this growing interest, one might argue with Philip Steinberg (2015) that the maritime space is "hidden in plain sight," in the sense that while we may occasionally see ships passing by offshore or along inland waterways, while the shipping container is a pervasive presence around us (Martin 2016), and while some of us get a passing glimpse of increasingly securitized and closed-off port facilities (Eski 2016), the maritime and what constitutes it remain obscure to most. This is because, despite the centrality of shipping to our everyday consumption, ships and the maritime infrastructures that support them have faded away from our quotidian experiences. The demand for efficient infrastructures able to withstand the pressures of significantly higher volumes of global trade has led to the relocation of ports away from populated urban centers and, hence, from public view (Birtchnell, Savitzky, and Urry 2015). In contrast, the airplane and the airport have become central to our movement across long distances and are firmly placed in our imaginations (Adey 2010).

Considering these developments, one might ask what the obscure empirical niche of stowing away in a global and yet invisible industry can possibly illuminate about the issues of borders, migration, and mobilities. In the first instance, shedding light on stowaways redresses the impression that mass migration via boats constitutes the only form of illegalized and risky movement across the seas. As this chapter shows, stowing away onboard cargo ships is also a life-and-death gamble and a heavily policed form of movement. In relation to the central theme of this book, the practice of stowing away speaks strongly to the notion of via-politics. As the next section demonstrates, the contemporary cargo ship is not merely a means of concealed transport for stowaways (see chapter 4, this volume, for the way concealed and cramped transport shape political imagination). For it also engenders communities of young men around ports who are drawn to the idea of stowing away and, in the process, form a strong sense of identity qua stowaways.[2] They collectively generate an impressive body of shared knowledge geared toward navigating the risks associated with their adventures across the high seas. However, the ship does not only serve as the linchpin for the formation of stowaways' identities and their risk-mitigating knowledge. It is also the object and site of production of an equally fascinating body of governmental knowledge by actors who seek to prevent, control, manage, and govern stowaways in the global shipping industry. This governmental knowledge is central to the vast assemblage of stowaway governance that has developed over centuries involving various actors dispersed across the globe, some of whom are discussed here (see Senu 2018, 209–23, on this governing assemblage). At the center of this chapter, therefore, are the rival knowledges of stowaways and those who seek to govern them, which are brought to life through the mobilities of cargo ships (see chapter 9, this volume, for rival knowledges in the context of the Alpine frontier).

The numerous actors involved in the governance of stowaways I have begun to allude to offer crucial insights into the ways in which various commercial and nonstate actors engage in forms of mobility control and constitute an efficient private governance of the issue, predominantly motivated by economic liabilities or benefits. As such—and this is the second reason why the governance of stowaways merits further scholarly attention—it also sheds critical light on the extreme scenarios that play out at times when economic rationalities meet border and migration control imperatives, with the ship as a mobile site of enforcement (Walters 2006). The extreme scenarios I am referring to here involve getting rid of stowaways at sea, often on makeshift rafts made from oil drums, by some seafarers who effectively sit at the end of a long chain of governance and control of stowaways. The significant economic cost of stowaways to the shipping industry, itself premised on states' practices of immigration control, creates the condition for the occurrence of such crimes, which remain hidden and forgotten due to the relative isolation of the ship across the maritime terrain. The ship also brings stowaways into contact with seafarers who are often of different nationality, race, and class than the stowaways, likely contributing to the devaluation of stowaways' lives in the face of substantial economic costs.

Hence, the issue of stowaways offers an excellent case for foregrounding the role of vehicles (in this case, the cargo ship) in engendering communities and identities, modulating behavior, and serving as a site of governance and contestation as well as production of rival knowledges. It also reveals how efforts to smoothly govern the issue from afar play out at sea in radically disturbing ways not originally planned by governing actors sitting in offices on shore (Stenson 2005; McKee 2009), and it also brings to the fore the "deadly life of logistics" (Cowen 2014) where the lives of stowaways become mere obstructions to the smooth international flow of goods. Throughout this chapter, I draw on data from my extensive research into the issue of stowaways, which involved analyses of stowaway incident reports, and technical and legal documents, as well as interview data from conversations with seafarers, various relevant actors in the shipping industry, and the stowaways themselves (Senu 2018). The interviews with stowaways, which I conducted with Tanzanians and Ethiopians stowing away from South Africa and Djibouti respectively, are particularly unique to the extent that there has not been any comparable work that brings their accounts to the fore with such fascinating insight into their shared knowledge and risk-mitigating strategies as well as experiences at sea.

The remainder of this chapter is organized into two sections. In the first section, I briefly revisit how the ship has figured in the social sciences, and I identify relevant attributes of the contemporary cargo ship that facilitate the global governance of stowaways. In particular, its attributes as a site of governance/contestation and object/site of knowledge production are highlighted. Here, the role of various private actors in generating governmental knowledge on stowaways is detailed, as are their practices of governing the issue through notions of risk. Their officially sanctioned practices of prevention, control, disembarkation, and repatriation informed by their collective knowledge of stowaways are discussed before moving on to the contestation of these formal governing practices on board ships. In the second section, I highlight how individual stowaways mobilize their collectively forged risk-mitigating knowledge to navigate the perceived risks posed to them, in particular their abandonment on makeshift rafts on the high seas. The chapter concludes by highlighting why stowaways matter in further enriching the understanding of the viapolitics of migration, borders, and their control.

The Contemporary Cargo Ship and the Private Governance of Stowaways as Risk

Erving Goffman's (1970) "total institutions" and Foucault's (1986) "heterotopias" often come to mind when one thinks about ships conceptually. Nonetheless, it is doubtful how much use these concepts are in understanding contemporary cargo ships, much less the issue of stowaways. Instead, they point to a time when ships were significantly more present in the public imagination and yet somehow considerably more isolated while at sea. Contemporary ships hardly capture public imaginations and are largely obscured, as discussed earlier. Yet, with advances in communication technologies across long distances, ships have become noticeably and continuously connected to shore through tools such as satellite phones and email. It is beyond the scope of this chapter to discuss how the evolution of communication technology on board, from Morse to the current availability of the internet, transformed the cargo ship. Nonetheless, as John King (2000, 52) states, "Communications technology brought a ship far out at sea into direct contact with people on shore, so that it could no longer be regarded as a completely independent unit."

What this virtual proximity to shore has entailed is the transformation of the ship from an isolated domain, where the shipmaster reigned sovereign, to a site of governance/enforcement and knowledge production embedded in the wider shipping infrastructure. While contemporary ships remain disciplined spaces with a clear hierarchy, where the captains or shipmasters sit at the top (Sampson 2013, 77–79), the masters' authority has been gradually eroded through technologies that allow shoreside personnel to exercise significant levels of monitoring and influence (King 2000; Sampson 2013, 89; Sampson, Turgo, and Acejo 2019, 9). However, there is also a limit to such monitoring and influence from shore inasmuch as seafarers are able to hide what takes place on board—something very pertinent to the issue of stowaways, as we will see later on.

Ships are also locales where various international and national laws apply in relation to a number of issues, including safety, environmental protection, and living and working conditions.[3] Of relevance to the topic of stowaways during the period when ships were the only means of transoceanic travel: immigration controls were exercised on board, whereby ships had the responsibility of verifying that their passengers were properly documented and were also made responsible for the cost associated with the return of inadmissible passengers (see Blue 2013; Scholten 2015).

While contemporary cargo ships do not transport humans, this liability remains in place in relation to stowaways. The history of stowaways in shipping is as variegated as it is long and deserves its own historiography. While the motivations of individual stowaways would certainly vary, stowing away as a concealed resort to mobility has emerged from the need to avoid the cost of travel, migration controls, or both. In that sense, stowing away is structurally ingrained into any means of exclusionary transport, including trains and airplanes. As such, the oft-held opinion that the history of stowaways is as old as shipping itself is convincing. However, it is also a history that has continued to evolve—from the predominant nationalities of stowaways at particular periods, to frequent embarkation ports, to how they have been dealt with in shipping. For instance, while European ports used to be hot spots for European stowaways in the past (see Donald 1928), it is stowaways from various African countries boarding ships in different ports on the continent who constitute the majority of present-day stowaways (Facilitation Committee 2010, 2013). Furthermore, how they are construed and managed onboard has also undergone profound changes, for instance, from the relatively distant past when they used to be forced to work their passage to the present, where their presence is not seen as a source of free labor but as a breach in ship security (see Senu 2018, 54–58, 101–3, on how stowaways have been construed as a security problem since the early 1990s and more so after 9/11).

Despite such variations over stowaways' long history in shipping, there are also parallel continuities. Such continuity is, perhaps, epitomized through the enduring practice of stowaway searches. For instance, compare the following two excerpts from instructions to seafarers on how to conduct stowaway searches from starkly different timelines:

> When the ship is fairly out, the search for stowaways is ordered. . . . The Captain, Mate, or other Officer, attended by the clerk of the passenger broker, and as many of the crew as may be necessary for the purpose, then proceed below, bearing masked lanterns or candles, and armed with long poles, hammers, chisels, etc. that they may break open suspicious looking chests and barrels. (*Illustrated London News* 1850)

> Always carry out a thorough stowaway search in a systematic manner. A ship specific check list should be available and the ship divided into sections or areas and systematically searched prior to departure. Breaking the ship into three areas for example and searching them under the guidance of an officer is the most efficient method of ensuring an effective search is carried out. . . . The master should acknowledge that he is satisfied that a thorough stowaway search has been carried out, keep a record of the fact and enter a remark in the official log book. (Standard P&I club 2009, 4)

The actual practicalities of a stowaway search procedure need to be tailored to the specificities of a particular ship and are far too extensive to detail here.[4] However, I would like to draw attention to the second excerpt, which points to the need for the captain to record in the official logbook that a stowaway search had been conducted. The official logbook on board is a crucial document that would be examined as evidence in various eventualities such as injuries, oil spills, grounding, collision, and so on. In relation to stowaways, recording the completion of stowaway searches as well as the maintenance of security watches in ports is the evidence that the ship has taken the necessary precautions to prevent stowaways; not having done so will risk annulling the insurance cover provided by the P&I clubs. It is precisely this technology of insurance that places P&I clubs at the core of the private governance of stowaways.

The global governance of stowaways is not an entirely private affair. States, through their immigration regulations, and the International Maritime Organization are also critical actors.[5] However, the role of P&I clubs in turning the cargo ship into a site of governance cannot be emphasized enough. Since the centuries-old state practices of rendering the ship responsible for the cost and return of stowaways has continued, P&I clubs have categorized stowaways among the liabilities against which they insure their members since at least the 1920s (NEPIA 1924, 55). This has led to their considerable stake in the issue and concomitant governing roles. Since they more often than not cover (i.e., reimburse) the significant cost of stowaways, they are keen on ensuring that ships take preventive measures.[6]

However, the governing role of these P&I clubs is not limited to prevention but also encompasses different types of intervention throughout the entire geography of a typical stowaway journey, as the quote opening the chapter demonstrates. This geography typically starts from embarkation ports, after which stowaways are found on board or reveal themselves a few days into the voyage. The stowaways will stay on board any number of days (sometimes months), depending on factors such as the time it takes to reach the next port of call, whether and how quickly port states cooperate in allowing disembarkation, whether it is decided to take the stowaways back with the ship during a return voyage, how quickly travel documents can be obtained, and so on. Hence, P&I clubs provide detailed guidelines on how to manage the stowaways' presence on board. This is particularly important in cases where stowaways remain onboard for long periods, as in the following example: "Four [Vietnamese] stowaways at one stage were found.... That was the start of about a four or five months ordeal of roaming around the whole world, literally with these four young people without any country at all accepting to take them ... which caused us lots and lots of delays and problems on the commercial side, on the medical side, and all of that" (Captain Karim, Egyptian).

The clubs provide guidance on every aspect of managing the stowaways' stay on board, from detention, supervision, treatment, and maintenance to interpersonal interactions. The management of interpersonal interactions is, in fact, of crucial importance to the clubs as a result of concerns over safety and security, but importantly over concerns that crew members could be tempted to assist stowaways to escape into port states, with serious implications for the ship. As a result, P&I clubs strongly advise captains to ensure interactions be-tween the crew and stowaways are limited.

> One of the things that we strongly recommend for various reasons is that
> stowaways are not put to work onboard, and the reasons are several. One is
> [working on board] is a potentially dangerous and skilled job which a stow-
> away doesn't necessarily have the ability to do. . . . But another problem is
> that if the stowaway was to work alongside the crew for a period of time and
> eat with them, it's far more likely that there will be the ability to tell the sto-
> ries and to build a friendship. Then, individual crew members may feel that
> they should assist. (Sarah, deputy claims director, P&I club B)

Ships are not just vehicles; they are mobile spaces of dwelling, where ani-mosities as well as solidarities can be forged over the course of a long voyage (see the introduction and chapters 2 and 4, this volume). In the above quote, we see how such solidarities become risks to be managed. However, in scenarios involving the unauthorized disembarkation of stowaways, the clubs and even the shipping companies would not even know about the presence of stowaways in the first place. Unauthorized disembarkations are organized by captains and their crew in a clear demonstration of the limits of the clubs' ability to govern the presence of stowaways on board from a distance. The following account of a captain about his experience with stowaways when he was a third mate provides a good example: "I was straightaway told not to—I remember the conversation—no documenting anything. So, it was off the record, absolutely off the record that they were onboard. . . . They were given one boiler suit each. Then they were escorted, and the chief mate was given the task to go out with them out of the dock. They went out [at] 11:00 or 11:30 at night. The chief mate came back on his own" (Captain Rajav, Indian). Such practices by certain seafarers, which radically deviate from those suggested by P&I clubs, would effectively annul the insurance cover and constitute a risky gamble. They also highlight the limitations of shoreside monitoring and influence enabled by the communication technologies mentioned earlier. In most cases, however, seafarers abide by the recommended practices, which was also reflected in my interviews. In typical cases, the clubs seek to disembark stowaways with mini-mum disruption. One of the most important tools to mediate this process is the stowaway questionnaire or form. Insurance clubs and their correspondents provide stowaway questionnaires and guidelines for onboard interrogation of stowaways and associated evidence collection, effectively rendering the vessel an important site of knowledge production on stowaways.

Even before beginning the interrogation, seafarers are advised to collect any physical evidence from the area where the stowaways had been hiding, including identification documents, tools, and drugs as well as food leftovers and packaging, which may provide some clue about where the stowaways boarded. Mobile phones carried by the stowaways are also important sources of information, as hints about the port of embarkation as well as the nationalities of the stowaways can be found from the country codes in the contacts list, call logs, and pictures stored on the phones. This is due to the reluctance of stowaways to reveal their true nationalities to obstruct disembarkation—a point I return to shortly.

During the interrogation itself, shipmasters are expected to find out where and how stowaways boarded the vessel, when they boarded, where they hid, and so on. All these details are meticulously recorded and subsequently passed on to the P&I clubs and their local correspondents, who then widely circulate the information gathered within the shipping industry as "lessons learned" through loss prevention bulletins. As the name makes abundantly clear, these bulletins are intended to prevent further economic loss to the clubs and their members by communicating the latest boarding techniques, hiding spots on board, behavioral patterns of stowaways, and any useful information that will help to prevent stowaway cases in the future as well as to render their handling smoother. Information from disparate incidents is also compiled, numerated, categorized, and maintained at various repositories (see Senu 2018, 168–72, for a detailed discussion on this).

More importantly, the interrogations on board are used to identify the nationalities of stowaways and kickstart the disembarkation process. Here, the role of communication technologies becomes evident as the information acquired on board is immediately passed on to parties on shore while the vessel is still at sea. Time is of the essence here, and it is precisely the need for establishing the nationalities of stowaways as quickly as possible that makes the stowaway questionnaires provided by P&I clubs and their correspondents extremely detailed. Specific questions include marital status, spouse's name, parent's names, permanent home address, occupation, last school attended, name of headmaster, name of capital of country of origin, name of president, name of currency used in country of origin, the colors of national flag, height, hair color, eye color, any tattoos, scars, vaccination scars, religion, tribe, chief, and subchief (Gard n.d.; P&I correspondent's stowaway questionnaire, author's source). All these details, including body marks, are used to deduce the nationalities of the stowaways, as they can be reluctant to divulge that information to frustrate repatriations, as the account below makes clear.

It's very much detective work, because they can tell you anything. I mean, that's why, with the questionnaires, we have a lot of questions.... As I say, then we can pass those questionnaires to the correspondent in Tanzania, and then they can look at the answers and say, "Actually, I think he's from Kenya. The fact that he said whatever he said. That's a tribe based in Kenya, not in Tanzania," for example.... Unless you are fortunate enough to come across a piece of paper that you might find or a mobile phone or something like that, near enough all of them, all of them lie. (Nick, senior claims executive, P&I club A)

The role of P&I correspondents is critical in identifying the nationalities of stowaways. Insurance clubs have local correspondents in different parts of the globe, and those in particular regions, such as Africa, from where most stowaways originate (Facilitation Committee 2010, 2013), have amassed a great deal of expertise on the practices, behaviors, and peculiarities of stowaways from the continent. Characterizing the networked operation involved in disembarking stowaways, while a ship can be en route to Asia, the information collected on board is passed on to correspondents in Africa for verification. Meanwhile, correspondents at the next port of call in Asia will have already kickstarted the disembarkation-repatriation machine, using information being forwarded from the ship to arrange for temporary travel documents obtained from embassy or consulate officials. They will also arrange inland transport to airports, book flights, solicit the service of security escorts to accompany the stowaways, liaise with the ship's local agent, and so on. In this sense, ensuring the smooth operation of the logistics of transporting goods demands that the uninvited and disruptive presence of stowaways be neutralized through the logistics of removal and deportation.

In this logistics of removal and deportation, there is also a kind of relay-run operation that is coordinated among correspondents in various regions of the globe. The increasingly limited number of countries that are prepared to allow the disembarkation of stowaways as well as the likelihood of connecting flights during repatriation necessitate such transnational coordination of activities, as one correspondent elaborated.

Well, what happens is, there are other parties or correspondents that are around the world that will deal with stowaways. But the problem is—you're probably aware of this—not all countries will allow stowaways to be disembarked.... They do take stowaways off from Brazil and Argentina. And like I said, our counterparts, they deal with it. And what happens is, normally, the stowaways will go from Brazil or Argentina to Johannesburg, being the hub for East and West Africa.... So, they'll come from Brazil and Argentina, we'll take over from Johannesburg, and then take them on to Cameroon or whatever the place is, Ghana, anywhere. (Zack, P&I correspondent, South Africa)

Hence, the network of P&I correspondents around the world's coastlines enables an efficient governance of stowaways. The correspondents also have local knowledge of immigration regulations and working relationships with authorities, which help in obtaining permissions to disembark and repatriate stowaways. As one P&I club representative put it, "They are our eyes and ears, and we rely an awful lot on correspondents to assist, to give us the right advice, to mitigate costs, keep costs to an absolute minimum" (Sarah, deputy claims director, P&I club B).

The correspondents deal directly with stowaways on the ground and, as such, they also have to contend with the various acts of resistance by stowaways during the disembarkation and repatriation process. Stowaways tend to be more assertive in ports and airports as opposed to their more pliant demeanors at sea, highlighting the significance of the ship and the isolated maritime environment within which it operates in exacerbating the vulnerabilities felt and experienced by stowaways and modulating their behaviors in the process. Stowaways are well aware that they have some leverage inside ports, where some try to literally swim or run their way into a country.

They were very good [during their time at sea]. They were not troublesome.... The local police came onboard. Now it kind of turned surreal because the guys were taken from their cabin ... and were not handcuffed. They were just frog-marched to the gangway by the local police. There were three or four local police, and they were told to go down the gangway and get into a waiting police van. As they got to the top of the gangway, they all ran, and they all ran throughout the port. That's the last we ever saw or heard of them. (Captain Bill, British)

Stowaways also exert some leverage in airports when they are being repatriated. For example, they often demand pocket money in return for their cooperation, which sets them on a collision course with the security escorts accompanying them, who sometimes resort to the use of force as a result: "He say until he get 2,000 [USD], 2,500 maybe, he been fight already you know. They may beat you. But in the end, they give that money, 1,000.... Yeah, they beat me. They put that, the chain [handcuffs].... Because they say, me, I want too much money, you see. Other people, when they go there, they get only 500. Me, I want 3,000, you see" (Charlie, Tanzanian stowaway, interpreted by Mohab).

Such behaviors and practices by stowaways do not occur in a vacuum but are grounded in their own shared body of knowledge (Senu 2018, 75–99), which stands in opposition to, and also in mutual permeation with, the industry's governmental knowledge. The stowaways' tactical knowledge is constituted through shared experiences, observations, beliefs, assumptions, and myths, and is used to circumvent obstacles the stowaways face both on shore and at sea. They draw from their shared knowledge to survive the vagaries of life on shore, circumvent preventive measures in ports, avoid detection during stowaway searches, and minimize the risk of victimization at sea, as well as navigate the disembarkation and repatriation process. The sharing of experiences and subsequent accumulation of collective knowledge are fostered through the communities the stowaways I interviewed formed around ports in South Africa and Djibouti. For these stowaways, the ship holds an important symbolic significance and serves as the core around which their identities qua stowaways crystalize. My interviews indicate a strong sense of identity among my participants, who explicitly identified as stowaways and saw stowing away as both "a means of escape and unannounced entry" (Walters 2008) and also a way of life. The trope "stowaway life" was often invoked in their narratives. "A stowaway life is repetitive, you know, but I also suggest that you also talk to the others I suggested. Because some of them have more experiences than I do, and they also know a lot more about the experiences of others" (Moses, Ethiopian stowaway, author's translation).

The ship provides a common purpose for the stowaways and the basis for associated identity formation. It represents hope for a better, albeit notoriously elusive, future and a way out. However, stowaways are also keenly aware that the "stowaway game is hard," as Barrack, a Tanzanian stowaway, characterized it, in which their physical safety and lives hang in the balance.

Navigating Risks at Sea

Whereas stowaways often assume more assertive postures during disembarkations and repatriations, they are acutely aware of their heightened vulnerabilities at sea. Thus, they draw on their shared knowledge to manage the risks they face. They undertake their own forms of risk assessment before deciding to board a ship due to perceived and experienced violence and victimization at sea. Here, it should be noted that victimization of stowaways at sea is not the norm but the exception, although it does certainly occur relatively more often than industry insiders assume (see Senu 2018, 128–30). However, as a body of knowledge geared toward risk mitigation, the accounts of stowaways are bound to accentuate and memorialize such exceptional incidents more prominently. It should be noted from the outset of this section that much of what stowaways describe, in particular in relation to seafarers of certain nationalities being prone to violent behavior, is difficult to fully examine within the scope of this chapter and is simply recounted here.[7] Nonetheless, stowaways' accounts provide important insights into the risk-mitigating practices they enact on and around the ship.

The stowaways I interviewed had a well-articulated categorization of ship types that are to be avoided based on considerations of the vessel's next destinations, the nationalities of the seafarers on board, and the ship's flag as well as the ship's condition as an indication of the state of the owning company. That is, seafarers working aboard ships that the stowaways deem substandard are expected to be under duress from their companies and, hence, predisposed to be violent toward stowaways. However, it is the nationalities of seafarers and the national composition of the crew that are by far the most important risk signifiers for the stowaways.

The stowaways were explicit about avoiding seafarers of certain nationalities or what the Tanzanians called "full ngome"—a juxtaposition of "full" to the Swahili word "ngome," which they explained to me as roughly translating to "fortress" or "garrison." The consensus was that seafarers of the same nationality would have an "entrenched mindset" or unity of mind and solidarity that would predispose them to conspire to resort to unofficial, secretive, and deadly methods of removing stowaways. Certain nationalities, such as Chinese seafarers, stood out in the accounts of the stowaways as being deemed likely to get rid of stowaways on makeshift rafts. Consequently, as part of their risk assessment practices, my participants were explicit about their attempts to avoid boarding ships that they thought were crewed by a single-nationality crew or nationalities they deemed problematic.[8]

> One nation very dangerous. Oh! Dangerous too much, my friend.... So, that's why I told you, you supposed to watch it first before you take it. If full ngome, dangerous.... Full ngome nice, Japanese from Asia. Japanese, Singapore is nice. Indonesia ... is nice. Problem Chinese, South Korea, and the other like India, Sri Lanka. Dangerous too much. They gonna kill you. (Mbongo Mzulu, Tanzanian stowaway)

As far as I am concerned, it was after I was dumped [into the sea] that I started to worry. Before that, I was not scared at all. I had even stowed away on a Chinese ship where the entire crew was Chinese. Even them, they did not do anything bad to me. I never thought the Turkish would do that. In fact, I was scared of the Chinese, because I knew that they had dumped people before that I know of. (Eyoel, Ethiopian stowaway, author's translation)

The apprehensions of the stowaways do not stop at the ships' gangway, however. They recognize that they are isolated and are usually outnumbered by seafarers, who are often equally apprehensive about the sudden appearance of strangers on board. The initial contact between the two parties is often fraught with fear and anxieties on both sides. The accounts of both stowaways and seafarers reveal this sense of trepidation, which is particularly intensified when a lone seafarer suddenly runs into stowaways.

I remember that [the seafarers] said, when they saw [the stowaway]— actually, they were a bit scared because in Nigeria there were rumors about pirates and all that. . . . They were scared, and they were taking, what do you call them? They were taking pieces of metal as if the stowaway was going to attack. (Chief Engineer Lamptey, Ghanian)

The first [seaman] who caught us was terrified and shut the door on us and run away. So he called the other [seamen], and they took us to the captain. (Yonathan, Ethiopian stowaway, author's translation)

For the stowaways, their concerns stem from the possibility of violent reactions by seafarers. Hence, they are careful when coming out of hiding. Their fears are based on personal experiences and shared accounts. While some seafarers may react out of fear, anger and frustration also drive violent reactions, as seafarers know all too well about the complications stowaways entail. The stowaways are thus very particular about how they make their presence known at sea, which includes avoiding coming out of hiding during the night. "When you stow away [on] a ship, don't come out in the night, you know. Stay there until in the morning, dangerous. . . . So, you can come in the night and there is somebody who won't believe you are [a] human being. So, he can even put you in the water, thinking maybe you gonna harm him, you know. So, he say don't come in the night" (Sadik, Tanzanian stowaway, interpreted by Mohab).

Stowaways are also fearful that individual seafarers, particularly those who are not among the officers, who are commonly known in maritime parlance as "ratings," would likely be violent toward them, since they assume that individual ratings might be held to account for failing to find stowaways during the stowaway searches. As a result, they try to avoid running into ratings when they come out of hiding and, instead, head directly to the bridge.

> They shouted, "Stowaway! Stowaway!" and they all came towards me. During that time, I feared that they might beat me. So I ran to the bridge.... Because some of them might just push you overboard or beat you up. But if the officers saw you, they would either take you to the captain, or he might even be there already.... There is something I myself experienced [in the past].... First, they asked me where I was hiding. I think they were the ones who were assigned to search that area during the stowaway search.... They said, "No, you were not hiding there," and started beating me. Because they would be held accountable since they were assigned to search that area. (Eyoel, Ethiopian stowaway, author's translation)

As these accounts reveal, for the stowaways, the more concerning aspect of their initial interactions with ratings is the prospect of being pushed overboard. These are again based on shared accounts, experiences, and rumors that are used to mitigate risks at sea. For instance, one of my participants stated that the reason he sought to avoid ratings was due to what he had heard from his compatriots. He stated, "I have heard from those who were before me about such incidents. There were a couple of boys who were thrown overboard near Tanzania without the knowledge of the captain. But I am not aware of any tangible incidents. All I know is that [the stowaways] have this attitude towards the ratings" (Yonathan, Ethiopian stowaway, author's translation).

A Viapolitical Gaze on Stowaways and Ships

As the editors of this volume argue in their introduction, vehicles are often overlooked in the studies of migration and borders. The issue of stowaways in shipping, while having been grossly overlooked, brings forth fully the role of ships in modulating practices and behaviors, engendering communities and identities, serving as sites of governance and contestation as well as enabling the generation of elaborate bodies of rival knowledges. Accordingly, it lends empirical depth to the conceptualization and exposition of the notion of viapolitics, which sees vehicles and the wider networked infrastructure in which they are embedded as contested domains of intervention and resistance.

The contemporary cargo ship brings disparate actors into an assemblage of governance in which private economic actors, such as P&I clubs and their correspondents, play central governing roles through insurance coverage. However, as I have tried to show here, this is contested throughout by the stowaways, as they come into conflict with economic actors such as seafarers and P&I correspondents, who are constrained by time and financial pressures. The onboard dynamics at sea include the added dimension of fear for both groups of strangers, that is, seafarers and stowaways. In extreme scenarios, stowaways have been forced off ships onto makeshift rafts in the middle of the ocean—knowledge that is always at the back of every stowaway's mind who dares to embark on such a risky undertaking. As we have seen in the previous section, the stowaways, therefore, enact their shared knowledge throughout the entire geography of their journeys to mitigate the risks they face. However, the stowaway journey is also equally animated by the interventions of P&I clubs and their local correspondents as well as seafarers on board, whose practices are informed by their collective governmental knowledge of stowaways, which they use to mitigate primarily economic but also safety- and security-related risks posed by stowaways.

Therefore, the issue of stowaways in global shipping provides an excellent demonstration of the status of vehicles and the broader transport infrastructures in which they are embedded as lively domains of interventions and contestations involving various cooperating and antagonistic actors. More importantly, it also highlights the violence and victimization that take place across vehicles and their infrastructures. Therefore, the seemingly obscure issues of stowaways and contemporary cargo ships merit more scholarly attention.

Notes

I would like to thank the editors of this volume for their comments on earlier drafts of this chapter. I am also very grateful for the generous funding I received from The Nippon Foundation to undertake my doctoral research on stowaways. Note that in the epigraph and throughout the chapter, pseudonyms are used.

1 For exceptions to this oversight, see Mason 1987; Jarvis 1988; Ort 1991; Nourse 1993; Steglich 1999; van Munster 2005; Walters 2008; Migreurop 2011; Maccanico 2012; Martin 2012; Maquet and Zortea 2013; Scholten 2015.

2 The stowaways in South Africa and Djibouti that I interviewed were all men. While a few reports have mentioned cases involving women stowaways (Dentlinger 2003;

Heads 2010; Christie 2016, 120), in the words of one Tanzanian stowaway in Cape Town, "Female stowaways are 'very rare' and . . . they would have to be 'pure ghetto' to survive in the Beachboy areas" (Christie 2016, 120). This statement alludes to the brutal aspect of the stowaway communities in both South Africa and Djibouti, where violence is not uncommon (see Bouyalew and Soribes [2010] and Christie [2016] for a glimpse into the lives of stowaways on shore in the two countries).

3   International regulations are ratified and enforced to varying degrees by individual states qua flag state and port state. See Sampson (2013, 29–31) for a brief introduction to "the role of the flag state" and Ozcayir (2004) for a thorough exegesis of port state jurisdiction and control.

4   See Jones (2014, 35–41) and Gard (n.d., 8–10) for a detailed list of activities involved.

5   See Senu (2018, 212–23) for a full discussion of all the important actors involved.

6   Based on data from interviews and documents, the cost directly covered by P&I clubs can vary from $12,000 to $50,000 per stowaway. However, these figures do not include the deductibles the members have to pay, or any cost to members associated with time and business lost.

7   For a more detailed discussion, including explanations for the maltreatment of stowaways at sea, see Senu (2018, ch. 7).

8   The stowaways' categorization of different nationalities of seafarers and crew composition on board is too nuanced and complex to fully map out here. See Senu (2018, 79–97) for a full discussion.

References

Adey, Peter. 2010. *Aerial Life: Spaces, Mobilities, Affects.* Oxford: Wiley-Blackwell.

Alderton, Tony, Michael Bloor, Erol Kahveci, Tony Lane, Helen Sampson, Michelle Thomas, Nik Winchester, Bin Wu, and Minghua Zhao. 2004. *The Global Seafarer: Living and Working Conditions in a Globalized Industry.* Geneva: International Labour Organization.

Anim-Addo, Anyaa, William Hasty, and Kimberley Peters. 2014. "The Mobilities of Ships and Shipped Mobilities." *Mobilities* 9 (3): 337–49.

Basaran, Tugba. 2015. "The Saved and the Drowned: Governing Indifference in the Name of Security." *Security Dialogue* 46 (3): 205–20.

Birtchnell, Thomas, Satya Savitzky, and John Urry, editors. 2015. *Cargomobilities: Moving Materials in a Global Age.* New York: Routledge.

Blue, Ethan. 2013. "Finding Margins on Borders: Shipping Firms and Immigration Control across Settler Space." *Occasion: Interdisciplinary Studies in the Humanities* [online] 5 (5): 1–20.

Bouyalew, Benyam, and Fernando Soribes. 2010. *Benyam.* Kindle ed. Valencia: Association Abay.

Bueger, Christian, and Timothy Edmunds. 2017. "Beyond Seablindness: A New Agenda for Maritime Security Studies." *International Affairs* 93 (6): 1293–1311.

Christie, Sean. 2016. *Under Nelson Mandela Boulevard: Life among the Stowaways.* Johannesburg: Jonathan Ball.

Cowen, Deborah. 2014. *The Deadly Life of Logistics: Mapping Violence in Global Trade.* Minneapolis: University of Minnesota Press.

Dentlinger, Lindsay. 2003. "Namibia: 9 Stowaways Found Off Coast Detained." *AllAfrica,* November 13. http://allafrica.com/stories/200311130373.html.

Donald, John. 1928. *The Stowaways and Other Sea Sketches: True Tales of the Sea.* Perth: Milne, Tannahill and Methven.

Eski, Yarin. 2016. *Policing, Port Security and Crime Control: An Ethnography of the Port Securityscape.* New York: Routledge.

Facilitation Committee. 2010. "Formalities Connected with the Arrival, Stay and Departure of Persons: International Group of P&I Clubs Data on Stowaway Cases." In *Report of the Facilitation Committee on Its 36th Session.* London: International Maritime Organization.

Facilitation Committee. 2013. "Formalities Connected with the Arrival, Stay and Departure of Persons: International Group of P&I Clubs Data on Stowaway Cases." In *Report of the Facilitation Committee on Its 38th Session.* London: International Maritime Organization.

Foucault, Michel. 1986. "Of Other Spaces." *Diacritics* 16 (1): 22–27.

Gard. n.d. "Gard Guidance on Stowaways." Accessed August 6, 2013. http://www.gard.no/Content/13385148/Guidance%20on%20stowaways.pdf.

Goffman, Erving. 1970. "The Characteristics of Total Institutions." In *A Sociological Reader on Complex Organizations,* 2nd ed., edited by Amitai Etzioni, 312–56. New York: Holt, Rinehart and Winston.

Grey, Michael. 2003. "The 'Image' of the Shipping Industry: Editorial." *WMU Journal of Maritime Affairs* 2 (1): 1–3.

Heads, Michael. 2010. "Befriending Stowaways—Revisited." *Gard News,* no. 199 (October). http://www.gard.no/web/updates/content/5645663/befriending-stowaways-revisited.

Illustrated London News. 1850. "The Tide of Emigration to the United States and to the British Colonies." July 6, 16.

Jarvis, Robert M. 1988. "Rusting in Drydock: Stowaways, Shipowners and the Administrative Penalty Provision of INA Section 273 (d)." *Tulane Maritime Law Journal* 13 (1): 25–49.

Jones, Steven. 2014. *Stowaways by Sea: Maritime Security Handbook.* London: Nautical Institute.

King, John. 2000. "Technology and the Seafarer." *Journal of Maritime Research* 2 (1): 48–63.

Maccanico, Yasha. 2012. "Securitising Maritime Transport: Shipping Merchandise and Dealing with Stowaways." *Statewatch Journal* 22 (1): 9–13.

Maquet, Paloma, and Julia Zortea. 2013. "Sanctions for Stowaways: How Merchant Shipping Joined the Border Police." *Statewatch Journal* 23 (2): 38–42.

Martin, Craig. 2012. "Desperate Mobilities: Logistics, Security and the Extra-logistical Knowledge of 'Appropriation.'" *Geopolitics* 17 (2): 355–76.

Martin, Craig. 2016. *Shipping Container*. New York: Bloomsbury.

Mason, Mary. 1987. "Alien Stowaways, the Immigration and Naturalization Service, and Shipowners." *Tulane Maritime Law Journal* 12 (2): 361–71.

McKee, Kim. 2009. "Post-Foucauldian Governmentality: What Does It Offer Critical Social Policy Analysis?" *Critical Social Policy* 29 (3): 465–86.

Migreurop. 2011. *At the Margins of Europe: The Externalisation of Migration Controls*. Paris: Migreurop.

NEPIA. 1924. *Rules of the North of England Protecting and Indemnity Association*. Newcastle, UK: M.S. Dodds.

Nourse, David A. 1993. "Detention of Stowaways: Who Should Bear the Cost?" *USF Maritime Law Journal* 6 (2): 435–48.

Ort, Beate A. 1991. "International and US Obligations toward Stowaway Asylum Seekers." *University of Pennsylvania Law Review* 140 (1): 285–366.

Ozcayir, Oya, ed. 2004. *Port State Control*. 2nd ed. Abingdon, UK: Informa Law from Routledge.

Sampson, Helen. 2013. *International Seafarers and Transnationalism in the Twenty-First Century*. Manchester, UK: Manchester University Press.

Sampson, Helen, Nelson Turgo, and Iris Acejo. 2019. "'Between a Rock and a Hard Place': The Implications of Lost Autonomy and Trust for Professionals at Sea." *Work, Employment and Society* 33 (4): 648–65.

Scholten, Sophie. 2015. *The Privatisation of Immigration Control through Carrier Sanctions: The Role of Private Transport Companies in Dutch and British Immigration Control*. Leiden: Koninklijke Brill NV.

Sekula, Alan. 2002. *Fish Story*. 2nd ed. Düsseldorf: Richter Verlag.

Senu, Amaha. 2018. "The Global Assemblage of Multi-centred Stowaway Governance." PhD diss., Cardiff University.

Senu, Amaha. 2020. "Migration, Seafarers and the Humanitarian-Security-Economic Regimes Complex at Sea." In *Global Challenges in Maritime Security*, edited by Lisa Otto, 75–94. Geneva: Springer.

Standard P&I Club. 2009. *Standard Safety: Special Feature—Stowaways*. London: Charles Taylor.

Steglich, Elissa. 1999. "Hiding in the Hulls: Attacking the Practice of High Seas Murder of Stowaways through Expanded Criminal Jurisdiction." *Texas Law Review* 78 (6): 1323–46.

Steinberg, Phillip. 2015. "Maritime Cargomobilities: The Impossibilities of Representation." In *Cargomobilities: Moving Materials in a Global Age*, edited by Thomas Birtchnell, Satya Savitzky, and John Urry, 35–47. New York: Routledge.

Stenson, Kevin. 2005. "Sovereignty, Biopolitics and the Local Government of Crime in Britain." *Theoretical Criminology* 9 (3): 265–87.

van Munster, Rens. 2005. *The EU and the Management of Immigration Risk in the Area of Freedom, Security and Justice*. Odense: Faculty of Social Sciences, University of Southern Denmark.

Walters, William. 2006. "Border/Control." *European Journal of Social Theory* 9 (2): 187–203.

Walters, William. 2008. "Bordering the Sea: Shipping Industries and the Policing of Stowaways." *Borderlands* 7 (3).

FOUR

Boxed In: "Human Cargo" and the Technics of Comfort | Julie Y. Chu

A ship is a habitat before being a means of transport.
—ROLAND BARTHES, *Mythologies*

From Noah's Ark to Spaceship Earth, the moving vehicle and its cramped quarters have long served as a microcosm of the best and worst of social life. Writing at the dawn of mass transport in the early nineteenth century, the French economist and social theorist Constantin Pecqueur touted the intimate spaces of the railcar and the steamship as ideal models of liberty and equality, where all the classes of society could be brought together "into a kind of living mosaic" to "prodigiously advance the reign of truly fraternal social relations" (cited in Schivelbusch 1986, 70–71). In contrast, the tight spaces of contemporary transport increasingly spark dystopian visions of the unraveling of the West's most cherished liberal principles. This is where unruly plane passengers exemplify the breakdown in rational, civic order by exploding in "air rage" over ever-shrinking legroom and overhead bins in scenes one journalist described as "befitting the pages of 'Lord of the Flies'" (Rosenbloom 2014). Meanwhile, across the Mediterranean as well as the Indian Ocean, boats crammed with migrants left adrift and sinking at sea continue to make international headlines and escalate public outcries over the lack of humanitarian response among potential host nations (chapter 8, this volume).

In all these cases, the moving vehicle clearly is more than a means of transport, as the introduction to this collection notes. Yet if it is a habitat, as Roland

Barthes ([1957] 1972) once argued, it is also a distinctive and often politicized one of enclosure and movement—a nonplace of captive travelers, where everyone is a stranger and no one is expected to feel quite at home. This chapter examines the moving vehicle as a space par excellence for grappling with the dis/orders of stranger sociality and with the limits of what moral philosophers since Hume and Smith have described as the political good of "fellow feeling" or sympathy. Whether encouraging an enlightened traveling public or a threatening irrational crowd, the cramped space of mass transport has been both milieu and medium for cultivating moral imaginations of how to deal with strangers and how, in the process, to live the good life. It is, moreover, a lightning rod for questions of personhood and its relationship to such liberal ideals as civility, humanity, and freedom.

Perhaps nothing captures these concerns better than the figure of "human cargo," whose unseemly return to contemporary scenes of transport has been hailed repeatedly in recent debates over both air rage and migrant shipwrecks alike. Such invocations are commonly accompanied by visceral descriptions of passengers crammed like cattle and breathing foul air in vessels designed to maximize the transporter's carrying capacity and profit margins. In recent air rage controversies, for instance, journalists and consumer advocates typically highlight the uncomfortable condition of passengers by citing the same litany of technical details: in the past decade (2010–20), space between seats has plummeted from an average of thirty-five inches to thirty-one inches while seat width has decreased from twenty to seventeen inches (Elliott 2015; McCartney 2014; Muskal 2014; Patterson 2012; Post 2014). Across the seas, recurring descriptions of "pitiful human cargo" also focus on the physical discomforts aboard barely seaworthy vessels with their waterlogged cabins, poor ventilation, and overcrowded bodies jostling for a bit of floor to sit and rest. The infrastructural problems of the migrant ship make it a "fetid floating coffin," as one journalist put it, in language intentionally reminiscent of the cramped horrors of the transatlantic slave ship (Birrell 2015). Similar invocations of bodies crammed like goods into the back of cargo trucks can be found in debates over the "crisis" of unauthorized crossings of the US-Mexico border (Shooster 2017; Sang 2018).

While physical misery has been an object of sympathy and humanitarian reform since the late eighteenth century—and well-studied as such by many scholars (Crowley 1999; Halttunen 1995; Lacquer 1989)—what I would like to examine in greater detail here are the peculiar technical and aesthetic fixations that shape this kind of politics of dis/comfort.[1] Such fixations, as I will show, make it possible to conceive of the problem of moving strangers in terms of the material culture of transport, where cramped conditions—and their distinctive rhythm of "turbulent stillness" (Martin 2011)—become iconic of the improper arrangement of intermingling bodies, vehicles, and infrastructure. I am especially interested in the presumed metric of comfort that governs these debates over the in/human, the un/civilized, and the un/free in the movement of migrants and other travelers. Once referring only to spiritual and emotional support, the notion of comfort came to denote the self-conscious embodied satisfaction with one's physical surroundings during a time of expanding consumer culture in eighteenth-century Anglo-American societies (Crowley 1999, 2001). As a middle ground between necessity and luxury, comfort provided a new idiom for linking the material aspirations of a rising bourgeois class to a moral project of modern self-fashioning and embodied rights premised on prevailing standards of decency and ease. In this chapter, I examine how this relatively novel redefinition of comfort has come to inform the politics of mobility since the late eighteenth century when abolitionists first successfully and iconically invoked the physical terrors of the slave ship to argue for the rights of all passengers to certain minimum standards of the humane in transport, in contradistinction to the movement of nonhuman things.

It is important to note that as a rights-claiming concept, comfort is not just a pragmatic matter of material satisfaction and technical utility; it is also aesthetic and affective as a key sign of the good life capable of moving people to help themselves and to help (or impede) others. This latter point notably appears in Adam Smith's discussion of approbation in *Theory of Moral Sentiments*, where Smith argues that what often moves people into sympathy and action is not rational utility per se but rather "the propriety and beauty" of utility as an aspirational means; that is, as a pleasing vision of "the perfect machine," artfully fitted for "conveniency or ease," which one can imagine and strive for regardless of the actual satisfaction of ends ([1759] 2011, 153–54). In fact, in his parable of the poor man's son, Smith points to such aspirations in travel as one of the catalysts for moral action. Forced to "walk a-foot, or to endure the fatigue of riding on horseback," the poor man's son, as Smith tells us, is enchanted by the sight of "his superiors carried about in machines," which he imagines could enable him to "travel with less inconveniency." And it is with "the distant idea of this felicity" in mind that the poor man's son comes to share a sensibility of comfort with his superiors and to aspire for its signs, through "the pursuit of wealth and greatness" (155). In the contemporary era, we do not need to look further than popular ads for luxury cars or first-class air travel to see Smith's theory of aspirational comfort and its distinctive techno-aesthetics at work.

In the remainder of this chapter, I focus mainly on the other end of the spectrum: those cramped vehicles of lowly travel where technical breakdown, sensory displeasure, and the figure of "human cargo" dominate. I come to this interest as an anthropologist who has spent over a decade doing fieldwork among Chinese transmigrants from Fuzhou made infamous in international media and political debates as the unfortunate subjects, as well as perpetrators, of many human smuggling disasters: from the *Golden Venture* boat drownings off the coast of New York in 1993 to the Dover incident in 2000, when fifty-eight migrants suffocated in the back of a cargo truck making its way from Belgium to England (Chu 2010). Perhaps the most notorious cases of all have involved Chinese human smuggling along transoceanic shipping channels, in which these migrants were guided into standard metal containers with limited provisions and makeshift ventilation to endure ten- to fifteen-day journeys aboard giant cargo ships. More than any other mode of transport, container smuggling crystallized the politicized yet porous boundaries between cargo and passenger mobilities; it did this by showing how an increasingly liberalized system of free trade could be repurposed by people otherwise subjected to an illiberal regime of immigration control. And in doing so, it challenged our prevailing assumptions of a world of smooth and speedy circulations by pointing to the lurching rhythms and hidden stasis of travelers crowded together and sometimes lost among the transnational flow of goods. One way to police and reinstate the distinction between passenger and cargo mobilities is through invocations of dis/comfort as a measure of the human in the vehicle and moreover, of that human's promise as sociable stranger or un/free subject capable and deserving of rights in a broader political community. As I will show, one cannot easily separate these questions of the human in transit from the moving vehicle and its infrastructures in contemporary migration politics. In this sense, I join this collection's call to attend to viapolitics—that is, to the ways in which "vehicles, routes and journeys matter not just because they shape migration worlds; they matter because the ship as well as the city, and the road as well as the agora, have provided a locus for problematizations of the human and the possibility of politics" (Walters 2015, 472).

The specific political possibilities that cramped transport invoke, which occupy the remainder of this chapter, hinge on an unspoken technics of moving strangers through which a sense of dis/comfort is key. By technics, I mean to get at more than the technological aspects of transport in shaping politics under cramped conditions. Rather, I draw from Lewis Mumford's ([1934] 2010, 3) distinction between technology and technics, the latter referring to the dynamic interplay of social milieus and technological innovation, in which technology-as-tool is only ever as efficacious as its cultural translation and social assimilation into an already existing complex of "ideas, wishes, habits, goals." Unlike technology per se, technics focuses on the resonances and relations of various elements—both human and machine, organic and nonorganic—in a sociotechnical ensemble. Moreover, it gestures to relations that are not only utilitarian and functional but also poetic and affective. Finally, it suggests how all these relations find coherence, as well as develop transmutations, only under specific material and historical conditions.[2]

This chapter makes a similar argument about the technics of moving strangers across oceans and into shared sociopolitical worlds. I do this by looking at the ways in which modes of transport and their metrics of comfort have come to orient how we deal with both, first, the pragmatics of travel and, second, the poetics of the vehicle as a powerful symbol for garnering sympathy, as well as revulsion, toward distant and intimate others. To trace the formation of this mobile world of tight quarters and stranger dis/comforts, I start by returning to the figure of "human cargo" as it comes into recognition as a political problem and through which the reform of moving vehicles and their infrastructures promises resolution in the name of the (human) passenger's right to comfort. I then examine one aspect of these technics in greater detail by homing in on the politics of ventilation and its related suspicion of smells in the policing of strangers boxed in together and on the move. The conclusion returns to a general discussion of the cramped vehicle and the insights enabled by attending to its technics in relation to migration politics, stranger sociality, and moral imaginaries of the good life.

Human Cargo, Passenger Comfort

In Alex Rivera's (2003) remarkable documentary project, the *Borders Trilogy*, three video snapshots of mobile subjects—moving from a realist to surreal to magical real mode—build a composite portrait of the off-kilter energies commingling between a liberal regime for expanding free trade in goods and the illiberal one for restricting the movement of people. The trilogy opens with a two-minute film titled "Love on the Line" that soberly observes people gathered for regular transnational picnics through the open slats of an imposing metal fence cutting across the beach and into the Pacific Ocean between the United States and Mexico. A woman defiantly kisses a man through another partial opening. Slapping his hand against the thick columns of the fence, this man later says to the camera, "This is solid. . . . You can't cross through. But there are things that aren't solid and *they* can cross through."

In the second segment, "Container City, USA," images of the American flag hanging in a quiet neighborhood are accompanied by horror film music and a sinister voice-over proclaiming that "America is being attacked by *invaders* from faraway lands." These invaders turn out not to be people but the growing stack of shipping containers encroaching on prime shoreline real estate next to a Newark, New Jersey, town.

This query into the relation of people and things culminates in the third film, "A Visible Border," which focuses on a single haunting image captured at the Mexico-Guatemala border using technology developed by the company American Science and Engineering, Inc. Juxtaposed against the faraway distorted sounds of a telephonic voice explaining the company's history and signature surveillance products, a blurry close-up of an incandescent black-and-white image slowly zooms out to reveal an X-ray scan of a container truck concealing ghostly human silhouettes among its stacks of cargo. A caption under the image explains, "The immigrants seen in this image were headed to the United States. They were in a shipping container, disguised as bananas for import."

In many ways, Rivera's documentary is exemplary of what I have sketched above as the study of moving strangers as technics. With its evenhanded treatment of the relation between humans and machines, along with its astute eye for their uncanny effects as part of larger ensembles of regulation, the film ultimately zeroes in on a tacit distinction in transport that we have come to take for granted—that passengers and cargo have different natures and means of movement. This assumption slowly starts to unravel as the figure of the border takes on different resonances and palpable forms through the interplay of metal fences and affective bodies, trade pacts and port overflow, X-ray scanners and cargo trucks. Reciprocal effects between humans and nonhumans abound in these various concretizations of the border. The metal fence turns out to be more than an inert technical object for keeping people out; it is also a poetic vehicle for relaying the immaterial bonds of love across the United States and Mexico.

As Rivera well understood, the ghostly X-ray scan has come to be one of our most iconic images for hailing the return of "human cargo" in the contemporary era. Less object of regulation than lightning rod for political discourse, "human cargo" has become a phantasmagoria for conjuring the technics of retrograde infrastructures and devalued migrant worlds, of cramped transport by convoluted sea routes and slow-going roads, rusty freighters and crammed trucks. These are conveyances supposedly more suitable to durable goods rather than to impatient modern people in the global age of speedy and abundant air travel. As William Walters (2012, 8) noted of the transit patterns in migration today, "A mere fifty years ago, as the age of mass air travel was dawning, no one would have predicted that migrants would once more return to the sea in such numbers.... But it is not just the ship, in its various forms and states of disrepair, that populates imaginations of irregular migration today.... Think of the public display of X-ray images of trucks, and containers, their interiors made to disclose diaphanous figures huddled together in adversity." Noting past associations of visually cramped interiors with human abjection in travel, he goes on to ask, "Does it risk trivializing the scale of inhumanity and killing that was the Middle Passage to note the eerie resemblance between these ghostly X-rayed images and Thomas Clarkson's famous diagram of the slave ship *Brookes* (1789)—a diagram whose mass circulation was to prove so instrumental in assembling a public against slavery?" (8).

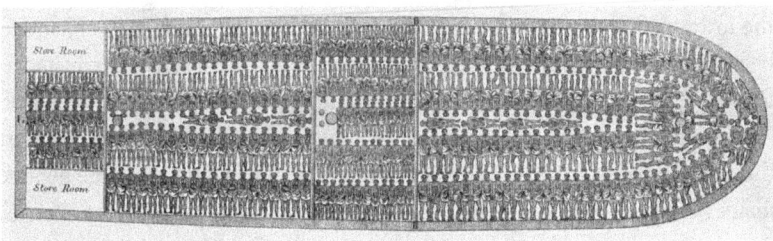

FIGURE 4.1 · Diagram of the slave ship *Brookes.*

FIGURE 4.2 · X-ray scan of human cargo, as featured in Alex Rivera's *Borders Trilogy,* screenshot.

Crusaders against human trafficking certainly have no qualms about drawing such comparisons when describing the contemporary movement of people-as-cargo as newfangled forms of slavery. Since 1993, when the *Golden Venture* freighter grounded off the coast of New York with nearly three hundred unauthorized Chinese on board, moral panics about "human cargo" have routinely pointed to the unsavory condition of transport as iconic signs of migrant abjection and enslavement. Conjuring the ghosts of the Middle Passage, a *Newsweek* article titled "The New Slave Trade" first described the *Golden Venture* in 1993 as a "dismal rust bucket" where migrants were trapped in "the darkened hold" with "barely enough room to lie down" and with "no shower, and . . . only one toilet for 281 people" (Liu 1993). In a more recent 2011 case in which two cargo trucks hiding 517 people were captured by X-ray scanners in Mexico, popular images and descriptions of the migrants as "crammed like cattle" and "stacked like wood" continued to raise the specter of the slave ship as a dehumanizing vehicle of commodity capture. This comparison of migrant transport to slavery continues to figure prominently in the Mediterranean crisis, especially as a rationale for militarizing the seas and for preventing further refugee flows into Europe.[3]

In many cases, as already shown by the story of the *Ocean Lady* featured in the introduction to this book, the very materiality of the cramped vehicle can become merged with the ontology of migrant bodies themselves. For instance, following a slew of Chinese boat smuggling incidents in Canada in 1999, Alison Mountz (2010) observed how government lawyers successfully argued against the asylum claims of most of these migrants by marshaling the same generic images of rusting boats as key evidence of the applicants' suspect dispositions. Can someone recently transported along such decrepit channels be trusted to become the kind of law-abiding, autonomous individuals citizen-subjects are expected to be in a liberal democracy like Canada? The answer, as Mountz noted, was a definitive no.

The relation of *human* to *cargo* has an interesting and ambiguous history. As late as 1941, the US Supreme Court formally declared that people, like goods, were an "article of commerce" and that this issue was "settled beyond question" (Bilder 1996, 745). Since then, this legal construct has gone largely unnoticed and unchallenged in both US courts and the broader public sphere. Under the laws of commerce, humans and nonhumans, passenger and cargo, may be different in degree but not necessarily in kind as articles holding commodity potential. This conceit does not seem so controversial when we think of such common industries as travel and life insurance today, which are in the business of pricing the value of both mobile people and mobile things.

In fact, far from being distinct and oppositional terms, cargo and passenger have long been elastic categories for describing a range of human and nonhuman mobilities. Derived from Spanish and Latin terms for burden, charge, and to load, *cargo* has been used variously to refer to a freight of goods, a load of travelers, and the moving vessel carrying the load. Similarly, *passenger*—coming from Middle English and French terms for passing and temporary—could point not just to the person being transported but also to the ship or other vehicle doing the transporting. This porousness among travelers, products, and vehicles probably did not seem so strange when it was still common to see people mixed in with goods in a ship's compartment and then off-loaded together through the same dock and checkpoint.

So what makes "human cargo" such a lightning rod these days? Here it may be useful to return to the iconic image of the slave ship *Brookes* that has been the referent for so many macabre descriptions and political rants about contemporary migration and travel. While all sorts of images and writings conveying the evils of slavery were circulated by British and American abolitionists throughout the late eighteenth century, the diagram of the *Brookes* seems to have been singularly powerful when it was introduced in 1789 because of the uniquely objectivist standpoint from which it made the physical miseries of the Middle Passage legible (Rediker 2007; Wood 1997). Instead of the usual baroque styles and sentimental appeals popular in abolitionist campaigns, the image of the *Brookes* offered a sober realist rendering of the precise architechtonics and financial calculations that went into maximizing the ship's capacity for the capture and delivery of humans for sale. Following the graphic conventions of naval architecture plans at the time, this was a work about the technorational horrors of slavery from the "system-building" perspective of merchant capitalists and transport engineers (cf. Law 1987). It meant to foreground the ruthless logic of capital in structuring the experience of the slave trade, a logic uniquely captured by the business of transporting people-as-cargo (as opposed to plantation life per se) in which economic efficiency was key. Here what appears from the shipowner's perspective as a winning design for maximizing profit comes to be seen as unconscionably cramped and cruel through the successful humanitarian reframing of the vehicle as a space of fellow feeling with suffering strangers.

Two metrics of the ship's design especially galvanized public imaginations of the brutalities of slave transport—one concerning the spatial allocation of living cargo on the vessel and the other, the material infrastructure of slave provisioning and waste management during the journey. The first metric concretized the degradations of crowding on board by making explicit the ratio of slaves to each tonnage of ship weight (two slaves to one ton) and the dimensions of each space of stowage per body (a maximum of six feet long by one and one-third feet wide with only two and one-half feet of height or headroom). The second metric captured the ship's metabolic dysfunctions in the feeding and "airing" of its stock of "living cargo" through descriptions of the deathly stench and "contagious disorders" circulating from the overcrowded slave decks into the sailors' quarters. In linking the handling of slaves to the perilous conditions of lowly seamen, these descriptions would also begin to disassociate the "human" from "cargo" in transit infrastructures.

Just two years after the 1807 passage of the first British law banning the slave trade, this association of comfort with human dignity and entitlement in transport would start to be codified through a series of increasingly detailed passenger laws in both England and the United States. The same cold calculations that inspired horror over the *Brookes*—its spatial allocation, its management of food, waste, and air—emerged as the key practical targets of legal reform. For instance, against the brutal slave ship metric of two slaves to one ship ton, successive passenger laws in England would expand the ratio from one person to two tons in 1809 to one person to five tons in 1823. In the United States, similar passenger laws have been hailed as the beginning of state recognition of the migrant as a person with natural rights to comfort and convenience rather than as cargo with commodity potential to be maximized (Dillingham 1911). Over the first half of the nineteenth century, the passenger would take on increasingly detailed embodied presence in law as a subject entitled to a certain minimum of square footage, hygiene standards, daylight, and fresh air, not to mention the detailed lists of daily staples and drinks. By 1849, US passenger law even demanded that ships meet a specific discriminating sense of taste: "at least fifteen pounds of good navy bread, ten pounds of rice, ten pounds of oatmeal, ten pounds of wheat flour, ten pounds of peas and beans, thirty-five pounds of potatoes, one pint of vinegar, sixty gallons of fresh water, ten pounds of salted pork, free of bone, all to be of good quality, and a sufficient supply of fuel for cooking."[4]

By articulating a new entitlement to comfort in travel, such laws not only helped cultivate our contemporary assumptions that passenger = human = rights while cargo = nonhuman = price, but were also important technical projects for drawing together all kinds of forces—lawyers, portholes, upholstered seats, good navy bread, air vents, head tax collectors, quarantine rooms—into the distinct worlds of passenger versus cargo infrastructure, which we have all come to know and now take for granted. Today it may be easy to assume that the illegality of "human cargo" is the result of people simply moving via the wrong channels in this dual system of shipping and travel. Such facts of law and its violation are hard to dispute. However, in tracking the techno-aesthetic chain of associations back from the ghostly X-ray of migrants to the slave ship *Brookes*, it should be clear that before the parallel regimes of passenger versus cargo transport could take legible and durable form, other infrastructures of mobility first had to be destabilized and broken into their constituent parts. This crucially included the successful decomposition of the slave ship into a set of questionable calculations and material arrangements, which in turn led to the disaggregation of passengers and their human/izing claim to comfort from the sociotechnical complex of cargo with its lower standards of perishability in transit.

Bad Airs: The Politics of Ventilation

Since the slave ship *Brookes* captured public imaginations, the cramped vehicle as political problem has been crucial to the concretization of comfort as a privileged measure of the human and the lawful in transport. This can be gleaned most obviously from the cushioned interiors of vehicles and port terminals designed for passengers as opposed to the more stripped-down spaces organized for cargo shipping. Yet comfort can also be materialized in less visible and architectural forms, less as a thing-like substance than as the sensible effect of a shifting confluence or friction of forces. In this section, I would like to further elaborate on the necessary rapport and reciprocal relations between heterogeneous elements—both machinic and organic, technical and social, thing-like and phantasmic—crucial to the production of comfort as a sensible sign of migrant il/legality and humanitarian claims. To do this, I take a look at one of the more embedded and diffused operations of the moving vehicle and its related infrastructures—what I am calling its politics of ventilation.

Stifling air and foul stench have long been signs of migrant disorder and of necessary reform in transportation (as well as, later, in housing) since the heydays of the abolitionists and passenger rights advocates discussed above. In 1849, the revised US passenger law formally subtitled, "An act to provide for the ventilation of passenger vessels, and for other purposes," made it clear that fresh air was an essential component of comfort and convenience due to passengers.[5]

Air circulation became a legal right of the migrant-as-person to be secured by the state through new infrastructural demands on transport providers for ample open doors, windows, and hatches on lower decks and for a minimum of two ventilators with "an exhausting cap to carry off the foul air…[and] a receiving cap to carry down fresh air." Yet it was not until the early twentieth century, after innovations in electric-powered ventilation and cooling systems, that the pervasive stench of long-distance travel would shift from a common condition of passengers, largely irresolvable through law, to an incriminating sign of only the most lowly migrants. Interestingly, this capacity to disperse foul smells in passenger transport would come from breakthroughs first made in the cargo shipping industry, particularly via new technologies of refrigeration for moving perishable foods like dressed meat (Cronon 1991).

Today, the degradations of foul air are not only experienced by those being smuggled, they are also materially and discursively reinforced by an elaborate infrastructure of state surveillance and border control. Often the poetics and pragmatics of smell become intimately entangled in the policing of unauthorized migrants. Since the discovery of container smuggling in the late 1990s, for instance, immigration officers and customs inspectors have routinely relied on techniques and technologies for detecting the olfactory signature of human waste as a means of identifying stowaways in and around cargo ports of entry. A booming industry in stowaway detectors, including carbon dioxide monitors and special sniffer dogs, now work with border police to search for the distinctive chemical profile of the odiferous human hidden among non "human cargo" in shipping containers. As an article reviewing a profiling technology, "the zNose 4200," noted:

> In recent years, smugglers have put humans inside cargo containers to slip them into the country. The presence of "human cargo" might be signaled by the odor of human waste, which contains a high percentage of E. coli bacteria. E. coli produce a very recognizable olfactory image, which is dominated by the chemical indole. The presence of molds and fungus in cargo containers can contaminate and even damage sensitive cargo. These life-forms produce distinctive olfactory images and unique, detectable chemicals called microbial volatile organic compounds. (Staples 2004, 25–26)

Such an effluvia of stench and garbage has become so indexical of the Chinese stowaway in border enforcement that one reporter concluded, "even if they make it here alive, they are easy to spot…because of the smell of waste they create [while in transit]" (Grossberg 2006).

Through the sensory associations of odor with criminalized discomfort, what both aspiring migrants and state authorities recognized were the reciprocal effects that occurred when bodies and vehicles came together in the act of traveling. Mode of transport was more than a simple instrument or prosthesis of the traveling person. Rather, something like a shipping container actively shaped the traveler both materially and symbolically, just as passengers gathered in the container transformed its various properties, from its air quality and chemical composition to its uses and meanings. The merger of container with human passengers even produced new life forms like the *E. coli* in human waste and new technologies like stowaway detectors, which together could then act as new mediators of il/legality in global shipping and border control.

This is not to suggest that there is something entirely novel in the privileging of smell in the policing of contemporary migration. As part of the technics of moving strangers, odor has a long semiotic-material legacy as a key differentiator of the uncivilized, contagious masses, with their animalistic and threatening smells, from the deodorized modern world of disciplined, self-possessing individuals, who claim more enlightened and delicate senses of hygiene, well-being, and comfort (Corbin 1988; Classen, Howes, and Synott 1994; Elias 2000). Moreover, far from being technologically dependent, efforts in the policing of "bad airs" often point to the relative autonomy of the poetics of aroma from the pragmatics of ventilation.

While the abolitionist movement and later the passenger laws first invoked the stench of overcrowding to call for infrastructural changes in long-distance transport, by the last decades of the nineteenth century, anticoolie campaigns and legislation, especially against the Chinese in the United States, would show how the same problem of odor could be recast as the incorrigible sign of bad strangers, threatening to a national body and its civilized ways of life. As passengers traveling on some of the same ships and routes that formerly served the slave trade, Chinese coolies occupied a peculiar position of ambivalence in Western moral imaginaries of freedom, humanity, and labor. As a transitional figure at the cusp of slavery's demise, the coolie served both as a new model of free labor (mostly for the British) and as a threatening vestige of the unfree (mostly for Americans) (Lowe 2006, 202). Yet despite such disagreements over the coolie's status as laborer, there appeared to be widespread consensus about how to deal with the coolie-as-passenger on dangerously overcrowded ships (and trains, as shown in chapter 1, this volume) that continued to defy humanitarian and legal standards of comfort. Whereas the cramped conditions of the slave ship inspired all sorts of material and structural reforms, it is striking how similar horrors of coolie transport did less to further such efforts than to direct public attention to the backward nature of the Chinese, who appeared on the one hand to be ignorant victims of their more savvy and ruthless countrymen (McKeown 2008) and on the other to be a distinctive race of insensible bodies inured to their own physical discomforts as well as to the suffering of others (Lye 2005; Hayot 2009).

In his widely read account, *Chinese Characteristics*, the late nineteenth-century American missionary Arthur Smith argued that "it is in traveling in China that the absence of helpful kindness on the part of the people towards strangers is perhaps most conspicuous" (1894, 209). Smith traced this Chinese apathy not only to cultural limitations of a "barbaric" civilization but also to the racial distinction of Chinese bodies themselves, which he argued made them much more tolerant of physical discomfort than they would be if they "had an outfit of Anglo-Saxon nerves" (94). This Chinese incapacity to feel, for both their own pain and that of others, was made especially clear in Smith's discussion of the problem of cramped space and its attendant bad airs. After offering various examples of Chinese indifference to physical confinement and noxious overcrowding, Smith summed up the inhuman limit of Chinese bodies by noting, "we must take account of the fact that in China breathing seems to be optional" (92–94). Just a few years after Smith published his account, a similar line of argument would appear in anticoolie campaigns to ban all Chinese migration to the United States.[6]

In diagnosing the continual problem of bad air in cramped transport among the Chinese, the moving vehicle no longer appeared to be an external force impinging on the traveler's sense of freedom, humanity, or comfort. Instead, it became a symptom of a degraded race and its innate insensibilities to overcrowding and poor ventilation. In turn, the solution was not in fixing the ship and its infrastructure but in banning its passengers from bringing their alienating habits and lowly standards onto Western shores, where they threatened to undermine the good life. This powerful reduction of the cramped vehicle to the bad, unsympathetic stranger not only supported a half century of Chinese exclusion laws and other race-based restrictions on immigration to the United States. Its legacy can also be glimpsed in contemporary invocations of rusty ships and smelly containers to disqualify migrant claims to asylum and other rights, as evident in the Canadian response to Chinese stowaways discussed earlier (Mountz 2010) as well as in the current debates over security and un/freedom across the Mediterranean and at the US-Mexico border.

Conclusion

Before we can feel much for others, we must in some measure be at ease
ourselves. If our own misery pinches us very severely, we have no leisure to attend to that of our neighbour; and all the savages are too much
occupied with their own wants and necessities, to give much attention
to those of another person.
—ADAM SMITH, *The Theory of Moral Sentiments*

The list of the stresses, indignities, and perceived injustices airline
travelers are expected to accept as a matter of course these days can
be overwhelming... but the real test of civility comes at 34,000 feet
in the air. The days when airlines enticed passengers with the promise
of comfort—meals, blankets, pillows, reading materials, movies—
throughout their flying journey are long gone. Passenger, comfort
thyself.
—ANNA POST, "I'm an Etiquette Expert"

In September 2014, the diagram of the *Brookes* returned to public attention as
part of two separate jokes about cramped space and the discomforts of air travel
in the media. Following a series of passenger fights over legroom that forced
three American flights to make emergency landings in little more than a week
in August, the Pennsylvania newspaper *Lancaster New Era* ran an editorial cartoon showing an elderly couple responding to a framed image of the *Brookes*
hanging on a gallery wall with the comment, "Must be where the airlines got their
ideas for passenger seating" (Gordon 2014). Meanwhile on *The Late Show with Stephen Colbert*, the television comedian performed a similar joke in a segment called
"Coach-Class Conflicts," in which he satirically raved about a "truly revolutionary
new seating design" by showing the diagram of the *Brookes* superimposed on the
frame of an airplane. Extolling the capitalist virtues of shrinking passenger space
in his usual faux-conservative elite bluster, Colbert noted of the design, "Not only
can you pack twice as many people into coach, you can fill the cargo hold with
spices and molasses to bring back from the colonies" (Fiorillo 2014).

Soon after these jokes appeared, public outrage over the use of the *Brookes*
became so intense that the Lancaster newspaper issued an immediate apology
and retraction of its editorial cartoon. By way of explanation, the newspaper
acknowledged how the comparison of cramped vehicles was not only "just plain

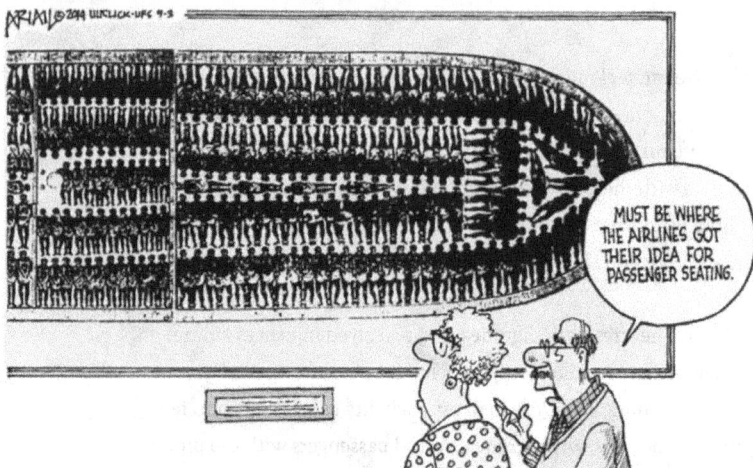

FIGURE 4.3 · *Lancaster New Era* editorial cartoon. Source: Robert Ariail.

FIGURE 4.4 · Screenshot from *The Late Show with Stephen Colbert.*

wrong" but also "deeply hurtful to our African American community and all those who understand the horrors inflicted on the men and women forced into the slave trade" (Kirkpatrick and Roda 2014; cf. Taibi 2014). While Colbert did not respond to the controversy, media pundits and bloggers would raise similar issues of racial insensitivity and poor taste in his invocation of the *Brookes* to examine the discomforts of air travel.

In the aftermath of the controversy, the cartoonist of the retracted illustration tried to explain how he did not mean "to trivialize slavery" but only wanted to "make a hyperbolic point about our modern day condition" by comparing airline seating with the most extreme and famous example that he could think of (Gordon 2014). Such hyperbole, after all, was not unusual in common jokes and gripes about the discomforts of flying, especially after three decades of airline deregulation and industry cutbacks of in-flight services and amenities in the United States. As one frequent flyer quipped to a reporter more than a decade ago: "Hell is the middle seat in the back row of a 757 with the smell of rancid lasagna wafting in the air" (Berger 1999).

By way of conclusion, I would like to consider how this analogy with hell could be read appreciatively by the reporter (and his audience) as humorous criticism of air travel while a similarly hyperbolic comparison with the *Brookes* only sparked widespread outrage and controversy. We might also ask how the same slave ship analogy continues to capture public imaginations of the current migrant crisis across the Mediterranean despite some serious critiques of the historically wrong and politically harmful implications of this comparison (Davidson 2015). Why are European publics unmoved by similar criticism of the slavery analogy, especially when these comparisons make no claims to comedic exaggeration as they appear in the somber, realist form of news coverage and political commentary?

To answer these questions, we must consider not only the technical matter of the vehicles at stake in these comparisons but also their implicit technics as a working social ensemble of heterogeneous parts spanning the human and the nonhuman, the practical and the aesthetic, the infrastructural and the fantastical. Above all, the technics of moving strangers has medium specificity; it is something that comes into articulation in a distinct cultural-historical milieu. In this chapter, I have tried to show this by tracing the emergence and uptake of comfort as an organizing symbol and measure of the in/human in transport, through which the slave ship *Brookes* first successfully captured public imaginations of the cramped horrors of the vehicle and, in the process, helped shape a new physical and moral landscape of travel. This is a landscape organized through dueling imaginaries of immigration versus trade in which, as we now all assume is the norm, human = passenger = rights while nonhuman = cargo = price. This separation of the human from cargo was not necessarily politically progressive and pro-immigrant in disposition. While I trace the successful articulation of comfort as a liberal right inspiring structural reform through abolition and passenger laws, I also show how it morphed into a racialized sign of insensible, bad strangers by the late nineteenth century in anticoolie campaigns calling for the banning of all Chinese from US borders and claims to higher standards of living.

In all these cases, the problem of comfort was never just a technical one of cramped transport. The technical was in fact always already entangled with an existing social repertoire of ideas, habits, and aspirations; that is, it had aesthetic and affective capacities as part of moral imaginaries of the good life. Whether through the iconic image of slave ship *Brookes* or through recursive signs of stench and garbage in container smuggling, both public sympathy and revulsion have been mobilized effectively, as I have shown, through sensory invocations of discomfort in travel. More than just a means of transportation, the vehicle is better thought of here as both medium and milieu for cultivating sensibilities of proper intimacy and distance with others, whether in the form of the sympathetic stranger or alienating "human cargo".

Air rage debates point to yet another way for imagining and intervening in the problem of passenger discomfort. In the aftermath of the three legroom incidents in 2014, the proliferation of etiquette guides and consumer advice for passengers suggested that if travelers could not afford to pay for more space in business or first class, then they should expect to bear the discomforts of their low-fare seats by working on their own civility and self-control (Post 2014; Rosenbloom 2014). Despite some critiques of mercenary airline practices in these discussions, the general consensus seemed to be that there is little anyone can do about ever-diminishing space in economy cabins since it is the natural outcome of market competition to meet consumer demands for the cheapest ticket. As one journalist put it, "unless you pay for extra space, be prepared to love your seatmates like yourself—or face the consequences" (Muskal 2014; cf. Elliott 2015; Patterson 2012). Besides giving tips on politeness, guides also encouraged passengers to discipline and arm themselves against discomfort by buying noise-canceling headphones, learning yoga breathing exercises, and, in general, finding ways to "tune out" and "avoid human contact" (Hewitt 2007; Rosenbloom 2014; cf. Von Hoffman 1999; see also Marks 2014; BBC 2015). Ironically, while the seeming indifference of the coolie to cramped conditions appeared to be a racial sign of the bad stranger in the past—not to mention the present-day illicit migrant—here the anesthetized, isolated passenger is praised as the ideal civilized subject rising above the poor coping skills and resulting rudeness of their fellow bargain-hunting travelers stuffed into airplane coach cabins.

Ultimately, in the misfiring of airplane jokes about the *Brookes*, what may have been lost in translation was not only the hurtful history and effects of slavery but also the remediated promise and power of the diagram's original shock-and-awe as capitalist critique. Instead, through the emerging consumer logic, not to mention the shrugging jokes, that you get what you pay for in travel, the techno-aesthetic work separating passenger rights from price threatened to dissolve back into each other. In this respect, the return of "human cargo" may no longer seem like such a problem but just an unavoidable cost—albeit one charged against some much more than others (read: the insensible migrant, the budget consumer)—in our contemporary world of moving strangers.

Notes

An earlier and longer version of this chapter appeared in *International Journal of Politics, Culture and Society* 29 (2016): 403–21. I am grateful to Sarah Wade-West for her excellent editorial work on this chapter.

1 Chapter 1, this volume, examines similar fixations in relation to early twentieth-century US deportation trains, whose design, Blue argues, was the result of a balance between costs, on the one hand, and the need to exercise greater train-board control and supervision, on the other.
2 For a cogent example of technics as more than technology, see Mumford's ([1934] 2010, 16–17) discussion of the clock and the emergence of a clockwork world.
3 See Hayot (2009) and Eng, Ruskola, and Shen (2011) for more detailed historical discussions of the association of Chinese insensibility with Western moral imaginations of the human, strangerhood, and sympathy.
4 See Blunt (1848, 454).
5 "An Act to Provide for the Ventilation of Passenger Vessels, and for Other Purposes," May 17, 1848, U.S. Statutes at Large, 9:220. https://www.loc.gov/law/help/statutes-at-large/30th-congress/session-1/c30s1ch41.pdf.
6 For instance, see the American Federation of Labor (1901, 22) pamphlet, "Some Reasons for Chinese Exclusion," which argued that the problem of bad air in Chinese residences was not a structural one of poor ventilation or lax enforcement but rather a racial puzzle about insensible bodies accustomed to "the dense and poisonous atmosphere" of cramped spaces.

References

American Federation of Labor. 1901. "Some Reasons for Chinese Exclusion." S.doc.137. Washington, DC: American Federation of Labor. http://pi.lib.uchicago.edu/1001/cat/bib/9494809.
Barthes, Roland. (1957) 1972. *Mythologies*. New York: Macmillan.

BBC. 2015. "Mediterranean Migrant Deaths: EU Faces Renewed Pressure." April 20. http://www.bbc.com/news/world-europe-32376082.

Berger, Warren. 1999. "Life Sucks and Then You Fly." *Wired*, August 1. http://www.wired.com/1999/08/flying/.

Bilder, Mary Sarah. 1996. "The Struggle over Immigration: Indentured Servants, Slaves, and Articles of Commerce." *Missouri Law Review* 61 (4). http://papers.ssrn.com/abstract=1524772.

Birrell, Ian. 2015. "Voyage of the Damned: Pitiful Human Cargo Fleeing Jihad and Slavery." *Mail Online*, July 18. http://www.dailymail.co.uk/news/article-3166490/Voyage-damned-Beaten-bowels-fetid-floating-coffin-just-hour-certain-death-pitiful-human-cargo-fleeing-jihad-slavery-man-helped-save.html.

Blunt, Joseph. 1848. *The Shipmaster's Assistant and Commercial Digest.* New York: Harper and Brothers.

Chu, Julie Y. 2010. *Cosmologies of Credit: Transnational Mobility and the Politics of Destination in China.* Durham, NC: Duke University Press.

Classen, Constance, David Howes, and Anthony Synott. 1994. *Aroma: The Cultural History of Smell.* New York: Routledge.

Corbin, Alain. 1988. *The Foul and the Fragrant: Odor and the French Social Imagination.* Cambridge, MA: Harvard University Press.

Cronon, William. 1991. *Nature's Metropolis: Chicago and the Great West.* New York: W. W. Norton.

Crowley, John E. 1999. "The Sensibility of Comfort." *American Historical Review* 104 (3): 749–82.

Crowley, John E. 2001. *The Invention of Comfort: Sensibilities and Design in Early Modern Britain and Early America.* Baltimore, MD: Johns Hopkins University Press.

Davidson, Julia O'Connell. 2015. "Rights Talk, Wrong Comparison: Trafficking and Transatlantic Slavery." *OpenDemocracy*, May 26. https://www.opendemocracy.net/en/beyond-trafficking-and-slavery/rights-talk-wrong-comparison-trafficking-and-transatlantic-sl/.

Dillingham, William Paul. 1911. *Reports of the Immigration Commission.* Washington, DC: Government Printing Office.

Elias, Norbert. 2000. *The Civilizing Process: Sociogenetic and Psychogenetic Investigations.* Rev. ed. Oxford: Blackwell.

Elliott, Christopher. 2015. "Airplanes' Space Wars Are Shifting to the Human Rights Front." *Washington Post*, September 17. https://www.washingtonpost.com/lifestyle/travel/airline-space-wars-are-shifting-to-the-human-rights-front/2015/09/17/d54999f4-5bce-11e5-8e9e-dce8a2a2a679_story.html.

Eng, David L., Teemu Ruskola, and Shuang Shen. 2011. "Introduction: China and the Human." *Social Text* 29 (4, no. 109): 1–27.

Fiorillo, Victor. 2014. "Lancaster Newspaper, Stephen Colbert Make Slave Plane Joke." *Philadelphia Magazine*, September 11. http://www.phillymag.com /news/2014/09/11/lancaster-newspaper-stephen-colbert-airplane-slave -ship/.

Gordon, Taylor. 2014. "Pennsylvania Newspaper Apologizes for Running Slave Ship Cartoon." *Atlantic Black Star*, September 16. http://atlantablackstar .com/2014/09/16/pennsylvania-newspaper-apologizes-running-slave-ship -cartoon/.

Grossberg, Josh. 2006. "Container Stowaways Reported Easy to Find." *Daily Breeze*, April 19.

Halttunen, Karen. 1995. "Humanitarianism and the Pornography of Pain in Anglo-American Culture." *American Historical Review* 100 (2): 303–34.

Hayot, Eric. 2009. *The Hypothetical Mandarin: Sympathy, Modernity, and Chinese Pain*. New York: Oxford University Press.

Hewitt, Ed. 2007. "Air Rage: Why the Caged Bird Sings." NBC *News Online*, October 31, https://www.nbcnews.com/id/wbna21384567.

Kirkpatrick, John A., and Barb Roda. 2014. "To Our Readers: An Apology for a Deeply Hurtful, Offensive Editorial Cartoon." *LancasterOnline*, September 11. http://lancasteronline.com/news/local/to-our-readers-an-apology-for-a-deeply -hurtful-offensive/article_d12d2752-392c-11e4-bf22-001a4bcf6878.html.

Lacquer, T. 1989. "Bodies, Details, and the Humanitarian Narrative." In *The New Cultural History*, edited by A. Biersack and L. A. Hunt, 176–204. Berkeley: University of California Press.

Law, John. 1987. "On the Social Explanation of Technical Change: The Case of the Portuguese Maritime Expansion." *Technology and Culture* 28 (2): 227–52.

Liu, Melinda. 1993. "The New Slave Trade." *Newsweek*, June 20. http://www .newsweek.com/new-slave-trade-193676.

Lowe, Lisa. 2006. "The Intimacies of Four Continents." In *Haunted by Empire: Geographies of Intimacy in North American History*, edited by Ann Stoler, 191–212. Durham, NC: Duke University Press.

Lye, Colleen. 2005. *America's Asia: Racial Form and American Literature, 1893– 1945*. Princeton, NJ: Princeton University Press.

Marks, Tod. 2014. "Knee Defender Puts Blame on Passengers." *Consumer Reports*, September 15. http://www.consumerreports.org/cro/news/2014/09/knee -defender-battle-puts-blame-on-passengers/index.htm.

Martin, Craig. 2011. "Turbulent Stillness: The Politics of Uncertainty and the Undocumented Migrant." In *Stillness in a Mobile World*, edited by David Bissell and Gillian Fuller, 192–208. New York: Routledge.

McCartney, Scott. 2014. "Airline Seat Battles: Be Kind, Don't Recline?" *Wall Street Journal*, September 3. http://www.wsj.com/articles/airline-seat-battles-be-kind -dont-recline-1409780915.

McKeown, Adam M. 2008. *Melancholy Order: Asian Migration and the Globalization of Borders*. New York: Columbia University Press.

Mountz, Alison. 2010. *Seeking Asylum: Human Smuggling and Bureaucracy at the Border*. Minneapolis: University of Minnesota Press.

Mumford, Lewis. (1934) 2010. *Technics and Civilization*. Chicago: University of Chicago Press.

Muskal, Michael. 2014. "Recline Rage: Why Airline Seating Is Provoking Mid-flight Fights." *Los Angeles Times*, September 2. http://www.latimes.com/nation/nationnow/la-na-nn-cramped-seats-recline-airline-20140902-story.html.

Patterson, Thom. 2012. "Airline Squeeze: It's Not You, 'It's the Seat.'" CNN, June 1. https://www.cnn.com/travel/article/airline-seats/index.html.

Post, Anna. 2014. "I'm an Etiquette Expert. The Feds Should Ban Seat Lock Devices on All Planes." *Washington Post*, August 28. https://www.washingtonpost.com/posteverything/wp/2014/08/28/im-an-etiquette-expert-the-feds-should-ban-seat-lock-devices-on-all-planes-its-just-good-manners/.

Rediker, Marcus. 2007. *The Slave Ship: A Human History*. London: Penguin.

Rivera, Alex, dir. 2003. *The Borders Trilogy*. New York: SubCine.Com.

Rosenbloom, Stephanie. 2014. "A Recipe for Air Rage." *New York Times*, September 28. http://www.nytimes.com/2014/09/28/travel/a-recipe-for-air-rage.html.

Sang, Lucia I. Suaraez. 2018. "Nearly 200 Illegal Immigrants Found in Just Three January Smuggling Busts." Fox News, February 2. https://www.foxnews.com/us/nearly-200-illegal-immigrants-found-in-just-three-january-smuggling-busts.

Schivelbusch, Wolfgang. 1986. *The Railway Journey: The Industrialization of Time and Space in the Nineteenth Century*. Berkeley: University of California Press.

Shooster, Jay. 2017. "The San Antonio Smuggling Tragedy: Don't Let Trump Hijack the Story." *Huffington Post*, August 4. https://www.huffingtonpost.com/entry/the-san-antonio-smuggling-tragedy-dont-let-trump_us_59848426e4b0f2c7d93f5511.

Smith, Adam. (1759) 2011. *The Theory of Moral Sentiments*. Kapaau: Gutenberg.

Smith, Arthur Henderson. 1894. *Chinese Characteristics*. New York: Fleming H. Revell.

Staples, Edward J. 2004. "Safeguarding Ports with Chemical Profiling." *Industrial Physicist*, June/July.

Taibi, Catherine. 2014. "Newspaper Apologizes for Offensive Cartoon Comparing Airplanes to Slave Ships." *Huffington Post*, September 14. http://www.huffingtonpost.com/2014/09/14/newspaper-airplane-slave-ships-lancaster-cartoon_n_5818446.html.

Von Hoffman, Nicholas. 1999. "Come Fly with Me." *Wall Street Journal*, December 17. http://www.wsj.com/articles/SB945388911433767425.

Walters, William. 2012. "From Borderlands to Viapolitics: An Essay on Migration and Its Routes of Power." Keynote lecture at conference New Borderlands or Cosmopolitanism from Below? Carl von Ossietzky University, Oldenburg, Germany, December 7.

Walters, William. 2015. "Migration, Vehicles, and Politics: Three Theses on Viapolitics." *European Journal of Social Theory* 18 (4): 469–88.

Wood, Marcus. 1997. "Imaging the Unspeakable and Speaking the Unimaginable: The 'Description' of the Slave Ship Brookes and the Visual Interpretation of the Middle Passage." *Lumen: Selected Proceedings from the Canadian Society for Eighteenth-Century Studies* 16: 211–45.

PART II

Trajectories, Routes, and Infrastructures

FIVE

Infrastructures of Escort:

Transnational Migration, Viapolitics,

and Cultures of Connection in

Indonesia | Johan Lindquist

Writing more than two decades ago, during the final years of Suharto's rule, Saya Shiraishi (1997) offered *pengantar*—meaning both "introduction" and "escort"—as an elegant pun and entry point for understanding Indonesia's New Order. Indonesia is characterized by a politics of connection and patronage rather than a politics of communication and identification based on general rights. As such, proximity to power and recognition are critical dimensions of economic and political life (Siegel 1997, 44; see also Morris 2007, 380). More specifically, the network, or *jaringan*, is the primary form of access to power and resources—at least in an urban or translocal context—and the pengantar (the escort) is the point of access. From the perspective of her own temporary embeddedness in upper-middle-class Jakarta, Shiraishi elaborates on the intimate nature of the politics of connection by illuminating the relationship between comfort and coercion in what is widely termed *antar-jemput*; *antar* (the root of pengantar) meaning to accompany someone somewhere, and *jemput* meaning to pick someone up. Taken together, antar-jemput highlights the importance of escort in the context of mobility.

Shiraishi describes her own arrival at Jakarta's Sukarno-Hatta airport and the mass of people she is faced with upon exiting the terminal, half of whom she imagines as family members waiting for relatives returning home. The rest, she suggests, make their living off those who are not expecting anyone (Shiraishi 1997, 18). While this points to the importance of having an escort, the more one fears outside danger, the stronger the grip of the escort (35). Allowing oneself to be escorted thus enables mobility and access to resources, but creates a relationship that is based on dependency and is potentially coercive.

This chapter takes antar-jemput as a starting point for understanding not only elite forms of mobility in urban centers such as Jakarta, but also low-skilled, documented migration from rural Indonesia to countries across Asia and the Middle East. In particular, the chapter argues that escort in the context of migration takes the form of brokerage, as a wide range of actors become engaged in regulating, aiding, and profiting from migrant mobility. More generally, this forms the basis for the development of a migration infrastructure—a sociotechnical platform for mobility (Larkin 2013; Xiang and Lindquist 2014)—that includes recruitment, documentation, transport, temporary housing, reception, and physical encapsulation centered on the protection (*perlindungan*) of the migrant.

As has been widely noted, protection potentially sets the stage for extraction and, in broader terms, the shaping of a "racket" (Tilly 1985; Barker 1998; Wilson 2015). In Indonesia, this is evident through modes of territorialization in contexts ranging from brothel villages (*lokalisasi*) to urban security regimes (*siskamling*; Barker 1999a, 111). In light of this, the current migration infrastructure points to a tendency to territorialize migration corridors (*jalur*) within a general economy of labor circulation. These jalur draw together human actors and infrastructure in a complex and patchwork process of "orchestration" (chapter 3, this volume), as migrant bodies are encapsulated—"isolated from broader social relations and access to social resources"—and thus controlled and commodified (Xiang 2013, 84).

The chapter describes how mobility is shaped by cultural, economic, and political forces across an uneven terrain that depends on individual actors, modes of transportation, and physical structures. This situates the chapter in an emerging field of scholarship that approaches migration as a sociotechnical process. In an attempt to move beyond binaries that focus on either migrant experience or migration governance, scholars have increasingly recognized the importance of developing an empirical and conceptual space that is attentive to the brokers and infrastructures that make migration possible (e.g., Lindquist, Xiang, and Yeoh 2012; Xiang and Lindquist 2014). Research dealing with migration industries (Gammeltoft-Hansen and Sørensen 2013), apparatuses (Feldman 2012), and logistics (Altenried et al. 2018), as well as with viapolitics (Walters 2015; introduction, this volume), develop a comparable mode of attention, as migration is reconceptualized as a process, a system-in-the-making.

In line with the volume's focus on viapolitics, this chapter uses the culturally specific concepts antar-jemput (escort) and jalur (track, channel, or corridor[1]) as an entry point for describing how the migration process is socially embedded. This should be considered in relation to work that has focused on how previously unregulated migration routes have been transformed into state-sanctioned corridors in the wake of deportation and refugee programs in Europe (Kasparek 2016, 6; Drotbohm and Hasselberg 2015, 553; chapter 7, this volume). While such research has focused on the role of the state in Europe, this chapter focuses on the Global South and develops a broader approach that situates the emergence of migration corridors at the intersection between culture, market, and state. This shifts our attention away from a strict focus on state borders as the key site for regulating mobility, to an open-ended and interconnected set of translocal processes beginning on the village level. More specifically, the Indonesian case allows us to approach the territorialization and encapsulation of mobility, or migration infrastructure more broadly, not strictly as a racket in political-economic terms, but also in relation to both the enduring relationship between the state and rural peripheries and regional cultures of mobility. The focus on escort reveals Indonesian migration as a historically contingent form that should be considered in relation to the enduring problem of the rural-urban divide. This leads back to the indirect rule of the Dutch colonial state, which relied on a wide range of intermediaries and technologies to mediate between villages and urban centers of power (Barker 1999b; Lindquist 2018b).

Rural populations have historically been infantilized by the Indonesian state in a didactic process of nation-building centered on development projects as diverse as family planning and television programming (Kitley 2002; Niehof and Lubis 2003). As villagers have increasingly been valued as an overseas labor reserve since the 1980s—a process that intensified after the 1997 economic crisis—the geographical divide between the rural and the urban has, in an important sense, become necessary to reorganize (Cremer 1988; Lindquist 2010). These state-sanctioned labor deployment programs, also evident in countries such as the Philippines and centered primarily on female domestic workers, aim to move migrant workers directly from rural areas to employment sites abroad. The expansion of migration infrastructure appears as a response to this, as villagers are transformed into migrants, while the enduring relationship between parent (state) and child (villager) is retained (cf. Shiraishi 1997, 31–32). Along these lines, the Indonesian government and nongovernmental organizations warn prospective migrants, through media and outreach campaigns, about the importance of using formal recruitment corridors.

Traveling alone is generally considered inappropriate, dangerous, or even strange across Indonesia and large parts of Southeast Asia, particularly for women. In fact, immobility often appears to be a way of avoiding vulnerability (cf. Anderson 1972; Errington 1989, 54, 134, 251; Allerton 2013). Shiraishi's description of her arrival at the Jakarta airport illustrates as much. More to the point, a culture of mobility has taken shape centered on the vulnerabilities of traveling alone and the comfort and security of traveling with someone or in a group. From this perspective, antar-jemput, which shares the didactic element that characterizes the state's concern with rural populations more generally, offers an entry point for conceptualizing migration infrastructure in Indonesia, not strictly as an apparatus for the regulation and extraction of labor or the management of a particular population, but as a historically embedded cultural form. This, in turn, allows us to move beyond an approach to migration based on facile dichotomies such as freedom and control.

The Rise of Documented Migration

In the wake of the 1997 Asian economic crisis there was a dramatic rise in documented transnational migration from Indonesia to countries across Asia and the Middle East, most notably Malaysia and Saudi Arabia—within a decade the annual number of documented migrants quadrupled to around 750,000 annually—the vast majority of whom were female domestic workers (Hugo 2012, 399). The collapse of the Indonesian rupiah, the fall of the New Order regime in 1998, the intensification of the Malaysian deportation regime, and the more general rise of a system of circular migration across Asia and the Middle East further shaped these flows.

In Indonesia, documented migration has taken shape during the past two decades through an expansive migration bureaucracy and a growing number of licensed recruitment companies, with most having multiple branch offices in key recruitment areas. These recruitment companies, in turn, depend on vast and unstable networks of petugas lapangan (PLs, field agents), informal labor recruiters who are the actual links between recruitment companies and the villages that are the primary sources of migrant labor across Indonesia (Lindquist 2010; Palmer 2016).

In comparative terms, there are a few notable points about Indonesian documented migration. First, while private labor brokers have characterized Asian migration since the colonial era (Houben 1999), the number of informal brokers engaged in Indonesia's documented labor migration industry is arguably unparalleled in relation to other countries across the region. Second, the list of required documents for Indonesian migration is extensive: birth certificate, letter of permission from husband or parents, *kartu keluarga* (family card), two different ID cards, medical certificate, letter of permission to have a passport made, a special twenty-four-page migrant passport, and a *surat keterangan jalan* (travel permit) certifying that the individual is a documented migrant (Lindquist 2018a). Third, the encapsulation of migrants, not only in the context of departure but also upon their return, appears unprecedented internationally (Kloppenburg 2013, 111). Most notably, at the Jakarta Sukarno-Hatta airport, between 1999 and 2014 there was a specific reception terminal for returning migrants, a model that was, for a time, reproduced on a smaller scale at other airports across the country. Despite being properly documented, returning migrants were not free to leave the terminals of their own accord but, rather, were compelled to purchase tickets for minivans that escorted them home. Encapsulation, particularly of women, was written into government directives, ostensibly in the name of protection from *preman* (thugs), who were seen as having the ability to divert and exploit migrants. A similar process was evident in deportation programs from Malaysia to Indonesia. Migrants en route were thus not to be left alone.

The ubiquity of brokers, the demand for paperwork, and the encapsulation of migrants should be considered together in the context of the culture of antar-jemput and the expanding migration infrastructure that organizes migrant mobility. This illustrates how the Indonesian state's enduring concern with controlling rural populations depends on collaborations with formal and informal brokers throughout the recruitment process, as well as the patchwork nature of migration infrastructure and the cultural forms that are integral to its functioning.

Departure

It is just before dawn as we drive along the main east-west road that cuts through Lombok (an island located just east of Bali), from the main commercial town of Mataram in the east toward the ferry port to Sumbawa in the west. A landscape of sound surrounds us as we pass men dressed for prayer walking to their local mosques. Together with Ibrahim, who works for P. T. Sinar, one of the most successful licensed recruitment companies on the island, I am on my way in a white minivan to pick up nine men who are ready to depart Lombok. In a few days, P. T. Sinar will be sending a group of two hundred migrants recruited from around the island to work on a palm oil plantation in Pahang, in West Malaysia, on two-year contracts, a job order that they had three months to fill. First, however, the men have to be accompanied to a rundown hotel to take part in a government-regulated, predeparture training before being escorted to the airport the following day for the flight to Kuala Lumpur in Malaysia, where they will be picked up by the plantation staff and driven directly to their workplace on the estate.

The transportation of these and other men to the hotel is a logistical feat that involves traveling along decrepit north-south roads lacking public transportation—in places, the road is so bad that it is literally impossible for cars to use. A complex network of PLs is therefore put to work to pick up and transport the migrants. In fact, it is not unusual for low-level PLs to double as motorcycle taxi (*ojek*) drivers who ply the route between the main road and villages, transporting people, goods, and information. As we travel along the road, we stop to pick up one of the PLs, Jusri, who has personally recruited five of the migrants. Jusri is a former migrant who quickly turned to recruitment when it became apparent that being a PL was far more lucrative than plantation labor. His recruits all live in the vicinity of his village, and he is well known in the area as a reliable recruiter. He wearily tells me about all the work he has put into the recruitment process, including repeat visits to prospective migrants' homes and escorting them to and from government offices, not to mention the cost of purchasing snacks and cigarettes.

On rural Lombok, a white minivan with tinted windows signals migrant transport. As we turn north off the main road and dramatically reduce our speed on the poor road—sometimes moving at only ten kilometers per hour—people stare as we pass. After an hour we turn onto an even smaller road and eventually stop at a house where two men are waiting with their backpacks leaning against the wall. A crowd of twenty people is waiting to see them off. Ibrahim and Jusri get out and greet the men, one of them quite young, probably still a teenager. A woman grabs his arm and begins to weep as he pulls away to get into the van. We do not waste time and quickly leave. This scene is repeated in similar form as we drive to other villages to pick up other men, but at the final stop there are two men and no one to send them off. There is apparently a problem with debt in the village.

As we drive back toward the main road in silence, with the men and their bags crowded in the back of the minivan, we encounter two young men standing near the middle of the road, holding up buckets, ostensibly to collect money for a local mosque under construction. It appears that they are particularly aggressive toward the van compared to the cars ahead. Ibrahim scowls as he swerves to avoid hitting them, and turns to me and asks rhetorically, "You know what they say about Lombok? It is the island of a thousand mosques [*pulau seribu masjid*] . . . and a million thieves [*sejuta maling*]."

By 10 a.m., about five hours after departing, we are back in Mataram, and drive to the local hotel that has the monopoly on housing predeparture migrants and hosting their compulsory government-sanctioned briefing sessions. The briefing has already started; a few hundred men, recruited by several companies, are in the decrepit auditorium, being informed about their rights, but primarily being lectured about their responsibilities as migrants. The men will spend a couple of nights in cramped quarters at the back of the hotel before being shuttled in minivans to the airport a couple of days later to take the direct flight to Kuala Lumpur.

Transport and Passage

The migrant minivan is ubiquitous throughout the migration process. While many PLs use motorbikes to transport prospective migrants one at a time—to government authorities, such as the immigration office, to produce passports; to clinics, for medical certification; or to recruitment companies upon departure— the minivan allows recruiters to scale up, as it is possible to fit more than ten migrants at a time into a vehicle. For the PLs and the recruitment company, the minivan, usually a Toyota Kijang, is a sign of success that signals a good reputation while representing a particular quality of travel. One PL told me that he bought a Kijang so that migrants would feel *aman* (safe, secure) when he escorted them to Mataram.

The minivan is also clearly valued by migrants themselves. The two times I traveled in minivans together with groups of departing women, the atmosphere quickly became bustling and lively (*ramai*), as the comfort of being escorted in the minivan apparently reinforced the positive dimensions of the migration decision (cf. Silvey 2018, 200). On another occasion, when I joined a PL to pick up migrants who were departing for Malaysia, one of the relatives angrily complained that we had arrived in a *bemo*, a minibus used for public transport

FIGURE 5.1 · Migrant minivan on Lombok. Source: Johan Lindquist.

refurbished to cram in as many passengers as possible. She adamantly claimed that the passengers would all become sick and vomit if they were forced to sit cramped and facing the side of the road. More importantly, the mundane form of transport did not match the gravity of the migrants' departure. To be picked up is a form of statement—by whom and how one is transported suggests the quality of the PL's connections to the world beyond the village.

While minivans are rare in rural areas, throughout urban Indonesia those run by private companies—positioned between public buses and private automobiles—have become a ubiquitous form of semipublic, door-to-door transport for the growing middle class in the context of intercity travel. In her ethnographic research on cross-border medical travel between Pontianak in Kalimantan in Indonesia and Kuching in East Malaysia on Borneo, Meghann Ormond (2015, 94) describes how the minivan driver "enacts a therapeutic environment within the van" through the production of comfort and the distribution of Malaysian vitamins to the passengers, while Ismail Fajarie Alatas (2016), in his work on the rise of Indonesian pilgrimage to the Hadramawt Valley in Yemen, describes how Yemen-based Indonesians, in collaboration with travel agents, engage in the antar-jemput of pilgrims. This form of escort, however, is most evident in the context of *antar-jemput anak sekolah*, the business of picking up and dropping off schoolchildren in major urban centers. As Shiraishi (1997, 26–27) has suggested, this process has a didactic dimension by which children learn to accept the protection and comfort of escort. In the context of migration, this urban phenomenon is thus transferred to a rural population previously imagined as immobile or, more specifically, produced as such through a history of colonial and postcolonial travel regulations aimed at capturing labor and regulating identity.[2]

The minivan is used not only during departure but also upon return. As noted, returning migrants at the Sukarno-Hatta airport, particularly women, were until recently compelled to pass through a specific migrant terminal, which they were not allowed to leave by themselves. Instead, most were escorted to their home villages by government-licensed transport companies. In government directives that regulate return, the importance of safety (*keamanan*), comfort (*kenyamanan*), and protection is highlighted (Kloppenburg 2013, 136). As stated in one of the documents, "each phase of the return process, from leaving the airplane until arriving at the home village, can be experienced as safe and comfortable by migrants coming from abroad" (quoted in Kloppenburg 2013, 114).[3]

For migrants' return trip, transport companies have been required to use dark-blue Isuzu minivans with dark windows, and official stickers identifying them as special migrant vehicles must be placed on the windows. Minivans en route may only stop at registered roadside restaurants, where migrants are counted and required to sign a form (Kloppenburg 2013, 130). In the context of transporting migrants away from the migrant terminal in Jakarta, Sanneke Kloppenburg notes how the "tips" that drivers receive from their passengers are used to pay off thugs on local roads. The transport companies' mandate is to deliver migrants to their front door—as the van becomes a mobile capsule connecting to other capsules in the regulation of the migration process. This means leaving the main highway and using smaller roads, where drivers inevitably are stopped intermittently and asked for money in order to pass. The tip money is thus "a lubricant for literally keeping the buses in motion when they enter local areas" (157). Similar stories were pervasive in my own fieldwork on Lombok.

Anecdotal accounts suggest that local forms of roadside extraction multiplied after the fall of the New Order, with the increasing opportunity to territorialize extraction in the wake of political decentralization. On Lombok's key thoroughfares, young men ostensibly ask for mosque donations. Drivers such as Ibrahim show them disdain but often feel compelled to comply. People traveling on small roads are generally *orang kenal* (people who are known), but on the main road there is more traffic of strangers who should, ideally, pay a toll.

Migrants—people passing through—are thus perceived as goods or commodities to be taxed. When I once commented on how people dared walk along the road as cars and motorbikes sped by, the man by my side replied, "If there is an accident, it is always the person driving who is at fault." This is a logic of territoriality rather than general responsibilities and rights, one that is generally respected by the police. Local inhabitants have the right to walk along or on the side of the road, unlike the car, which is just passing through. The same logic shapes the demands for donations, as it does payments to government officials at specific passage points such as ports and airports.

Curiously, the minivan also appears in the context of migrant smuggling from the Middle East via Indonesia to Australia. In Luke Mogelson's (2013) widely publicized *New York Times* article, in which he, together with a photographer, pays to be smuggled to Australia, the author appears dumbfounded by the mode of transport, as they leave their safe house in Jakarta in preparation for departure:

> We all crammed into a new car with tinted windows, driven by a squat Indonesian man with long rapier-like pinkie nails that tapered into points, who belched every couple of minutes and chain-smoked flavored cigarettes. . . . We stopped at three gas stations along the way and linked up with other drivers. By the time we made it out of the city [Jakarta], several hours later, we led a convoy of six identical cars, all packed with asylum seekers. It seemed a bit conspicuous, and sure enough, as we climbed a narrow, winding road up a densely forested mountain, people came out to watch whenever we passed a shop or village. It was maybe eight or nine at night when our driver got a call that caused him to accelerate abruptly and career down a side road that led into the woods. The other cars followed. Pulling to a stop, shutting off the lights and engine, our driver spun around and hissed: "Shh! Police."

The migrants and drivers were, indeed, apprehended, but then, for reasons Mogelson does not comprehend, the former were allowed to leave and make their way back to Jakarta by way of public transport. The drivers and vehicles remained at the police station, the story suggests, to settle the debt.

Despite its tinted windows, the minivan clearly reveals more than it obscures, not only to the police but to most everyone it passes. This is the case for government-licensed vehicles, licensed recruitment companies, PLs, and, apparently, even migrant smugglers. It would appear that the transport of migrants calls for a particular look that communicates itself as such. The self-identification of the minivan as a mode of migrant transport places it in a particular jalur, or corridor, in the context of documented migration. In 1990s Jakarta—characterized by an authoritarian state—most elite antar-jemput took place with a car, clearly separating them from the dangers of the street. As Shiraishi (1997, 27) put it, "the commuters in their automobiles and the pedestrians live in two separate worlds." Today, in relation to both middle-class mobility and low-skilled migration, it is possible to see how this distinction must be understood in broader terms. From this perspective, the Indonesian migration infrastructure can be conceptualized as an infrastructure for antar-jemput.

Like the motorcycles and minivans that move migrants from rural villages to urban hubs for further transport abroad, much of the temporary housing that has become necessary with the expansion of documented migration is refurbished and a patchwork: former schools, clinics, and decrepit hotels that have been integrated into a developing migration infrastructure. Although there is a stark contrast between how men and women are treated in this process, all migrants are encompassed by a broad state-centered moral project that Tania Murray Li (2007) terms the "will to improve," as villagers are transformed into migrants in a didactic process that is evident in a wide range of state interventions leading back to the colonial era. Nowhere does this appear more formalized than in another temporary space, namely, the reception terminal for migrants returning from abroad.

Return

"The airport is the new bus terminal." This is a phrase I have often heard during the past decade. It refers not only to the movements of growing numbers of migrants but also to the thugs and forms of extraction that are increasingly pervasive at airports, and which had previously been associated with bus stations. The deregulation of the airline industry and the rise of low-cost carriers, such as AirAsia and Lion Air, have increased the range of destinations and made flying inexpensive, thus transforming migrant flows, not least to Malaysia, who increasingly travel by plane rather than overland (cf. Hirsh 2016). Provincial airports have become increasingly connected to international destinations, such that the Lombok airport regularly sees trucks arrive packed with family and friends, either to see migrants off or to wait for them to return.

Shiraishi's account suggests that thugs, or preman, real or imagined, were evident in some form at Sukarno-Hatta airport in the 1990s. Indeed, the opening in 1999 of a special migrant terminal, informally called Terminal 3, was a response to public outcries against the abuses that migrants faced upon returning from overseas. While the actions of the government acknowledged extortion as a problem—for instance, through exhorbitant porter costs or ticket prices—the solution was imagined in terms of infrastructure. As described by Rachel Silvey (2007), Terminal 3 produced a spatial distinction between returning migrants (TKI, *tenaga kerja Indonesia*, or migrant workers in general, and TKW, *tenaga kerja wanita*, or female migrant workers) and general passengers, ostensibly in the name of protection.

In collaboration with licensed travel companies, the terminal was meant to create a safe and reasonably priced system of transport (a jalur) to migrants' home villages, often long distances from Jakarta. It quickly became evident that this spatial segregation in fact tended to organize and intensify abuses against migrants by creating an enclosed environment for extraction. Largely in response to protests, the old terminal was closed and a new one opened in 2008. Formally called the Building for the Registration of the Return of Indonesian Migrant Workers (informally it was called Terminal 4), it was located a fifteen-minute drive from the main airport, adjacent to an urban village.

In 2009—during the first of my three visits—between four hundred and one thousand migrants, nearly all of them women, passed through the terminal each day. This was due to the fact that most migrants who returned via Sukarno-Hatta airport had been domestic workers in the Middle East, and were thus women. Furthermore, as women they were more easily identified as migrants because of their Middle Eastern style of dress. Kloppenburg (2013, 114–19) has shown how migrants were not only identified but also self-sorted into specific corridors that led them to Terminal 4 after passing through immigration. In the baggage areas there were signs pointing toward the "special lane for Indonesian migrant workers" (*jalur khusus* TKI). Even if government officials were able to make qualified guesses, they could not know with any certainty which passengers were migrants, and, in fact, there was no regulation forcing returning migrants to pass through Terminal 4. It is clear from Kloppenburg's account, however, that migrants rarely resisted this sorting but tended to follow the identified lanes.

As migrants left the main airport by bus for Terminal 4, the travelers were warned by officials to bring only the money they needed for the trip, thus preparing them for the dangers of the trip home (Kloppenburg 2013, 121; see also Silvey 2007, 272). This way of reassuring migrants while highlighting their vulnerability was evident throughout the return process. Some signs and banners promised that the workers would be taken care of, while others stated that extra charges were not allowed, suggesting the possibility that one might very well be asked to pay additional fees to keep moving homeward (Silvey 2007, 275). As noted, this was also evident in government directives concerning the transport companies and on the return trip itself (Kloppenburg 2013, 127).

A large banner reading "Selamat datang pahlawan devisa" (Welcome home, foreign revenue heroes) was draped over the entrance to Terminal 4, which was a cavernous space the size of a football field. Near the entrance a half-dozen kiosks with computers signaled where migrants should line up to be registered. Inside the building were half a dozen moneychanger booths (with far worse exchange rates than even at the main airport terminals), a couple of cell phone shops, a bank office, two small restaurants, a travel agency, a gift shop selling electronics and stuffed animals, a large waiting area for the migrants (with different sitting areas marked according to the returning migrants' home provinces), a clinic, a room for the licensed transportation companies, an office for insurance claims, and government offices, as well as a room for "TKI *bermasalah*" (Indonesian migrant workers with problems). Sleeping rooms for women who had to stay overnight were located on the second floor. During a period beginning in 2012, the Jakarta office of the International Organization for Migration opened an office there in which they identified and offered support to victims of trafficking, who, following the logic of documented return, were escorted home after a period of rehabilitation.

Upon arrival, migrants were registered. The data collected included names, passport numbers, home addresses, recruitment companies being used, and the reasons for returning home. One of the good things about the new terminal, compared to the old one, an official told me, was that "data collection was well-ordered" (*penataan teratur*). As returning migrants waited in line, moneychangers came out and stopped at an invisible line, waving and yelling to the migrants to change money. Once migrants passed the data-collection kiosk, they faced a second series of kiosks selling bus tickets. A majority of the migrants were sent directly to purchase bus tickets to their home addresses. Generally, as explained below, seeking alternative transportation home, even rides from friends and relatives, was not allowed. The fares for each destination were clearly listed on a signboard. For migrants who lived on Lombok, or even farther afield, this trip could take up to forty-eight hours. Each van took nine people, and migrants were driven all the way to their houses in a door-to-door process. The twenty-nine licensed transport companies (in 2009)—many of which were part of larger conglomerates that included recruitment companies—took turns filling the vans.

Government officials I spoke with made it clear that their main priority was to return migrants safely to their home addresses. This meant that migrants could neither be picked up by family members—who were not permitted to enter the terminal—nor return to their recruitment companies in Jakarta.[4] According to both Silvey (2007, 273) and Kloppenburg (2013, 126), while it was possible to change certain types of data contained within a passport, it was particularly difficult to alter the home address. The burden of proof was on the migrant who wanted to return to a different address to show that either her parents or husband lived there. The reason given was that there was a risk that women migrants could be intercepted and *recycled* (the Indonesian term)—that is, involuntarily sent abroad again by brokers through illicit channels.

Indeed, when I spent time in the terminal witnessing the registration process, an official would open the migrant's passport and enter the data listed therein into a computer. He would then ask for the migrant's address and compare it with the one in the passport. If the addresses were inconsistent, the migrant was asked to report to the office for "Indonesian migrants with problems." While I was observing in that office for a couple of hours, one official told a few of the migrants sitting there that it was important for them to return home to their families and their *kampung halaman* (home village), that one should not return to the recruitment company or join anyone else. He joked that the minivan would carry them all the way to their village, but could not enter their actual houses.

The migration terminal became a prototype that was reproduced across Indonesia. I don't want to dwell on the effectiveness of these new terminals in terms of protection, but rather note the enduring importance of the term and, more specifically, the concepts of escort and safe return. In effect, this reveals that the state recognizes the dangers of traveling alone but responds to the threats primarily through an infrastructure of escort and encapsulation, which is evident during both departure and return. Training centers, terminals, and minivans become nodes in corridors that move migrants along particular jalur.

Deportation

The deportation process of undocumented workers from Malaysia to Indonesia follows a logic strikingly similar to that of the return of documented migrants. In contrast to arrivals at Jakarta's airport terminal, however, the vast majority of the deportees are men who were arrested in Malaysia as undocumented workers on construction sites and palm oil plantations across the country. During the past decade, an increasingly regulated deportation infrastructure has developed, whereby these undocumented migrants are transported by public ferry from Johor, in western Malaysia, to Tanjung Pinang, on Bintan (Indonesia), through an agreement between the Indonesian and Malaysian governments. This has been the largest and most formalized deportation program to Indonesia, particularly because of the extent of the Malaysian deportation regime. Upon arrival, the men are received by the Department of Social Affairs and held in a temporary reception center before being shipped by Pelni (the national shipping and passenger company) to the port of Tanjung Priok, in Jakarta. Since 2006 the frequency of deportations has varied, from several times a week to once every other week, but the structure has remained the same. As in the context of documented migrants returning via airport reception terminals, the deportees, most of whom are men and destitute, have not been allowed to leave on their own because of fears that they will be recycled and trafficked back to Malaysia (e.g., Lindquist 2013; McNevin 2014).

Unlike the forms of coercive viapolitics that characterized the transportation by train of Chinese coolies across the United States, described in chapter 1, this deportation process is mostly framed in the paternalistic language of protection. Even the most influential NGO activist dealing with migration and deportation issues in Tanjung Pinang agreed with the official government position of forced encapsulation, claiming that the risk that these deportees would be intercepted and retrafficked was too great, since most did not have any money and wanted to return to Malaysia. Their desire to return to Malaysia rather than to their home villages with nothing to show for their time abroad was evident in their requests for support from the activist—for instance, her help in obtaining a passport—which generally related to the migrants' desire to find a way to cross the border again.

Another woman in the same NGO had taken the ship to Tanjung Priok several times. When the deportees boarded the ship, they were locked up until the boat departed, after which they were allowed to move about with the rest of the passengers. She told me that she herself had seen how recruiters among the regular passengers approached these migrants and strongly encouraged them to exit through the regular gate at Tanjung Priok rather than the one for deported migrants. More generally, the mismatch between the number of deportees placed aboard ship and the number who actually arrived at Tanjung Priok's holding area worried many of the responsible government officials I talked to, while what could be done in response was often unclear.

Once in Tanjung Priok, the regular passengers exited first through the main gate, while the deportees came last and were directed through a separate entrance by an official using a loudspeaker system.[5] Once inside the large waiting room, which had been officially inaugurated in August 2006 by Indonesia's president, Susilo Bambang Yudhoyono, as a *ruang tamu* TKI, or Indonesian migrant waiting room, the migrants were directed to sit in the sections that were signposted according to their respective home provinces. In one corner there was a small, makeshift health clinic, while banners on the wall read "Coordinating Post for the Sending Home [*pemulangan*] of Migrant Workers Deported from Malaysia" and "We Will Facilitate Return to Your Area of Origin [*daerah asal*]." As the names of provinces were called one by one, migrants lined up in front of a desk with two officials. The migrant-cum-deportees were photographed and asked for their addresses, ages, places of origin, and where they had been in Malaysia. As far as I understood, the information collected was not used for any further purpose other than data collection itself, and the fact that they were deportees was not held against them.

The deportees were then transported to a public bus station in North Jakarta, from where they were sent back to their home provinces on buses chartered by the government. Once the deportees arrived at their own province's department of manpower office, they were driven back to their home villages. "We cannot force

FIGURE 5.2 · Indonesian migrant waiting room, Tanjung Priok harbor, Jakarta. Source: Johan Lindquist.

the migrants to return," an official I talked to told me, "but we prefer this process because it is our responsibility toward the family members and the migrants themselves. Once the migrant has returned home, he is free to do what he wants."

The similarities between the deportation process and the return home of documented migrants is striking, in terms of their encapsulation, the importance of escorting them all the way home (*antar pulang*), the organization of the spaces where they wait—spatially organized according to home province—and the collection and checking of data, in particular their place of origin. While the idea of home as a safe space is widely valued in migration policy internationally, usually uncritically so (Walters 2004), the Indonesian case points to a strikingly institutionalized concern with regulating mobility between the space of migration and the kampung, home, or village (cf. Lindquist 2013). The Indonesian state's need to protect migrants from the dangers of being en route not only suggests that rural populations remain infantilized or that migrants are seen as exploitable by a wide variety of actors, but also points to broader anxieties concerning its ability to govern.

The Viapolitics of Escort and Circulation

Why is it considered strange to travel alone in Indonesia? Beginning with this question—difficult if not impossible to respond to properly—rather than the organization of migration per se, allows us to take antar-jemput, the infrastructure of escort, as a starting point for describing and conceptualizing documented (and sometimes undocumented), low-skilled Indonesian transnational migration. Understanding travel and mobility as rooted in antar-jemput complicates liberal dichotomies of state power versus individual freedom, and introduces a complex continuum between control, exploitation, comfort, desire, trust, and care in the context of migration (Silvey 2018, 200).

Although rooted in colonial relations, the mediation of migration has intensified with the rise of state-sponsored, documented, circular migration that developed in Indonesia in the 1980s and, in particular, since the 1997 Asian economic crisis. In this process, there has been an expansion of migration bureaucracy with related demands for migrant documentation. As a result, migrants have faced an increasingly regulated migration infrastructure as they are escorted and controlled by a large number of actors, usually in the name of protection. As in Barker's description of the rise of siskamling, the Indonesian system of urban policing developed during the New Order, there has been an explicit attempt by the state to transpose or deterritorialize certain forms of localized authority, which have then been reterritorialized through licensing, regulations for migrant mobility, housing, transport, documentation, and terminal buildings (Barker 1998). One might identify this as a form of jalur, a corridor that ideally moves migrants from the village, to employment abroad, and back to the village again. As we have seen, however, these jalur are patchwork, unstable, and depend on forms of brokerage centered on contingent relationships between actors, technologies, and physical structures.

With the expansion of migration infrastructure, as a system-in-the-making, forms of mediation have evolved and become increasingly complex, while others appear to be collapsing, most notably the special migrant terminal at the Jakarta airport. The ideal form of migration and mobility, however, remains centered on antar-jemput. These contemporary forms of migration and mediation should not be understood strictly in relation to the transformation of the Indonesian migrant worker into an export commodity, or the rise of a global demand for migrant workers. Historical processes have shaped the rural-urban divide and associated forms of mobility in Indonesia, which takes a particular form through the cultural economy of antar-jemput and the ensuing production of migration jalur.

In closing, the migration corridors that have taken shape across Asia in the Middle East in the past few decades have become a global laboratory for circular labor migration. This chapter has described in detail how circularity, arguably the dominant spatial metaphor of contemporary international labor migration governance, depends on complex and contingent relationships between diverse actors and material forms within and across cultural milieus. If we want to understand how migrations—ranging from documented labor to deportation programs—are taking shape in practice in the contemporary world, it is thus critical to move beyond overly general categories of analysis and carefully consider the specific relations that take shape between the particular and the universal. It is in this space that viapolitics is revealed.

Notes

This is a shortened and rewritten version of a previously published article: "Infrastructures of Escort: Transnational Migration and Economies of Connection in Indonesia," *Indonesia* 105 (2018): 77–95. I thank William Walters and Charles Heller for helpful comments on an earlier version of this chapter.

1　In earlier publications I have translated *jalur* as "channel" (Lindquist 2018a), but in order to bring the analysis in line with other discussions outlined in the volume, I use the term "corridor" here.

2　While the Dutch cultivation system policy was in effect, the Javanese peasant economy became organized on a territorial basis by the colonial state, as the village became the primary unit for the extraction of labor and taxes. The creation of travel passes further regulated labor mobility and positioned the village chief in a mediating position of power, not least when it came to the recruitment of migrant labor (Breman 1990, 16; Barker 1999b, 127–28; Termorshuizen 2008, 94).

3　On how a certain politics of dis/comfort has informed and continues to inform the social realities and imaginaries of migration, see also chapter 4, this volume.

4　In her article on Terminal 3, Silvey (2007, 276) noted the large number of family members waiting outside the terminal for returning migrants. Some had camped out for days, having only received a letter or a quick phone call revealing on what approximate day they would be returning. Although the names of arrived migrants were read over a loudspeaker system, uncertainty reigned, as many names were common or difficult to discern. Many migrants, not knowing that family members were waiting for them, came out with tickets for a return home to their village, which they had been forced to purchase on the inside.

5　I witnessed this particular episode in May 2007.

References

Alatas, Ismail Fajarie. 2016. "The Poetics of Pilgrimage: Assembling Contemporary Indonesian Pilgrimage to Hadramawt, Yemen." *Comparative Studies in Society and History* 58 (3): 607–35.

Allerton, Catherine. 2013. *Potent Landscapes: Place and Mobility in Eastern Indonesia.* Honolulu: University of Hawai'i Press.

Altenried, Moritz, Manuela Bojadžijev, Leif Höfler, Sandro Mezzadra, and Mira Wallis. 2018. "Logistical Borderscapes: Politics and Mediation of Mobile Labor in Germany after the 'Summer of Migration.'" *South Atlantic Quarterly* 17 (2): 291–312.

Anderson, Benedict. 1972. "The Idea of Power in Javanese Culture." In *Culture and Politics in Indonesia*, edited by Claire Holt, 1–69. Ithaca, NY: Cornell University Press.

Barker, Joshua. 1998. "State of Fear: Controlling Criminal Contagion in Suharto's New Order." *Indonesia* 66: 6–43.

Barker, Joshua. 1999a. "Surveillance and Territoriality in Bandung." In *Figures of Criminality in Indonesia, the Philippines, and Colonial Vietnam*, edited by Vicente L. Rafael, 95–127. Ithaca, NY: Southeast Asia Program.

Barker, Joshua. 1999b. "The Tattoo and the Fingerprint: Crime and Security in an Indonesian City." PhD diss., Cornell University.

Breman, Jan. 1990. *Labour Migration and Rural Transformation in Colonial Asia.* Amsterdam: Free University Press.

Cremer, Georg. 1988. "Deployment of Indonesian Migrants in the Middle East: Present Situation and Prospects." *Bulletin of Indonesian Economic Studies* 24 (3): 73–86.

Drotbohm, Heike, and Ines Hasselberg. 2015. "Deportation, Anxiety, Justice: New Ethnographic Perspectives." *Journal of Ethnic and Migration Studies* 41 (4): 551–62.

Errington, Shelly. 1989. *Meaning and Power in a Southeast Asian Realm.* Princeton, NJ: Princeton University Press.

Feldman, Gregory. 2012. *The Migration Apparatus.* Palo Alto, CA: Stanford University Press.

Gammeltoft-Hansen, Thomas, and Ninna Nyberg Sørensen, eds. 2013. *The Migration Industry and the Commercialization of International Migration.* London: Routledge.

Hirsh, Max. 2016. *Airport Urbanism: Infrastructure and Mobility in Asia.* Minneapolis: University of Minnesota Press.

Houben, Vincent. 1999. "Before Departure: Coolie Labour Recruitment in Java, 1900–1942." In *Coolie Labour in Colonial Indonesia: A Study of Labour Relations in the Outer Islands of Indonesia, c. 1900–1940,* edited by Vincent Houben and Thomas Lindblad, 25–42. Wiesbaden: Harrassowitz.

Hugo, Graeme. 2012. "International Labour Migration and Migration Policies in Southeast Asia." *Asian Journal of Social Science* 40 (4): 392–418.

Kasparek, Bernd. 2016. "Routes, Corridors, and Spaces of Exception: Governing Migration and Europe." *Near Futures Online* 1 (March). http://nearfuturesonline .org/wp-content/uploads/2016/01/Kasparek_Final_PDF.pdf.

Kitley, Philip. 2002. *Television, Nation, and Culture in Indonesia.* Athens: Ohio University Press.

Kloppenburg, Sanneke. 2013. "Tracing Mobilities Regimes: The Regulation of Drug Smuggling and Labour Migration at Two Airports in the Netherlands and Indonesia." PhD diss., University of Amsterdam.

Larkin, Brian. 2013. "The Politics and Poetics of Infrastructure." *Annual Review of Anthropology* 42: 327–43.

Li, Tania Murray. 2007. *The Will to Improve: Governmentality, Development, and the Practice of Politics.* Durham, NC: Duke University Press.

Lindquist, Johan. 2010. "Labour Recruitment, Circuits of Capital, and Gendered Mobility: Reconceptualizing the Indonesian Migration Industry." *Pacific Affairs* 83 (1): 115–32.

Lindquist, Johan. 2013. "Rescue, Return, in Place: Deportees, 'Victims,' and the Regulation of Indonesian Migration." In *Return: Nationalizing Transna-*

tional Mobility in Asia, edited by Biao Xiang, Brenda Yeoh, and Mika Toyota, 122–40. Durham, NC: Duke University Press.

Lindquist, Johan. 2018a. "Infrastructures of Escort: Transnational Migration and Economies of Connection in Indonesia." *Indonesia* 105: 77–95.

Lindquist, Johan. 2018b. "Reassembling Indonesian Migration: Biometric Technology and the Licensing of Informal Labor Brokers." *Ethnos: Journal of Anthropology* 83 (5): 832–49.

Lindquist, Johan, Biao Xiang, and Brenda Yeoh. 2012. "Opening the Black Box of Migration: Brokers, the Organisation of Transnational Mobility, and the Changing Political Economy in Asia." *Pacific Affairs* 85 (1): 7–20.

McNevin, Anne. 2014. "Beyond Territoriality: Rethinking Human Mobility, Border Security and Geopolitical Space from the Indonesian Island of Bintan." *Security Dialogue* 45 (3): 295–310.

Mogelson, Luke. 2013. "The Impossible Refugee Boat Lift to Christmas Island." *New York Times*, November 15. http://www.nytimes.com/2013/11/17/magazine/the-impossible-refugee-boat-lift-to-christmas-island.html.

Morris, Rosalind. 2007. "Legacies of Derrida: Anthropology." *Annual Review of Anthropology* 36: 355–89.

Niehof, Anke, and Firman Lubis, eds. 2003. *Two Is Enough: Family Planning in Indonesia under the New Order, 1968–1998*. Leiden: KITLV Press.

Ormond, Meghann. 2015. "*En Route:* Transport and Embodiment in International Medical Travel Journeys between Indonesia and Malaysia." *Mobilities* 10 (2): 285–303.

Palmer, Wayne. 2016. *Indonesia's Overseas Labour Migration Programme, 1969–2010*. Leiden: Brill.

Shiraishi, Saya. 1997. *Young Heroes: The Indonesian Family in Politics.* Ithaca, NY: Southeast Asia Program.

Siegel, James. 1997. *Fetish, Recognition, Revolution.* Princeton, NJ: Princeton University Press.

Silvey, Rachel. 2007. "Unequal Borders: Indonesian Transnational Migrants at Immigration Control." *Geopolitics* 12: 265–79.

Silvey, Rachel. 2018. "From Java to Saudi Arabia and Dubai: Precarious Itineraries of Indonesian Domestic Workers." In *Departing from Java: Javanese Labour, Migration and Diaspora*, edited by Rosemarijn Hoefte and Peter Meel, 188–208. Copenhagen: NIAS Press.

Termorshuizen, Thio. 2008. "Indentured Labour in the Dutch Colonial Empire, 1800–1940." In *Dutch Colonialism, Migration and Cultural Heritage: Past and Present*, edited by Gert Oostindie, 261–314. Leiden: Brill.

Tilly, Charles. 1985. "War Making and State Making as Organized Crime." In *The Formation of Nation-States in Western Europe*, edited by Peter Evans, Dietrich Rueschemeyer, and Theda Skocpol, 169–87. Cambridge: Cambridge University Press.

Walters, William. 2004. "Secure Borders, Safe Haven, Domopolitics." *Citizenship Studies* 8 (3): 237–60.

Walters, William. 2015. "Migration, Vehicles, and Politics: Three Theses on Viapolitics." *European Journal of Social Theory* 18: 469–88.

Wilson, Ian. 2015. *The Politics of Protection Rackets in Post–New Order Indonesia: Coercive Capital, Authority, and Street Politics.* London: Routledge.

Xiang Biao. 2013. "Transnational Encapsulation: Compulsory Return as a Labor-Migration Control in East Asia." In *Return: Nationalizing Transnational Mobility in Asia,* edited by Xiang Biao, Brenda Yeoh, and Mika Toyota, 83–99. Durham, NC: Duke University Press.

Xiang Biao and Johan Lindquist. 2014. "Migration Infrastructure." *International Migration Review* 48: S122–S148.

SIX

Routes Thinking | Maribel Casas-Cortes

and Sebastian Cobarrubias

Despite the revival of wall imagery when envisioning and depicting migration control strategies, many of the actual practices of border work happen far beyond those conventional fenced borders through mobile devices and itinerant strategies. This chapter examines these practices in the specific context of the EU migration regime. This regime has largely displaced and outsourced its borders to non-EU countries long enough to unfold and establish a distinct logic for the control of certain populations on the move (Zolberg 2003; Vaughn-Williams 2008; Bialasiewicz 2012; Zaiotti 2016). What we call "routes thinking" refers to a spreading common sense—an emergent episteme—on border management among policy makers, border agents, and international organizations. Within this framework, bordering practices and border-like spaces are reproduced along hypothetical migrants' itineraries (see also chapters 7 and 9, this volume). This form of routes thinking allows for the operationalization and legitimation of expanding borders across spaces and times of any traveler's trajectory under the suspicion of illegality. In this way, a viapolitical infrastructure of *illegalization* is constructed at those moments and places when members of undesired populations (as perceived by the EU) are said to be moving inappropriately. The establishment of routes, as a way to read migrant trajectories and make them targetable, constitutes the viapolitical moment when it comes to routes thinking. As Walters, Heller, and Pezzani explain (introduction, this volume), the identification of routes is a way to make the changing and mutable trajectories of migrants apprehendable, making the movements into a specific object.

Our previous work has signaled how these processes of border externalization are unfolding profound spatial reconfigurations of the border and state practices (Casas, Cobarrubias, and Pickles 2011, 2013, 2015). This chapter reflects upon our research on externalization policies and puts them into conversation with the notion of viapolitics. The analytical findings in this chapter are grounded in a multisited research project titled EU Borderlands: Mapping Changing Geographies of Jurisdictions and Sovereignties, which included both ethnographic interviews and archival research on EU border practices in Africa.[1] Focusing on the case of Spain's border policies in North and West Africa, attention was given to the implementation of the migration routes strategy elaborated by the European Commission under the Global Approach to Migration and Mobility, which is a policy framework introduced by the EU in 2005, intended to expand the functioning of borders and migration management far beyond the edge or the immediate neighborhood of the EU.[2] Whether they were policy makers, think tank members, border guards, or NGO representatives, interviewees shared a geographical and cultural shift in thinking about the where and how of border work. This emerging way of approaching migration control is what we call routes thinking, one that embraces mobile surveillance across extranational territories through dispersed infrastructures of contention. Routes thinking requires the creation of viapolitical instruments for the managing of migrant trajectories, leading in turn to significant transformations: distinct ways of imagining and visualizing border spaces and border practices, as well as alternative forms of implementing foreign relations.

Building on spatial readings of border externalization and mobile borders, this chapter further develops the notion of routes thinking as a critical lens to unpack the viapolitical strategy of governing migrant trajectories. To do so, the chapter builds upon some of the analytical concepts that we have developed in our own research: mainly, the deployment of a "Euro-(con)centric geographical imaginary" and the emergence of a "mapping migration matrix." These concepts help to make sense of the complex, emerging border geographies we describe: practices of contention and selective exclusion carried out on oceans and in lands lying thousands of kilometers away from the EU's territorial borders. The chapter traces the institutional genealogy of how this emergent border regime evolves from a model based on concentric circles to one framed in terms of routes thinking. The role of cartography becomes key in constituting the current logics of migration management: we think of maps not as providing a mere representation of routes, but as practices that bring them into being, and which are also instrumental in the contestation over routes. In fact, we briefly introduce an experiment by a migrant rights' collective to produce a countercartography of migration management maps, reflecting on how this experience speaks about contesting institutional routes thinking. Finally, the chapter concludes with some reflections on the colonial power dynamics underpinning routes thinking.

Genealogies of Containment: Euro-(con)centric Imaginaries of Mobility Control

Ethnographic work at different locations of the border regime (Rabat, Vienna, London, Brussels, Madrid) led us to study the origins of recent spatial displacements of territorial borders: when did migration control start to be imagined as operating far away from apparent destination countries? Based on archival research in EU documents initially proposing this form of remote migration management, we unfold a genealogy of border externalization that uncovers a Eurocentric cartographic imaginary at work that underpins practices of contention thousands of kilometers away from its borderlines.

While working on this genealogy, an official document proposing to divide the world into concentric circles caught our attention: the EU's "Strategy Paper on Immigration and Asylum Policy," by the Council of the European Union (CEU 1998a).[3] This document has been analyzed sporadically by authors tracing the history of the EU's inclusion of migration policy in its foreign policy (Boswell 2003; Barbero 2010). We started to take it seriously after encountering the work by Abdelkrim Belguendouz (2009, 2005). In his critique of the role of migration policy in the relations between North Africa (especially Morocco) and the EU, he argues the document's foundational importance for understanding the current EU border regime. During the Austrian presidency of the EU in 1998, this official document was distributed to different branches of the European Union Council (it was addressed specifically to the K4 committee of Interior Ministries). An initial draft was leaked to the press, and NGOs alerted the public to its controversial nature. This 1998 document classifies territories worldwide and populations therein into four concentric circles. It evokes a geographical vision of how mobility should be distributed in the world, with hierarchical access to mobility. The implication is that everyone belongs to a particular geographical circle, each one with different rights or restrictions for moving in and out (the right to move is conditional on that category).

The "Strategy Paper on Immigration and Asylum Policy" of 1998 proposes four concentric circles to encompass the entire globe (figures 6.1 and 6.2),

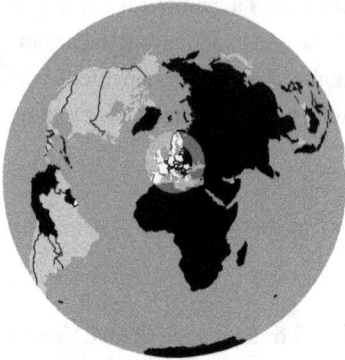

1 EU member states / Schengen zone

As the integration of the European Union proceeded, the twenty-odd members of the EU pooled their sovereignty together and created a zone of free movement for goods, capital and people called the Schengen zone. The zone allows you to move, work and study freely in any of its member countries. Considered one of the success stories of the EU, Schengen has come under increasing critique since the so-called financial and refugee crises.

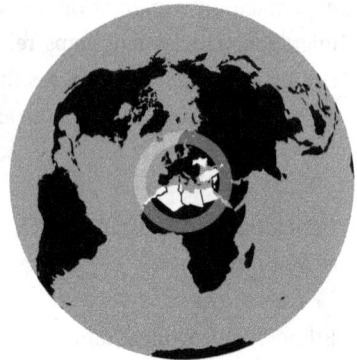

2 European Neighborhood Partnership

EU candidate countries are potential members of the EU, and must meet Schengen criteria. They are considered countries of transit until membership. Countries of the European Neighbourhood Policy (ENP). These countries, which are adjacent to the European Union, are offered a chance to participate in the EU's Single Market and regulatory frameworks, but in exchange are asked to manage and police any undocumented migration passing through their territories, potentially on it's way to the EU. Integration to EU structures is made conditional on their cooperation in border security.

FIGURES 6.1–6.2 · Visualization of concentric circles of the European Union's migration policy, by Maribel Casas-Cortes, Sebastian Cobarrubias, and Tim Stallman. Source: CEU (1998a).

3 Transit Zone

The transit zone includes many of the ENP countries (which have stronger trade links with the EU), along with other countries, which are seen from the EU as needing to police migrants who are "transiting" through their countries on the way to the EU. Countries of the third circle are considered to be points of transit for migrants on their way to the first circle. These countries are not offered integration into EU Markets and frameworks.

4 Source Countries

The countries of the 4th circle are seen as migration "source" countries, briefly referred to in the 1998 strategy as "the Middle East, China, and black Africa." The EU approach toward these countries includes border security as in the transit countries but is complimented by programs that encourage people to "stay in their circle." These projects of "dissuasion" can include development projects; PR campaigns on the dangers of irregular migration as well as signing agreements to allow for rapid deportation of these countries' nationals form the EU.

Countries highlighted on this map are those considered part of the "4th circle" for EU purposes, but as the stars indicate, not all countries that actually make up the top sources of undocumented migrants to the EU are treated as part of the 4th circle by EU policy.

☆ Stars indicate the countries that were identified as top sources of illegal entries in 2016 (Frontext FRAN report).

classifying all countries of the world as either: (1) desirable destinations and zones of mobility; (2) countries of transit adjacent to the EU; (3) countries of transit further away; or (4) sources of undesirable population flows.

The first circle is formed by the EU member states capable of fulfilling Schengen standards of control, and other countries, which "do not cause emigration" but have become "target countries on account of their advanced economic and political situation" (CEU 1998a, points 60 and 116).

The second circle would consist of "transit countries" which no longer generate emigration but which "on account of a relatively stable internal economic and political situation accept only very limited control procedures and responsibility for migration policy." This second circle would include the neighbor countries of the Schengen/EU territory, that is, the associated states and "perhaps also the Mediterranean area." These countries' systems of control should gradually be brought into line with the first-circle standards (CEU 1998a, points 60 and 118).

The third and fourth circles would contain the countries of emigration. The third circle would include countries of both emigration and transit, that is, the CIS area (former Soviet Union), Turkey, and North Africa.[4] These countries would be required to "concentrate primarily on transit checks and combatting facilitator [migrant smuggler] networks." The fourth (outermost) circle would consist of countries of emigration apparently deemed somewhat beyond the reach of European "political muscle." (Mention is made of the Middle East, China, and "black Africa.") These countries are to be encouraged to "eliminate push factors" of migration (CEU 1998a, points 60 and 119).

A reward would follow if a country meets the obligations arising from its assignment to a particular circle. "For example, the second circle must meet Schengen standards as a precondition for EU membership; for the third circle, intensified economic cooperation is linked to the fulfilment of their obligations; and [for] the fourth circle, the extent of development aid can be assessed on that basis" (CEU 1998a, point 61; FECL 1998).

This "*Euro (con-)centric* vision of mobility" (Casas-Cortes and Cobarrubias 2019) literally puts the EU in the center, dictating who can move where but also designating—or at least heavily influencing—which country is in which circle. Quite remarkably, this model is proposed as a replacement of "fortress Europe"—a concept explicitly mentioned in the 1998 strategy paper (CEU 1998a, point 60)—in the attempt to reduce migratory pressure. While this vision of control and contention of worldwide human flows is based on analytical assumptions that, from an empirical perspective, appear questionable at best, it reveals a spatial imaginary that will have enduring consequences.[5] Its designation of worldwide territories beyond the EU in terms of their role in an imagined global migration system has for the most part remained intact, despite (or perhaps because of) never having been a representation of the EU border regime as it actually ever existed.

This early vision of migration control based on concentric circles scandalized many, including several EU member state governments, due to what was at the time perceived as an unnecessarily restrictive and discriminatory approach to migration. Yet, while the policy proposal itself was officially voted down in 1998,[6] slowly but surely this vision became the organizing framework for EU policy on migration management.[7] It is a vision where everyone, in a sense, belongs in their circle in relation to migration into and out of the EU, with few exceptions. This understanding of mobility is based on designating the members of specific territories and populations as having different entitlements to move. These distinct entitlements, by extension, also grant the EU and its member states the right to intervene in different countries utilizing strategies considered best adapted to each circle (e.g., economic integration, policing, or development aid). By doing this, the focus shifts from border crossings at national limits to a more global method of migration control. It becomes necessary to pay attention to the points of origin and transit of those flows from places labeled as sources of undesired mobility. This vision of migration control was made explicit and officially approved through the Global Approach to Migration (GAM) framework in 2005 with its routes strategy connecting points of origin, transit, and destination.[8] While the GAM was initially considered a new policy framework that was less repressive in its approach to migration, there is an important connection between the 1998 Austrian strategy paper and the GAM. It is in this forgotten Austrian strategy paper, in fact, that the terms *origin, transit,* and *destination* countries first appear in a section called "Global Approach," next to the section introducing the notion of concentric circles. The GAM's principal contribution, then, is to articulate a routes strategy that connects work across countries in different circles.

For the European Commission, the routes approach was something distinctly new, and while "it may seem obvious now to pursue migration management in this way ... the routes strategy was not evident. It took the EU some time to develop this approach."[9] In the process, migrant itineraries were traced (even if not accurately) as part of the routes initiative, in turn, transforming them into objects of policy. Segments of these routes were then parsed into origin, transit, and destination countries and then further reduced to manageable or governable categories (border crossings, transit points, bus stations, and other actionable locales). All those parceled geographies are assigned specific goals for governmental and state action.

How did a migration routes strategy with governmental units such as origin, transit, and destination emerge from a vision of global concentric circles? Building on a vision of the world divided into delimited zones of uneven mobilities, a distinct way of imagining migration control came alive: securing the territorial lines of a border appeared as a limited way to deal with the big picture of mobility. This global conception of mobility contributes to a broader spatial approach to migration: tracking when and where illegalized bodies begin and continue to move. This is the rationale to organize migration management around itineraries, mapping them and coordinating transnational border cooperation projects to intervene. The target/goal becomes both those bodies on the move and the infrastructures facilitating movement along those mapped migratory journeys. If global journeys cut across concentric circles, these journeys become a source of concern and should be managed in order to identify undesired mobilities. Military missions, interrogation tactics, detention, and deportation along those routes are then legitimate and necessary. Spatially speaking, migration control practices can be located anywhere, including far beyond conventional borderlines. This helps to explain the proliferation of multinational police operations acting in states designated by the EU and its member states as origin and transit countries where migration flows are either initiating or crossing on their way to destination countries.

Spain has been at the forefront of this process of border externalization, inaugurating routes thinking as a way of envisioning migration control. Since 2006, the Spanish Guardia Civil has launched several programs, all falling under the umbrella term of Seahorse operations (Project Seahorse, Seahorse Network, Seahorse Cooperation Centres, and the West Sahel and Blue Sahel projects) which have focused on detecting and stopping irregular migration from West African countries.[10] Funded by the European Commission, these transnational police efforts have included the participation of numerous African and European states as well as EU institutions such as Frontex (especially through the better known Hera operations) and are considered in Madrid as well as in Brussels as exemplars of transnational border coordination among origin-transit-destination countries to "promote regional and interregional cooperation on the management of migration flows in the Maghreb and Sub-Saharan Africa" (EuropeAid 2010, 12).

The rollout of Seahorse operations took place after the border fence jumps at Ceuta and Melilla in 2005, which led to a general acceleration of police and defense planning for migration on the part of Spanish forces. After the military response at the fences, migrants' boats started to go toward the Canary Islands. This is when the Spanish Guardia Civil launched a series of bilateral operations beyond Morocco with countries such as Senegal and Mauritania (operations Atlantis, Cabo Blanco, and Goree; BOE 2006). This was followed by an accelerated implementation of Project Seahorse, which established the initial experiments in a multipartner state series of joint patrols by border and coast guards, police training missions, and donations of equipment (EuropeAid 2007, 12). These were followed by Seahorse Network, which established a more formal means of communication among the different participating gendarme forces via secure satellite networks and the establishment of "local contact points" (Guardia Civil 2009). Afterward, the Seahorse Cooperation Centres aimed at transforming local contact points into coordination centers modeled on the Centro de Coordinacion Regional de Canarias (Guardia Civil 2009), the main node coordinating border surveillance from the Straits of Gibraltar down to the West African coast and Cape Verde.[11]

What needs to be foregrounded here is that these operations highlight a shifting spatial approach toward the management of borders and a distinct spatial strategy in the attempts to channel and manage human mobility. Seahorse operations seek to trace migrant itineraries from their places of origin through their various key transit nodes and routes. According to a member of the General Directorate of External Relations and Migration Unit, part of the Spanish Ministry of Interior:

Not too long ago, the border used to be patrolled by two members of the Guardia Civil walking for hours along the beach, who would be caught by surprise when spotting ships only a few meters away from the coast. Nowadays, coastal border patrolling is done by teams of Guardia Civil personnel seated in rooms with lots of radar screens, and when they see a ship, they click with the mouse and drag a helicopter, or whatever is needed, to that area. This sends a signal/message to the concrete unit in the field to intervene in a given exact location.

. . . On the basis of a risk analysis, we establish where it is important to work. For example, we interviewed [detained migrants, and they] tell us, "Well, I come from this place because there was a war where my tribe was being targeted," and another says, "I came from this place on foot. . . ." On foot! . . . How?! . . . and on the basis of that information about places at war and itineraries, we began to work more in transit and origin. We had to go to the place where migration began in order to be efficient.[12]

These operations thus need to be understood as the latest step in an evolution in border management: from police units patrolling small segments of a coastline to a high-tech upgrading of surveillance for large areas of the border, and finally to renewed efforts to monitor and intercept migrants in other countries. The result is a deepening of institutions and practices that ensure that "the communication continues, as do the patrols, *to keep the route closed*."[13] "Keeping the routes closed" or "cutting the routes" were the expressions we heard repeatedly during our interviews with the border authorities, not only in Madrid but also in Brussels, Vienna (headquarters of ICMPD[14]), and Rabat. At the institutional level across distinct countries and agencies, routes thinking and its

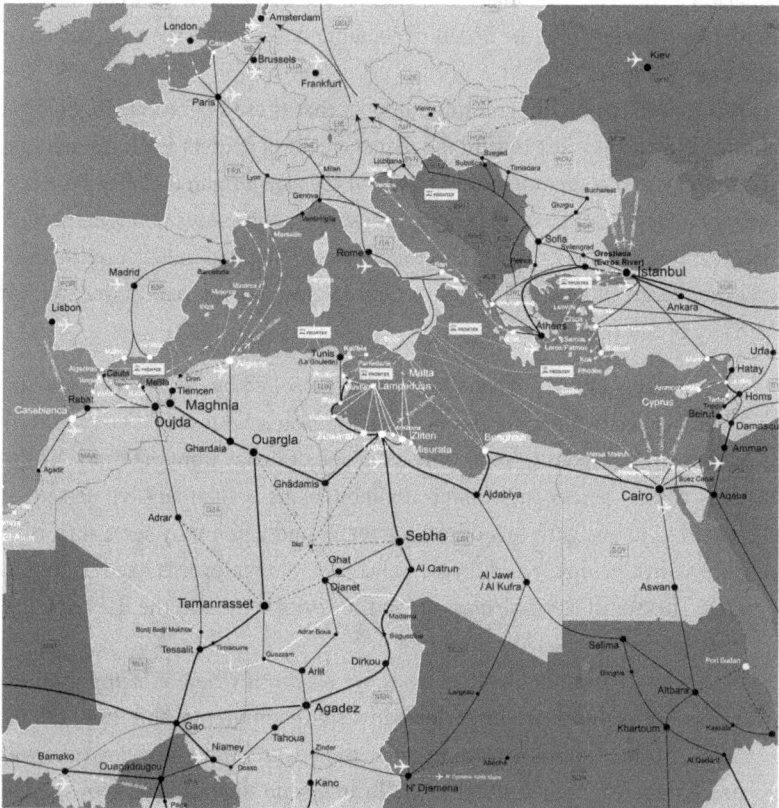

FIGURE 6.3 · i-Map, 2012. Dialogue on Mediterranean Transit Migration map of irregular and mixed migration flows. Source: International Centre for Migration Policy Development.

consequent policies of extraterritorial and itinerant borders were starting to sink in as the new normal.

This emerging episteme was captured by the flurry of routes maps, especially the i-Map (see figure 6.3), which were hanging in many of the offices we visited during our research fieldwork. These maps are important not so much for their empirical accuracy or lack thereof, but rather for their role in constructing and legitimizing this global migration control regime. The aesthetic politics of visualizing routes in particular ways as knowable and visible objects that exist "out there" is a fundamental iteration of routes thinking. The next section explores the ways cartographies do not simply represent but bring into being, or constitute, the space of the route as a field of government.

Cutting the Routes: A Mapping Migration Matrix

The goal of tracking and cutting routes has thus spread among EU migration policy circles, expert security actors, and border authorities. This thinking in terms of routes has been possible in great part thanks to the series of maps and cartographic representations of human flows (such as the i-Map), most of which are assumed to originate in Africa and Asia and imagined to move always toward "EU"rope. These are official cartographies produced by and circulating among policy makers, border authorities, and security think tanks and reprinted by media outlets. These cartographic iterations of routes, often technologically slick and expert-looking maps, the networks of organizations reproducing them, and the forms in which the knowledge produced by them travels from one institutional site of border management to another constitute what we call a "mapping migration matrix."[15] We contend that this matrix is creating a shared language of expertise and a geographical imaginary of illegality beyond borders, through the consolidation of a method, communities of creation, and reiteration. While these institutional maps deploy the professionalism and neutrality associated with expertise, we signal how they are driven by a restrictive logic of containment toward mobility. They crystallize and further support the EU's strategy of migration routes management introduced in the first versions of the GAM (2005), where border enforcement is envisioned as most efficient when implemented at different points of origin, transit, and destination along a specifically traced route. This routes management approach establishes a connection between the expert-driven production of maps on irregular migration and border control operations.

If for EU migration policy circles, efficient migration management entails going beyond the place and time of a port of entry physically located on the border, then it is necessary to establish transnational cooperation in order to locate where the migrant is in the process of moving toward an assumed destination point in Europe. Collaboration with the border authorities of other countries would then be necessary to intercept irregular migrant flows. The shifting itineraries of migrants (though defined by the EU, member states, and collaborating institutions, not by migrants themselves) become the object of migration management policy, and thus the attempt to map and define the spaces of routes becomes a political goal. The objective is to trace and manage the journey, which is how the route has become a migration management concept and strategy.

One of the earliest and most prominent examples of this mapping practice was developed by the International Centre for Migration Policy Development (ICMPD). Since 2003, the ICMPD has visualized migrant routes with the intent of managing them (chapter 7, this volume). Their i-Map project, an online cartography, has become a reference point for other institutions conducting border management from a distance. The map does not trace border walls or empirically represent individual journeys; rather, it focuses on clustering flows into distinct routes that can be managed as shared itineraries with clear points of origin, transit and destination. Initially, the European Commission designated four main routes traversing the African continent: the West African/Atlantic Route, the Western Mediterranean Route, the Central Mediterranean Route, and the East African/Horn of Africa Route. More recent iterations of i-Map show how the representation and naming of routes evolve according to perceived transformations of migrant itineraries. The i-Map's visual work has inspired similar routes mapping projects by agencies relevant to the EU's border regime such as Frontex or the International Organization for Migration (IOM).[16] Behind the neutral and technological façade of these experts' maps, it is possible to identify a controversial spatial politics able to convey certain mobilities as a disproportionate and shared problem for and among receiving countries. Here, it is helpful to recall the notion of "cartopolitics" (Bueno Lacy and Van Houtum 2015; Cobarrubias 2019), which thinks of maps as playing a crucial role in naturalizing geopolitical arbitrariness. Building on the notion of cartopolitics, we argue that current representations of migration flows, assuming unidirectionality toward the EU, lead to the production of an arbitrary geographic imaginary that produces illegality beyond borderlines. Such professional yet simplified cartographic portraits of migratory routes justify the budgets and political prioritization for EU member states in conducting border work beyond their territorial limits.

In visualizing targets as fluctuating routes, these maps do not provide a straightforward empirical representation of the exact numbers of people moving through the routes, nor is the directionality of the routes accurate, as Europe is often assumed to be the sole destination. Such maps—which are widely disseminated among border authorities and migration experts and eventually make their way to the media—produce, spread, and normalize a particularly restrictive way of thinking about migration control.

Regardless of their level of accuracy and complexity, maps are capable of shaping and reinforcing geographical realities. The reiteration of migratory route maps as a way to represent a problem and suggest points of intervention helps to operationalize routes thinking at the EU level, complementing the efforts to displace border control practices to presumed places of origin or transit along a route. EU and non-EU countries are engaged in multiple interventions and projects along migratory routes, some of which are veritable military deployments that have been ongoing for years. For instance, through the different Seahorse operations, since 2006 Spanish border authorities have deployed border personnel, satellite technologies, military vessels, aircraft, and border posts to Senegalese and Mauritanian waters and inland territories (these have coincided with the Frontex Hera operations, the longest running in Frontex history). While those are thousands of miles away from the official borders of Spain, the goal is legitimated because they are intended to patrol potential migrant boats (fishing boats retooled for possible migration) or overland transit migrants.

Given the success of these operations in terms of apprehending migrants in the Atlantic, a similar, though further developed, technological infrastructure and modus operandi for surveillance have been applied to the Mediterranean. This effort has at times been known as Seahorse Mediterranean and has been incorporated into the pan-EU border surveillance network EUROSUR. Similar strings of operations and projects can be found along other routes.[17] Thus the visualization and implementing of routes thinking can travel to different routes with the understanding that origin, transit, and destination sections can be managed using tactics tried along other routes.[18] These sequences of operations and projects are built on a perception of following a route along its hubs to more successfully close or reroute it, and also, attempting to transport elements of one route's management scheme to another route.

All of these projects show how outsourcing borders is not a solo enterprise. While the EU and its member states are very invested in these policies, non-EU governments must agree to these efforts and cooperate with them in order for this approach to migration control to work. Most of the time, although EU efforts with third countries are portrayed as creating a "connected global border management community" (Frontex n.d.) and "capacity building" (ICMPD web-site, n.d.), collaboration only comes under certain conditions: development aid, entrance to EU markets, or diplomatic support. Thus the creation of a viapolitical infrastructure is tied to other attempts at political or economic integration (and geopolitical alignment in a context that includes the increased presence of actors such as US military forces, and the economic and political involvement of Chinese development policy).

Thus, a cross-national institutional architecture is also working in parallel to the police and military projects mentioned above, often through diplomatic processes involving countries whose territories align with specific routes. For instance: for the East African route there is the Khartoum Process (whose main participants include Germany, Italy, Eritrea, and Sudan), and for the West African route, the Rabat Process (whose main participants include Spain, France, Morocco, and Senegal). These processes (referred to as Regional Consultative Processes) include political and diplomatic meetings, but also exchanges between migration and police officials in participating countries, the spread of migration management techniques from EU-funded international bodies (such as the IOM and ICMPD), and more generally the development of a network of migration control. All those actors begin to construct a common vision of policy and to envision their route as a space.

These transnational relations and intercontinental deployments become a logical counterpart to a cartographic mind that presents different migratory routes as a specific entity crossing multiple countries that must be dealt with transnationally to be efficient. These cartographic representations operational-ize the migratory route management strategy. As such, these maps further inter-nalize the logic of the concentric circles as a real geography of competing and interacting zones of mobility. The maps enable policy makers and law enforce-ment to focus on the route as a unit of control. Nonetheless, that imagined space of the route is often contested by those partner countries that coconstruct it, as well as by the very migrants who allegedly follow those routes.

Counter Cartographies of the Big Brother Map

Back in 2012, members of a pro-migration group based in Zaragoza (Spain) were staring at the detailed cartography of irregular migration flows visible in the public versions of the i-Map. Someone at this meeting of La Red de Sin

Papeles said, "What a Big Brother map!" Mainly from Senegal, Mali, Mauritania, Morocco, and Algeria, many of these no-borders activists had successfully trespassed on recent EU-led migration control operations deployed to manage migratory routes in Atlantic and Mediterranean waters. The reactions to this detailed and flashy portrayal of irregular migration flows were intense. Everyone at La Red de Sin Papeles's meeting fumed and retorted verbally at what was felt to be a limited, obscuring, yet intimidating map of a key part of their lives.

After the initial furious reaction upon discovering the existence of i-Map, a decision was made to organize a series of workshops for collaboratively drawing "our own map of routes." The mapping process was technically simple. The base of the i-Map was traced on very large paper around which or upon which a dozen or so people could sit at a time (see figure 6.4). Different members of the groups shared and compared stories of mobility and its interdiction and what were the most important things for them during those journeys. The legend generated reflected themes like time spent in a locale, money earned and spent, friendships and relationships developed, feelings of fear or of safety, encounters with authorities, and more. The journeys were marked by important human experience, sometimes empowering, sometimes tragic, rather than by icons for hubs, irregular entry, or means of smuggling and served as a vector of analysis for members for the group, including the request by those labeled as migrants that all members, including locals, place themselves on the map. The rich reflections coming out of these workshops shifted the usual eyewitness stories of so-called illegal and risky crossings of the border: instead of a dramatized and often self-blaming narrative, a more empowering self-portrait emerged that was able to pin down the lack of political will on the part of governments to allow people to move. Visually, the obstacles people faced while traveling are shown by a series of icons incorporated into a map legend. The contrast between these two maps, the countermap visually mimicking the i-Map, is a graphic example of what Walters, Heller, and Pezzani (introduction, this volume) refer to as trajectories versus routes. The migrant trajectories mapped by La Red reflect the "embodied paths of movement traced in space that emerge from the clash between migrants' movement and the friction they encounter" (introduction, this volume). In contrast, maps like i-Map attempt to transform these trajectories into routes, as objects upon which management and control efforts can be exercised. Even if the actual map might be rolled up inside a closet, the final product itself is not central, but rather the reimagining of identities and political demands that emerged through the mapping process.

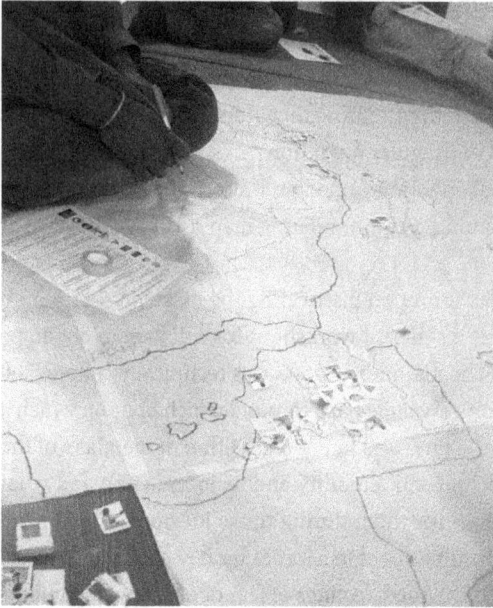

FIGURE 6.4 · Photo of countermapping workshop, Zaragoza 2012. Source: Authors' collection.

If the mapping migration matrix contributes to a geographical imaginary of illegality, countercartographies refer to those graphic and collaborative efforts working toward a no-borders ethic.[19] These maps visually show the limits of the seemingly overpowering border regime as well as the obstacles it puts in the way of people's freedom to move, thereby empowering a politics of disobedience toward restrictive and arbitrary border politics. These countercartographies can include long-term collective projects by migrant rights associations, artists, and NGOs as well as simpler mash-up-style maps evoking and facilitating freedom of movement. Especially in the case of the latter maps, these can be sent, texted, or emailed among migrants along their journeys or sent to peers and family to build collective knowledge of travel and make their paths smoother. The "It Is Obvious from the Map" collection showcased a series of maps (see figures 6.5 and 6.6) that speak to the turbulence of migration movements tres-passing those sophisticated networks of migration control (Casas-Cortes and Cobarrubias 2018).

These drawings, whether more artistically refined or more doodle, challenge the accuracy of official route maps and point to the many alternative ways to or around Europe (in this case), many of which are not visible on official maps (chapter 7, this volume) and highlight the many different forms of travel, often perfectly legal, that are used along any given route. Countercartographies of the border regime include mapping initiatives that try to contest the Big Brother feeling conveyed by border management maps.

We have reflected elsewhere upon the meta-cartographic discussion that led to the mapping project by the Zaragoza collective in the framework of a "clash of cartographies" (Casas-Cortés et al. 2017). Still, we return to it because of its evocative power to produce a counterargument. The story of the Zaragoza collective turns the self-representation of the i-Map as a kind of omnipresent gaze upside-down: it points to how some of the very migrants traversing the targeted routes are themselves observing, analyzing, and countermapping with other alternative lines, and most importantly, alternative visions of mobility.

Therefore, the i-Map's great conceit is that it suggests a spatial truth that it can capture and comprehensively represent, and which can then be prescriptive. This effort is always a reactive one—a response to something that is already there, but which is also always more complex, convoluted, pliable, mutable, and tactical than the map can ever succeed in representing. So there is a continuous dialectic between the autonomy of migrant mobilities and the tactics of control, involving reciprocal responses and alternating tactics, but the map's efforts to instruct bordering is, like bordering itself, always playing "catch up" (Cobarrubias 2019). Routes thinking is grounded on this very notion of chasing and catching up with turbulent mobility. In this process, though, routes thinking is establishing a unique space of governance that trespasses across the very border it purports to uphold.

Routes Thinking, a Viapolitics of the Frontier?

The viapolitical geography of the route constitutes a whole apparatus tracing not only bodies in motion but all the components that make up the "via," such as means of transport and hubs. Routes thinking creates a unique political space that allows for international and interregional arrangements to cut across bureaucratic and legal obstacles. The viapolitical regime of the route cannot be contained within the limits of the nation-state, international sanctions, regional budgets, and so on, but requires creative and semilegal arrangements in both the political and financial spheres.

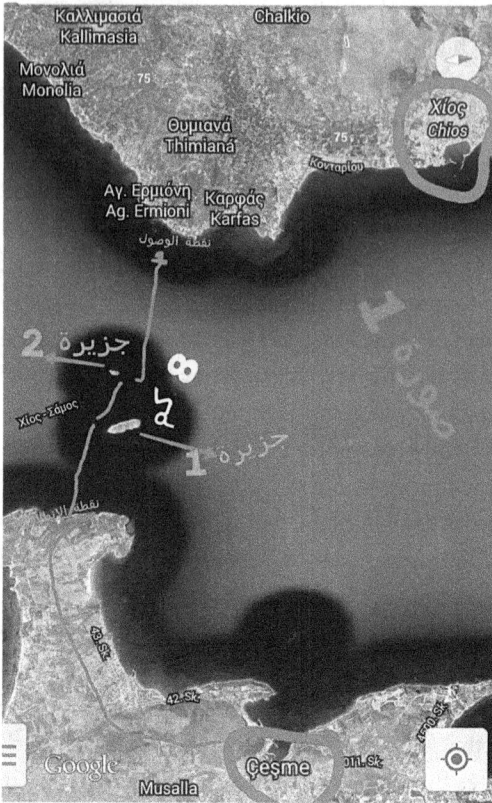

FIGURES 6.5–6.6 · Zoomed-in annotated maps of personal or group trajectories, from the "It Is Obvious from the Map" exhibit. Source: Sohrab Mohebbi and Thomas Keenan.

A systemic and repetitive set of geographic imaginaries, budgetary decisions, policy experiments, police force cooperation missions, diplomatic arrangements, discourses combining human rights with migration control, and political agreements allows institutional networks to avoid many conventional procedural controls. The solidification of routes thinking has required multiple adaptations of legal and financial instruments to fit this specific geography of governance. This includes establishing common working relationships along a route that traverses not only multiple countries but multiple regions, at times, needing to incorporate countries or organizations that have been blacklisted. In addition to the processes of technical and operative coordination mentioned above, routes management is grounded in a growing process of informalization of legal and political arrangements. This political geography of the via is based on the creation and/or diversion of financial and legal instruments to be used for migration control along a route, such as the series of Memorandums of Understanding that have allowed Spanish gendarmes and Frontex to operate in Senegalese and Mauritanian waters in the context of the Seahorse projects mentioned above.[20] These types of agreements do not require legislative approval from their respective partners, and they are not classified, but neither are they public documents (thus requests for access often fall short; see Casas-Cortes, Cobarrubias, and Pickles 2016; López-Sala 2012). A similarly informal agreement has facilitated the sudden ability for foreign troops to deploy to Niger without that country's parliamentary approval in violation of the Nigerien constitution. This has been occurring in a confused context where antiterrorism mixes with militarized migration control (see Le Point Afrique 2018; Penney 2018).

The route as a tool to objectify migrant trajectories is specific for territories imagined as external, purportedly outside of an EU space that is imagined as already/better managed. Routes management becomes a device to make foreign, non-EU, even uncooperative spaces readable for intervention (Scott 1998).[21] In this sense, not only is routes thinking a type of viapolitics that turns turbulent movement into something that can be compartmentalized and managed, but it constitutes a mode of intervention in frontier territories. The spatial logic of routes thinking enables visions of broad development, police, legal, and military deployments to move through the fragmented space of a route. Of course, this route space coexists—without replacing—with existing jurisdictions, borders, legal entities, territorial sovereignties, and so on. Nonetheless, migratory routes management and the thinking it entails promote a way of dealing with states considered unable to deliver efficient control of their own borders. For "EU"rope, these can appear as unreadable governments due to either lack of transparency, distinct communication style, or unwillingness to go along.

This management of travel and its infrastructures connects current border externalization practices with a broader historical period, well before the establishment of the nation-state when colonial settlers were consolidating sovereign territories. We propose an analogy between routes thinking and the historical imaginary of the settler frontier into indigenous territory. When advancing the settler-frontier, nonlocal actors were somehow understood as preparing territories for modern forms of sovereign control. Similar to Turner's (1921) frontier thesis, different waves of actors followed one after another along the "via(s)" of rivers and indigenous trails until frontier spaces were consolidated into ever-increasing layers of modernity.[22]

The externalized frontier of routes management prepares the ground for more conventional forms of migration control. The attempts to control via(s), such as cooperation along transnational routes and the focus on hubs, is also complemented by staples of border control such as port of entry checkpoints and improvements in national documentation. Routes management works in tandem with more common types of border logic. The final goal may not be direct territorial domination but an incorporation into a harmonized system of population management through the exchange of knowledges, laws, police forces, and equipment.

Distinct from the historical analogy of the settler-frontier as a rolling out of civilization, the actual implementation of routes management is not simply a rolling out of EU power and requires the cooperation of partner governments along the route. Still, despite the talk of cooperation, routes thinking prefers opaque deployments of migration management, consisting of political priorities primarily articulated by the EU and member states being pushed on receptive partners. These spatial power dynamics resonate with historical and current colonial processes such as the pacification of a frontier. Scholars working on Native American studies and Palestine studies have developed a critical understanding of settlement processes (Salaita 2016), which can be very pertinent to further explore this spatial analogy and fully grasp the political implications of border externalization as a desire for control of movement at origin and transit points.

By emphasizing the control of movement over the control of borderlines, and through the "transformation of trajectories into routes" (introduction, this volume), such policies create a unique geography of governance, one that attempts to reflect the space-times of migrant travels themselves. That routes-based geography, though, must overlap with existing legal geographies (including states; existing readmission agreements or the lack thereof; and regulations on transport, crime, and documentation). It is in this legal clutter and geopolitical messiness that routes management attempts to constitute itself.

Such a constitution of the route as a space of governance is one of the most important achievements of routes thinking. In other words, it is not only the ability or effectiveness of the route in stopping or managing migration that is to be considered. Rather, routes thinking can lead to the formation of its own political space made out of states, nonstate actors, international organizations, networks of police contacts, technologies, and vehicles deployed. It is in these emergent infrastructures that a key operation of the viapolitical is at work: the establishment of a technology of governance able to mobilize across distinct institutional regimes and jurisdictions. Herein is another similarity to the settler-frontier logic and its modus operandi, which moved in and out of the rule of law but always functioned as a tool of law (Benton 2010).

Routes thinking entails a highly restrictive and selective view of human mobility. Through a series of policies, and human and nonhuman actors, routes thinking attempts to make turbulent movements knowable and targetable, stretching operations across external terrains as in a frontier. Contrary to a neutral portrait of borders in motion, externalized border drifting is grounded in a neoimperial political agenda of controlling certain mobilities beyond territorial limits. The EU's current practices of remote border control (Zolberg 2003) are indeed normalizing a geographical imaginary of illegality beyond the borderline, taking bordering work to a global or at least intercontinental scale. The logic of routes thinking means that illegality can be presumed preemptively, well before any border has been trespassed. Processes of border externalization deepen this repurposing of borders not only for containing territories but also for intercepting human mobility and classifying populations beyond specific territories, through the logic of the route. As such, the displacement of migration control based on exclusionary genealogies of contention and Eurocentric geographical imaginaries confirms the forceful critiques by indigenous, anticolonial, and promigrant movements of borders as institutions of ingrained racism: "You call it illegal trespassing, I call it White Power" (graffiti on border wall, Arizona). When speaking of the externalization of migration policy, the insights provided by the popular slogan "the border crossed us" definitely resonate, both in its insinuation that borders actively move and in its message that b/ordering[23] is fraught with a racist politics of othering.

Border externalization then appears as a colonial logic of ordering territories and populations therein, dating from the high imperialism of the late nineteenth century. Direct intervention on the part of the EU in places of supposed origin and transit of migrant trajectories—through development projects, the creation of civil registries, international military deployments, or foreign police operations—has led to critical readings of externalization and border cooperation as a form of neocolonialism (Akkerman 2018; Prestianni 2018; Bunyan 2016). The attempts to manage or contain populations of the Global South have thus included an embracing and deeper incorporation of territories and economies of the Global South into a broader process of geopolitical alignment and structure (Heller 2017). Processes of externalization, though, imply more than a rollout of imperial power if the agency of African nation-states (as well as nonstate actors), with their diverse and at times divergent reasons behind their participation in border cooperation with the EU, is also taken into account (Cassarino 2018; Paoletti and Pastore 2010). The security focus and interests of cooperating states in transit and origin countries can in turn influence and solidify the security priorities of the EU and member states, thus producing a two-way traffic in influence, even if highly unequal. This amalgam of geopolitical incorporation plus divergent directionalities of policy influence coconstitute the border empire.[24]

In the i-Map for example, Europe-bound migrations are represented in flashy migratory routes erasing African national borders. This is reminiscent of the boundary-making power that Europeans have historically exerted on the African continent, from colonial times onward. This geographic imaginary, embraced by the EU and its member states, portrays a displaced border space, which ignores and overrides African nation-state borders as well as intra-African mobilities.[25] That imagining only makes sense in the historical context of a colonial erasure of previously existing polities and societies as well as the multiple mobilities and itineraries within, from, and to the African continent. Again, Africa becomes a kind of living space for Europe to design, order, and profit from (Salaita 2016).

We propose to embrace this twist on our understanding of borders: from stable lines to be crossed to institutional practices actively b/ordering populations in an unending war on mobility. That is, borders as actively and consistently crossing us to the point that they dictate political allegiances, our corresponding entitlements or lack thereof. Seen in this way, this powerful and normalized device of mandatory membership and social stratification—the national border—could become a scandal for many, even from differing ideological positions. This national border becomes unmoored from a particular territory, actively seeking out those it attempts to exclude before they have taken their journey. The scandal in this regard is not whether or how borders are crossed, but the fact that borders are actively crossing us. If b/ordering then is a central component of contemporary forms of empire, then asserting and enacting the right to mobility and residence throughout human trajectories (whether in origin, transit, or destination) becomes a fundamental modality of anti-decolonial resistance in the present.

Notes

1 This fieldwork was conducted with the support of National Science Foundation Grant no. BCS-1023543 from 2010 to 2013.

2 The word *Mobility* was added to the title only after 2012.

3 This study refers to immediate origins of recent EU frameworks and member state policies. A longer history of this vision of mobility would be necessary to show flows of human mobility within and between different European empires and how the development of racial categories coincided with the management of intraimperial human mobility (see Anderson 2013).

4 It is important to note that the geographic designation of countries as pertaining to one circle or another is not very precise in the strategy paper. Especially with regard to the second and third circles, a particular region may overlap circles. This is particularly the case for southern and eastern Mediterranean countries.

5 Many of the migration dynamics assumed by the document have been revealed as flawed: in the first place, the document implies that everybody intends to get to circle 1, thus ignoring movement within and across circles, especially south-to-south migrations; second, the document suggests that no one leaves the EU, and that there is no migratory movement from circle 1 to circles 2, 3, or 4, an omission that has

been noted in some critiques of the lack of vision of emigration policy by southern European countries, where southern European emigrants are traveling to countries that were once assumed to be origins of migration, not destinations (Mavrodi and Moutselos 2016).

6 Immediately after this strategy paper (CEU 1998b) was voted down during the Austrian presidency, another EU Council document serving as a brief on the issue of migration and asylum for the incoming German presidency of the EU made suggestions as to how the strategy on concentric circles could be followed up on. The language and goals of this new document build on that contention logic, for instance: an initial list of countries was to be produced "with action plans comprising measures which can be taken *against* such countries," the goal being to "*reduce* this influx" of asylum seekers and migrants (CEU 1998b). Despite more recent attention to human rights in the EU's border apparatus, the initial architecture of its externalized borders saw transit and origin countries as targets, legitimating all means under the primary goal of reducing influx.

7 Many of the ideas underpinning this policy proposal were further pursued outside the EU framework by an intergovernmental network, the High Level Working Group on migration, which elaborated many of the original ideas of the strategy paper into action plans focused on particular countries (the action plan for Iraq being notable).

8 Both were reinvigorated in 2015 after the Arab Spring and related uprisings around the Mediterranean and their aftermath. This impasse received the name "migration crisis," but many scholars have reframed the roots of the imminent and massive human suffering as the "European border crisis" (Tazzioli and De Genova 2016).

9 EU Commission-Directorate General of Home Affairs, interview with author, Brussels, February 2011.

10 Seahorse operations designate a series of interventions financed by the European Commission, specifically by EuropeAid, under its funding programs AENEAS (2004–6) and the Thematic Programme on Cooperation with Third Countries in the Areas of Migration and Asylum (first phase 2007–10 and second phase 2011–13). The operational management of Seahorse is carried out by the section Jefatura Fiscal y de Fronteras of the Spanish Guardia Civil. For a detailed engagement with this case, see Casas-Cortes, Cobarrubias, and Pickles (2016).

11 Spanish Ministry of Interior, interview with author, Madrid, March 2012.

12 Spanish Ministry of Interior, interview.

13 Spanish Guardia Civil, interview with author, Madrid, February 2012, emphasis added.

14 The International Centre for Migration Policy Development (ICMPD, founded in Vienna in 1993) was created to provide advice on migration and asylum issues and was one of the earliest institutions that proposed cooperation on border management between EU and non-EU countries. The ICMPD, though independent from the EU and member states, has been a key implementation partner in border management

with third countries. Its roles have included debating border strategy, creating forums between EU and non-EU agencies on migration management; developing a pool of EU experts on undocumented migration for deployment to third countries; and drafting border and migration policy.

15 For a more detailed exploration of the cartographic politics at work in these maps, see Casas-Cortés et al. (2017), Casas-Cortes and Cobarrubias (2019), and Cobarrubias (2019).

16 See Migratory Map, FRONTEX, https://frontex.europa.eu/along-eu-borders /migratory-map/, as well as FRONTEX 2020; Missing Migrants, IOM, https:// missingmigrants.iom.int/, and visual https://missingmigrants.iom.int/sites/default /files/Mixed_migration_routes_to_Europe_2.pdf; and Displacement Tracking Matrix, IOM UN Migration, https://dtm.iom.int/.

17 Another route that has been an important focus of border cooperation missions is the Central Mediterranean. In this case, EU and member state work with Libya has continued post-2011, even in the midst of a civil war there, including the training and equipping of coast guards, and attempts at strengthening the southern border of the country with a string of attempted projects and budget lines. This has been followed by operations in Niger as a transit country, considered a model of collaboration by the EU Commission and hosting a number of EU-funded projects (Akkerman 2018, 55).

18 This spreading and consolidation of routes thinking has been strengthened by agreements between EU and African Union countries following the EU-AU Valetta summit of 2015. These have allowed political relationships, training, equipment, and funds to flow to specific transit or origin countries such as Eritrea, Niger, and governing entities in Libya, in some cases allowing states with dubious human rights records to emphasize their international cooperation with migration policy goals (Prestianni 2016).

19 Countercartography, as a term and practice, has developed its own literature and traditions that go from retooling conventional cartographic forms to thoroughly questioning the aesthetics and representational language of maps, almost always with a goal of questioning relations of social power or supporting the organizational efforts of marginal groups (see Harris and Hazen 2005; Mogel and Bhagat 2007; Dalton and Mason-Deese 2012; orangotango 2018; chapter 9, this volume).

20 As an example of the financial instruments created to act upon routes, the Emergency Trust Fund for Africa is EU funds that avoid requirements for EU parliamentary approval and can detour monies from the European Development Fund to security-related migration projects (Webber 2017).

21 We should note that while this imaginary projects a kind of less controlled outside versus inside of the EU, recent events have challenged this. The treatment of Greece and EU candidate countries in the Balkans speaks to a kind of internal periphery along the countries of the so-called Balkan route (see chapter 7, this volume). The reemergence of internal borders and the management of intra-EU routes has also broken down this neat outside-inside distinction at the level of practice, if not imaginary. The Franco-Swiss-Italian border region is instructive in this regard. At the

Franco-Spanish border, recent practices of informal deportation by French police in Spanish territory have even led to the term "internal externalization" as a way to think through this complexity (Barbero and Donadio 2019).

22 On a related note, see chapter 1, this volume, on the process of Indian removal.

23 Based on the work of Houtum, Kramsch, and Zierhofer (2005) and Houtum and Naerssen (2002), *b/ordering* refers to the demarcation of spaces and populations as an active and ongoing process. B/ordering, in this reading, is understood as a three-part process including bordering, ordering, and Othering.

24 For the concepts of border empire and border imperialism, see Harsha Walia (2013), *Undoing Border Imperialism*. For more on Euro-African relations as key to understanding the neocolonial reach of recent EU policies, see Gaibazzi, Dünnwald, and Bellagamba (2017).

25 This erasure of African national borders is far from the call to "scrap the borders" that Mbembe (2017) makes in an impassioned plea to remake Africa as a "vast area of freedom of movement."

References

Akkerman, Mark. 2018. *Expanding the Fortress: The Policies, the Profiteers and the People Shaped by EU's Externalisation Programme*. Amsterdam: Transnational Institute.

Anderson, Bridget. 2013. *Us and Them? The Dangerous Politics of Immigration Control*. Oxford: Oxford University Press.

Barbero, Iker. 2010. "Las transformaciones del estado y del derecho ante el control de la inmigración = Estatuak eta zuzenbideak immigrazioa kontrolatzeko izan dituzten aldaketak." *Cuadernos*, 3. Bilbao: Ikuspegi, Inmigrazioaren Euskal Behatokia (Ikusoegi: Basque Observatory of Immigration).

Barbero, Iker, and Giacomo Donadio. 2019. "La regulación de las fronteras en la estrategia de externalización interna del control migratorio en la UE." *Revista CIDOB d'Afers Internacionals*, no. 122.

Belguendouz, Abdelkrim. 2005. "Expansion et sous-traitance des logiques d'enfermement de l'Union Européenne: L'exemple du Maroc." *Cultures et Conflits* 57: 155–219.

Belguendouz, Abdelkrim. 2009. "Le Maroc et la migration irrégulière: Une analyse sociopolitique." CARIM, Analytic and Synthetic Notes. http://cadmus.eui .eu//handle/1814/10799.

Benton, Lauren A. 2010. *A Search for Sovereignty: Law and Geography in European Empires, 1400–1900*. Cambridge: Cambridge University Press.

Bialasiewicz, Luiza. 2012. "Off-Shoring and Out-Sourcing the Borders of Europe: Libya and EU Border Work in the Mediterranean." *Geopolitics* 17 (4): 843–66.

BOE. 2006. *Boletin Oficial del Estado*, 243 (October 11): 35161–162.

Boswell, Christina. 2003. "The 'External Dimension' of EU Immigration and Asylum Policy." *International Affairs* 79 (3): 619–38.

Bueno Lacy, Rodrigo, and Henk Van Houtum. 2015. "Lies, Damned Lies and Maps: The EU's Cartopolitical Invention of Europe." *Journal of Contemporary European Studies* 23 (August): 477–99.

Bunyan, Tony. 2016. "Analysis: The EU Goes to War with African 'Elite.'" *State-Watch Bulletin*, July 24.

Casas, Maribel, Sebastian Cobarrubias, and John Pickles. 2011. "¿Se estiran las fronteras más allá de los territorios de soberanía?" Geopolítica(s). *Revista de Estudios Sobre Espacio y Poder* 2 (1): 71–90.

Casas-Cortes, Maribel, Sebastian Cobarrubias, and John Pickles. 2013. "Re-bordering the Neighbourhood: Europe's Emerging Geographies of Non-accession Integration." *European Urban and Regional Studies* 20 (1): 37–58.

Casas-Cortes, Maribel, Sebastian Cobarrubias, and John Pickles. 2015. "Riding Routes and Itinerant Borders: Autonomy of Migration and Border Externalization." *Antipode* 47 (4): 894–914.

Casas-Cortes, Maribel, Sebastian Cobarrubias, and John Pickles. 2016. "'Good Neighbours Make Good Fences': Seahorse Operations, Border Externalization and Extra-territoriality." *European Urban and Regional Studies* 23 (3): 231–51.

Casas-Cortes, Maribel, and Sebastian Cobarrubias. 2018. "'It Is Obvious from the Map!': Disobeying the Production of Illegality beyond Borderlines." *Movements: Journal für Kritische Migrations und Grenzregimeforschung* 4 (1): 29–44.

Casas-Cortes, Maribel, and Sebastian Cobarrubias. 2019. "Genealogies of Contention in Concentric Circles: Remote Migration Control and Its Eurocentric Geographical Imaginaries." In *Handbook on Critical Geographies of Migration*, 193–205. Cheltenham, UK: Edward Elgar.

Casas-Cortés, Maribel, Sebastian Cobarrubias, Charles Heller, and Lorenzo Pezzani. 2017. "Clashing Cartographies, Migrating Maps: The Politics of Mobility at the External Borders of EUrope." *ACME: An International E-Journal for Critical Geographies* 16 (1): 1–33.

Cassarino, Jean Pierre. 2018. "Beyond the Criminalisation of Migration: A Non-Western Perspective." *International Journal of Migration and Border Studies* 4 (4): 397.

CEU. 1998a. "Strategy Paper on Immigration and Asylum Policy, from the Austrian Council Presidency to the K4 Committee." Brussels, July 1, 9809/98 CK4 27, ASIM 170, Limite. Initial leaked draft. Subsequent drafts are coded 9809/1/98, Rev 1 Limite, CK4 27, ASIM 170; and 9809/2/98, Rev 2 Limite, CK4 27, ASIM 170. Council of the European Union.

CEU. 1998b. "Strategy on Migration and Asylum Policy, from Incoming German Presidency." Brussels, December 21, 1465/98 Limite ASIM 260. Council of the European Union.

Cobarrubias, Sebastian. 2019. "Mapping Illegality: The i-Map and the Cartopolitics of 'Migration Management' at a Distance." *Antipode* 51 (3): 770–94.

Dalton, Craig, and Liz Mason-Deese. 2012. "Counter (Mapping) Actions: Mapping as Militant Research." *ACME: An International E-Journal for Critical Geographies* 11 (3): 439–66.

EuropeAid. 2007. "AENEAS Programme. Programme for Financial and Technical Assistance for Third Countries in the Area of Migration and Asylum: Overview of Projects Funded 2004–2006." European Commission.

EuropeAid. 2010. "Migration and Asylum Programme. Thematic Programme on Cooperation with Third Countries in the Areas of Migration and Asylum: Overview of Projects Funded 2007–2008." European Commission.

FECL. 1998. "EU Strategy Paper on Asylum and Immigration: Show of 'Political Muscle.'" FECL 56. Fortress Europe Circular Letter.

Frontex. n.d. "Non-EU Countries." Frontex: European Border and Coast Guard Agency website. https://frontex.europa.eu/we-build/other-partners-and -projects/non-eu-countries/.

Frontex. 2020. *Risk Analysis for 2020*. Luxembourg: Publications Office of the European Union. https://doi.org/10.2819/450005.

Gaibazzi, Paolo, Stephan Dünnwald, and Alice Bellagamba, editors. 2017. *EurAfrican Borders and Migration Management: Political Cultures, Contested Spaces, and Ordinary Lives*. New York: Palgrave Macmillan.

Guardia Civil. 2009. "El director general de la policia y de la guardia civil clausura la IV Conferencia Euro-Africana sobre Inmigracion Irregular." Press release, Oficina de Relaciones Informativas y Sociales, October 22.

Harris, Leila, and Helen Hazen. 2005. "Power of Maps: (Counter) Mapping for Conservation." *ACME: An International E-Journal for Critical Geographies* 4 (1): 99–130.

Heller, Charles. 2017. "Reflections on Containment: Critical Perspectives on the Euro-Mediterranean Border Regime." *Movements Journal* Lecture, at the Deutscher Kongress für Geographie conference, October 10, Tübingen, Germany.

Houtum, Henk van, Olivier Thomas Kramsch, and Wolfgang Zierhofer, editors. 2005. *B/ordering Space*. Aldershot: Ashgate.

Houtum, Henk van, and Ton van Naerssen. 2002. "Bordering, Ordering and Othering." *Tijdschrift Voor Economische En Sociale Geografie* 93 (2): 125–36. https:// doi.org/10.1111/1467-9663.00189.

ICMPD. n.d. "Capacity Building." https://www.icmpd.org/our-work/capacity -building/.

Le Point Afrique. 2018. "Forces étrangères au Niger: Tout le monde n'est pas d'accord." https://afrique.lepoint.fr/actualites/forces-etrangeres-au-niger-tout -le-monde-n-est-pas-d-accord-09-02-2018-2193685_2365.php.

López-Sala, Ana. 2012. "The Political Design of Migration Control in Southern Europe." In *European Migration and Asylum Policies: Coherence or Contradiction?*, edited by Cristina Gortázar Rotaeche, 209–23. Bruxelles: Bruylant.

Mavrodi, Georgia, and Michalis Moutselos. 2016. "Immobility in Times of Crisis? The Case of Greece." In *South-North Migration of EU Citizens in Times of Crisis*, edited by Jean-Michel Lafleur and Mikolaj Stanek, 33–48. New York: Springer.

Mbembe, Achille. 2017. "Scrap the Borders That Divide Africans," *Mail & Guardian*, March 17. https://mg.co.za/article/2017-03-17-00-scrap-the-borders-that-divide-africans.

Mogel, Lize, and Alexis Bhagat, editors. 2007. *An Atlas of Radical Cartography*. Los Angeles: Journal of Aesthetics and Protest Press.

orangotango, kollektiv. 2018. *This Is Not an Atlas*. Bielefeld: transcript.

Paoletti, Emanuela, and Ferruccio Pastore. 2010. "Sharing the Dirty Job on the Southern Front? Italian-Libyan Relations on Migration and Their Impact on the European Union." Oxford: International Migration Institute Working Paper Series.

Penney, Joe. 2018. "Drones in the Sahara." *The Intercept* [blog], February 18. https://theintercept.com/2018/02/18/niger-air-base-201-africom-drones/.

Prestianni, Sara. 2016. "Steps in the Process of Externalisation of Border Controls to Africa, from the Valletta Summit to Today." ARCI Immigrazioni. http://www.integrationarci.it/wp-content/uploads/2016/06/analysisdoc_externalisation_ARCI_ENG.pdf.

Prestianni, Sara. 2018. "The Dangerous Link between Migration, Development and Security for the Externalisation of Borders in Africa." Rome: ARCI Reports. https://www.arci.it/documento/the-dangerous-link-between-migration-development-and-security-for-the-externalisation-of-borders-in-africa-case-studies-on-sudan-niger-and-tunisia/.

Salaita, Steven. 2016. *Inter/Nationalism: Decolonizing Native America and Palestine*. Minneapolis: University of Minnesota Press.

Scott, James C. 1998. *Seeing Like a State: How Certain Schemes to Improve the Human Condition Have Failed*. New Haven, CT: Yale University Press.

Tazzioli, Martina, and De Genova, Nicholas. 2016. "Europe/Crisis: Introducing New Keywords of 'the Crisis' in and of 'Europe.'" *Near Futures Online*, no. 1. http://nearfuturesonline.org/europecrisis-new-keywords-of-crisis-in-and-of-europe/.

Turner, Frederick Jackson. 1921. *The Frontier in American History*. New York: Henry Holt.

Vaughn-Williams, Nick. 2008. "Borderwork beyond Inside/Outside? Frontex, the Citizen-Detective and the War on Terror." *Space and Polity* 12 (1): 63–79.

Walia, Harsha. 2013. *Undoing Border Imperialism*. Anarchist Interventions 06. Oakland, CA: AK Press.

Webber, Frances. 2017. "Europe's Unknown War." *Race and Class* 59 (1): 36–53.

Zaiotti, Ruben, ed. 2016. *Externalizing Migration Management: Europe, North America and the Spread of "Remote Control" Practices*. Routledge Research in Place, Space and Politics Series. New York: Routledge.

Zolberg, Aristide. 2003. "The Archeology of 'Remote Control.'" In *Migration Control in the North Atlantic World: The Evolution of State Practices in Europe and the United States*, edited by Andreas Fahrmeir, Olivier Faron and Patrick Weil, 195–223. New York: Berghahn.

SEVEN

Historicizing the Balkan Route:

Governing Migration through

Mobility | Sabine Hess

and Bernd Kasparek

For European publics at large and activists and researchers following contemporary migration toward Europe, the term *Balkan Route* has come to be nearly synonymous with the events of what we and many others refer to as the Summer of Migration (Kasparek and Speer 2015) in 2015. It captures the different aspects associated with these extraordinary months in Europe, that is, the arrival of around one million refugees and migrants on the Greek shores of Europe, their subsequent transit from Greece and across the countries and jurisdictions that are so thoughtlessly summarized as the Balkans, and their final arrival in Austria, Sweden, and especially Germany. The common imaginary invoked in popular illustrations of the Balkan Route is—as in so many contemporary depictions of migrations—a mass of people walking on dirty roads, or along railway tracks, even though this is certainly not an accurate representation of the modes of transport that a majority of those traveling the Balkan Route in these months of 2015 and 2016, especially during its heyday, have used.

We find a much more faithful description of the modes of travel and the vehicles used in the fittingly titled essay "Some Tips for the Long-Distance Traveler" by Ghaith Abdul-Ahad, which was published in the *London Review of Books* in October 2015. Referencing a hand-drawn diagram (figure 7.1), the opening paragraph—worth quoting in full—describes the surprising ease of travel made possible by contemporary transnational logistics of human mobility:

> A Kurdish friend of mine in Sulaymaniyah in northern Iraq recently posted an image of a hand-drawn diagram on his Facebook page. With little arrows and stick figures and pictures of a train and boat or two, the diagram shows how to get from Turkey to the German border in twenty easy steps. After you've made the thousand-mile trip to western Turkey, the journey proper begins with a taxi to Izmir on the coast. An arrow points to the next stage: a boat across the Aegean to 'a Greek island', costing between €950 and €1200. Another boat takes you to Athens. A train—looking like a mangled caterpillar—leads to Thessaloniki. Walking, buses and two more worm-like trains take you across Macedonia to Skopje, and then through Serbia to Belgrade. A stick figure walks across the border into Hungary near the city of Szeged. Then it's on to Budapest by taxi, and another taxi across the whole of Austria. At the bottom of the page a little blue stick figure is jumping in the air waving a flag. He has arrived in Germany, saying hello to Munich, after a journey of some three thousand miles, taking perhaps three weeks, at a total cost of $2400. (Abdul-Ahad 2015)

This description and the hand-drawn diagram that accompanies it are distinctly viapolitical (introduction, this volume), as they foreground the particular vehicles and infrastructures that are central to migrants' journeys. This account as well as the stages and means of transport depicted in this simultaneously "aspirational and operational map" that serves to guide the movement of precarious travelers (Keenan 2019) resonates with the experience of many researchers and activists who were involved with the movements along the Balkan Route in those months. We would, however, like to highlight how starkly it contrasts with the usual notions that are associated with so-called migratory routes (introduction and chapter 6, this volume). If we follow the descriptions of the technocrats and practitioners of migration control in the EU, migratory routes are never characterized by such ease and such visibility. Rather, we are told, the routes of illegalized migrants are a realm of shadows, controlled by transnational criminal organizations of smugglers and human traffickers, extorting and exploiting those who are forced to travel in concealed compartments of vehicles, and readily abandoned when confronted by border guards or law enforcement.

We do not intend to downplay the misery and suffering that have indeed been part and parcel of illegalized mobility to and across Europe over the past decades and that is again the main feature nowadays. Rather, we want to use the

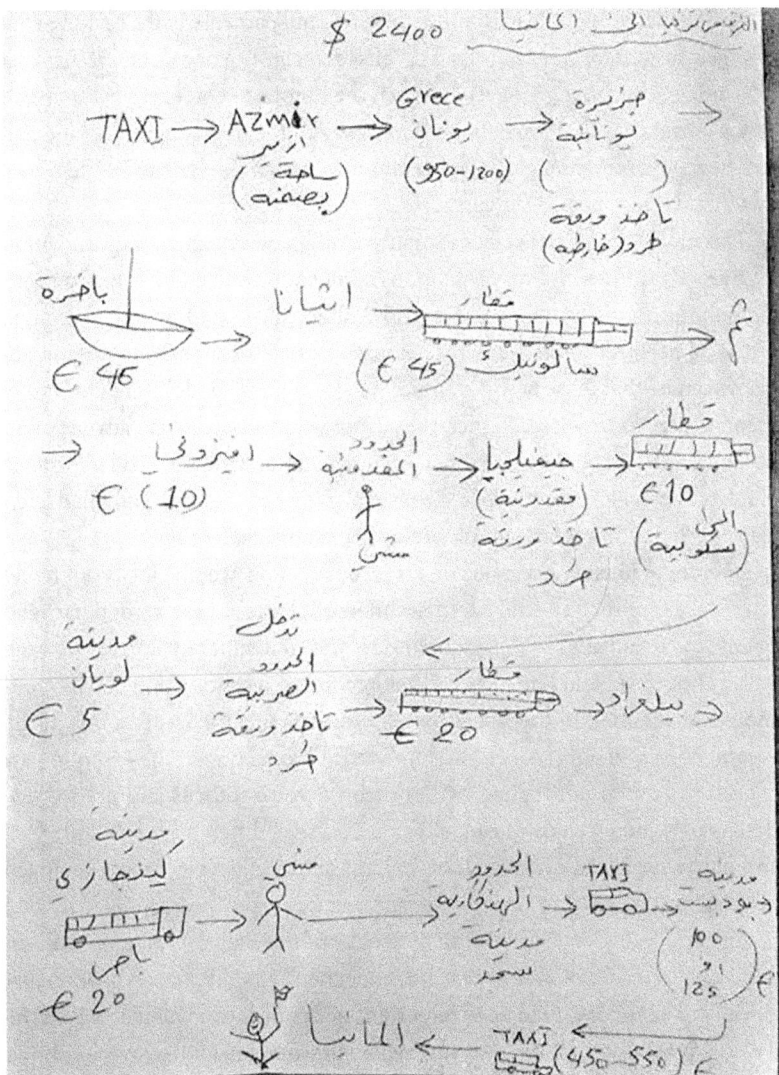

FIGURE 7.1 · Hand-drawn diagram shared on Facebook detailing the Balkan Route from Iraq to Germany. Source: "Some Tips for the Long-Distance Traveller" (Abdul-Ahad 2015).

exceptionality of the Balkan Route in 2015–16, and particularly the period of the "formalized corridor" (Speer 2017), as a lens for reconstructing its emergence as a new mode of governing migration within the European border regime from the 1990s onward. At that time, the epistemology of the migratory route emerged as a new governmental gaze and rationale in which the Balkan Route of the previous decades played a pivotal role.

This mode of a spatialized governance of migration by the European Union of course constitutes the very conditions of migration and flight to Europe with all their horrific consequences (see also Walters 2009, 496). Through a longer historical perspective on the Balkan Route as a path of migrations and mobilities, we argue that these new governmental geopolitical modes were not simply theoretically constructed. Rather, they emerged precisely at the advent of an EU migration and border regime and in its encounter with a particular instance of migration, which twenty years ago had already been captured and had been made visible as an object of governance by the term *Balkan Route*.

In order to pursue this genealogical reconstruction, we first focus on the recent Balkan routes and analyze their different phases. In the second part and against the dominant presentism of most of the contemporary literature on the Balkan Route, we take the recent developments as a starting point to turn our analytical attention to the last decades, reconstructing the route as one of the pivotal objects of governance and knowledge production of the emerging EU migration and border regime. We draw on diverse sources and preoccupations, partly produced by ourselves in the course of different research projects and partly produced by colleagues. In light of recent developments, archived old empirical material has received new importance and meaning. A vast body of data and knowledge about the dynamics of the Balkan Route in 2015–16 exists due to the work of activists and researchers who themselves spent many months either on the road or at important nodes of the movement across the Balkans, providing an important yet fragile infrastructure of solidarity (see, inter alia, Moving Europe, and moving-europe.org). Since then, a lively and critical academic debate, centered in the Balkans, has developed, providing important insights and analyses we are grateful to be able to draw upon (see especially the contributions in Bužinkić and Hameršak 2018). Through our recent research project Transit Migration 2 on the de- and restabilization of the European border regime (transitmigration-2.org), which we carried out in 2016 in Turkey, Greece, and Serbia, we have contributed to this debate. Last, we draw on nearly two decades of academic and activist research into the European border and migration regime as it has emerged since the 1990s and the collective knowledge production of the Network for Critical Migration and Border Regime Studies (kritnet) in this field (Transit Migration Forschungsgruppe 2007; Hess and Kasparek 2010; Hess et al. 2016).

The Summer of the Balkan Route

Well, we came from Turkey to Greece with the boat. From the Greek island, we came to Athens. After Greece, the governments sent us to other countries, with buses and trains. The worst [problem] was public transport. There were too little cars and buses. In Macedonia, generally, it was a very difficult situation. It was not easy to get on a bus. People from the government came. There was one person that had stayed in one place for twenty, twenty-five days, and could not move forward with the train. Trains came every day, but there were so many people, you could not just enter. For me, it was OK. OK means, I managed. But a friend of mine got stuck, and when I arrived in Germany, I sent money.
—Interview with a twenty-three-year-old man from Afghanistan, who had stayed in Turkey for two years and in summer 2015 came to Europe; interview conducted by author in Göttingen, Germany, 2018

The Balkan Route of 2015 and the first months of 2016 can roughly be separated into four phases that we outline in greater detail in the following paragraphs: a clandestine phase, the open route, the formalized corridor, and a return to a clandestine mode after the closure of the corridor. Even though we cannot pinpoint precisely the time during which our interviewee was trapped in Macedonia, he seems to refer to the phase of the open route. The fact that he was able to openly board a train in Macedonia indicates to us that his journey took place after the Macedonian government allowed for the transit of refugees in June 2015, while the chaos and arbitrariness highlights that the logistics of the corridor had not been fully worked out yet.

Before 2015, transit migration across the Balkans took place in a more or less clandestine manner due to the illegalization of most parts of the migration movements as an effect of the restrictive EU border and migration regime. This was especially the case for Macedonia. In their reconstruction of the emergence of the Balkan Route in Macedonia and Serbia (Beznec, Speer, and Stojić Mitrović 2016), our colleagues of Transit Migration 2 describe how increased clandestine crossings of the space of the Macedonian state had already started in early spring of 2015, and constituted the initial phase of the Balkan Route in 2015–16: clandestine, illegalized, and largely invisibilized movements to the north, without access to transportation, and always under the threat of being discovered and subsequently detained. Despite the irregularity of the movements, as "Macedonian authorities mostly just allowed people to move, knowing the goal of migrants was to cross through Macedonia and leave the country as soon as possible, an informal 'transit economy' soon developed in the southern border region [of Macedonia]" (Beznec, Speer, and Stojić Mitrović 2016, 17). Bicycles were being sold (at elevated prices) to migrants aiming to cycle to the northern border, and apparently there was also a practice of buying the bikes back (at reduced prices) and returning them to the south to be sold again. Authorities largely turned a blind eye to these movements and the associated economy.

This tacit acceptance of transit was institutionalized in June 2015, when the recent Serbian asylum legislation was copied and passed into Macedonian law:

> Parliament passed amendments to the Law on Asylum and Temporary Protection in June [2015] which introduced a so-called seventy-two hours paper....
> Asylum seekers could now "register an intention to apply for asylum at the border entry points, in which case the asylum-seeker is provided with a travel permit valid for seventy-two hours, for the purpose of traveling to a police station to formally register the asylum claim."... After the new legislation came into force, refugees were able to legally transit through the country, and use public or private housing and transport. (Beznec, Speer, and Stojić Mitrović 2016, 17ff.)

This legislative change was the final event that led to the establishment of what has been described as the "open route" (El-Shaarawi and Razsa 2018). Already in spring 2015, the new coalition government of SYRIZA and ANEL in Greece had partially decriminalized the provision of transportation for unregistered migrants in Greece (Kasparek and Maniatis 2017, 75), and thus allowed for facilitated travel across Greece toward the Macedonian border. This meant that both ferries and buses became available as means of transport. Together with the new Macedonian legislation and the already existing Serbian legislation, the Balkan Route was at that point indeed open between Greece and Hungary. After reentering the Schengen area and the subsequent registration as asylum seekers in Hungary, migrants and refugees were then relatively free to continue their journey toward Austria, Germany, and Scandinavia, in most cases relying on smugglers and their services.

Instances of vehicular death played a pivotal role in the transitions from one phase to the next. In April 2015, fourteen refugees who were walking on train tracks in Macedonia were hit by a train and died. Such accidents had happened before, but this particular incident became a catalyst for grassroots organizations of solidarity, raising the issue of transiting refugees nationally, and finally leading to the passing of the new asylum legislation and the introduction of the de facto transit visa. The still at times deadly but decidedly less risky crossing of the few kilometers of open sea between Turkey and the Greek Aegean islands, as opposed to the murderous passage of the Central Mediterranean, now allowed for completely unknown patterns of migration, as epitomized by elderly people leaving dinghies on the Greek shores only to continue their journey in wheelchairs. Also, the percentage of women and children on the route increased visibly (see Muižnieks 2016).

Similar to the Macedonian case, the discovery of seventy-one suffocated refugees in a truck in Austria in late August 2015 led to the obstruction of movement at the Austrian-Hungarian border due to intensified police controls. This, however, created back pressure all the way to Budapest. Not only were there suddenly long traffic jams at the internal Schengen border between Austria and Hungary, more importantly, the smugglers ceased their operations, leaving thousands of refugees stranded at Budapest Keleti train station. The Hungarian government reacted ambivalently, at one time allowing refugees access to trains bound for Austria, at another time attempting to lure refugees into trains bound for detention centers and disallowing access to international trains (see Kasparek and Speer [2015] for a detailed account). This led to the initiation of the March of Hope in the night from September 4 to 5, 2015, when thousands of refugees started to leave Budapest on foot with the declared aim of walking all the way to Austria. These scenes, televised globally, led to the next phase of the Balkan Route. The Austrian and German governments decided to keep their national borders open for the refugees on the move and provided for buses and trains. Germany suspended the Dublin regulation for Syrian nationals and thus transformed the open Balkan Route into a "formalized corridor" (Speer 2017).[1] In an earlier article, Bernd Kasparek (2016b) describes this formalized corridor as "a highly efficient infrastructure of transit" that had been established across the Balkans, reaching from the ports of Piraeus and Thessaloniki to several regional distribution centers in Germany. He highlights the role of the transit camps as a main architectural feature, "geared towards processing migrants as fast as possible," as well as the connecting lines of transport, and concludes, "By this time it was no longer just a route, but rather a corridor, i.e., a narrow and highly organized mechanism to channel and facilitate the movement of people that only states seem capable of providing. . . . Migrants didn't travel the route any more: they were hurriedly channeled along, no longer having the power to either determine their own movement or their own speed" (Kasparek 2016b).

The phase of the formalized corridor is what today is mostly associated with the notion of the Balkan Route. Like other authors, we utilize the term *corridor* to point out the exceptional character of organized logistics implicit in that period. This notion specifically resonates with the term *humanitarian corridor*, which is often employed in a military context as a negotiated agreement to let civilians escape from cities or regions under siege in an organized manner.

Other authors have taken the analysis of the ambivalence and exceptionality of the corridor as a device for facilitating movement while exerting a new mode of control over the movement at the same time. Santer and Wriedt describe the corridor as a "passageway enabling legalized and therefore relatively safe movement across borders for thousands of refugees" but contend "that at the same time it remained inscribed within a violent migration management system" (2017, 148). Petrović discusses the suspension of law within the corridor—a formal and necessary condition for the ambivalence of the corridor—under a paradigm of "humanitarian exceptionalism," concluding, "The very formation of a humanitarian corridor was an attempt at introducing control over migratory movements by creating a refugee 'flow' and confirming sovereignty with administrative control wherein care for refugees was mixed with the suspension of legal framework with the use of humanitarian exceptionalism" (2018, 59ff.). He points to the "paradoxical" character of this mode of security-humanitarian policy, combining "humanitarian compassion, care, surveillance and racism" (59).

Hameršak and Pleše, in their analysis of the corridor, go one step further and understand the corridor—viapolitically intriguing—"as a specific form of detention" whereby infrastructures of mobility turn out to be sites of containment and hypercontrol: "The corridor could be conceived as detention consisting of locked trains, buses and walking columns of refugees guarded and directed by the police, as well as the camps becoming some form of convergence point for different pathways of movement and a kind of obligatory stopping points" (2018, 24ff.).

Likewise, El-Shaarawi and Razsa not only affirm the speed at which travel along the Balkan Route during the phase of the corridor was possible (echoing Abdul-Ahad's friend from Kurdistan), but also underline the enormity and complexity of the task of closing the route even if the states had reestablished some degrees of state control over the movements of migration with the formalized corridor: "Nonetheless, seven months were required for the EU to muster the resources, policing strategies, international agreements, and political pretexts necessary to re-impose the border regime" (2018, 4).

Thereby, the corridor, with its hydraulic emphasis on flows and of movement, created like a self-fulling prophecy its ongoing momentum: any interruption of the motion created greater pressure for the obstacle to be overcome, and any measure to accelerate the movement north created suction, pulling in yet more people. This is certainly true for the last months of 2015, when the corridor was traveled by hundreds of thousands of people and the states along the route could do nothing but facilitate the flow through the ad hoc provisioning of stationary as well as mobile infrastructures. The question that posed itself to the states then was: How could this self-perpetuating movement be stopped again?

True to the hydraulic assessment, two approaches emerged. A regional coalition under the auspices of the Austrian government opted for slowly reducing the flows. In a coordinated manner, access to the corridor and thus the movement to the north was restricted to three nationalities (Syria, Iraq, Afghanistan), and at a second stage even Afghans were not admitted to the corridor anymore. In order not to imperil the overall stability of the corridor, these restrictions were imposed, within twenty-four hours, at all border crossings that the corridor had previously let disappear: a true management of flows along the route. This thinning of the corridor was the precondition for the final closure—the second approach—of the entire corridor by cutting off the very source of movement through the closure of the Greek-Macedonian border at Eidomeni (Anastasiadou et al. 2018) in February 2016, the conclusion of the EU-Turkey agreement in March 2016 (Hess and Heck 2017), and the creation of the hot spot zones on the Greek Aegean islands through spring of 2016 (Antonakaki, Kasparek, and Maniatis 2016).

Through these measures, the corridor ceased to exist, and the normalcy of the border and migration regime of the EU's southeastern nieghborhood was seemingly restored. This was echoed, for example, in the assessment by the European Union's border agency that "the flow of migrants across the Western Balkans continued to reflect the influx on the Eastern Mediterranean route, yet at a lower level compared with previous years given the continuing efforts made on the route to curb the number of irregular crossings. The total number of irregular crossings in 2017 stood at 5728" (Frontex 2017).

However, widening the perspective to a longer period cautions us about the validity of such an assessment. Indeed, even though the very term Balkan Route these days is mostly associated with the years 2015 and 2016, its history is much longer. The presentism exhibited in many writings and analyses of the 2015–16 Balkan Route needs to be critically interrogated by a historical reconstruction rereading the emergence of the EU border and migration regime as being highly entangled with the route that was turned into one of EU's pivotal objects of migration governance in the 1990s, which we outline in the following section.

Historicizing the Balkan Route

Regional studies remind us of the multiply layered histories of the Balkans concerning transborder mobilities, migration, and flight reaching back as far as the times of the Habsburg and Ottoman empires. Central transportation and communication infrastructures used today by transcontinental movements of migration were established during the heyday of Western imperialism, so neatly encapsulated in the Orient Express, the luxury train service connecting Paris with Istanbul that started operating in 1883, or the construction of the Berlin-Baghdad railway between 1903 and 1940 as an infrastructural manifestation of Germany's colonial claim to the Middle East. During World War II, a different Balkan Route existed, bringing European refugees not just to Turkey, but even farther to refugee camps in Syria, Egypt, and Palestine, operated by the Middle East Relief and Refugee Administration.

In the 1960s, direct trains departing from Istanbul and Athens (known as the Istanbul, Akropolis, and Hellas Express) carried thousands of prospective labor migrants to the cities and factories of Germany and Austria, giving rise to its very own iconography of masses at trains and train stations. Connected with the Fordist labor migration regime of Germany and Austria is the famous Highway of Brotherhood and Unity, Autoput Bratstvo i Jedinstvo in Serbian, often referred to simply as the autoput, or by the Turkish term *sıla yolu*, the road home. This Yugoslav highway, constructed in the 1950s and 1960s, came to stretch over more than a thousand kilometers from the Austrian to the Greek border. Before the availability of cheap flights, it was the main infrastructure enabling transnational connections for labor migrants in Western Europe with their other homes in Yugoslavia, Greece, or Turkey. It was traveled extensively during summer vacations and gave rise to yet another viapolitical iconography of the crammed car overfull with belongings, presents, and persons.

Today, the autoput forms part of the Pan-European Transport Corridors, stretching from beyond Moscow and Helsinki all the way south to Istanbul and Igoumenitsa. The initiative to create this large-scale European transport infrastructure was taken at the European Transport Conference in Crete in 1994, giving rise to a manifest and physical interconnection of previously existing infrastructures. Misa and Schot (2005) have referred to such processes as the "hidden integration" of Europe, which they characterize as a contested process fraught with episodes of fragmentation, and contrast it with an understanding of European integration rooted in the realm of negotiations between nation-states.

This in so many respects applies to the routes and corridors of the Balkans. With reference to Étienne Balibar, El-Shaarawi and Razsa remind us of the intrinsic connection between the imaginary of Europe and the Balkans:

> Nowhere, perhaps, is the unsettling of Europe as productive, or as sorely needed, as in its "Balkan borderlands," which are sometimes interior and sometimes exterior to Europeanness. After all, the designation of things as *Balkan* is not only geographical but has an important, often discriminatory, history. The violence of the wars of Yugoslav succession (which precipitated the previous European refugee crisis in the 1990s) was represented as *Balkan* (and therefore primitive) in contrast to a civilized Europe. (2018, 2)

This European variant of Orientalism—the trope of the Balkans as the Wild East (cf. Wolff 1994; Todorova 2009)—became a rich source of negative stereotyping, playing a vital role in firmly connecting migration with the notions of organized crime in the public and political imaginaries of Western Europeans (Dietrich 1999). With the collapse of the Soviet bloc and the fall of the Iron Curtain, the process of European integration, which had just started to develop a dimension of justice and home affairs and thus an initially faint notion of Europeanized migration and border policies, was confronted with a completely new landscape of human mobility. The wars in the 1990s that accompanied the dissolution of Federal Socialist Yugoslavia and the consequent establishment of several new nation-states created the first large refugee movement since World War II within Europe, while the disintegration of the Albanian state in successive episodes created migratory movements across the Adriatic and to Greece. These were, however, largely dealt with nationally, for example, with Germany hosting around 300,000 people designated as victims of war (and thus categorized outside the German asylum system, which focused on individuals who were politically persecuted), or police interventions by the Italian state in Albanian ports in order to stop the movement across the Adriatic. While these events gave rise to the very first institutionalization of migration policies in various states of the European south (see Droukas 1998; Frangakis 2004, for the case of Greece), it was yet another migration from the southeast that became a foundational event for the emerging European border and migration regime.

Schengenland and the Balkan Route

Off the south Italian coast, close to Catanzaro Marina, a refugee ship ran aground this morning. Aboard were more than eight hundred persons, mostly Kurdish from Turkey and Iran. When the Coast Guard boarded the ship, the crew had vanished without a trace. The refugees are said to have paid more than five thousand Deutschmarks per person. During the six-day journey, they only received some bread and cheese to eat. It is the third ship with Kurdish refugees that has arrived in Italy over the last few weeks. At the end of October, border controls toward the EU member states were dropped in Italy, too. Many of the refugees wanted to continue their journey to France or Germany.
—*TAGESSCHAU*, December 27, 1997, our translation

This short clip of Germany's main TV news program, routinely reaching an audience of millions at eight o'clock in the evening, condenses the tropes of human smuggling, the advent of Schengenland, and the new reality of human displacement taking place in the neighborhood of the EU in thirty-five neat seconds. It goes on to explain that this particular ship (figure 7.2.) was just one of many, and indeed more were to follow in January 1998. The prominent placement of such news items in front of a national audience was not a coincidence, but part of a decisive discursive push for the institutionalization of a new European approach to migration.

A mere three months before the landing of the ship of unknown name on the Italian coast, the Treaty of Amsterdam was signed, scheduled to enter into force two years later, in 1999. Through Amsterdam, the Schengen Agreement, which had long grown beyond its initial five member states and now also included Italy, would be incorporated into the EU treaties proper. Taken together with the communitarization of migration and asylum policies, the EU had suddenly become territorial, and a securitized preoccupation with migration was at the heart of the new field of Justice and Home Affairs, or, as the Treaty of Amsterdam labeled it, the yet-to-emerge Area of Freedom, Security and Justice. The tentative formulation of an EU migration policy would, however, not

FIGURE 7.2 · Screenshot of *Tagesschau*, German public broadcaster ARD's daily news program, reporting the arrival of a ship carrying refugees at the Italian coast (December 27, 1997, 8′40″).

happen until the European Council in Tampere in 1999; common asylum policies would only emerge from the early 2000s onward, and the implementation of a common European policy on external borders as a technology of migration control would only gradually take place—inter alia—through the creation of the European border agency Frontex in 2004.

However, this process of Europeanization had already been anticipated somehow by the Schengen process launched in 1985, whose concrete mode of practical and pragmatic transnational police cooperation and preoccupation with technical solutions and expert knowledge had gained momentum during the 1990s. Instituting not necessarily a hidden, but certainly a secretive integration of Europe in the field of Justice and Home Affairs, and building on predecessors such as the ultrasecretive TREVI group (founded in 1976), it had developed into an existing apparatus, a bureaucracy, and a dispositif of police and border practitioners by the time of the signing of the Amsterdam Treaty. This advent of Schengenland went hand in glove with a new way of thinking and doing borders in conjunction with the government of migration: "In the form of Schengenland its [i.e., the EU's] relationship to the border has become much more immediate. Security must now operate not just on the deep interior of the European economic space, but on a horizontal plane, the space of mobile flows" (Walters and Haahr 2005, 112).

Largely thanks to the detailed research of Forschungsgesellschaft Flucht und Migration (Research group on flight and migration) into the early stages of the nascent European border and migration regime in the 1990s, we can reconstruct the encounter between Schengenland, the Balkans, and migration from the Middle East that the news clip cited above refers to. Helmut Dietrich's (1999) analysis allows us to connect the ship's arrival in Italy with the new modus operandi of the border. He highlights the role that the German federal minister of the interior at the time, Manfred Kanther, played:

> In the history of Fortress Europe, this staging of enormous potential threat based on the factually very small statistical numbers [of asylum claims by Kurdish persons in Germany in 1997] is unprecedented. Few will have forgotten the media drama in December 1997 and January 1998, when Kanther called attention to the ships with Kurdish refugees arriving on the shores of Italy, employing absurd exaggerations and horror scenarios, and forcing the Italian authorities to comply with Schengen's policies. The dramatization of the arrival of Kurdish persons in Italy was part of a campaign to achieve the passing of Action Plan Iraq. (Dietrich 1999, fn. 12, our translation)

The Action Plan Iraq that Dietrich refers to was one of the first concerted efforts of the European Union to counter migration to Europe. It was part of the deliberations of the Justice and Home Affairs Council in those months. The minutes of the 2,055th meeting of the Council on December 4 and 5, 1997, in Brussels record:

> The Council held an in-depth discussion of the problem caused by the mass influx of asylum-seekers and illegal immigrants, particularly from northern Iraq, which has been observed for some time in several Member States. This migration appears to be routed essentially either through Turkey, and thence through Greece and Italy, or via the "*Balkans route*," with the final countries of destination being in particular Germany, the Netherlands and Sweden. Several suggestions were put forward for dealing with this worrying problem, including the strengthening of checks at external borders, the stepping up of the campaign against illegal immigration networks, and pre-frontier

assistance and training assignments in airports and ports in certain transit third countries, in full cooperation with the authorities in those countries. (Council of the European Union 1997, 13, emphasis added)

The media campaign accompanying these deliberations clearly paid off, for in late January 1998, the General Affairs Council adopted Action Plan Iraq:

The Council approved a forty-six point action plan to tackle the growing problem of the influx of migrants from Iraq and the neighbouring region.... In late 1997 Member States reported a significant increase in the number of migrants originating in Iraq and the neighbouring region, many travelling by boat to the EU. Evidence suggests that recent arrivals include an increasing number of ethnic Kurds of Turkish as well as Iraqi nationality, and also a small but growing number of migrants of other nationalities using the same transit routes. Many of the migrants have sought asylum either on first arrival in the EU or in a subsequent Member State. Many are economic migrants but a substantial number is in need of protection. The migrants almost always make use of traffickers, of whom the majority appear to be part of organized crime networks, with contacts within the EU.... The EU recognizes that a key element in tackling the problem is to establish effective cooperation with the Turkish government, given that most of the migrants transit Turkey or originate from Turkey. (Council of the European Union 1998, 8)

We cannot reliably claim that this is the first instance of the term *Balkan Route* being used in the EU context. What we are, however, much more interested in is the new approach to the government of migration that the use of the term, and its related rationalities, exhibits. It precisely describes the "horizontal plane, the space of mobile flows," and the route emerges as the seemingly simplest of epistemological devices or knowable entities to approach this new modus operandi of the border. The physical demarcation of the border, that is, the intersection of borders and routes, remains a vantage point from which specific action needs to be taken ("strengthening of checks at external borders"), but additionally the semantics of the route now motivate targeting its very logistics ("illegal immigration networks") and its entire geographical expanse ("prefrontier assistance," "transit countries," "Turkey"). Furthermore, Dietrich (1999) succinctly identifies the securitizing aspect of this new framing by referencing a central concept of the Schengen control rationality: "Dangerous places now turn into dangerous routes."

The European parliament in February 1998 doubted the legality of the action plan and incredulously concluded:

> Given that for many people it is not feasible to flee to somewhere else in the region, the Member States must not cut off the possibility of refugees reaching the EU. The Action Plan—in paragraphs thirty-five (penalties against carriers: including those acting in good faith?) and thirty-nine (readmission agreements)—seems to be attempting to seal off the escaped routes [sic] as far as possible." (Committee on Civil Liberties and Internal Affairs 1999)

Apparently, the larger approach of migration control through the epistemology of the route had not yet reached the parliament. Over the years, however, the notion of the migratory route would become a central concept of the EU's approach to migration. While the 1998 Action Plan can be characterized as a reaction to an exceptional situation—the protracted conflict in Iraq after the Gulf War of 1990–91 was only the first harbinger of the violent destabilizations of entire regions that have become so characteristic of the present—over time, such analyses would start to shape the governmental conceptualizations of the EU with respect to migration and migration control policies in general.

The route approach was officially adopted and defined by the European Council at its extraordinary meeting in Hampton Court in London, in October 2005, with the Global Approach to Migration. The routes approach, or, as the commission would spell it out in 2007, the "migratory routes initiative" (European Commission 2007), would become the official rationale of the common European migration policy as established after Amsterdam (see also chapter 6, this volume). The extraordinary meeting had been called in response to the events at the Spanish exclaves of Ceuta and Melilla, where hundreds of migrants had repeatedly attempted—and at times succeeded—to cross the fences that constitute the only land border between the European Union and the African continent. To the heads of state and governments of the EU, this proved that the very intersection between borders and movements of migrations proved to be too narrow a space within which to exert control. The qualifying adjective "global" in the ambitious program's name thus not only carried the meaning of "all-encompassing" or "holistic," as the translation into, for example, German suggests, but indeed targeted the entire globe as a field for intervention: "Applying the Global Approach to the Eastern and South-Eastern regions neighbouring the EU according to the concept of 'migratory routes' also requires consideration of countries of origin and transit further afield. Attention must therefore also be paid to: Middle Eastern ENP [European Neighbourhood

Policy] partner countries (Syria, Jordan and Lebanon), Iran and Iraq; Central Asia (Kazakhstan, Kyrgyzstan, Tajikistan, Turkmenistan and Uzbekistan); and Asian countries of origin such as China, India, Pakistan, Afghanistan, Bangladesh, Sri Lanka, Vietnam, the Philippines and Indonesia" (European Commission 2007, 3).

With the Global Approach to Migration, which was relabeled the Global Approach to Migration and Mobility in 2011 (European Commission 2011), the policing tactics exhibited in Action Plan Iraq became official policy. However, the instruments necessary to implement such tactics, to operationalize such an approach, and to generate the requisite knowledge of the new object of the route, were developed in a different process, to which we now turn.

Knowing the Route

We in Europe feared a mass invasion of Russians. Albanians were leaving for Italy en masse in overcrowded boats, and nearly one million Iraqi Kurds had desperately been seeking to enter Turkey, pushed by Saddam Hussein. In Africa and Asia, many of the previous client states of the USSR or the USA, respectively, fell into anarchy, with mass displacements as a consequence.... In Western Europe, again, we were in the midst of what we conceived as a never ending asylum crisis, with new and growing forms of trans-continental inflows of applicants with weak claims, paralleled by a surge of anti-immigrant far-right political rhetoric. This all brought the migration issue on the top of the 1991 NATO, OECD and EC/EU agenda, and all this was before the devastating war in Bosnia with its brutal bleeding out of one fourth of its population into Central and Western Europe.
—WIDGREN, "New Trends in European Migration Policy Cooperation"

Eerily reminiscent of the present European and global constellation, Jonas Widgren, the founder and first director general of the International Centre for Migration Policy Development (ICMPD) between 1993 and 2004, describes the political context that gave rise to the new Europeanized approach to policing migration. Widgren had been involved in migration policy since the 1960s, with appointments at the UNHCR before 1990 and as coordinator of the rather informal Intergovernmental Consultations on Migration, Asylum and Refugees (IGC) between 1991 and 1993. He also worked for the European Commission. Both Dietrich (1999) and Fabian Georgi (2007) trace the development of the ICMPD to the IGC. Georgi (2007, 16) writes that prior to 1992, the IGC constituted a forum for fundamental strategy debates, but started to develop into a rather technical organization and a computerized network in order to coordinate experts and their working groups. The ICMPD grew out of this dissatisfaction, and was founded in the spring of 1993 upon the initiative of Austria and Switzerland in order to organize an intergovernmental forum where such debates could be continued with a focus on the building of Schengenland and the European border regime. According to Widgren (2002), the ICMPD, headquartered in Vienna, was founded with the clear aim of strengthening the regulatory capacities of the European states and at the same time pushing for the Europeanization of migration policies. Thus, it was at that time that Eastern Europe, especially after the implosion of the Soviet bloc, emerged as the central nearby problem space and forecourt of the EU in terms of border and migration policies (cf. Georgi 2007, 17). In the context of the upcoming EU enlargement, with the *acquis communitaire* as the central governmental accession technology the Eastern European countries had to adopt, the ICMPD came to the fore as the leading consultancy organization in the border and migration policy field, teaching and training the accession countries how to adjust.

In this respect, it was one of the initial central functions of the ICMPD to provide the official secretariat of the Budapest Process, an "informal dialogue" toward Eastern Europe that grew to a central political technology in the EU enlargement process and the externalization of the EU border and migration regime (Hess 2010, 102). The Budapest Process emerged out of the ministerial conference held in 1993 in Budapest, which was attended by representatives of thirty-five European governments, with the aim of establishing a "coordinated, geographically all-encompassing policy of controlling East-West migration in Europe" (Georgi 2007, 29, our translation). The recommendations of the conference consisted of restrictive visa policies and border controls, but also included information exchange, readmission agreements, and the criminalization of migratory logistics in the form of smugglers and transport enterprises (Georgi 2007, 29). The conference ushered in the creation of a steering committee, working groups, and a series of seminars and conferences, which continue to be organized to this day, involving more than fifty countries of origin, transit, and destination, as well as international and European organizations—all sitting around the same table. The practice of the Budapest Process and its main characteristics such as its informality, flexibility, and "pedagogical character," as Sabine Hess (2010, 108) called it, constituted its "success."

But the Budapest Process is more than a round of practitioners; rather, the ICMPD believed in its central role as knowledge network and the necessity to create an epistemic community with consensually agreed problem definitions, approaches, and solutions. At the heart of this enterprise was the production of migration as a knowable object in order to target it as a domain to be governed. In the context of the Budapest Process, this found its spatial expression in the rediscovery of the Balkan Route. "The Balkan region has long been a major migration crossroads even if there was little public notice until 2000," conclude Kolakovic, Martens, and Long (2002, 119) in their contribution to a survey titled "New Challenges for Migration Policy in Central and Eastern Europe" that tried to change the course of events and produced for the first time, with the help of apprehension statistics, a visible, qualifiable, and quantifiable agenda.

The vital role of the concept and object of the route is not to be underestimated in the process of constituting and extending this European epistemic community toward the southeast (see chapter 6, this volume, for the application of the route approach across the Sahara). The rediscovered Balkan Route within the Budapest Process created a common problem space that bound the multiplicity of actors together, and thus created a new governmental profile and "collective responsibilities" that hitherto did not exist (Hess 2010). Central to this binding together was the production and processing of data and knowledge on the movements of migration, thus enabling the gaze on the Balkan Route and giving it shape in the form of statistics, for example, on apprehension figures, or through the use of maps, published in recurring yearbooks. This specific knowledge-power complex was a highly strategic and indeed innovative answer to the challenges posed both by the enlargement of the EU and the rise of new movements of migration in the region. The ICMPD specialized in supporting the EU's effort outside the EU framework by means of such informal policy advice and the coordination of intergovernmental and transregional cooperation, initiating projects on visas, legislation, border control, apprehension, return, trafficking, and so on, and drawing in millions in EU funding (Hess 2014).

In the very words of the ICMPD in its report on the activities of the Working Group on South East Europe titled "How to Halt Illegal Migration to, from and through South East Europe":

> Taking into account the revitalization of the classical "Balkan route" for the smuggling and trafficking of migrants after the conclusion of the Dayton-agreements in 1996 and the rapid increase of illegal flows in the region in 1997–1998, Germany convened a Special Meeting on Illegal Migration to, through and from South East Europe, which was held in Budapest on the twenty-ninth and thirtieth June 1998 in the context of the Budapest process.

Delegations from thirty-one countries participated at the meeting, among them all countries in the South-Eastern region (with the exception of FRY, having been invited but having declined the invitation).... In the conclusions, the Participating States expressed their ... collective responsibility to counter illegal migration and trafficking in aliens on routes through South East Europe with concrete, quick, and practical deterrence and prevention measures. (ICMPD 2000, 3)

Spaces of Precarious Circulation

We are going into the game, one time, three times, ten times—so many
times until we succeed.

These words, which we heard in so many variations in Belgrade in autumn 2018, aptly describe the effects and outcomes of the policies we have sketched out above—historically and in conjunction with the Balkan Route of 2015–16. Many migrants are simply stuck en route, but this does not mean that they are stationary. They are trying to overcome the various blockages of the route north again, and again, and again.

Many who do not succeed in crossing the fenced borderscapes to Hungary or Croatia have come back to Belgrade many times; others have just arrived. Nongovernmental organizations estimate the arrivals from Macedonia and Bulgaria to be around thirty—each day. They are relying on the humanitarian, social, and economic artifacts that the extraordinary time of the Balkan Route in 2015–16 has left behind: infrastructures of medical treatment, legal counseling, one-stop centers with access to computers, hostels, and jobs specialized in the needs of this specific clientele, as well as the expanded Serbian camp infrastructure that in autumn 2018 was still characterized by its openness.

Most of our interlocutors made a distinction between the possible games. There is the taxi game for those who can still afford a cab ride to the border with a driver who has specific knowledge of border operations. But there is also the normal game, that is, using public transportation and hoping not to get caught. States in the region have, since 2016, further clamped down on the movements of migration. Hungary is fenced off to both Serbia and Croatia. The violence at its border and the harsh laws criminalizing migration within are known to everybody. Croatia followed a similar path, tightening border control with Serbia.

The route has rerouted itself, and as we write in spring 2019, it leads across Bosnia and Herzegovina, with people hoping to cross the small part of Croatia, between Velika Kladuša and Vinica, in order to reach Slovenia and move onward to Italy. Monitoring projects and NGOs have documented systematic pushback practices by Slovenian and Croatian police forces (cf. Border Violence Monitoring Network 2019), which however already occurred in 2015 (Bužinkić and Hameršak 2018).

The mobile detention of the corridor has given way to a seemingly uncoordinated practice of pushbacks and readmissions, resulting in a highly precarious, intensified mobility practice of transit migrants, who are forced to circulate back and forth within the western Balkan region under the constant threat of deportation. The Balkan Route, that is, not the corridor but the condition of circulation and movements, is still alive and has not been forced back into the shadows and invisibility that was characteristic of the route before 2015. The official closure has redirected and dispersed the movements, has slowed down the speed, and has heavily influenced the composition (with regard to gender, age, ability, financial means, and class background) of those moving. But people still, again and again, manage to pass through, even if the necessary investment in time, energy, endurance, and money has skyrocketed.

But the events of 2015 and the brief existence of the formalized corridor have left not only a repressive migration control infrastructure behind, but also a new landscape of camps that were constructed along the route of 2015 as transit camps and processing centers. For the case of Serbia, it seems as if the government wants to hang on to this function and use it to enable transit, in order not to be relegated to becoming the buffer zone outside the EU. The inherent mobile characteristic of the route, epitomizing movement, not stasis, and spelled out again and again in the Budapest Process, has created a boomerang effect.

One could interpret the developments in 2015 and onward as a clear sign that all the ambitious integrationist activities of the Budapest Process and many other intergovernmental rounds teaching Eastern European states how to install the best European migration and border policies somehow failed, giving way not only to the massive forces of migration in 2015 but also to the support of a plethora of pro-migration and humanitarian activities along the whole route. But the boomerang effect can also be read in this fashion: the EU was in fact quite successful in creating a common problem space, in proposing the multinational mode of governing migration in movement, and in inscribing the epistemology of the route into the politics of migration management in the Balkans. Finally, this has taught all the states involved that immobilizing migration is a losing proposition.

Certainly, the genealogy of the Balkan Route that we have started to sketch out in this contribution is only one strand of the web of history that is the long process of Europeanization of migration and border policies, and which has been described and discussed before (see also chapter 6, this volume). However, such histories have usually been written either from a perspective of institutional transformation and legal developments, or as a history of important summits, their protagonists, and their decisions. While a critical analysis of the EU's migration and border policies builds on such accounts, its main challenge is to introduce a perspective of migration on these developments. Government of migration relies on silencing its object and does not aim to enter into a dialogue with it. Critical analysis must not reproduce this silencing act.

This requirement does, however, pose an objective challenge, for there is no obvious approach to precisely weaving a narrative that accounts for both the myriad experiences across Europe's borders and the governmental desires directed at migration. The viapolitical investigation (introduction, this volume), not despite but precisely because of its seemingly idiosyncratic gaze, might well be such an approach. It certainly forced us to think more concretely about all the historical instances where the Balkan Route was implied, even if only in a decentered manner. Moving this particular via into the center of our attention opened a path toward an analysis that brought together the concrete experiences of the Summer of Migration, the governmental rationales aimed at its containment, the advent of Schengenland in its southeast, and the heightened role of new practices of knowledge production implicit in the endeavor.

Notes

This contribution is based on research carried out in the project Transit Migration 2 in 2016, funded by Fritz Thyssen Foundation.

1 "Dublin regulation" refers to the core of European asylum legislation that has established criteria to determine which EU member state is responsible for processing an asylum application. In most cases, it is the country of first entry into the EU, that is, countries at the southern borders such as Greece or Italy. This allocation is usually enforced, that is, asylum seekers who move to another EU member state and lodge another asylum application will be deported to the member state designated through the Dublin regulation (see Schuster 2011; Kasparek 2016a; Picozza 2017a, 2017b).

References

Abdul-Ahad, Ghaith. 2015. "Some Tips for the Long-Distance Traveller." *London Review of Books*, October 8. https://www.lrb.co.uk/v37/n19/ghaith-abdul-ahad /some-tips-for-the-long-distance-traveller.

Anastasiadou, Marianthii, Athanasios Marvakis, Panagiota Mezidou, and Marc Speer. 2018. *From Transit Hub to Dead End: A Chronicle of Idomeni.* Vol. 2. Munich: Bordermonitoring.eu. https://bordermonitoring.eu/berichte/2017 -Idomeni/.

Antonakaki, Melina, Bernd Kasparek, and Georgios Maniatis. 2016. "Counting Heads and Channeling Bodies: The Hotspot Centre Vial in Chios, Greece." Transit Migration 2. https://transitmigration-2.org/wp-content/uploads/2016 /10/ma+bk+gm--vial.hotspot.pdf.

Beznec, Barbara, Marc Speer, and Marta Stojić Mitrović. 2016. "Governing the Balkan Route: Macedonia, Serbia and the European Border Regime." Beograd: Research Paper Series of Rosa Luxemburg Stiftung Southeast Europe 5.

Border Violence Monitoring Network. 2019. "Border Violence Monitoring." https:// www.borderviolence.eu/.

Bužinkić, Emina, and Marijana Hameršak, eds. 2018. *Formation and Disintegration of the Balkan Refugee Corridor: Camps, Routes and Borders in the Croatian Context.* Zagreb: Institute of Ethnology and Folklore Research.

Committee on Civil Liberties and Internal Affairs. 1999. "Report on the Influx of Migrants from Iraq and the Neighbouring Region: EU Action Plan Adopted by the Council on 26 January 1998 (Hughes Procedure)." A4-0079/1999. European Parliament.

Council of the European Union. 1997. "2055th Council Meeting—Justice and Home Affairs—Brussels, 4 and 5 December 1997." 12888/97 C/97/375.

Council of the European Union. 1998. "2066th Council Meeting—General Affairs—Brussels, 26 January 1998." 5271/98 C/98/13.

Dietrich, Helmut. 1999. "Fluchtwege." *Antimilitarismus Information* 99 (11).

Droukas, Eugenia. 1998. "Albanians in the Greek Informal Economy." *Journal of Ethnic and Migration Studies* 24 (2): 347–65.

El-Shaarawi, Nadia, and Maple Razsa. 2018. "Movements upon Movements: Refugee and Activist Struggles to Open the Balkan Route to Europe." *History and Anthropology*, October: 91–112. https://doi.org/10.1080/02757206.2018 .1530668.

European Commission. 2007. "Applying the Global Approach to Migration to the Eastern and South-Eastern Regions Neighbouring the European Union." COM(2007) 247 final. Brussels.

European Commission. 2011. "The Global Approach to Migration and Mobility." COM(2011) 743 final. Brussels.

Frangakis, Markos. 2004. "Greece: The Political and Social Effects of Albanian Immigration." *International Studies Masters,* paper 69. https://fisherpub.sjfc.edu /intlstudies_masters/69.

Frontex. 2017. "Western Balkan Route." Migratory Routes. https://frontex.europa.eu /along-eu-borders/migratory-routes/western-balkan-route/.

Georgi, Fabian. 2007. *Migrationsmanagement in Europa: Eine kritische Studie am Beispiel des International Centre for Migration Policy Development (ICMPD).* Neuausg. Saarbrücken: AV Akademikerverlag.

Hameršak, Marijana, and Iva Pleše. 2018. "Confined in Movement: The Croatian Section of the Balkan Corridor." In *Formation and Disintegration of the Balkan Refugee Corridor: Camps, Routes and Borders in the Croatian Context,* edited by Emina Bužinkić and Marijana Hameršak, 9–42. Zagreb: Institute of Ethnology and Folklore Research.

Hess, Sabine. 2010. "'We Are Facilitating States!' An Ethnographic Analysis of the ICMPD." In *The Politics of International Migration Management,* edited by Martin Geiger and Antoine Pécoud, 96–118. New York: Springer.

Hess, Sabine. 2014. "Das Regieren der Migration als wissensbasierte Netzwerkpolitik: Eine ethnographische Policy-Analyse des ICMPDS." In *Formationen des Politischen: Anthropologie Politischer Felder,* edited by Asta Vonderau and Jens Adam, 241–74. Bielefeld: Transcript.

Hess, Sabine, and Gerda Heck. 2017. "Tracing the Effects of the EU-Turkey Deal: The Momentum of the Multi-layered Turkish Border Regime." *Movements: Journal for Critical Migration and Border Regime Studies* 3 (2). http:// movements-journal.org/issues/05.turkey/04.heck,hess--tracing-the-effects-of -the-eu-turkey-deal.html.

Hess, Sabine, and Bernd Kasparek, eds. 2010. *Grenzregime: Diskurse, Praktiken, Institutionen in Europa.* Berlin: Assoziation A.

Hess, Sabine, Bernd Kasparek, Stefanie Kron, Mathias Rodatz, Maria Schwertl, and Simon Sontowski, eds. 2016. *Der Lange Sommer der Migration: Grenzregime III.* Berlin: Assoziation A.

ICMPD. 2000. "How to Halt Illegal Migration to, from and through South East Europe." A Report on the activities of the Working Group on South East Europe of the Budapest Group. Prepared by the Secretariat of the Budapest Group for the meeting of the Working Group in Skoplje on 27–28 November.

Kasparek, Bernd. 2016a. "Complementing Schengen: The Dublin System and the European Border and Migration Regime." In *Migration Policy and Practice,* edited by Harald Bauder and Christian Matheis, 59–78. Migration, Diasporas and Citizenship. New York: Palgrave Macmillan.

Kasparek, Bernd. 2016b. "Routes, Corridors, and Spaces of Exception: Governing Migration and Europe." *Near Futures Online,* January. http://nearfuturesonline .org/routes-corridors-and-spaces-of-exception-governing-migration-and -europe/.

Kasparek, Bernd, and Georgios Maniatis. 2017. "Griechenland, Syriza und die Migration: Ein Interview mit Giorgos Maniatis." In *Der Lange Sommer der Migration: Grenzregime III*, edited by Sabine Hess, Bernd Kasparek, Stefanie Kron, Mathias Rodatz, Maria Schwertl, and Simon Sontowski, 72–83. Berlin: Assoziation A.

Kasparek, Bernd, and Marc Speer. 2015. "Of Hope: Hungary and the Long Summer of Migration." Bordermonitoring.eu, September 9. http://bordermonitoring.eu /ungarn/2015/09/of-hope-en/.

Keenan, Thomas. 2019. "Aspirational and Operational Maps of Migration." In *When Home Won't Let You Stay: Migration through Contemporary Art*, edited by Eva Respini and Ruth Erickson, 190–203. Boston: Boston Institute of Contemporary Art.

Kolakovic, Peter, Jonathan Martens, and Lynellyn Long. 2002. "Irregular Migration through Bosnia and Herzegovina." In *New Challenges for Migration Policy in Central and Eastern Europe*, edited by Frank Laczko, 119. Cambridge: Cambridge University Press.

Misa, Thomas J., and Johan Schot. 2005. "Introduction: Inventing Europe: Technology and the Hidden Integration of Europe." *History and Technology* 21 (1): 1–19.

Muižnieks, Nils. 2016. "Human Rights of Refugee and Migrant Women and Girls Need to Be Better Protected." Council of Europe, March 7. https://www.coe.int /en/web/commissioner/-/human-rights-of-refugee-and-migrant-women-and -girls-need-to-be-better-protected.

Petrović, Duško. 2018. "Humanitarian Exceptionalism: Normalization of Suspension of Law in Camp and Corridor." In *Formation and Disintegration of the Balkan Refugee Corridor: Camps, Routes and Borders in the Croatian Context*, edited by Emina Bužinkić and Marijana Hameršak, 43–62. Zagreb: Institute of Ethnology and Folklore Research.

Picozza, Fiorenza. 2017a. "Dubliners: Unthinking Displacement, Illegality, and Refugeeness within Europe's Geographies of Asylum." In *The Borders of "Europe": Autonomy of Migration, Tactics of Bordering*, edited by Nicholas De Genova. Durham, NC: Duke University Press.

Picozza, Fiorenza. 2017b. "Dublin on the Move." *Movements: Journal für Kritische Migrations- und Grenzregimeforschung* 3 (1): 71–88. http://movements-journal .org/issues/04.bewegungen/05.picozza--dublin-on-the-move.pdf.

Santer, Kiri, and Vera Wriedt. 2017. "(De-)Constructing Borders: Contestations in and around the Balkan Corridor in 2015/16." *Movements: Journal for Critical Migration and Border Regime Studies* 3 (1). http://movements-journal.org/issues /04.bewegungen/10.santer,wriedt--de-constructing-borders.html.

Schuster, Liza. 2011. "Dublin II and Eurodac: Examining the (Un)Intendend(?) Consequences." *Gender, Place, and Culture: A Journal of Feminist Geography* 18 (3): 401–16.

Speer, Marc. 2017. *Die Geschichte des formalisierten Korridors: Erosion und Restrukturierung des Europäischen Grenzregimes auf dem Balkan.* Bordermonitoring. eu. Munich: Ulenspiegel.

Todorova, Maria. 2009. *Imagining the Balkans.* Updated ed. Oxford: Oxford University Press.

Transit Migration Forschungsgruppe. 2007. *Turbulente Ränder: Neue Perspektiven auf Migration an den Grenzen Europas.* Bielefeld: Transcript.

Walters, William. 2009. "Europe's Borders." In *Sage Handbook of European Studies,* edited by C. Rumford, 485–505. London: Sage.

Walters, William, and Jens Henrik Haahr. 2005. *Governing Europe: Discourse, Governmentality and European Integration.* New York: Routledge.

Widgren, Jonas. 2002. "New Trends in European Migration Policy Cooperation." Lecture presented in the Migration Seminar Series at MIT, Harvard University.

Wolff, Larry. 1994. *Inventing Eastern Europe: The Map of Civilization on the Mind of the Enlightenment.* Stanford, CA: Stanford University Press.

PART III

The Geophysics of Migration

EIGHT

The Other Boats: State and Nonstate Vessels at the EU's Maritime

Frontier | Charles Heller and Lorenzo Pezzani

Since the beginning of what has been called the migration crisis in the Mediterranean, international media have been flooded with images of migrants' overcrowded boats crossing the EU's maritime frontier.[1] Closely following news concerning this subject, one is struck not only by the recurrence of similar—nearly interchangeable—images, but by the repeated recirculation of several iconic images in the press that come to signify boat migration in general but lose any reference to the context in which they were initially taken. This is the case of an image used in the *Guardian* on March 29, 2012, with the evasive caption: "Many migrants and refugees risk their lives to cross the Mediterranean from Africa to Europe. Photograph: AFP/Getty Images" (figure 8.1). This image, as the caption indicates, is not used to point to a specific event that can be dated, localized, and contextualized, but rather to a structural event: the precarious boat overloaded with "poor" and "colored" people breaching the borders of sanctified white and wealthy Europe. This image, and the many similar images that are used interchangeably, trigger a mental image for the viewers or readers of each article in which it drifts. It has become a "floating image" in Hito Steyerl's (2013, 171) terms, appearing hundreds of times, at many other dates and in different media. Unmoored, anonymous, perpetually dispersed, it echoes the conditions of the subjects it depicts.

Following the only specific element in the caption—"AFP/Getty Images," pointing to the ownership of the rights over the image as it drifts from medium

FIGURE 8.1 · Screen capture of the *Guardian* article "Migrant Boat Disaster: Europe's Dereliction of Duty," Philippa McIntyre, March 29, 2012.

FIGURE 8.2 · Screen capture of AFP image archive showing the migrants' boat, released by the French Navy on September 25, 2008.

to medium—we were, however, able to remoor this floating image to the conditions of its production. The online AFP image archive indicated that it was released on September 25, 2008, by the French Navy (figure 8.2). Here the image was accompanied by a longer caption, describing it as showing "a fishing boat carrying 300 illegal migrants in the Mediterranean Sea, before their interception on 24 September, by a French naval vessel patrolling for the EU border security agency Frontex. The French navy released the migrants to the Italian authorities on the island of Lampedusa."[2] Thus another boat was present on the scene, the fifty-four-meter-long *Arago* patrol vessel (P675), but that is left out of the frame (Ministère des Armées n.d.). The image of the intercepted boat represents the subjective perspective of a military officer who was looking down on the migrants from the vantage point of the large ship, a perspective that hints at the radical inequality in the different means of locomotion present on site and the differential access to mobility they signify: a mighty European military ship policing the high seas on one side, a derelict and overcrowded boat carrying passengers who have been stripped of their freedom to move on the other.[3] Furthermore, as we learn from several reports concerning this event, while one officer held a camera in his hand, his fellow crewmembers held machine guns—even shooting in the air, thus immobilizing migrants in space under the threat of violence while the camera was freezing the boat in time.[4] This highly militarized interception sparked criticism by NGOs and parliamentarians at the time, forcing the French military to respond and justify its action. While the French vessel was patrolling in the frame of an operation coordinated by Frontex, the European border guard agency, its action was triggered by a request from the Italian and Maltese coast guards that directed it toward the boat in distress. As it arrived on location, it found the passengers "in a situation in which their life was at imminent risk. In application of the international conventions on rescue at sea, the *Arago* rescued them, before handing them over to the Italian authorities."[5] As for the display and use of the crew's weapons, it was justified in response to aggressive behavior by some of the passengers and to ensure that the rescue operation would unfold without incident. The pixelated image as well as the different reports we have found tell us little about the identity of the passengers, what brought them to attempt the dangerous crossing, or what their fate was following disembarkation in Lampedusa. Were these passengers among the several thousand who, at the time, fled the region of Gafsa in southern Tunisia after the violent repression of an uprising that took place a few months before this image was taken (Boubakri 2013)?

Regardless of their origin and reasons for leaving, which are impossible for us to confirm, we can expect that once disembarked they faced a fate similar to that of many other illegalized migrants before and after them: precarious legal conditions, waiting in the limbo of the asylum process, enlisted into an overexploited labor force, or, if they were Tunisian nationals, being deported back to their country after Italy and Tunisia signed a repatriation agreement in January 2009 (Cassarino 2013).

This image and the event it captures are important in a number of respects that are central to the argument of this chapter. First, it exemplifies the "border spectacle" (De Genova 2013) that reveals the bodies—and vehicles—of illegalized migrants as they are apprehended by border controllers who themselves are rather kept in the shadows. In the process, the threat of illegalized migration and the securitization work of border control are simultaneously made visible and naturalized, following a circular logic. If migrants are being intercepted through militarized means, it is because they are a threat. If they are a threat, then they must be policed by all means. The sense of migration as threat is only exacerbated by the profusion of similar images that suggest an invasion of the European space by those who have been constructed as radically other—the racialized and impoverished migrants from the Global South. These racialized representations of migration at Europe's external maritime borders, which produce "a dominant associative notion of irregular migration to non-white bodies," shape in turn racialized border control within Europe, as "any non-white body on the move" is perceived as a potential illegal traveler that must be checked (Keshavarz and Snodgrass 2018). The spectacularization of the scene of border enforcement is thus both deeply enmeshed with and conceals multiple forms of violence that mark their trajectory before, at, and after the border.

As opposed to the framing offered by the border spectacle, our analysis of this image allows us to hint at the broader trajectory of struggle, migration, and violence that lie beyond the limits of the spatiotemporal boundary of the photograph. Furthermore, if the border spectacle offers us the vantage point of the ship of state, "there were other boats as well," as Enseng Ho (2014, 213) has noted when writing about the imperial history of the Indian Ocean, and much can be gained by returning the gaze. Looking back at the ships of empire past and present from the perspective of migrants crossing the sea as they encounter these "other boats," we seek to provide a critical counterpoint to the spectacularization of border apprehension that fuels the "myth of invasion" (De Haas 2008). In this way, the interchangeable images of "migrant boats" that haunt European imaginaries give way to myriad other vehicles (including airplanes, drones, and satellites), making other crucial aspects of this story emerge. As our brief reconstruction demonstrates, the (in)actions of these other vehicles that intersect with the trajectories of migrants' vessels are essential to the way the maritime frontier operates, and yet they are too often kept outside our visual but also theoretical frame. As such, while Mawani's contribution to this volume (chapter 2) brilliantly demonstrates that there is much to learn from a viapolitical gaze applied to migrants' boats themselves, their spatial organization, and the interactions between passengers, here we want to bring to the fore the different boats migrants sight and encounter—or, as we will see, don't encounter precisely because they intentionally remain out of sight—at the maritime frontier. These are not only the various ships of different agencies of European and North African states, tasked with policing migration, nor simply the boats of various NGOs that have taken to the sea in an attempt to put an end to the death of migrants. They are also merchant ships, fishermen's boats, and ferries or cruise ships, which, albeit formally unrelated to the politics of migration as such, constantly find themselves enmeshed in the political struggles surrounding migration for the very fact of crossing paths with migrants' boats. These moments of (at times violent) encounter and friction not only shape migrants' trajectories but impinge upon the behavior of all actors at sea.

Second, the French military's justification of this militarized interception/rescue is illustrative of the conflicting imperatives of security and humanitarianism that shape the (in)actions of vessels operating at the maritime frontier in terms of rationales, discourses, and practices. At sea, as at other borders that have become lethal to illegalized migrants seeking to cross them, the latter are simultaneously constituted as "a life to be protected *and* a security threat to protect against" (Vaughn-Williams 2015, 3). This ambivalence of migrant subjects is not only at work in discourses surrounding migration and borders, but inflects legal regimes and the practices of actors, starting from the presence and operational patterns of their vessels at sea. Border control agents such as the French vessel described above are constrained by international conventions, and activities designed to prevent illegalized migration can seamlessly be pulled into rescue activities that ultimately enable the movement of migrants. In turn, nongovernmental rescue boats deployed toward specifically humanitarian aims may find themselves embedded in security logics that they contest. Other actors at sea, such as merchant ships that are deployed according to an economic logic (Senu 2020), may find themselves enlisted for both humanitarian or security ends, as any ship transiting across the maritime frontier may be tasked with rescue by states, but also to push migrants back to countries in which their lives are at risk.

The logics of security and humanitarianism, as well as that of economic interest, are thus not the property of any single actor, but operate through all of them to different degrees in an always unstable balance (Fassin 2012; Cuttitta 2018). The shifting assemblages of these distinct and often conflicting logics offer a crucial perspective to understand the shifts that have occurred at the maritime frontier in recent years. It reveals that the conflict surrounding mobility across the Mediterranean over the last few years is to a large extent fought out over the responses to these precise questions: Which boats are being deployed—or simply present—in which areas of the sea? How do their activities and operational logics relate to migrants' crossings?

In this chapter, we use this perspective to chart key shifts that we have observed at the maritime frontier through our ongoing research within the Forensic Oceanography project, which has extended from 2011 to the present. We concentrate on two crucial moments of bifurcation in the Mediterranean border regime, each of which is either exemplified or crystallized by particular shipwrecks. The first is the moment of rupture in the border regime marked by the Arab uprisings in 2011, which led seafarers and European state agencies to adopt recurrent practices of non-assistance exemplified by the "left-to-die boat" case. The second corresponds to the lethal policies of non-assistance implemented by European states in terminating the Italian Mare Nostrum humanitarian and security operation at the end of 2014 with the aim of deterring migrants from crossing. We demonstrate that this policy led to shifting the burden of rescue onto ill-prepared merchant ships, contributing to a dramatic rise in the number of deaths at sea. In relation to both these moments, we underscore the way reconfigurations of the logics of security and humanitarianism translated into the (lack of) deployment of vessels by different actors and changing modes of lethal (in)action. Before charting these shifts, we first trace the deeper roots of the Mediterranean mobility conflict, further introduce the different actors operating at sea in response to migrants' crossings, and discuss the specific form of violence operating at and through the maritime frontier—which we call *liquid violence*.

The Mediterranean Mobility Conflict: A Clash of Boats with Lethal Outcomes

As accustomed as European publics may have become to the daily images of migrants' overcrowded boats, there is nothing natural about the highly politicized and militarized mobility conflict that plays out across the Mediterranean frontier and beyond, often with deadly consequences. While the Mediterranean had long been a conflictual sea and a laboratory for novel forms of identification and mobility control (Calafat 2019), European imperial expansion toward the sea's southern shores in the nineteenth century fundamentally altered the balance of forces, inaugurating key elements of the unequal mobility regime we still observe today. The genealogy of this becoming-border of the sea has yet to be reconstructed. It would need to rely on many boat stories such as the one with which we began this chapter. Among them, one might include that of the ships carrying Maltese emigrants to Tunis who were denied disembarkation by the Bey of Tunis for several months in the winter of 1837. His decision came after a series of incidents involving Maltese, one of the main European communities living in Tunisia, who were infamous for petty crimes. It was only after British warships arrived in the port to reinforce British insistence that the Bey open his ports again that he reluctantly accepted (Clancy-Smith 2010, 227). This episode is exemplary of the nineteenth-century dynamics in which north-south migration of poor Europeans prevailed and the power relations within which this movement was embedded, as North Africa started to be forcefully opened up to European colonial expansion and control.

While European settlers migrated in great numbers toward North African territories, the northbound movement of colonized populations toward metropolitan territories that increased after World War I was subjected to successive moments of the partial opening and closure of borders, which resulted in evasion and early cases of deaths at sea (Le Cour Grandmaison 2008). However, it was only at the end of the 1980s that illegalized migration across the Mediterranean and deaths at sea became a structural and highly politicized phenomena. It was then that, in conjunction with the consolidation of freedom of movement within the EU through the Schengen Agreement, visas were increasingly denied to citizens of the Global South. With the Europeanization of migration policies, a truly European color line was institutionalized, as the populations that were excluded from accessing European territory were marked out within a matrix of race and class. This process of categorization and illegalization didn't halt migrants' crossings. As a result of migrants' agency as well as the perpetuation of the systemic conditions underpinning migrants' movements toward Europe—including the need for migrant labor, global inequalities, and existing migrant networks—the movement of dispossessed migrants from the Global South continued but in an increasingly clandestine form.

Barred from access to formal means of transport in which their mobility would be controlled, would-be migrants first resorted to fishermen, who, knowing the sea, became occasional providers of the service of illegalized passage. As smuggling became increasingly criminalized during the 1990s, this service fell into the hands of more or less criminal organizations that ensured the continued capacity of illegalized migrants to reach the southern shores of Europe by boat (Monzini, Pastore, and Sciortino 2004; Monzini 2010). In response, the Mediterranean was progressively militarized through the deployment of patrol vessels from different states agencies—coast guard, police, military, Frontex—and transformed into a frontier area that allows border operations to both expand and retract far beyond the legal perimeter of the EU. Crucially, since the early 2000s, the EU has increasingly outsourced border control to authoritarian regimes in North Africa to contain migrants on their shores.

The policing of illegalized migration has taken a distinctly viapolitical form. In an important report submitted in 2003 to the EU Commission by CIVIPOL—a semipublic consulting company to the French Ministry of the Interior—the authors explain that in order to "hold a maritime border which exists by accident of geography," it is necessary to go well beyond an understanding of the maritime border as delimited by EU states' territorial waters (CIVIPOL 2003, 8, 71). To control the border, surveillance has to cover "not just an entry point, as in an airport, nor a line, such as a land border, but a variable-depth surface" (8). Recognizing the impossibility of monitoring the entire space of the sea and the totality of traffic that populates it, state agencies focus the attention of their mobile governmentality on the main vectors and lines of sea crossing—what CIVIPOL calls "focal routes ... which account for more than 70 percent–80 percent of detected cases of illegal immigration by sea" (9) and whose locations are dictated by geography: "straits or narrow passages where Schengen countries lie close to countries of transit or migration" (9, see also chapters 6 and 7, this volume). These nodes of logistical tension are the ones where "the surveillance required is highly intensive, detailed and semi-permanent in virtually constant areas" (66). However, rather than stopping the inflow of illegalized migrants, CIVIPOL itself acknowledges that "when a standard destination is shut off by surveillance and interception measures, attempts to enter tend to shift to another, generally more difficult, destination on a broader and therefore riskier stretch of water" (9). The dialectic between escape and control and the splintering of migrants' routes that result from it is one of the mechanisms that has led to rising numbers of migrant deaths.

As a result of these policies and militarized practices, once traveling at sea, migrants frequently find themselves in situations of distress. However, as soon as they enter the Mediterranean Sea, they enter a space of overlapping and conflictual international responsibility. The ocean's liquid element has long imposed constraints on states in terms of their modes of appropriation and control, but it also offers crucial potentialities to connect empires and trade on a global scale (Steinberg 2001). Over time, states have enshrined through international conventions a space over which no single polity can exercise exclusive sovereignty, and all states exercise partial rights and obligations, which often overlap and conflict with each other. At work is a form of "unbundled" sovereignty described by Saskia Sassen (2006), in which the rights and obligations that compose modern state sovereignty on the land are decoupled from each other and applied to varying degrees, depending on the spatial extent and the specific issue in question. As a result, illegalized migrants' boats crossing the Mediterranean frontier cut across various jurisdictional zones that crisscross the ocean—from exclusive economic zones to search and rescue (SAR) regions—and are caught between a multiplicity of legal regimes that depend on the contested juridical status applied to those on board (refugees, economic migrants, illegals, pirates, etc.). These overlaps, conflicts of delimitation, and differing interpretations are not malfunctions but rather a structural characteristic of the maritime frontier, one that both constrains and offers potentialities to migrants and states alike. Migrants departing from Libya may seek to navigate undetected until they reach the limits of the Maltese and Italian SAR areas in the hope of being rescued by European actors and disembarked on European soil. Conversely, in order to avoid engaging in rescue missions and bearing the burden of processing migrants' asylum requests following disembarkation (as entailed by the so-called Dublin regulation), coastal states have strategically exploited the partial and overlapping sovereignty at sea and the elastic nature of international law to evade their responsibility for rescue at sea (see Gammeltoft-Hansen and Alberts 2010, 18; Suárez de Vivero 2010), criminalized fishermen for rescuing migrants, and engaged in lengthy standoffs in which they have sought to refuse disembarkation (Senu 2020). All these practices have acted as a disincentive for seafarers to comply with their obligation to rescue any passenger in distress, leading to repeated cases of non-assistance to migrants crossing the sea.

The illegalization and precaritization of migrants' journeys, the splintering of their routes to more dangerous zones, and the practices of non-assistance are some of the main mechanisms that have led to the deaths of more than forty thousand migrants at sea since the end of 1980, turning the Mediterranean into the deadliest route for migrants in the world.[6] Most migrants' deaths across the Mediterranean frontier have occurred not only *at* sea but *through* the sea, which has been turned into a deadly liquid as a result of the EU's exclusionary and militarized policies. As in other "landscapes of deaths" that characterize global borders (Nevins 2002, 144; Weber and Pickering 2011), the sea's "geopower" (Grosz 2012) has become embedded in a form of killing that operates without state actors directly touching migrants' bodies, in which violence is rather inflicted in an indirect and mediated way, through water: it is the liquid element that mediates between the violence of state policies and the bodies and lives of migrants. In this process, the (lack of) deployment of specific boats—or the (lack of) mobilization of others, as well as their operational logics, also play a decisive role. The shifting logistics of border control and rescue (Mezzadra 2017), and the way they intersect with the logistics of maritime trade, leisure cruises, and fishing, are essential in modulating the modalities of liquid violence.

From the Collapse of Externalized Border Controls to Practices of Non-assistance

Through the combined measures described above, by 2009 the EU seemed to have succeeded in sealing off each of the main migration routes along its external border. Looking at the Mediterranean at the time, it could seem as if a major fault line of the world system had been pacified. This, however, was only the calm before the storm. The "delayed defiance" of the Arab uprisings, a rebellion against "domestic tyranny and globalised disempowerment alike, now jointly challenged beyond the entrapment of postcolonial ideologies" (Dabashi 2012, 18–19), opened a sequence of unprecedented challenges to the European border regime itself. By toppling or destabilizing the authoritarian regimes in North Africa that had served as the pillars of Europe's policy of externalized border control, these popular uprisings (and the foreign military interventions that accompanied them in the case of Libya) also made the European border regime vacillate. While European migration policies have long been characterized by constant instability, here a phase of heightened turbulence ensued.

Initially, state actors were caught off guard. With the power vacuum in Tunisia and Libya, Europe was left with no state partner to which it could entrust border control or send back migrants. Italian and Maltese police and coast guard vessels mostly patrolled areas close to European coasts, and both state and non-state vessels operating in the maritime space crossed by migrants feared being caught in lengthy standoffs or even criminalized for assisting migrants. As a result, practices of non-assistance were heightened between 2011 and 2013, with the left-to-die boat case with which we initiated the Forensic Oceanography project in 2011 constituting a paradigmatic example.[7] In this event, which occurred while more than thirty-eight warships were deployed off the coast of Libya in the context of NATO military intervention, seventy-two migrants fleeing the war zone were left to drift in the central Mediterranean Sea for fourteen days (see map 8.1). Sixty-three human lives were lost, despite the survivors calling Father Zerai (an Eritrean priest based in Rome) via satellite phone, despite distress signals sent out to vessels navigating in the area indicating the boats' position, despite being flown over by military aircraft, and despite several encounters with state and nonstate vessels. Already in their first day of navigation, the migrants approached fishing boats during the night. As they approached the first one, it drew in its nets and sailed away swiftly, almost making the migrants' small boat capsize. Soon they saw a second one, the crew of which told them "four hours, four hours" in Arabic, pointing in the direction of Lampedusa, before abandoning them in the darkness. While they continued their route with all possible speed, they ran out of fuel, and at daybreak the motor stopped. As they drifted, they saw in the distance large vessels that appeared to be merchant or passenger ships, but were unable to approach them. After approximately ten days of drifting, when almost half the passengers on board had already died, a warship came within ten meters of the passengers, before turning away. Dan Haile Gebre, one of the survivors we interviewed, vividly recalled that moment: "We are watching them, they are watching us. We are showing them the dead bodies, children. We drank water from the sea, we cried. The people on the boat took pictures, nothing else."[8] In failing to assist the drifting passengers while knowing their fate, the crew on board this military ship—which remains unidentified to this day—killed them without touching their bodies.

This instance of lethal abandonment was not an isolated event, nor can it be reduced to the individual behavior of the captains of the different boats and ships involved. The practices of non-assistance in which they engaged were rather the structural product of a "system of sanctions that punishes rescuers" (Basaran 2015, 206), making state (and nonstate) actors reluctant to act in accordance with their obligation to rescue migrants in distress. Military actors in particular sought to focus their activities on their security mission—at the time toppling the Khadafi regime. However, as crossings increased again in summer 2013 and public indignation rose in the face of the rising death toll, the principled reluctance to rescue migrants on the part of states, and the practices of non-assistance it gave rise to, became untenable. A sequence of rapid change in policies and practices ensued, playing out through conflicts surrounding the deployment of state vessels and their operational priorities.

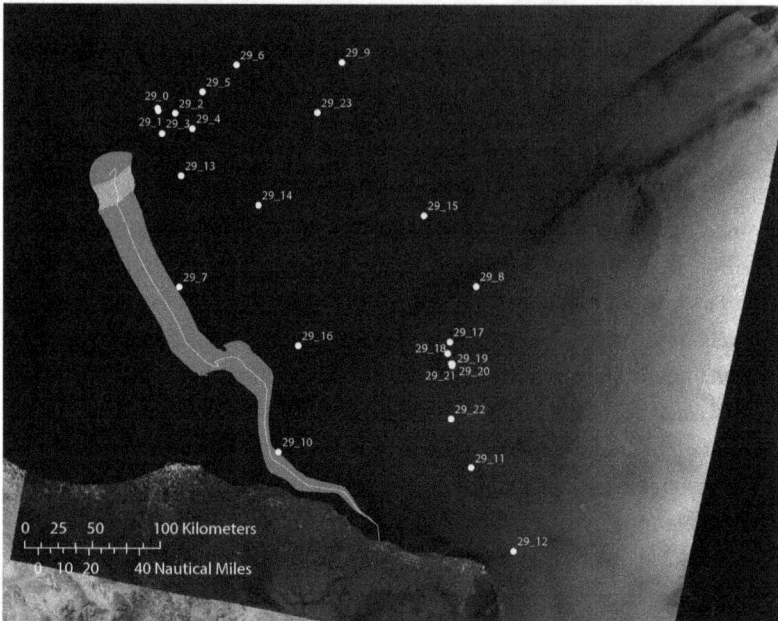

MAP 8.1 · Analysis of March 29, 2011, Envisat satellite image showing the modeled position of the left-to-die boat (diagonal hatching) and the nearby presence of several military vessels who did not intervene to rescue the migrants. Credit: Forensic Oceanography and SITU Research, "The Left-to-Die Boat" report.

From Military Saviors to the Becoming-Lethal of Rescue

On October 3, 2013, a boat carrying more than five hundred migrants sank less than one kilometer from the coast of Lampedusa, causing the death of at least 366 people and a public outcry (see Watch the Med 2013a). Not only did this boat manage to cross the multiple layers of surveillance surrounding Lampedusa undetected, but survivors of this incident also claimed that, a few hours before the boat capsized, two or three fishermen's ships ignored their calls for help (this has not been confirmed or disproven to date). On October 11, another boat carrying more than four hundred people sank after rescue deployment was delayed for over five hours as a result of the recurring conflicts between the Italian and Maltese coast guards, and more than two hundred people died (see Watch the Med 2013b). Since both of these tragedies involved practices of non-assistance, they initially appeared to be a tragic repetition of the left-to-die boat, with an even more exorbitant death toll. In hindsight, however, we can see that these shipwrecks were indexes of much deeper changes.

In the wake of these two tragic shipwrecks, migrants' deaths suddenly gained tremendous public visibility as the haunting underwater images of the Lampedusa wreck circulated in the international press, forcing policy makers to articulate their positions. The EU policy makers were swift to seize the opportunity to justify in the language of humanitarianism an increase in Frontex's budget and the launch of Eurosur, the European Border Surveillance System—that is, the continuation of a predominantly security-based approach to migration. The Italian authorities, however, went beyond humanitarian framing and made the rescue of migrants a central operational aim of the large-scale Mare Nostrum operation launched by the military (ANSAmed 2013). One 135-meter-long amphibious vessel, two frigates, two corvettes, four helicopters, three planes, and unmanned aerial vehicles patrolling for over one year just a few miles off the coast of Libya at the monthly cost of about 9.5 million euros: these figures provide an indication of the spectacular scale of Mare Nostrum.[9] In the framework of this humanitarian and security operation, Italian Navy ships proactively patrolled close to the Libyan shores to rescue migrants and disembark them on Italian territory, thus marking a clear shift away from the principled reluctance observed in previous years to initiate rescue operations. The October 2013 shipwrecks then marked a sharp turn toward what we may call, following William Walters (2011, 138), the humanitarianization of the border, a process through which humanitarianism became increasingly embedded within border control at both the discursive and operational levels. Now, instead of foregrounding the securitized scene of neutralizing the threat of migration through border control, Mare Nostrum activities focused public attention on the good "scene of rescue" (Tazzioli 2014), recasting the role of the state and the military as that of a merciful savior (Chouliaraki and Musarò 2017). However, the "humanitarian border spectacle" (Cuttitta 2014) was just as selective in the (in)visibilization of the maritime frontier as the primarily security-oriented spectacle that had preceded it: rescue by the military occluded the perpetuation of the EU's policies of exclusion that precaritize migrants' crossings in the first place, and migrants thus continued to die despite this large-scale operation. Furthermore, in the process of rescue, the military also facilitated the arrest of 330 alleged smugglers, and the large military ships allowed for the hosting of teams of police officers tasked with identifying and fingerprinting, thus extending for the first time onto the high seas the biopolitical regime normally applied on dry land.[10]

While the Italian operation thus remained highly ambivalent, the military did rescue more than 100,000 people over a year of activity. The break with the politics and practices of non-assistance and the strength of the humanitarian logic marked by Mare Nostrum proved short-lived, as the operation was soon criticized for allegedly constituting a "pull factor" for people crossing the Mediterranean. UK Foreign Office Minister Lady Anelay exemplified this position when she stated, "We do not support planned search and rescue operations in the Mediterranean. We believe that they create an unintended 'pull factor,' encouraging more migrants to attempt the dangerous sea crossing and thereby leading to more tragic and unnecessary deaths" (Daily Hansard 2014). Translated in more frank terms by François Crépeau, United Nations Special Rapporteur on the rights of migrants, this statement amounted to saying, "Let them die because this is a good deterrence" (United Nations Human Rights 2014). As the balance of the border regime tilted once again toward securitization, European member states refused to Europeanize Mare Nostrum as Italy had requested, and Italy terminated the operation at the end of 2014. On November 1, 2014, the Triton operation led by Frontex was launched instead, deploying fewer vessels in an area farther from the Libyan coast and with border control instead of rescue as the priority (see map 8.2). Through this operational shift, which we have reconstructed in detail in our "Death by Rescue" report (Heller and Pezzani 2016), the EU and its member states hoped to make migrant crossings more difficult, so as to deter migrants from crossing.

In reality, as predicted by the human rights community as well internal Frontex documents, migrants' crossings continued unabated, but instead of a fleet of state-operated vessels, a lethal rescue gap awaited them. Seeking to fill this gap, the Italian coast guard sought to coordinate rescue by relying on the different types of vessels present at sea, both state and nonstate, generating, however, considerable conflict in the process. A first series of conflicts arose in early November 2014, immediately after the beginning of Frontex's Triton operation, as a result of the Italian coast guard calling upon Frontex assets to operate rescue operations close to the Libyan coast. In response to this, on November 25, 2014, Klaus Rösler, Frontex director of operations, wrote a letter addressed to Italian border authorities to voice his "concerns about engagement of Frontex deployed assets in activities outside the operational area" and highlighting Frontex's border control mission (Rösler 2014). The mobilization of its state assets toward humanitarian ends was thus opposed by Frontex not only during the planning of its operation but in its implementation as well, an opposition that met strong criticism from members of the European Parliament, who demanded that the

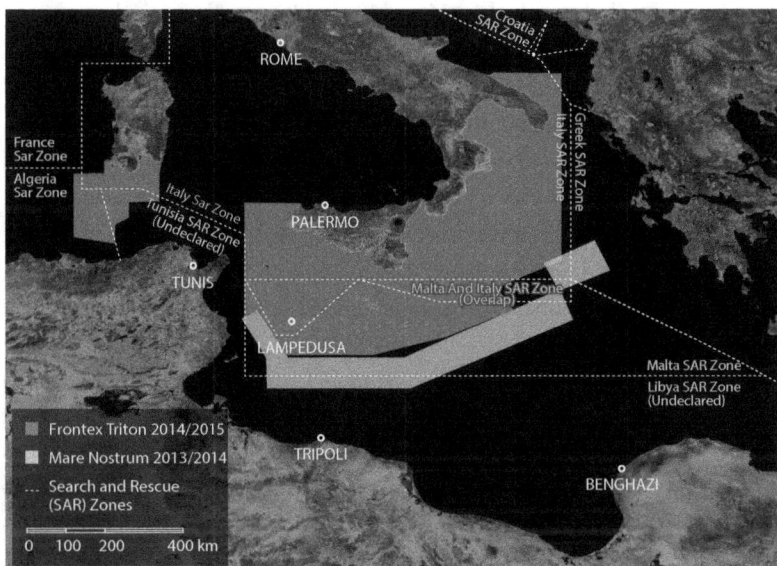

MAP 8.2 · Map comparing the zones of deployment of the Italian Navy's Mare Nostrum operation and the EU's border agency's (Frontex) Triton operation. Credit: Forensic Oceanography, "Death by Rescue" report. GIS analysis: Rossana Padeletti. Design: Samaneh Moafi.

Italian minister of interior "oblige Frontex to abide to its SAR duties enshrined in EU regulations" (Spinelli 2014).

Since the gap left by Mare Nostrum could not be filled by state assets, and this was already leading to a rising number of migrant deaths in early 2015, the Italian coast guard increasingly came to call upon a second actor to perform rescues: the large merchant ships transiting the area. While as we noted above, the coastal state policy had long discouraged merchant ships from making rescues, they had already been called upon to cope with the unprecedented number of crossings during 2014. Despite the significant costs incurred while rescuing migrants, which as Senu (2020) notes are only partially covered by insurance, in a context in which Italy accepted rescued passengers, merchant ships demonstrated a remarkable commitment to abide by their obligations and engaged in challenging rescue operations. In early 2015, however, with the retreat of state-operated vessels, the shipping industry became the largest SAR operator in the central Mediterranean, rescuing 11,954 people within the first five months of 2015. Tangled and zigzagging tracks, unequivocally signaling ongoing rescue operations, started to become more and more ubiquitous in that period on online vessel tracking platforms such as Marine Traffic. Rescue, then, was being privatized, but only partly and ambivalently. The Italian coast guard, as established by the international legislation on SAR, still maintained the full control and coordination of SAR operations even in these cases of rescue by proxy. In fact, instead of the privatization of rescue, we might speak in this instance just as adequately of the temporary nationalization of commercial shipping to operate SAR.[11] This development confirms Saskia Sassen's (2002, 173–74) argument that privatization should not be equated with a simple withdrawal of the state from its various regulatory functions, but rather understood as its "repositioning . . . in a broader field of power."

In this new position, the merchant shipping industry thus became, despite itself, a central actor at the EU's maritime frontier, not only at the operational level but also through its outspoken criticism of the EU's policy of retreat. The International Chamber of Shipping had already vocally denounced the ending of Mare Nostrum (*World Maritime News* 2014). In early 2015, as it was becoming clear that merchant ships were being made to carry a burden that was far too heavy, the shipping community warned EU member states unequivocally in an open letter that is worth quoting at length:

> The humanitarian crisis in the Mediterranean Sea is spiralling out of control. . . . There is a terrible risk of further catastrophic loss of life as ever-more desperate people attempt this deadly sea crossing. . . . We believe it is unacceptable that the international community is increasingly relying on merchant ships and seafarers to undertake more and more large-scale rescues. . . . Commercial ships are not equipped to undertake such large-scale rescues. . . . In the short term, we therefore feel that the immediate priority must be for EU and EEA Member States to increase resources and support for Search and Rescue operations in the Mediterranean, in view of the very large number of potentially dangerous rescues now being conducted by merchant ships. . . . In addition to increasing SAR resources, there is also an urgent need for EU and EEA Member States to develop a political solution. . . . The shipping industry believes that the EU and the international community need to provide refugees and migrants with alternative means of finding safety without risking their lives by crossing the Mediterranean in unseaworthy boats.[12]

This letter strikingly illustrates the role the shipping community came to play at this time, a role that underscores the multiple—and at times surprising—actors that came to oppose or forge alliances with each other in the mobility conflict raging across the maritime frontier. Here were shipping associations, in principle established to defend the commercial interests of the shipping industry, echoing the calls of many actors of the human rights community for state-led rescue missions and legal pathways for migration. It also demonstrates the shipping community's recognition of the danger to the lives of migrants implied by the involvement in rescue operations of its own ships, which are unfit for the task (*World Maritime News* 2014). However, this urgent call too was discarded by EU policy makers, and in April 2015, the interventions of merchant ships led to two shipwrecks that cost the lives of more than 1,200 people in a single week. In these two incidents, for which we have provided detailed reconstructions (Heller and Pezzani 2016), the actual loss of life occurred in the presence of merchant ships that were tasked with rescue, and partly as a result of their intervention, not because actors at sea refrained from assisting the passengers in distress as had been the case in the past. The survivors of the first April shipwreck described how their overcrowded fishing boat capsized due to its passengers' abrupt movement on deck in excitement at the sight of platform supply vessels approaching to rescue them, leading to the death of at least four hundred people. As for the shipwreck that happened just a few days later, survivors described to us how the 147-meter-long cargo ship *King Jacob* approached their twenty-one-meter-long fishing boat, loaded with over 850 people in the middle of the night (see figure 8.3 and map 8.3). The pilot of the migrants' boat,

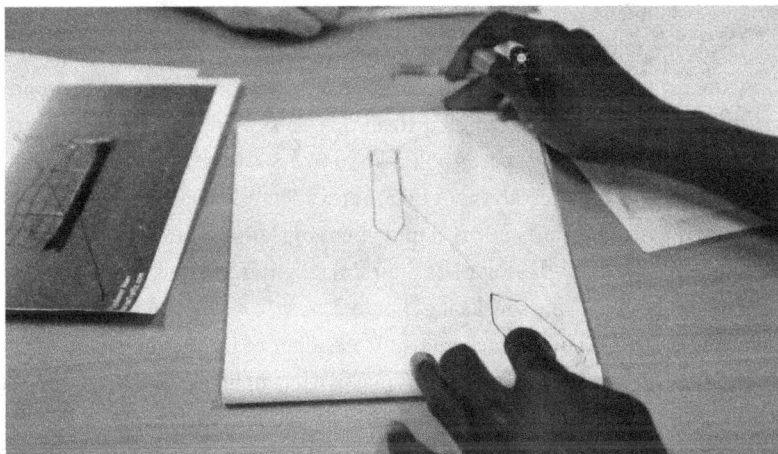

FIGURE 8.3 · Video still of an interview with a survivor of the April 18 shipwreck, showing his drawing of the collision between the migrants' boat and the cargo ship. Credit: Forensic Oceanography, "Death by Rescue" report.

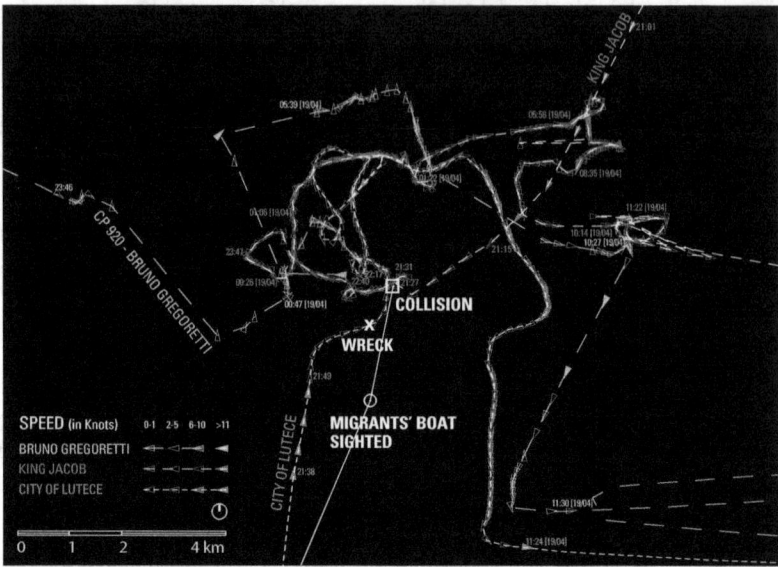

MAP 8.3 · The frantic tangle of automatic identification system vessel tracks in the Mediterranean following the April 18 shipwreck. Credit: Forensic Oceanography, "Death by Rescue" report. GIS analysis: Rossana Padeletti. Design: Samaneh Moafi.

however, maneuvered badly as the large cargo ship approached, colliding with the merchant ship. More than eight hundred people were pulled down with the sinking fishing boat.

While it could appear, as news media and politicians frame the event, that only the ruthless smugglers who overcrowded unseaworthy boats to the point of collapse are to blame, we argue instead that these shipwrecks were the outcome of the EU's carefully crafted policies of non-assistance. The ending of Mare Nostrum and its (non)replacement by Frontex's Triton operation, which materialized in profound shifts in the deployment of state-operated vessels at the maritime frontier and the logics of their (in)activities, created the conditions that made the April shipwrecks inevitable. The EU's responsibility was partly admitted by Jean-Claude Juncker (2015), president of the European Commission, himself, when in the wake of this massive loss of life he conceded, "It was a serious mistake to bring the *Mare Nostrum* operation to an end. It cost human lives." However, because policy makers chose to ignore warnings from multiple actors and implemented this policy with full knowledge of its lethal outcomes, this cannot be characterized as a mistake but rather as a form of "killing by omission" (Mann 2016).

From Privatized Rescue to Privatized Pushbacks

After the events described in this chapter, the operations, actors, and logistics of border control and rescue at sea continued to remain highly unstable and contested. Like the October 2013 shipwrecks, the twin April 2015 shipwrecks signaled another wave of impressive shifts in the assemblage of security and humanitarian logics shaping rescue and bordering practices at the maritime frontier. The EU continued (and still continues to this day) to refuse to launch a new proactive SAR operation—let alone rethink its exclusionary policy that creates the necessity for rescue in the first place. Instead, the EU strengthened its security-oriented operations by increasing Frontex's budget and by launching, on June 22, 2015, a European antismuggling operation named EUNAVFOR MED. At its core, this operation has the "neutralisation of ships and logistic infrastructures used by smugglers" (Garelli and Tazzioli 2018; see Sonnino 2016). Faced with this situation, a growing number of NGOs courageously stepped in with their own vessels to fill the lethal gap in rescue capabilities left by the ending of Mare Nostrum, progressively constituting a veritable civilian rescue fleet (see Stierl 2018; Cuttitta 2018). As of 2017, Italy and the EU embarked on a desperate attempt to seal off the central Mediterranean route. This undeclared operation, which we have called elsewhere Mare Clausum, has also played out through the contested logistics of rescue (pushing NGO vessels out of the sea by criminalizing civilian rescue) and border control (equipping the Libyan coast guard with new or repaired boats so that they intercept migrants).[13] As a result of these recent shifts, merchant ships have once again become a central and contested actor. This time, however, they are used to implement not only privatized rescue—despite the risks this entails—but privatized pushbacks, as they have been repeatedly tasked by the Italian coast guard with taking migrants back to Libya, despite the existence of ample documentation showing how they face untold violence and abuse there. Migrants, for their part, have attempted to resist this by hijacking on a few occasions the merchant ships that had rescued them and forcing them to sail to Europe, a new tactic that has already been judged a legitimate form of self-defense by an Italian court (DPU 2019).

As we have tried to demonstrate in this chapter, while the spectacularized images of migrants' intercepted and rescued boats discussed at the beginning of this chapter dominate media representations, it is by shifting the focus from migrants' boats to those of all the different vehicles that interact with them—or stay away precisely not to do so—that we can foreground the contradictory imperatives different actors at sea have to negotiate, the intense political conflicts they are embedded in, and the shifting modalities of liquid violence they give rise to. The struggles surrounding the (non)deployment of boats at the maritime frontier exemplify and allow one to chart all these different moments of profound change in the border regime. What emerges forcefully is that the mobility conflict opposing illegalized migrants' movements to the exclusionary policies of states is mediated by multiple—and at times surprising—actors and their vehicles, which by far exceed the state/migrant binary relation, and further include fishermen, merchant ships, and NGOs. The mobility conflict plays out on the ground—in our case, at sea—as a struggle over the logistics of border control and rescue, and it is only by bringing all these "other boats" (as well as the spatial and operational logics that shape their activities) to the fore that one can begin to unravel the tactical moves and reversals of the actors involved in "the Mediterranean battlefield of migration" (Mezzadra and Stierl 2019).

Notes

1 As has been amply noted (Bojadžijev and Mezzadra 2015), the so-called migration crisis should be rather understood as a crisis of European migration policies sparked by the unruly movements of illegalized migrants.

2 See document PAR2176581 accessible at AFP Forum (accessed April 2020), https://www.afpforum.com/AFPForum/Search/Results.aspx?pn=1&smd=8&mui=3&q=3163049804314535789_0&SearchUN=True&fst=PAR2176581&fto=3&cck=a72a9d#pn=1&smd=8&q=8876491078696444937_0&SearchUN=True&fst=PAR2176581&fto=3&mui=3&t=2&cck=a72a9d.

3 The ways in which this difference in the height of the perspectival point of vision signals the differential access to mobility was made acutely visible by Philippe Scheffner in his 2016 film *Havarie*, which visually repurposes a short clip of a migrants' boat shot from the vertiginous heights of a cruise ship.

4 See Del Grande (2008). See the reply of the French authorities (Assemblée National 2008).

5 See the reply of the French authorities (Assemblée National 2008).

6 See the list of migrant deaths at the European borders established by UNITED for Intercultural Action (n.d.).

7 For our reconstruction of these events, see our report on the Forensic Architecture site: https://forensic-architecture.org/investigation/the-left-to-die-boat.

8 The full interview of Dan Haile Gebre is available on the dedicated page on the Forensic Architecture site: https://forensic-architecture.org/investigation/the-left-to-die-boat.

9 For the list of units the Italian Navy deployed in the frame of Mare Nostrum, see Ministero della Difesa (n.d.).
10 See Ministero della Difesa (n.d.).
11 We thank Eyal Weizman for suggesting this formulation.
12 Letter of the European Community Shipowners' Associations (ECSA) and the International Chamber of Shipping (ICS) to the Heads of State/Heads of Government of EU/EEA Member States, March 31, 2015, http://www.ecsa.eu/images/NEW _Position_Papers/2015-03-31%20shipping%20industry%20general%20letter%20 eu%20heads%20of%20state.pdf (last accessed 12 April 2021).
13 See our "Mare Clausum" report (Heller and Pezzani 2018).

References

ANSAmed. 2013. "Immigration: Italy Launches Mare Nostrum, 400 More Saved." October 15. http://www.ansamed.info/ansamed/en/news/sections/generalnews/2013 /10/15/Immigration-Italy-launches-Mare-Nostrum-400-saved_9466386.html.

Basaran, Tugba. 2015. "The Saved and the Drowned: Governing Indifference in the Name of Security." *Security Dialogue* 46 (3): 205–20.

Bojadžijev, Manuela, and Sandro Mezzadra. 2015. "'Refugee Crisis' or Crisis of European Migration Policies?" *Focaal* (blog), November 12. https://www.focaalblog .com/2015/11/12/manuela-bojadzijev-and-sandro-mezzadra-refugee-crisis-or -crisis-of-european-migration-policies/.

Boubakri, Hassan. 2013. "Revolution and International Migration in Tunisia." Migration Policy Centre, Research Report, 2013/04. European University Institute, Robert Schuman Centre for Advanced Studies. https://cadmus.eui .eu/handle/1814/29454.

Calafat, Guillaume. 2019. *Une mer jalousée*. Paris: Le Seuil.

Cassarino, Jean-Pierre. 2013. "Tunisia's New Drivers in Migration Governance." Paper presented at the International Studies Association Conference, San Francisco, CA, April 3–6.

Chouliaraki, Lilie, and Pierluigi Musarò. 2017. "The Mediatized Border: Technologies and Affects of Migrant Reception in the Greek and Italian Borders." *Feminist Media Studies* 17: 26–52.

CIVIPOL. 2003. "Feasibility Study on the Control of the European Union's Maritime Borders." European Commission, April 7. http://www.ifmer.org/assets /documents/files/documents_ifm/st11490-re01en03.pdf.

Clancy-Smith, Julia. 2010. *Mediterraneans: North Africa and Europe in an Age of Migration, c. 1800–1900*. Berkeley: University of California Press.

Cuttitta, Paolo. 2014. "'Borderizing' the Island: Setting and Narratives of the Lampedusa 'Border Play.'" *ACME: An International E-Journal for Critical Geographies* 13 (2): 196–219.

Cuttitta, Paolo. 2018. "Repoliticization through Search and Rescue? Humanitarian NGOs and Migration Management in the Central Mediterranean." *Geopolitics* 23 (3): 632–60.

Dabashi, Hamid. 2012. *The Arab Spring: The End of Postcolonialism*. New York: Zed.

Daily Hansard. 2014. Column WA41. October 15. https://publications.parliament.uk /pa/ld201415/ldhansrd/text/141015w0001.htm.

De Genova, Nicholas. 2013. "Spectacles of Migrant 'Illegality': The Scene of Exclusion, the Obscene of Inclusion." *Ethnic and Racial Studies* 36 (7): 1180–98.

De Haas, Hein. 2008. "The Myth of Invasion: The Inconvenient Realities of Migration from Africa to the European Union." *Third World Quarterly* 29 (17): 1305–22.

Del Grande, Gabriele. 2008. "Lampedusa: Mitra sulle navi francesi di Frontex." *Fortress Europe* (blog), September 27. http://fortresseurope.blogspot.com/2006 /01/lampedusa-mitra-sulle-navi-francesi-di.html.

DPU. 2019. "I 'facinorosi' assolti." *Diritto Penale e Uomo* (blog), June 6. https:// dirittopenaleuomo.org/contributi_dpu/i-facinorosi-assolti/.

Fassin, Didier. 2012. *Humanitarian Reason: A Moral History of the Present*. Berkeley: University of California Press.

Gammeltoft-Hansen, Thomas, and Tanja E. Alberts. 2010. "Sovereignty at Sea: The Law and Politics of Saving Lives in the Mare Liberum." *DIIS Working Paper*, 1–31.

Garelli, Glenda, and Martina Tazzioli. 2018. "The Humanitarian War against Migrant Smugglers at Sea." *Antipode* 50 (3): 685–703.

Grosz, Elizabeth. 2012. "Geopower." *Environment and Planning D: Society and Space* 30: 971–88.

Heller, Charles, Pezzani, Lorenzo, and Situ Research. 2012. "Report on the Left-to-Die Boat." London: Forensic Architecture. https://forensic-architecture.org /investigation/the-left-to-die-boat.

Heller, Charles, and Lorenzo Pezzani. 2016. "Death by Rescue: The Lethal Effects of the EU's Policies of Non-assistance." Death by Rescue. https://deathbyrescue.org/.

Heller, Charles, and Lorenzo Pezzani. 2018. "Mare Clausum: Italy and the EU's Undeclared Operation to Stem Migration across the Mediterranean." Forensic Architecture. https://content.forensic-architecture.org/wp-content/uploads /2019/05/2018-05-07-FO-Mare-Clausum-full-EN.pdf.

Ho, Engseng. 2004. "Empire through Diasporic Eyes: A View from the Other Boat." *Comparative Studies in Society and History* 46: 210–46.

International Organization for Migration. n.d. "Missing Migrants: Tracking Deaths along Migratory Routes." https://missingmigrants.iom.int/.

Juncker, Jean-Claude. 2015. "Speech by President Jean-Claude Juncker at the Debate in the European Parliament on the Conclusions of the Special European Council on 23 April: 'Tackling the Migration Crisis.'" European Commission, April 29. http://europa.eu/rapid/press-release_SPEECH-15 -4896_en.htm.

Keshavarz, Mahmoud, and Eric Snodgrass. 2018. "Orientations of Europe: Boats, the Mediterranean Sea and the Materialities of Contemporary Mobility Regimes." *borderlands* 17 (2).

Le Cour Grandmaison, Olivier. 2008. "Colonisés-immigrés et 'périls migratoires': Origines et permanence du racisme et d'une xénophobie d'etat (1924–2007)." *Cultures et Conflits* 69: 19–32.

Mann, Itamar. 2016. 'Killing by Omission'. *EJIL: Talk!* (blog). 20 April 2016. https://www.ejiltalk.org/killing-by-omission/.

Mezzadra, Sandro. 2017. "Digital Mobility, Logistics, and the Politics of Migration." *Spheres: Journal for Digital Cultures* 4: 1–4.

Mezzadra, Sandro, and Maurice Stierl. 2019. "The Mediterranean Battlefield of Migration." *Open Democracy*, April 12. https://www.opendemocracy.net/en/can-europe-make-it/mediterranean-battlefield-migration/.

Ministère des Armées. n.d. "Arago (P 675)." https://www.defense.gouv.fr/marine/equipements/batiments-de-patrouille-surveillance/patrouilleurs/patrouilleurs/type-arago/arago-p-675.

Ministero della Difesa. n.d. "Mare Nostrum Operation." http://www.marina.difesa.it/EN/operations/Pagine/MareNostrum.aspx.

Monzini, Paola. 2010. *Smuggling of Migrants into, through and from North Africa.* Vienna: United Nations Office on Drugs and Crime.

Monzini, Paola, Ferruccio Pastore, and Giuseppe Sciortino. 2004. "Human Smuggling to/trough [*sic*] Italy." Centro Studi di Politica Internazionale. http://www.cespi.it/en/ricerche/human-smuggling-totrough-italy.

Nevins, Joseph. 2002. *Operation Gatekeeper: The Rise of the "Illegal Alien" and the Making of the U.S.-Mexico Boundary.* New York: Routledge.

Rösler, Klaus. 2014. Letter to Dr. Giovanni Pinto. Frontex, November 25. https://deathbyrescue.org/assets/annexes/6.Frontex_Letter%20to%20Giovanni%20Pinto_25.11.2104.pdf.

Sassen, Saskia. 2002. "A New Cross-Border Field for Public and Private Actors." In *Political Space: Frontiers of Change and Governance in a Globalizing World,* edited by Yale H. Ferguson and R. J. Barry Jones, 173–88. Albany: State University of New York Press.

Sassen, Saskia. 2006. *Territory, Authority, Rights: From Medieval to Global Assemblages.* Princeton, NJ: Princeton University Press.

Senu, Amaha. 2020. "Migration, Seafarers and the Humanitarian-Security-Economic Regimes Complex at Sea." In *Global Challenges in Maritime Security: An Introduction,* edited by Lisa Otto. Cham: Springer.

Sonnino, Antonello De Renzis. 2016. "Operazione Sophia." Informazione della Difesa, April 12. https://www.difesa.it/InformazioniDellaDifesa/Pagine/Operazione_Sophia.aspx?lang=en.

Spinelli, Barbara. 2014. "Alfano richiami Frontex al rispetto dei compiti di salvataggio in mare." *Barbara Spinelli* (blog), December 11. http://barbara-spinelli.it

/2014/12/11/alfano-richiami-frontex-al-rispetto-dei-compiti-di-salvataggio
-mare/.

Steinberg, Philip E. 2001. *The Social Construction of the Ocean*. Cambridge: Cambridge University Press.

Steyerl, Hito. 2013. *The Wretched of the Screen*. Berlin: Sternberg.

Stierl, Maurice. 2018. "A Fleet of Mediterranean Border Humanitarians." *Antipode*
50 (3): 704–24.

Suárez de Vivero, Juan Luis. 2010. *Jurisdictional Waters in the Mediterranean and
Black Seas*. Brussels: European Parliament.

Tazzioli, Martina. 2014. *Spaces of Governmentality, Autonomous Migration and the
Arab Uprisings*. London: Rowman and Littlefield International.

UNITED for Intercultural Action. n.d. "About the 'List of Deaths.'" http://
unitedagainstrefugeedeaths.eu/about-the-campaign/about-the-united-list-of
-deaths/.

United Nations Human Rights. 2014. "Europe/Migrants." Office of the High
Commissioner, October 30. http://www.ohchr.org/EN/NewsEvents/Pages
/DisplayNews.aspx?NewsID=15239&LangID=E.

Vaughn-Williams, Nick. 2015. *Europe's Border Crisis: Biopolitical Security and
Beyond*. Oxford: Oxford University Press.

Walters, William. 2011. "Foucault and Frontiers: Notes on the Birth of the Humanitarian Border." In *Governmentality: Current Issues and Future Challenges*,
edited by Ulrich Bröckling, Susanne Krasmann, and Thomas Lemke, 138–64.
New York: Routledge.

Watch the Med. 2013a. "At Least 366 People Dead in Wreck 1 km from Lampedusa."
October 3. http://watchthemed.net/reports/view/31.

Watch the Med. 2013b. "Over 200 Die after Shooting by Libyan Vessel and Delay in
Rescue." November 29. https://watchthemed.net/reports/view/32.

Weber, Leanne, and Sharon Pickering. 2011. *Globalization and Borders: Death at the
Global Frontier*. London: Palgrave.

World Maritime News. 2014. "ICS: Rescue of All Persons in Distress at Sea."
October 29. http://worldmaritimenews.com/archives/141521/ics-rescue-of-all
-persons-in-distress-at-sea-is-a-must/.

NINE

When the "Via" Is Fragmented and Disrupted: Migrants Walking along the Alpine Route | Glenda Garelli

and Martina Tazzioli

November 22, 2018, at the railway station in Oulx, located in the Alps, on the Italian side of the French-Italian border: since the beginning of 2018 the rail station in the small Italian town has been a crucial junction for migrants who want to cross into France. Outside the railway station, the migrants, who usually arrive equipped with small backpacks, are approached by volunteers who bring them to a temporary shelter, run by a local NGO, where they can stay overnight. From there they start walking along the main road or take the bus to reach the Italian village of Claviere, located two kilometers from the border on a mountaintop. From there, they try to cross into France, walking over the mountains for about six hours and eventually—if they are lucky and are not detected by the French police—reach the French city of Briançon. The Italian police monitor arrivals at the rail station but do not identify or stop migrants. The French police, on the other hand, push migrants back into Italy every single day. In fact, the majority of them end up having to go to Oulx more than once before eventually managing to cross and stay in France.

With the hardening of border controls along the coastal crossing point and on the trains (between the cities of Ventimiglia and Menton) since 2015, many migrants have had to reroute their journey from the coast to the Alps, which means hiking high mountain passes and walking in the snow during the winter. As the Alpine migration route is quite recent in comparison with other migrant crossing points at the Italian-French border (e.g., Ventimiglia on the coast), it has remained relatively marginal in the political debate, despite being a deadly frontier and regularly causing tension between French and Italian authorities.[1] Migrants who decide to try the Alpine route go to Turin, where they take the regional train that heads to Bardonecchia, the Italian outpost at the border. Some of them get off in Oulx; others, instead, reach the final destination, Bardonecchia, by train and then start walking into France up the Col de l'Echelle, a mountain pass that in winter is particularly dangerous and hard to cross.

The Alpine migrant route, we argue, illustrates the forcefully fragmented and decelerated nature of migrant journeys (Collyer 2007, Hess 2012), which include different means of mechanized transport—in this case, trains and buses—and walking long distances. As the vignette above shows, migrants' journeys are also disrupted in the sense that migrants are bounced back from the border and forced to try new routes or to try crossing again and again. The rough pathway to France is the result of capillary border controls and arbitrary pushback operations on the part of the French authorities, who carry out a proper migrant hunt (Chamayou 2012) across the Alps, as well as the extreme weather conditions of the mountain environment. In this context, both the French and Italian authorities are confronted with "migrants' untameable will to cross, irrespective of the snow, something that nobody can actually manage," as one of the volunteers in Oulx put it.[2]

In this chapter, we retrace the opening of the Alpine migration route at the French-Italian border by engaging with the emerging scholarship on viapolitics and mobilizing a particular analytical angle as part of that debate: the practices of migrants' forced walking and the fragmented and disrupted character of these journeys.[3] The chapter proceeds as follows. The first section engages with the emerging debate about migrant viapolitics, bringing attention to the fragmented nature of migrants' journeys and highlighting migrants' practices of walking as a fundamental dimension of viapolitics. The second section illustrates migrants' Alpine route at the French-Italian border, providing an in-depth analysis of the logistics of migrant crossing and of the struggle opened up at that border zone due to migrants' passage. The third section builds on the conditions that characterize migrants' hiking in the Alps to reflect on the shortcomings of various strands of literature on the practice of walking and illuminates the contribution to these conversations that a viapolitical analysis of migrant walking can bring. The fourth section contends that a critical account of migrants' forced walking

Altitudes

4 000 m.
3 000 m.
2 000 m.
1 000 m.

Voies empruntées par les migrant.e.s

Sentiers, chemins, etc.
Autoroutes
Routes
Voies ferrées

Contrôles migratoires de la police et la gendarmerie

dans une zone de la frontière terrestre à une ligne de 20 km

au sein des PPA   hors des points de passage autorisés (PPA)

(auto)routiers

ferroviaires

permanents   non permanents

Principaux espaces frontaliers où ont lieu les non-admissions[1]

1. Une même personne qui tente le passage depuis l'Italie vers la France, peut être arrêtée et reconduite côté italien à plusieurs reprises. En conséquence les chiffres doivent être analysés avec prudence.

Chambery

Grenoble

Gare de Modane 1 991 m
Tunnel de Fréjus 1 228 m

Col de l'Échelle 1 762 m

Briançon

Col de Montgenèvre 1 854 m

Gap

Sisteron

Digne-Les-Bains

La Durance
La Durance

Aix-en-Provence

Marseille

Toulon

Tunnel du Mont Blanc (11 381 m)
Aoste
Col du Petit Saint Bernard (2 188 m)

Col du Mont Cenis 2 081 m

Sestrière

Turin

Col Agnel 2 744 m

Le P.G.

Col de l'Arche 1 991 m

ITALIE

Col de la Lombarde 2 350 m

Col de Tende 1 871 m

Tunnel de Tende 1 371 m

Breil sur Roya

La Roya

FRANCE

Menton

Nice

Antibes

Cannes

Mer Méditerranée

Nombre de non-admissions notifiées depuis les Hautes Alpes[1]
2015 2016 2017

Nombre de non-admissions notifiées depuis les Alpes maritimes[1]
2015 2016 2017

0   25   50 km

Sources : Anafé, 2018 ; CGLPL, 2018 ; Police aux frontières

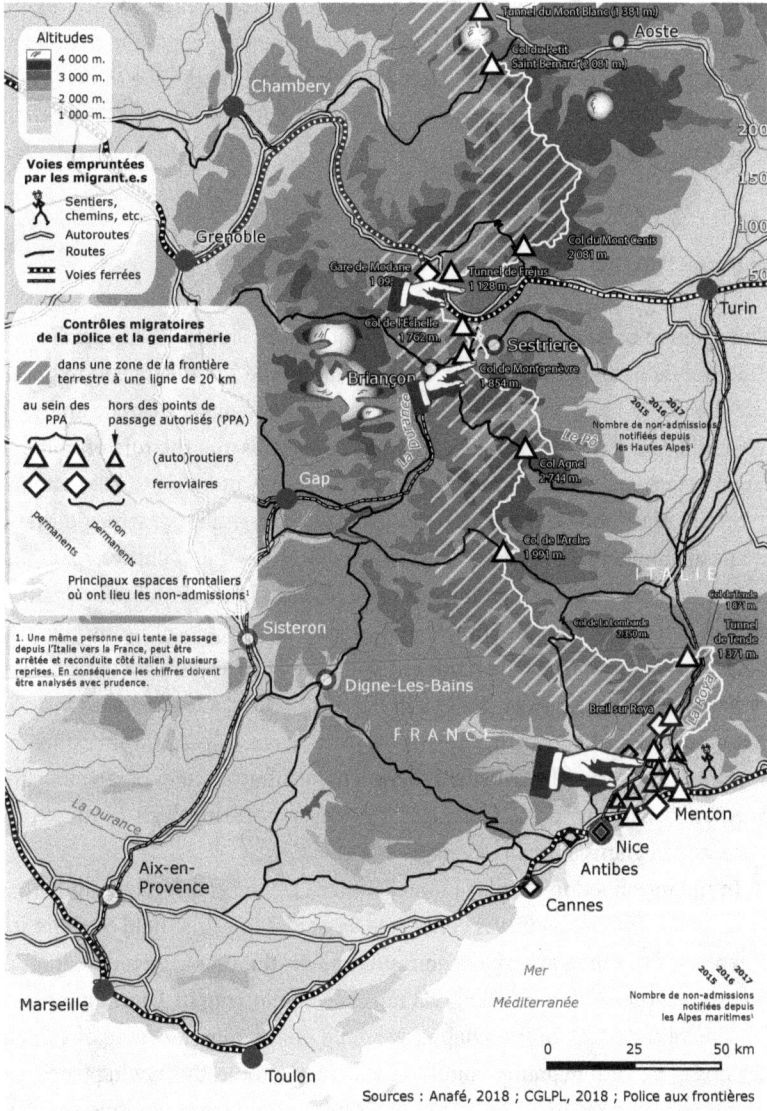

FIGURE 9.1 · Controlled crossings at the Franco-Italian border. Map by Olivier Clochard, in "Persona Non Grata: The Consequences of Security Policies at the Franco-Italian Border," ANAFE, January 2019.

needs to consider the specificity of the practical knowledge about crossing shared among migrants. The final part of the chapter challenges the naturalization of the mountains as a deadly frontier, while at the same time showing how the Italian and French police have transformed the Alpine route into a weaponized terrain for migrants in transit.

Between Fragmented Viapolitics and Forced Walking

The opening of a rough Alpine migrant route at the French-Italian border and the "mobile battlefield" that has emerged along the route between migrants and the actors involved in detecting and pushing them back can be analyzed from different points of view, such as police controls and the role of humanitarian actors and solidarity networks. Here we bring attention to the materiality of migrants' journeys and look at the contested terrain of struggle that it opens up. Building on William Walters's consideration that "vehicles, roads and routes merit a much more prominent place in critical thinking about migration politics" (2015, 471), we are interested in focusing on the conditions migrants experience en route and the fragmented nature of their journeys. The notion of viapolitics introduced by Walters in the same article, and expanded upon in this volume, constitutes a useful analytical tool, we suggest, for investigating migrants' journeys at the crossroads between the infrastructures of traveling, the constantly changing "field of struggles" (Mezzadra 2018) in which crossings take place, and migrants' mobility as such.

In the introduction to this volume, Walters, Heller, and Pezzani argue that, as far as the term *viapolitics* is concerned, *via* has a threefold field of reference: it expresses the time and space en route to a destination, a given medium of communication ("I am traveling via rail"), and, following its Latin etymology, the way or the road). In this chapter we build on the third meaning of viapolitics, engaging with migrants' condition of being en route, by drawing particular attention to the practices of hiking the Alps and interrogating how they are part of the broader fragmented, disjointed economy of migrant journeys. As we illustrate later in the chapter, the migrant Alpine route foregrounds some limits of an exclusive focus on means of transport and on the road as a spatial referent. In fact, an insight into the assemblages between practices of walking and means of transport—in our case, the bus and the regional train—highlights the fundamentally disrupted nature of traveling; and, most importantly, it highlights that means of transport also work as infrastructural obstacles to migrants' mobility. Or, better, it illustrates that trains and buses are used by the authorities for disrupting migrants' journeys—that is, identifying migrants on public transport, forcing them to get off even when they travel with regular tickets, and using local buses and trains to push them away from the border.

An engagement with migrants' viapolitics involves taking the scholarly debate around infrastructures into account. However, what does infrastructure mean in relation to migrants' mobility? In their seminal article, "Migration Infrastructure," Biao Xiang and Johan Lindquist refer to infrastructures as "the systematically interlinked technologies, institutions and actors that facilitate and condition mobility" (2014, 122; see also chapter 5, this volume). Work on migration and infrastructures enables taking stock of migrants' nonlinear geographies and of the mediations that are at play in the economy of migrants' mobility, and stressing that migrants not only move but are also moved (Cranston, Schapendonk, and Spaan 2018; Hiemstra 2013; Conlon, Moran, and Gill 2016; Xiang and Lindquist 2018). In particular, as William Walters has compellingly shown, a focus on the infrastructures of mobility allows researchers to undermine a state-centric approach to migration and reorient attention toward the governing and the knowledge of migration routes. Referring to the notion of deportation infrastructure, Walters argues in fact that "this challenges the ingression bias: the tendency to equate border regimes with mechanisms and spaces that are oriented to the anticipation, policing, and prevention of migratory movements *towards* the territories of the global North" (2018, 2814, emphasis in original; see also Casas-Cortes, Cobarrubias, and Pickles 2015).

Yet, in the pages that follow, we show that, first, such a literature is not sufficient to capture the fundamental disruptiveness in which migrants' mobility takes place, where forced walking plays a central role. More broadly, means of transport and infrastructures are used not only for facilitating mobility but also for obstructing, deviating, and decelerating the mobility of some. Second, we suggest that more attention should be paid to how migrants' desires and subjective drives intertwine with their experiences of journeying and influence the viapolitics of migration. The growing scholarship on migration and logistics enables exploring how infrastructures of circulation contain and channel both migration, on the one hand, and the persistent excess of migrants' movements and subjective drives with respect to border controls, on the other. For instance, Moritz Altenried and colleagues (2018, 294) highlighted that "the widespread use of logistical terminology—hot spots, hubs, platforms, corridors" is used "to establish a new geography and, in a way, a new rationality of migration management" that could channel "turbulent, unpredictable, and autonomous movements of mass migration" (see also Mezzadra and Neilson 2013; chapter 7, this volume). Similarly, Charmaine Chua and colleagues have pointed to counterlogistics movements that "interrupt the circulation of violence" and that, beyond disruption, also aim at "forging new solidarities and new modes of political engagements" (2018, 623–25).

Going back to viapolitics, we argue that both the dimension of circulation and that of infrastructure should be radically questioned in light of migrants' disrupted and fragmented journeys and, in particular, as we show in the next section, in light of migrants' forced walking practices. In his lecture series *Security, Territory, Population*, Michel Foucault has notably pointed to the crucial role of circulation in the so-called dispositifs of security, hence positing circulation as an element that was constitutive of governmentality in the eighteenth century: "The problem was circulation, that is to say, for the town to be a perfect agent of circulation. . . . It is simply a matter of maximizing the positive elements, for which one provides the best possible circulation, and of minimizing what is risky and inconvenient" (2007, 17–19). That is, circulation was at the same time managed and fostered, according to Foucault, in French towns of the eighteenth century. Foucault's considerations on the nexus between circulation, security, and biopower represent, we suggest, a significant reference for the debate on viapolitics, since he hints at the centrality of transport and infrastructural networks for making goods and people move. Many scholarly debates draw on Foucault's point about circulation, in particular in the field of political geography and mobility studies: the "spatial logic of security" (Klauser 2013, 99) would not be possible without a network of infrastructures of circulation (Bærenholdt 2013; Gill 2016).

However, for the purpose of this chapter, two things should be noted about Foucault's account of circulation. First, at a close glance, Foucault's focus on circulation is not followed by a similar in-depth insight into the infrastructures that make circulation possible. Second, as Foucault stresses, with security apparatuses it was "a matter of organizing circulation, eliminating its dangerous elements, making a division between good and bad circulation" (2007, 18). While hinting at this division in *Security, Territory, Population*, Foucault does not, however, develop an analysis of "bad circulation" and of the way in which the unruly and "bad" elements are managed; rather, he mainly draws attention to the good circulation, or, better, to the enhancement and channeling of circulation that can be productively incorporated and regulated through security apparatuses. For an analysis of "bad circulation," we have to turn to the earlier lecture series *The Punitive Society* (1972–73). There Foucault (2016, 163) engaged more closely with "bad circulation," dealing with the processes of criminalization of unruly mobility in the modern capitalist society, and highlighting the historical connections between the moralization of undisciplined conducts, labor force, and mobility controls.[4] In particular, in *The Punitive Society* Foucault focused on the criminalization of "popular illegalism" as conduct that at some point appeared to be incompatible with the economic interests of the emerging bourgeoisie.

Foucault's analysis of the governing of criminalized mobility could be used as an analytical grid for elaborating on what we could call the countergeographies of security apparatuses. Indeed, an insight into migrants' fragmented and disrupted journeys highlights how state authorities engage in obstructing migrants' mobility. At the same time, the countergeography of security apparatuses is also formed by migrants enacting tactics of mobility that involve using means of transport without being detected by the police, or avoiding these and walking instead.

In this regard, we suggest that an analysis of migrants' viapolitics, and of what we called elsewhere "logistics of migrants' crossing" (Garelli and Tazzioli 2018a, 2018b), should not take the dimension of circulation for granted. Rather, it requires addressing what Claudia Aradau and Tobias Blanke called "the political effects of securing circulation" (2010, 3). In other words, as the focus on the Alpine migration route shows, an analysis of migrants' viapolitics should start from the exclusionary and differential functioning of circulation and, more precisely, from the measures and tactics deployed by states for disrupting migrants' mobility.

The Alpine Migration Route

"The south Alpine border," Cristina Del Biaggio argues, "constitutes a new 'inner rim' dividing the south of the Alps from the north" (n.d., 4). We could expand on that, contending that such an inner rim actually divides migrants' imagination of Europe seen from Italy, as the Europe they aspire to is located beyond Italy, past that Alpine rim. Since October 2018, the number of migrants trying to cross into France has increased, according to estimates by local authorities in the Susa Valley.[5] This increase, they argue, was a response to the Security Decree enforced by the Italian government that drastically reduced legal guarantees for migrants and refugees in the country, effectively resulting in thousands of migrants being expelled from different housing structures (Matamoros 2018).

The cities of Oulx, Bardonecchia, and Claviere in the Susa Valley constitute the Italian outposts and at the same time the main signposts on the map for migrants who, coming by train from Turin, head toward Briançon, an Alpine French city located about twenty kilometers beyond the border. The Alpine passage has remained relatively invisible in the political debate in comparison with others along different routes, despite the muscular border enforcement on the French side. In March 2018, a group of activists and locals occupied a room inside the church in Claviere to offer temporary shelter to migrants in transit. They named it Chez Jesus (Jesus's place). Since the local priest opposed the occupation, they ironically and strategically played with the condition of being in a church, which, according to the law, is a space of sanctuary. For months, the presence of Alpine guides, activists, and locals at Chez Jesus was a fundamental logistical support for migrants in transit. Chez Jesus provided not only a space to stay but also a source of what we could call countermapping tips for fellow migrants about how to cross without getting lost while avoiding getting caught by the French police before reaching the city of Briançon. In fact, if we can speak of migrants' viapolitics in such a context, it is remarkable that their practices of walking and use of means of transport cannot be separated from the precarious and mobile infrastructures of support provided by this heterogeneous network of citizens. In some cases, migrants have also been helped in crossing, in particular through the support of members of the Italian and the French Alpine Rescue, which is in charge of rescuing people who find themselves in danger in the mountains (Darnault 2017; Tazzioli and Walters 2019). Notably, in December 2017 some French Alpine guides addressed a letter to the French president, Emmanuel Macron, pointing to the extreme risks that migrants run in crossing the Alps.[6]

In most cases, the support given by locals and activists at Chez Jesus consisted of a more indirect, but no less fundamental, network of support— including both mobile infrastructures and shared practical knowledge, such as cartographic tips about how and where to cross. Between March and September 2018, Chez Jesus worked as a crucial safe space in migrants' geographies. That is, it was incorporated into migrants' shared knowledge. Chez Jesus was a place where migrants could take a rest and also carefully view the videos made by other migrants about how and where to cross, as well as study the maps of the mountain paths that activists illustrated for them. In a context like Chez Jesus, migrants' viapolitics is situated within a broader economy of unstable "mobile commons" (Trimikliniotis, Parsanoglou, and Tsianos 2015; see also Papadopoulos and Tsianos 2013) formed by the intertwining of migrants' practices of walking, practical knowledge shared between migrants and locals, infrastructures of support, and countermapping practices.

From the village of Claviere, it takes migrants between five and six hours on foot, on average, to reach the French city of Briançon. Far from being a smooth road for migrants in transit, the Alpine crossing turns out to be an extremely rough path. Indeed, in order not to be spotted by the French police, migrants cannot follow the cross-country skiing path used by locals and tourists, which smoothly twists and turns through the forest. Instead migrants are forced to undertake multiple diversions and reroutings, which result in their getting lost in the mountains and taking life-threatening risks in snowy weather conditions or having to orient themselves in a snow-covered landscape.

In light of these conditions, migrants spend a lot of time walking, starting from when they leave Claviere. In most cases they are forced to return to Claviere more than once, as they are pushed back by the French authorities multiple times before eventually managing to reach Briançon. In fact, the village of Claviere is not only a transit point in migrants' geographies but also a place of temporary forced return: "This morning I had to walk back from the border for the third time in two days; the first two times the French police fingerprinted me and gave me a paper [expulsion order]. This time I have been spotted at night, and they just pushed me back, and I had to walk to come to Chez Jesus again."[7] This testimony of a Sudanese citizen that we met outside the church in Claviere illustrates well that migrants' routes across the Alps are characterized not only by extenuating and rough walking distances but also by migrants undertaking the same route or similar routes multiple times through that Alpine crossing point. The violent eviction of Chez Jesus on October 10, 2018, forced the migrants in transit to reinvent their logistics of crossing: to date they have to stop in the city of Oulx, which is located seventeen kilometers farther down, as there is no longer a shelter in Claviere. Even in this case, the reorganization of migrants' logistics of crossing involved the participation of diverse local actors, despite frictions and conflicts. At the end of October 2018, the municipality of Oulx authorized a local NGO, Talita Kum, to use a room next to the rail station to host the migrants in transit at night and to equip them with appropriate clothes.

The alternative to the Alpine route through Claviere for migrants who want to cross to France starts in the city of Bardonecchia, the final destination of the regional train from Turin. As soon as migrants get off the train, they are monitored by the local police. However, this does not hamper their movements. "The migrants who arrive here wish they were invisible. They try not to be spotted, as their goal is to move on to the border. They are a sort of *silent and uneven flow*."[8] The mayor of Bardonecchia is describing the peculiar nexus between the production of (in)visibility and migrants' logistics of crossing the Alps. In fact, despite migrants' sheer bodily presence in the streets of Bardonecchia and Oulx, no "border spectacle" (De Genova 2013) has been staged until now, neither by citizenry nor by local authorities. The partial invisibilization of migrants' passages makes of the Alpine frontier a quite different border zone from places like Ventimiglia or Lampedusa that instead constitute the spatial landmarks of what states named Europe's "refugee crisis"—a crisis characterized by hypervisibility and by governing through emergency (Tazzioli 2018a).[9] Nevertheless, the partial invisibilization of migrants walking from Bardonecchia to France and the relative lack of controls along the road on the Italian side of the border does not mean at all that migrants can cross easily. On the contrary, the walking path to the Col de l'Echelle can be highly dangerous in winter, due to weather conditions, and it requires proper alpine skills and equipment to hike that mountain. In four hours migrants can reach the border if they do not get lost, which happens quite often, and from there, if they manage to cross, they start the long descent toward the village of Nevache. But the weaponization of the Alpine crossing space is actually only in part the result of weather and environmental conditions. In fact, at the top of the pass the French police patrols the border, and on many occasions it has been supported by fascist volunteers from the group Generation Identitaire.

However, such a focus on contemporary migration should not lead us to conclude that the Alpine passage is not a new frontier and space of struggle. Or, better, while it is definitely a quite recent one for the migrants who have been trying to cross to France, the Alpine passage has a much longer history. In particular, the Susa Valley has been a space of refuge and transit for partisans who struggled for the liberation of Italy in the 1940s; then, in the 1970s, locals from the Susa Valley opposed the construction of infrastructure, and since the 1990s the valley has notably become the site of the NoTav political movement against a high-speed train. Accounting for such a temporal thickness of the frontier enables us to retrace its transformations over time and to highlight how that frontier has also been at the same time a space of struggle and solidarity practices (see Tazzioli and Walters 2019). Indeed, the abovementioned space of refuge that opened up in Claviere and the multiplication of migrant solidarity networks in the valley should be analyzed in light of the political memory of previous struggles that has been reactivated in the present.

A Viapolitics of Walking

By engaging viapolitics from the angle of migrant walking, we have two aims. First, we want to bring a critical geography emphasis on the via, the path that migrants have to undertake to move themselves to their aspired destination in the political and social context of different European crises, including the political crisis of international protection and hospitality. In other words, we take the expression "making your way to" literally and materially, by looking at how migrants who enter Europe through Italy have to walk their way to the place they imagine as a possible and desirable home, on the other side of the Alpine curtain. Second, our goal is to frame migrants' hiking path through the Alps within the migration politics that produces the challenging landscape of mountain crests as the only way to a desired home for migrants, and walking (hiking the Alps) as the only means of movement allowed to migrants who hope to get all the way to their destination. Within this framework, the angle of viapolitics allows us to shed light on some of the shortcomings of the literatures on walking developed in different disciplines by bringing to the center of the debate what, drawing from Peter Nyers's (2003) work on migrant cosmopolitanism, we could term the *abject ambulatory paths* of migrants' forced mobility.

Let us clarify the two meanings that the term *forced mobility* here covers for us. On the one hand, we refer to an approach to containing migration that works by imposing further mobilities on migrants. As we showed elsewhere (Tazzioli and Garelli 2018), the European border regime increasingly deploys a twofold containment approach that combines a variegated infrastructure of choke points (aimed at disrupting migrants' autonomous movement) with an informal but nonetheless persistent politics of keeping migrants on the move, a politics that enforces a perennial transience that exhausts migrants' bodies and resources, finally hampering their ability to accomplish their journey. The Alpine scene of migrant hiking is a viapolitical enactment of this way of governing migrants by forcing their mobility: it routes migrants' journey from Italy to France through the risky landscape of the Alps and imposes hiking as the means of crossing the Italy-France border.

Moreover, by rerouting migrants' journey to France onto the challenging Alpine path, this politics decelerates the pace of border crossing. As Joseph Nevins shows, slower means of transport equal greater risks: slowing migrants down is an approach to governing migrant flows and shows the "uneven distribution of the speeds of life and death as they relate to mobility" (2018, 33, 40). However, speed is not the main point we want to stress here: migrants are not only decelerated in their crossing, but, more importantly, they are forced to undertake convoluted routes, to multiply their movements in the attempt to cross the border, and finally to undertake more dangerous journeys. Moreover, what it takes for migrants to cross into France along the imposed Alpine path is a relentless capacity to be on the move yet again—after getting lost, being hampered by weather conditions, and being spotted and chased away by police forces patrolling the mountainous French border. Following migrants' hiking in the Alps, in other words, means "riding the routes" migrants are forcefully channeled through and studying the permutations of the "itinerant borders" (Casas-Cortes, Cobarrubias, and Pickles 2015) that keep following them across valleys and mountains (see also chapter 6, this volume).

The substantive literature that the practice of walking has given rise to in the social sciences and humanities is of little help in analyzing the viapolitics of migrants' walking. For as variegated as this literature is, when it is approached from the vantage point of migrants in the Alps, it looks like it proposes a homogeneous and rigid canon, where what we call in this chapter the abject ambulatory paths of migrants seem completely out of place—a sign, maybe, that viapolitics may bring a fundamental contribution to the literature on walking, by engaging with the political materiality that dramatically changes the defining characters of walking in terms of who is walking, in which conditions, along which path, and based on whose decision. The romantic ambulatory culture that has dominated different disciplinary conversations (e.g., Berman 1988; Careri 2002; de Certeau 1984), in fact, tends to give a homogenous portrayal of the walker: an adventurous and exploratory hero who deliberately engages with a peripatetic, unpredictable, and self-directed *flânerie* across a (mainly) urban landscape—a landscape that is instead planned to direct movement across space in controlled and standardized ways (Cresswell 2010, 20).

This portrayal starkly contrasts with the migrant walker, a subject who is forced to walk (and even hike), who is routed away from the city and its urban infrastructure, and, most importantly, a subject who is enduring—but certainly not decadently enjoying—the deceleration of his or her mobility and the unpredictability of the path that hiking in the mountains (and even mountains patrolled by border guards) imposes (on the experience of walking in the context of US forced mobility, see also chapter 1, this volume). Moreover, while these literatures portray the walker as a rebellious subject staging a peripatetic practice against the oppressive and/or capitalist ordering of the city space, they don't engage with a study of walking in terms of power relations. The romanticization of the walker-hero, in fact, posits walking as an exodus (albeit rebellious) from the power struggles that spatial orders ingrain into any particular territory. Migrants' Alpine hiking can't even begin to be understood if we ignore the power relations that forced migrants to take this path in the first place and the fact that their walking is inextricably bound to the survival and organizing strategies they have to improvise in order to survive the police chase to stop their hike to France.

We may need to look elsewhere to find some anchors for studying the viapolitics of migrant walking. Historically, for instance, it is probably helpful to look back in time—certainly before Romanticism praised walking as a virtuous experience, that end in itself that stood as the mobility referent to Romantic poetry and philosophy. Before Romanticism, in fact, "the actual process of travel, especially on foot, was considered a drudge—literally a *travail*—that had to be endured for the sole purpose of reaching a destination" (Ingold 2004, 321). This certainly resonates with migrants' forced hikes: a goal-oriented, burdensome, risky activity—certainly not an enjoyable stroll. The association of leisure with walking (at least in the Western imaginary these literatures on walking mainly draw from) is in fact a nineteenth-century Romantic addition, as Ingold (2004, 322) remarks. Before then, he adds, walking was disregarded as the mobility practice of the poor or the criminal. Here we see some useful parallels with migrant hiking in the Alps: the forced hiking migrants have to endure along the Alpine path, in fact, is a testimony to the unequal distribution of the freedom to move across Europe and of the exclusion of migrants and refugees from legal, safe, and direct ways for crossing borders and reaching their destinations.

Another interesting indication on how to further the scholarly conversation about walking in light of migrants' forced hiking comes from disability studies. Here walking is critiqued and assessed as a normative imaginary where the practice of walking is embodied in the stereotype of the masculine, abled body (Taylor 2009; Oliver 1996.). Thinking about these important contributions, we want to suggest that a viapolitics of migrant walking helps us break out of the one-sided typology of the white, self-indulgent, male citizen strolling through a twentieth-century Euro-Atlantic city as the paradigmatic figure of the walker.

The Unevenness of Migrants' Shared Knowledge Chain

Migrants' viapolitics is not formed only by infrastructures, means of transport, and struggles. It is also constituted by the circulation of practical knowledges among migrants themselves and, as we illustrated above, between locals and migrants. The long and rough walking distances, the dangers and risks along the route, and the exhausting pushbacks that force migrants to undertake the same route multiple times have become part of a collective memory shared by migrants in transit. How do migrants orient themselves across the Alps? And how do they know where they can stop and transit through without being in danger? As one local in Bardonecchia significantly put it in December 2018, "We do not know why, but, in comparison to last year, now there are by far less migrants who try to cross from Bardonecchia through the Col de l'Echelle. The majority tries via Oulx-Claviere. This is perhaps because migrants started to spread the news that here it is dangerous when it snows, unlike in the summer."[10] That is, due to the extreme weather conditions and the highly risky route on the Col de l'Echelle that many experienced in the winter of 2018, Bardonecchia became quite a dangerous spot on the virtual map that migrants share by circulating information and personal stories about logistics, feasibility, and risks that concern their journeys.

Most of this shared knowledge consists of detailed practical information about how to move, about the means of transport that should be used, about where to stop and where not to go. As part of that, migrants also share the average walking time needed to cross the Alps and reach the French city of Briançon. Smartphones and mobile phones in general are of course fundamental for generating what we call migrants' knowledge chain; relatedly, migrants' use of Google Maps and of Mapme is widespread also along the Alpine route, where migrants download the map before they start walking (Garelli and Tazzioli 2018c; Gillespie, Osseiran, and Cheesman 2018; Latonero and Kift 2018). Thus, connectivity and mapping constitute the digital backbone of the logistics of migrant crossing and, at the same time, of the production of migrants' shared knowledge. However, the role of digital technologies should not be overstated. Nor should technologies be considered as the exclusive way through which migrants share knowledge about the logistics of journeys. In fact, as we realized in conversations with migrants in transit across the Alps and elsewhere (for instance, in Ventimiglia), in many cases information is shared by word of mouth: many hear bits of information from other migrants inside the reception centers about the Alpine route, and particularly when they arrive in Turin, they are able to gather more detailed information, in particular in the area of the main rail station.

Such a chain of migrants' knowledge is by no means a smooth flow of information. On the contrary, it is characterized by a series of interruptions, disconnections, and fragmentations. These depend on connectivity or service problems, police monitoring, and the quick transformation of border control tactics, which are adapted by the authorities on the basis of new migrants. In this sense, the chain of knowledge and the virtual map that migrants generate turns out to be quite disjointed. In this regard it is worth stressing that if migrants share knowledge, this does not necessarily mean that this knowledge is always accurate or even helpful. On this point, the Alpine environment considerably alters migrants' practical knowledge, in particular as far as walking conditions and feasibility are concerned: indeed, what is valid on flat landscapes (in terms of risks, walking distances, and time and equipment needed) does not apply in the same way on the mountain. For instance, at the rail station in Bardonecchia, migrants often count on a short distance to reach the French border, as shown on the map—about six kilometers.

However, on mountainous terrain and particularly during the winter, such a short distance requires many more hours of hiking than on flat terrain, and also requires the use of technical equipment. Moreover, the knowledge shared to support migrants' hiking is rendered unstable: continually changing police enforcement strategies, in fact, often force migrants to walk at night and to reroute their path unexpectedly. French authorities' tactics of mountain border enforcement have an adverse impact on the knowledge of the path that migrants can count on. In fact, the fundamental knowledge that migrants, activists, and locals share to support those who want to attempt the hike to France can't possibly incorporate the element of police patrolling, with its tactical changes of location, approach, and enforcement technique. It is important to underscore that it is this politics of terrain—the patrolling of the Alps as a border, the changing police strategies aimed at stopping migrants before they cross into France—that turns the Alps' weather conditions and geo-atmospheric features into potentially lethal terrain. Local authorities and politicians insist that it is important to dissuade migrants from attempting the crossing because the Alps are a dangerous landscape. However, the transformations that weather conditions like blizzards, rainstorms, and thaws ingrain on the terrain are not lethal per se. They have, in fact, very often been successfully faced precisely thanks to the maps, videos, and pictures that migrants have been able to rely on through the shared knowledge chain described in this section. As one of the occupants of Chez Jesus put it: "The mountains are not the problem, the snow is not an emergency. The problem is the border that forces these migrants to cross from here and in these conditions" (interview quoted in Tazzioli 2018a).

We should also consider that it is not even just a question of lack of adequate knowledge of the particular hiking conditions. Rather, migrants' journey experiences and desires contribute to craft their cartography of crossing as well as to enhance their resolution to cross into France: "We crossed the Sahara desert and we made it through the Mediterranean Sea. These mountains won't stop us, or at least we are almost there—we cannot but try."[11]

To some extent, this constantly interrupted chain of knowledge echoes the fragmented logistics of crossing that we described above. Therefore, as this section has shown, an analysis of migrants' viapolitics requires grappling with the production and the circulation of migrants' practical knowledge. The latter gives rise to a sort of *virtual shared map* of migrants' logistics of crossing. As we mentioned above, migrants' walking across the Alps is supported, directly and indirectly, by a network of local people, NGOs, and activists. Such support is not only logistical or humanitarian (e.g., giving food, clothes, and temporary shelter to migrants in transit) but also consists in the practical information and mountain expertise that locals have acquired and that, in part, they share with the migrants (e.g., practical advice about the sudden changes of the weather). Plus, a sort of virtual infrastructure of communication was recently put in place among the different actors involved in supporting and monitoring migrants' passages in the Susa Valley: the municipalities, the local Red Cross, and the two NGOs that are currently operating in Oulx and Bardonecchia activated a WhatsApp group chat through which they constantly exchange information about the migrants who are pushed back at the border, those who got lost, and those who sleep in the temporary shelters. Therefore, in speaking of migrants' shared knowledge, we should consider multiple layers: migrants' disrupted chain of knowledge, consisting of information shared among migrants themselves via digital technologies and through word of mouth; migrants' virtual maps, formed by the articulation of the information provided by locals and activists with the knowledge shared among migrants about safe places to stop and unsafe passages; and the virtual infrastructure of knowledge about the migrants, for supporting but also for monitoring them, a knowledge that is generated through cooperation among different local actors.

Mountainous Weapons for Migration Containment

May 2018, Durance River, high Alps, French-Italian border: the body of a young woman is found dead at the Pellers dam, ten kilometers south of Briançon. It is the body of a Nigerian woman who—according to the activists from Chez Jesus who had assisted her days before—slipped into the river after she had to abandon the group she was walking with to run away from the French police, which engaged that night in one of their raids to spot migrants trying to cross into France and push them back to Italy (CarovaneMigranti 2018). After surviving the many dangerous crossings visa policies force migrants to undertake (Albahari 2015; Carling 2007; Ferrer-Gallardo and van Houtum 2014), it was on the Alpine heights that this young woman lost her life. The Sahara Desert, the Mediterranean Sea, and finally the Alps were the enforced dangers this person had to face in order to reach France, the place where she wanted to move.

Migration containment—an ultimate containment in the case of border deaths like the one just described—works also by channeling mobility across dangerous landscapes, with no other tool left to migrants to confront them but their bodies. In fact, migrants' physical exhaustion (and even death) is not caused by the landscape itself (see introduction, this volume). It is not the snow, the altitude, or temperatures that turn the Alps into a life-threatening frontier for migrants. It is important to denaturalize the landscape as we discuss the viapolitics that characterize migrants' pedestrian crossing of the Alpine landscape. The naturalization of the terrain has always represented a tool for political domination—in colonial empires, in development programs, in racial stereotyping, and in migration policies where some or all of these elements are at play. The naturalization of the Alps as an arduous terrain for migrants' crossings (and fatalities) demands critical attention exactly in relation to the politics of mobility it underpins—a politics of attrition (Theodore 2011) against the mobility of migrants across Europe, the politics that forcefully routes migrants along a via (a path, i.e., the Alpine route) that highly restricts their chances of succeeding. The Alpine route could easily become a safe passage for migrants, as the work of volunteers and activists supporting migrants in the Alpine valleys suggests.

Quoting Stuart Elden, we could say that what makes the Alpine route so arduous for migrants is the "relation between the geophysical and the geopolitical" (2017, 9) that is enacted in this mountainous landscape. The geophysical challenges the Alps pose to someone on foot, in fact, highly depend on the ways in which that person's mobility is regulated—catered to or obstructed, facilitated or impeded—as the dichotomous cases of the tourist and migrant hiker clearly show. It is literally the geopolitics of migration that turns the Alps into an attrition tool for the particular group of forced hikers that migrants end up being in the Alps at this particular time. In fact, migrants are forcefully channeled through the Alps and obliged to zig-zag across a hostile landscape because safer, smoother, and more direct routes of mobility from Italy to France are closed to them.

"The desert and rocky terrain," continues Elden in the article cited above about the US-Mexico border, "becomes part of the border, itself a weapon against migration, in a similar way to how Frontex has effectively turned the Mediterranean into Europe's southern border" (2017, 10). The viapolitics of migrants' forced walking on the Alpine route is rooted in this weaponization of the migratory path, of the via, and in the geopolitics that force migrants to improvise themselves as inexperienced, underequipped mountain hikers. Therefore, if on the one hand it is true that, as Geoffrey Boyce (2016) noticed, rugged landscapes limit and disrupt state surveillance operations, on the other hand, attention should be paid to how terrain itself is shaped and turned into a weapon against the migrants (see also introduction, this volume).

Conclusion

The fragmented nature of migration geographies is particularly glaring along the Alpine route. Indeed, the weaponization of the migratory path at the Alpine border is enacted there through the assemblages of police tactics—which involve a sort of migrant hunt, turning migrant bodies into mobile microtargets (Chamayou 2012) across the mountains—environmental barriers, and repeated border pushbacks to obstruct, decelerate, and deter migrants' passage. Migrants' walking along the Alpine route illuminates the rough and convoluted routes that migrants must take to get to their destinations. In this respect, this chapter has argued for the need to politicize migrants' abject walking as part of an inquiry on migrant viapolitics. In particular, through a focus on the obstructed migrant passages at the Alpine French-Italian border, this chapter has revolved around two elements that materially underpin the viapolitics of migration. First, we have drawn attention to the knowledge that is shared among migrants and between migrants and activists, and which gives rise to a sort of virtual map, which includes the temporary safe shelters where migrants can stop, places to avoid, and information about the journey. Such practical knowledge is, however, highly uneven and fragmented, due to the constant reorganization of police tactics, the criminalization of migrant solidarity networks, and the technical difficulties in sharing updated information in real time (information that covers the changes both in environmental conditions and border control tactics). Second, we have highlighted migrants' "incorrigibility" (De Genova 2010) and resolution in crossing to France, showing how migrants' subjective drive troubles the cartography of border control and of humanitarianism: migrants try to cross, sometimes refusing to stay in a safe shelter, and their determination to make it can never be fully calculated by police tactics. In fact, as Nicholas De Genova

(2016, 50) put it, "The autonomy and subjectivity of human mobility always instigates the reaction formations of bordering that convert particular forms of human mobility into the bordered social formations that we come to know (only retrospectively) as 'migration.'" In bringing attention to the weaponization of the environment, we should caution, however, about not corroborating state authorities' narrative about the Alps as a dangerous place for migrants in transit (a narrative that justifies the necessity to stop migrants from undertaking the Alpine route based on weather and environmental conditions; see e.g., Rocci and Ricca 2017). The threat that mountains pose to migrants is, to a large extent, the outcome of mountains being turned into the frontier that migrants in transit to France are forcefully channeled through.

Notes

1 While the total number of migrants who have lost their lives at the Alpine border remains unknown, Médecins sans Frontières (2017) reported they were aware of twenty migrant deaths in 2017 in the Alps.

2 Interview with local volunteers who manage the temporary shelter in Oulx, November 22, 2018.

3 We engage with the debate about the politics of migrant walking from the angle of forced walking (i.e., the Alpine hiking paths imposed on migrants by the EU border regime). For the angle of practices of freedom and claim making associated with migrant marches, see, e.g., chapter 7, this volume). The empirical material presented here is the result of fieldwork in Oulx, Bardonecchia, and Claviere conducted in March, July, and November 2018, including interviews with the mayors of Bardonecchia and Oulx, the priest of Bussoleno, two local NGOs and doctors, some NoTav activists, and some of the migrants in transit.

4 "Now, the circulation of individuals around wealth is still feared, but moral [nomadism] is equally feared" (Foucault, 2016, 163).

5 The increase in crossing the Susa Valley marks a rerouting of migrants' crossing away from the coast inland, with a prominence of crossing points in the Alps where train stations are (e.g., Bardonecchia, Chiasso, Como, Trieste).

6 "Migrants: Lettre ouverte au Président de la République," change.org, accessed July 6, 2021, https://www.change.org/p/migrants-lettre-ouverte-au-pr%C3%A9sident-de-la-r%C3%A9publique.

7 Interview with S., a Sudanese migrant, met outside the Claviere church, July 19, 2018.

8 Interview with the mayor of Bardonecchia, November 23, 2018.

9 On the coexistence of hypervisible border zones and invisibilized ephemeral spaces, see the collective mapping project Europe's Migrant Spaces (Tazzioli 2018b).

10 Interview with S. M., a citizen of Bardonecchia, who has mobilized, together with others, to support migrants in transit, November 22, 2018.

11 Interview with two Sudanese migrants outside the rail station in Bardonecchia, March 29, 2018.

References

Albahari, Maurizio. 2015. *Crimes of Peace: Mediterranean Migrations at the World's Deadliest Border*. Philadelphia: University of Pennsylvania Press.

Altenried, Moritz, Manuela Bojadžijev, Leif Höfler, Sandro Mezzadra, and Mira Wallis. 2018. "Logistical Borderscapes: Politics and Mediation of Mobile Labor in Germany after the 'Summer of Migration.'" *South Atlantic Quarterly* 117 (2): 291–312.

Aradau, Claudia, and Tobias Blanke. 2010. "Governing Circulation: A Critique of the Biopolitics of Security." In *Security and Global Governmentality: Globalization, Governance and the State*, edited by Miguel de Larrinaga and Marc Doucet, 44–58. London: Routledge.

Bærenholdt, Jorgen. 2013. "Governmobility: The Powers of Mobility." *Mobilities* 8 (1): 20–34.

Berman, Marshall. 1988. *All That Is Solid Melts into Air: The Experience of Modernity*. Harmondsworth, UK: Penguin.

Boyce, Geoffrey. 2016. "The Rugged Border: Surveillance, Policing and the Dynamic Materiality of the US/Mexico Frontier." *Environment and Planning D: Society and Space* 34 (2): 245–62.

Careri, Francesco. 2002. *Walkscapes: Walking as an Aesthetic Practice*. Barcelona: Gustavo Gili.

CarovaneMigranti. 2018. "Frontiera Italo Francese del Monginevro: Cronache di una Morte Annunciata." Facebook, May 15. https://www.facebook .com/carovanemigranti/posts/il-comunicato-di-chez-jesus-rifugio -autogestitoclavierefrontiera-italo-francese-/1272966476180346/.

Carling, Jorgen. 2007. "Migration Control and Migrant Fatalities at the Spanish-African Borders." *International Migration Review* 41 (2): 316–43.

Casas-Cortes, Maribel, Sebastian Cobarrubias, and John Pickles. 2015. "Riding Routes and Itinerant Borders: Autonomy of Migration and Border External-ization." *Antipode* 47 (4): 894–914.

Chamayou, Grégoire. 2012. *Manhunts: A Philosophical History*. Princeton, NJ: Princeton University Press.

Chua, Charmaine, Martin Danyluk, Deborah Cowen, and Laleh Khalili. 2018. "Introduction: Turbulent Circulation: Building a Critical Engagement with Logistics." *Environment and Planning D: Society and Space* 36 (4): 617–29.

Collyer, Michael. 2007. "In-Between Places: Trans-Saharan Transit Migrants in Morocco and the Fragmented Journey to Europe." *Antipode* 39 (4): 668–90.

Conlon, Dominique, Dierdre Moran, and Nick Gill, eds. 2013. *Carceral Spaces: Mobility and Agency in Imprisonment and Migrant Detention.* Surrey, UK: Ashgate.

Cranston, Sophie, Joris Schapendonk, and Ernst Spaan. 2018. "New Directions in Exploring the Migration Industries: Introduction to the Special Issue." *Journal of Ethnic and Migration Studies* 44 (4): 543–57.

Cresswell, Tim. 2010. "Towards a Politics of Mobility." *Environment and Planning D: Society and Space* 28 (1): 17–31.

de Certeau, Michel. 1984. *The Practice of Everyday Life.* Berkeley: University of California Press.

De Genova, Nicholas. 2010. "The Queer Politics of Migration: Reflections on 'Illegality' and Incorrigibility." *Studies in Social Justice* 4 (2): 101–26.

De Genova, Nicholas. 2013. "Spectacles of Migrant 'Illegality': The Scene of Exclusion, the Obscene of Inclusion." *Ethnic and Racial Studies* 36 (7): 1180–98.

De Genova, Nicholas. 2016. "The 'Crisis' of the European Border Regime: Towards a Marxist Theory of Borders." *International Socialism* 150: 31–54.

Del Biaggio, Christina. (n.d.). "The South Alpine Border Theatre: Actors and Scene of the Rematerialization of a Frontier-Line." Unpublished manuscript.

Elden, Stuart. 2017. "Legal Terrain—the Political Materiality of Territory." *London Review of International Law* 5 (2): 199–224.

Ferrer-Gallardo, Xavier, and Henk van Houtum. 2014. "The Deadly EU Border Control." *ACME: An International E-Journal for Critical Geographies* 13 (2): 295–304.

Foucault, Michel. 2007. *Security, Territory, Population: Lectures at the Collège de France, 1977–78.* New York: Picador.

Foucault, Michel. 2016. *The Punitive Society: Lectures at the Collège de France, 1972–1973.* New York: Picador.

Garelli, Glenda, and Martina Tazzioli. 2018a. "The Biopolitical Warfare on Migrants: EU Naval Force and NATO Operations of Migration Government in the Mediterranean." *Critical Military Studies* 4 (2): 181–200.

Garelli, Glenda, and Martina Tazzioli. 2018b. "The Humanitarian War against Migrant Smugglers at Sea." *Antipode* 50 (3): 685–703.

Garelli, Glenda, and Martina Tazzioli. 2018c. "Migrant Digitalities and the Politics of Dispersal: An Introduction." *Border Criminologies* (blog), May 22. https://www.law.ox.ac.uk/research-subject-groups/centre-criminology/centreborder-criminologies/blog/2018/05/migrant.

Gill, Nick. 2016. "Mobility versus Liberty? The Punitive Uses of Movement within and outside Carceral Environments." In *Carceral Spaces: Mobility and Agency in Imprisonment and Migrant Detention*, edited by Dominique Moran, Nick Gill, and Dierdre Conlon, 31–48. New York: Routledge.

Gillespie, Mark, Souad Osseiran, and Margie Cheesman. 2018. "Syrian Refugees and the Digital Passage to Europe: Smartphone Infrastructures and Affordances." *Social Media + Society* 4 (1): 1–12.

Hess, Sabine. 2012. "De-naturalising Transit Migration: Theory and Methods of an Ethnographic Regime Analysis." *Population, Space and Place* 18 (4): 428–40.

Hiemstra, Nancy. 2013. "'You Don't Even Know Where You Are': Chaotic Geographies of US Migrant Detention and Deportation." In *Carceral Spaces: Mobility and Agency in Imprisonment and Migrant Detention*, edited by Dominique Moran, Nick Gill, and Dierdre Conlon, 57–75. Surrey, UK: Ashgate.

Ingold, Tim. 2004. "Culture on the Ground: The World Perceived through the Feet." *Journal of Material Culture* 9: 315–40.

Klauser, Francisco. 2013. "Through Foucault to a Political Geography of Mediation in the Information Age." *Geographica Helvetica* 68 (2): 95–104.

Latonero, Mark, and Paula Kift. 2018. "On Digital Passages and Borders: Refugees and the New Infrastructure for Movement and Control." *Social Media + Society* 4 (1). https://doi.org/10.1177%2F2056305118764432.

Matamoros, Cristina Abellan. 2018. "Italy's New Security Decree Clamps Down on Immigration." *Euronews*, November 30. https://www.euronews.com/2018/11/29/italy-s-new-security-decree-clamps-down-on-immigration.

Médecins sans Frontières. 2017. "Out of Sight: Informal Settlements." February 8. https://www.msf.org/italy-migrants-and-refugees-margins-society.

Mezzadra, Sandro. 2018. "In the Wake of the Greek Spring and the Summer of Migration." *South Atlantic Quarterly* 117 (4): 925–33.

Mezzadra, Sandro, and Brett Neilson. 2013. *Border as Method, or, the Multiplication of Labor*. Durham, NC: Duke University Press.

Nevins, Joseph. 2018. "The Speed of Life and Death: Migrant Fatalities, Territorial Boundaries, and Energy Consumption." *Mobilities* 13 (1): 29–44.

Nyers, Peter. 2003. "Abject Cosmopolitanism: The Politics of Protection in the Anti-deportation Movement." *Third World Quarterly* 24 (6): 1069–93.

Oliver, Michael. 1996. *Understanding Disability: From Theory to Practice*. Basingstoke, UK: Macmillan.

Papadopoulos, Dimitris, and Vassilis Tsianos. 2013. "After Citizenship: Autonomy of Migration Organisational Ontology and Mobile Commons." *Citizenship Studies* 17 (2) 178–96.

Rocci, Carlotta, and Jacopo Ricca. 2017. "Presidio alla stazione di Bardonecchia per dare aiuto ai migranti che tentano la traversata delle Alpi." *La Repubblica*, December 6. https://torino.repubblica.it/cronaca/2017/12/06/news/presidio

_alla_stazione_di_bardonecchia_per_dare_aiuto_ai_migranti_che_tentano
_la_traversata_delle_alpi-183207779/.

Taylor, Astra, dir. 2009. *Examined Life* (documentary). Zeitgeist Films.

Tazzioli, Martina. 2018a. "Crossed Boundaries? Migrants and Police on the French-Italian Border." Open Democracy, April 3. https://www.opendemocracy.net
/beyondslavery/martina-tazzioli/crossed-boundaries-migrants-and-police-on
-french-italian-border.

Tazzioli, Martina. 2018b. "Towards a Genealogy of Europe's Migrant Spaces: A
Map-Archive of Border Zones." *Border Criminologies*, November 15. https://
www.law.ox.ac.uk/research-subject-groups/centre-criminology/centreborder
-criminologies/blog/2018/11/towards-genealogy.

Tazzioli, Martina, and Glenda Garelli. 2018. "Containment beyond Detention: The
Hotspot System and Disrupted Migration Movements across Europe." *Environment and Planning D: Society and Space*, February 19. https://doi.org/10
.1177%2F0263775818759335.

Tazzioli, Martina, and William Walters. 2019. "Migration, Solidarity and the Limits
of Europe." *Global Discourse* 9 (1): 175–90.

Theodore, Nik. 2011. "Policing Borders: Unauthorized Immigration and the Pernicious Politics of Attrition." *Social Justice* 38 (1–2): 90–106.

Trimikliniotis, Nicos, Dimitris Parsanoglou, and Vassilis Tsianos. 2015. *Mobile Commons, Migrant Digitalities and the Right to the City*. London: Springer.

Walters, William. 2015. "Migration, Vehicles, and Politics: Three Theses on Viapolitics." *European Journal of Social Theory* 18 (4): 469–88.

Walters, William. 2018. "Aviation as Deportation Infrastructure: Airports, Planes,
and Expulsion." *Journal of Ethnic and Migration Studies* 44 (16): 2796–2817.

Xiang, Biao, and Johan Lindquist. 2014. "Migration Infrastructure." *International
Migration Review* 48 (1): 122–48.

Xiang, Biao, and Johan Lindquist. 2018. "Postscript: Infrastructuralization: Evolving
Sociopolitical Dynamics in Labour Migration from Asia." *Pacific Affairs* 91
(4): 759–73.

TEN

Deportation and Airports

Clara Lecadet and William Walters

Croydon Aerodrome, 1939: Grounding Air Deportation

A photograph published in the *Daily Mail* on March 31, 1939 (see figure 10.1), shows a man being carried by his arms and legs by a cohort of men in uniform (Frankl 2017). The scene takes place at Croydon Aerodrome in the suburbs of London. The civilian suit worn by the man being carried like a parcel contrasts with the uniforms worn by the others, who bear the insignia of power and authority. Nonetheless, the man's raised head, the curve of his body, and his tensed limbs suggest a resistance, a revolt against what fate had in store for him. His name was Oskar Goldberg, and he had reached England in a private plane with a small group of Jewish refugees fleeing former Czechoslovakia, which had been invaded by the Germans. Throughout the previous day there had been an extraordinary scene at Croydon. Nearly four hundred Jewish refugees had arrived in a stream of airliners, the biggest influx the aerodrome had ever witnessed. As refugees were not guaranteed sanctuary on English soil, his group was on the point of being deported. Indeed, they were to be returned on the same plane that had brought them from Warsaw via Copenhagen. But their protests, as well as the presence of reporters, prevented this from happening.

The picture sums up the unwillingness, and sometimes the refusal, to accept refugees fleeing the Nazi advance in the lead-up to World War II; the brutal measures taken against them; and the strategies employed by the refugees to avoid deportation. It also demonstrates the power of pictures. This photograph

FIGURE 10.1 · Oskar Goldberg, a refugee from German-occupied Czechoslovakia, being forcibly deported from Croydon airport, UK, March 30, 1939. Source: Wiener Library, London (VII-B-0004-WL25)/Zuma Press. Photographer: Weston (*Daily Mail*).

testifies to the violence meted out to refugees while simultaneously becoming in itself part of the process that it disrupts by providing publicity for it. The picture of Oskar Goldberg about to be deported is strangely familiar, since it anticipates others of foreigners being brutally expelled in the context of migration policies that have been consistently strengthened since the 1970s in many European countries. But something is incongruous here in the context of the early stages of World War II, as it shows that airplanes have long been a means of deporting foreigners who are not accepted into a given country. While trains have been used for purposes of immigrant control and deportation in the United States since the end of World War I (see chapter 1, this volume), and became emblematic of deportation and the atrocities committed during the Nazi period, the use of airplanes as a means of deportation at that time has rarely been documented.

This archive picture features in the attempt to retrace the genesis of what we have elsewhere called air deportation (Walters 2019). Like others that followed, it helps to reconstitute the policy and micropolitics of deportation by air and the necessarily scattered history of control measures, as well as highlighting the moments of resistance that played their part in such expulsions. Since the interwar period, the development of civil aviation has brought about profound changes in both the flow and number of flights, but it has also completely altered airport space and its infrastructure. Globalization has been marked by an increase in air traffic and also, by contrast, in the control and limitation of movement of foreigners, largely from poor areas of the planet. How does the picture of Oskar Goldberg enable us to reflect on the way in which aviation has become a major tool in deportation, a key element of political communication for governments, as well as a strategic issue for those trying to resist it, above all for those who are vulnerable to deportation or who have already been deported? How might this "surviving picture," to use Didi-Huberman's (2002) expression, both shed light on a forgotten event that we have identified as the early stages of the air deportation system and help us to understand better the issues of the present?

Airport/Deport

The background of air deportation is the system of civil aviation that emerged during the interwar years and which today forms a key infrastructure of globalization. Historians and geographers have shown in some detail the ways in which the creation of airline companies, the forging of air routes, airline advertising campaigns, and much else all illustrate the close associations that existed between civil aviation, national power, and identity (Kranakis 2010), but also the political dream of revitalizing imperial rule through the skies (Bhimull 2017, Pirie 2017, Caprotti 2011). Scholars and publics typically associate air power with the military capabilities of states. But these studies of civil aviation lend support to the case for a wider conception of air power, one not confined to the military domain. Given that civil aviation allows the state to mobilize deportation on a routine and worldwide basis, and given that contemporary deportations are inscribed within a hierarchical geopolitics that bears a profoundly colonial and postcolonial imprint (Walters 2002; De Genova 2010), there are good reasons to see deportation as a key element of this wider conception of air power.

These deportations have become a key component of the government of migration and acquired a communitarian dimension in the European Union with the adoption of the Return Directive in 2008. This implies that air deportation is still enacted at the national level but can also be the object of negotiation and joint operations involving different European countries. The vast majority of deportations from Europe are by air and involve airports of one kind or another. For example, of the 25,375 deportations officially conducted from Germany in 2016, *Deutsche Welle* (2017) reports that 94 percent were by air. This chapter argues that the airport is not simply a gateway or a neutral infrastructure that just happens to provision the deportation programs of European governments. Instead, airports are complex spaces that interact with and mediate deportation. If they have sometimes been used by governments seeking to turn deportation into a sovereign spectacle, they are also settings for antideportation protests by activists and solidarity movements. They are securitized zones that deportees themselves negotiate and sometimes leverage to obstruct their own removal. They are logistical hubs that are served by nearby detention centers, which in many countries are clustered in a carceral geography around these zones of flight. Airports also possess detention areas in their own right (Makaremi 2018). And they are places where busy flows of population mix, requiring careful measures to segregate, control, channel, and sometimes hide deportations. While ferries and buses form a backbone for the deportation infrastructure in many regions of the world—a point illustrated by Lindquist's discussion (chapter 5, this volume) of movements of undocumented workers from Malaysia to Indonesia—aviation plays a pivotal role in Europe's deportation regime.

This chapter argues that the airport offers a privileged window for critical research on deportation. As such, it deepens the insight of viapolitics set out in the introduction to this book: that vehicles and their infrastructures deserve more attention in critical research on migration. Our aim is to ground air deportation, that is, to move from seeing the flight merely as a moment of passage, or the plane as a vehicle that flies almost effortlessly into the clouds, to a view in which the materiality of forced movement, and all its complications and entanglements, comes into view. Despite the growth of a large and rich literature on deportation (De Genova and Peutz 2010; Kanstroom 2007), as well as the boom in border studies (Parker and Vaughan-Williams 2009), an analysis of the role of airports within the deportation activities and movements of states has yet to be systematically undertaken. Airports appear periodically in deportation scholarship but usually only as background or incidental features. At the same time, while there is an important interdisciplinary literature on airports and aerial life (Salter 2008; Adey 2010; Aaltola 2005), it has had little to say about deportation. The point that airports are border spaces that control, filter, and distribute mobility and surveil populations is by now well made. Yet the airport's place in border infrastructure has rarely been theorized from the angle of removals (Alpes 2015; Walters 2018). Hence in thinking about deportation at the level of airports, we aim to bridge these literatures.

Our focus on airports underscores a methodological and political point and builds on calls to give more attention to the journeys (Peutz 2006) and transport forms of deportation (Walters 2016; Feys 2019; chapter 1, this volume). It moves us away from a state-centric and Eurocentric view in which deportation is theorized from the inside to the outside, from the "here" to the "nowhere" or the "over there." Instead, we want to sketch a transversal space and to hint at the existence of a whole aerial geography of deportation that is presently off the map of migration studies. This aerial geography highlights a series of powers, authorities, and operations that, while uneven and fragmentary, are exercised across space and time, and not simply concentrated in a moment of expulsion.

To deepen understanding of the airport/deportation nexus, we present a series of stories, figures, and vignettes. These fragmentary episodes map loosely onto the way airports can feature in three different phases of a deportation journey: departure, transit, and arrival. We pay special attention to the scene of arrival/reception and the airports of the countries of destination. This is for tactical reasons: arrival promises to bring into focus the issues, paradoxes, and tensions that arise surrounding the countries and places of destination. Our use of fragments reflects a desire to think from contexts, settings, and encounters rather than a quest for a general theory. But it is also because this mode of knowledge mirrors in a certain way its very object. Air deportation is not a domain that lends itself to participant observation or the even gaze of social research. On the contrary, one is dealing with a fractional geography of glimpses, encounters, incidents; where leak, rumor, and scraps of testimony offer us bits and pieces, but the whole remains necessarily out of reach. Our aim is not a systematic overview so much as a series of cuts.

Stansted, 2002: Deportation, Pomp, and Circumstance

The TV cameras arrived at London's Stansted airport on September 20, 2002 (*The Times* 2002). They had been tipped off by the UK Home Office about the pending group deportation of forty-eight men, women, and children to the Czech Republic whose claims for asylum had been rejected. Under the glare of the cameras, the group was boarded onto the chartered plane for Prague. According to *The Times*, some smiled defiantly while others shielded their faces. This was Operation Elgar in action, a Home Office project to generate usable media images of forced deportation on the expectation that the circulation of such images to the countries of origin of the expelled would deter future arrivals.[1] Human rights organizations condemned the action for making a spectacle out of people's misery, making a circus out of deportation, and stripping vulnerable subjects of their dignity. Such criticisms did not deter the Home Office. In 2004 the Home Office repeated the action, this time contracting Associated Press TV news to film the forced departure of approximately two dozen Afghan people from Gatwick airport (Fekete 2005, 20; cited in Tyler 2018). Again, the idea was that not just unwanted migrants should be sent home but TV images as well. In transmitting people and images, the UK would signal its toughness and decisiveness in immigration enforcement. Just as data doubles have become important shadows within digitalized border controls, these returnees would be shadowed and even preceded by their media images. If the camera had been an ally in frustrating the deportation of Oskar Goldberg, under the auspices of Operation Elgar, it was now to be a weapon of immigration enforcement.

Scholars argue we should treat the pervasive images of boat migration not as a second-order reality but as an absolutely constitutive part of oceanic borderscapes and border spectacles (De Genova 2013), entangled in the complex politics of compassion, resentment, hostility, and fear that animates this phenomenon. Something similar can be said of the phenomenon that interests us here: air deportation. There is a flux of expulsion that is structured, speeded, and equally obstructed through its unavoidable contact with routes and hubs of commercial aviation, but there is also, bound up and interacting with these movements, a flux of images. The latter includes the kind of staged media coverage just mentioned, as well as the stories and photographs of journalists who were granted special permission to go behind the scenes with particular deportation charter flights (*Telegraph* 2009).

But, operating as a counterforce to these officially sanctioned images, there is a whole play of stolen glimpses, fragments, and leaks: a student who livestreams her own interruption of a deportation flight (BBC News 2018); activists who film themselves obstructing a charter flight by anchoring its undercarriage with their bodies (Britton 2019); a passenger who records blurry images and angry confrontations in the cabin; the reenactment of a forced removal operation in which the expellee is bound and trussed for movement like cargo (Lee 2011); a computer-aided simulation in which, by contrast, there are no humans at all, just the haunting image of the infrastructure of detention spaces and departure areas, a waiting plane on the tarmac, and darkened cabin doors (Bridle 2015); or an online map of deportation flights—one of the very few cartographies of deportation routes we have seen—whose method was not unlike that used to make visible the furtive disappearances of terror suspects known as "extraordinary rendition" (Englebert et al. 2017).

These officially sanctioned images and counterimages dance around one another in a play of secrecy and revelation (Fischer 2005). There is something about the nature of contemporary aviation that overdetermines this agonistic play of images. Intensive security protocols make the airport a highly segmented, fractured, and uneven space. Signs in passport and customs areas remind the traveler: no photography! The play of images we describe is freighted with the sense that the airport itself is a place not just of arrival and departure, or norms and exceptions (Salter 2008), but of appearance and disappearance, of front stages and backstages, cosmopolitan freedoms and strict prohibitions. Overarching all this is the suspicion, fostered by multiple reports and anecdotes, that it is in the least visible areas that the worst violence is inflicted on the expellees (Makaremi 2018). In such an environment, it is perhaps hardly surprising that the very act of recording and transmitting scenes of deportation carries the potential to become a political stake in its own right (Bridle 2015), or that the business of disappearing people should provoke such determined efforts to generate a trace, to bear witness to these airborne acts of removal. But if the moment of departure appears to crystallize these issues, often decisive for the future of deportees and/or for countries themselves in terms of the production of images or their obliteration, the journey itself, its stages and any interruptions, seem to make up what the German documentary producer Ralf Jesse, at an exhibition in Berlin in 2011, called *Blackbox der Abschiebung: Bilder und Geschichten von Leuten, die gern geblieben wären*" (The black box of expulsion: Portraits and stories of people who would have liked to stay). His installation, a cube carpeted with rubbish bags and in which a rather kitsch family living room was reconstructed, with a television in the middle, attempted to show the rejection of undocumented foreigners from the perspective of discarded waste, the use of deportation as a political tool and a public spectacle, the opposition between the domestic vision of the state (as shown here in the house) sovereign on its own soil, and an indeterminate outer area brought in here by televised images.[2] Using reports from Kosovo, Russia, and Nigeria, it aimed to give back to people made invisible by deportation a face and a story, the theme of the black box suggesting that the representation of the deportation of undocumented foreigners rested on a partial vision of reality, hiding what was to come after it.

Rotterdam Airport, 2013: In the Hangar

Airports can be used to stage and display deportation, but they are also used to conceal it. This much we learn by reading the official monitoring reports that document what European governments, in anodyne language, call "return" procedures (Pirjola 2015). A special transport van carrying four detainees and their security escorts from the Rotterdam detention center arrived at one of the hangars at Rotterdam The Hague Airport at 8:40 a.m., October 17, 2013 (CPT 2015). There the Dutch escort team met up with their security and immigration counterparts from Germany and Slovenia who were bringing their own deportees to the flight. Frontex staff were also present. This was a joint return operation (JRO), a component of the Return Directive we mentioned earlier, and a recent innovation in air deportation piloted by Frontex. JROs utilize charter flights that gather deportees and security and immigration officials from two or more EU member states. In this instance, the plane's destination was Lagos, Nigeria. But it would stop en route in Madrid where deportees from Spain and Bulgaria also boarded.

By the time the van arrived, there were more than one hundred people in the hangar, creating a certain amount of "confusion" (CPT 2015, 15). For this reason, the detainees and their escorts were kept in the van for some time, a reminder that detention can take mobile as well as fixed forms; a reminder also of the role that vans, like airplanes, play not just in locomotion but in the "encapsulation" of migrant bodies (chapter 5, this volume). Eventually the detainees would be transferred one by one onto the waiting Boeing 737. The confusion was no doubt related to the large numbers involved and multiple nationalities and immigration agencies present. But perhaps it also reflected the fact that there had been a change in the boarding procedure for this particular JRO. No longer were the deported to be shuffled through the airport terminal. This was the first time the whole boarding operation at Rotterdam had been conducted inside the hangar, a space that, in the words of the monitors, "completely concealed the aircraft" (CPT 2015, 15n24). One reason that governments have created the charter flight system is that it insulates air deportation from the eyes and interventions of fellow passengers as well as from activists (Walters 2016; Fekete 2011). But here we see that such a move involves not just a different kind of plane but changes in the ways that bodies and spaces mix within airport space. We associate hangars with storage and repair. Vast in size, they form an essential part of the infrastructure of aviation yet one that the regular passenger only glimpses momentarily from the window of a taxiing plane. They are places for ground crews and mechanics, not passengers. But in the case of this JRO, the hangar is repurposed to become a tactical element within deportation infrastructure and a place for deportees. Not only does deportation appropriate aviation in order to move people across vast distances, forging corridors of expulsion whose aerial geography reinscribes global hierarchies of rich and poor. It also operates on local scales as well, in this case forging new pathways and routes between detention centers and airports, and even within airports. Hangars hide deportees just as container ships hide smuggled people (chapter 4, this volume). Only the latter's mixing of people and cargo is deemed scandalous.

Schiphol, 2012: Passengers in Transit

Jama Warsame had never been to Somalia (Sniderman 2013). Yet in February 2012 he found himself sitting in the back of a plane, accompanied by two Canadian government escorts, heading for Somalia, the country to which Canada was intent on deporting him. Warsame was born in Saudi Arabia to two Somali parents. At a young age he had moved with his parents to Canada where he grew up. Warsame acquired a significant criminal record, including convictions for assault, robbery, and drug possession. For the Canadian government, this was grounds to seek his deportation—a move consistent with the growing trend of many states to expel noncitizens convicted of serious offenses. The case went to the UN Human Rights Committee, which ruled that Warsame's deportation would violate his right to life, expose him to cruel and unusual punishment, and violate his right to remain in his "own country." Despite this verdict, and perhaps determined to prove its resolve on issues of crime and immigration enforcement while dog whistling to racist sentiments within sectors of the electorate, the Canadian government pressed ahead with the deportation.

However, the aerial geography of Warsame's deportation was not straightforward. How could it be, when so few major airlines were prepared to fly into Somalia? And when that destination was deemed safe enough for the expellee but too dangerous a place to send Canadian government officials? Warsame's escorts had been instructed to take him only as far as Nairobi, following a change of planes at Schipol in the Netherlands. Warsame was by no means the only expellee to take this route. An investigation by the Canadian Broadcasting Corporation revealed that it was not uncommon for Canada to deport people to Somalia without paperwork (CBC 2014). The practice was to hire third-party contractors in Nairobi to complete the journey, collaborating with a regional airline called African Express. According to one former director of the Canadian Border Services Agency, the fee for this last leg of the deportation journey could vary, but the going rate was about $25,000, a sum that would be carried by the Canadian escorts and handed over *in cash* to an airline official in Nairobi.

But Warsame never got as far as Nairobi. In Schipol airport, as his escorts hustled him between flights, he struggled to get the attention of a Dutch immigration official who, according to Warsame, "was acting like he didn't want to hear me" but then relented. Deeming Somalia—and eventually Canada—an unsafe country, the Netherlands ultimtely granted him a temporary stay. His asylum case was rejected by the Dutch government. Schipol was to have been a transit point en route to Somalia. Instead, it became a gateway to statelessness.

In breaking down in a place deemed a transit airport, Warsame's journey reveals to us what is masked by the common image of deportation as a straight line, an almost instantaneous and direct movement from a country of expulsion to one of return. In many cases, there may well be a straightforward plane journey. Especially when people leave under voluntary or assisted voluntary status, they put themselves on regular flights and travel much like regular passengers.[3] But in many other cases, what exists are complex trajectories involving liaisons among multiple immigration and police authorities as well as private security and airline officials, temporary detentions and holding areas, and a certain tactical know-how as to which airports (Council of the European Union 2000), which consulates, and which airlines are better suited to the task of involuntary movement. What exists are complex administrative and diplomatic arrangements that, whether they take the form of readmission agreements or new devices like the EU's harmonized travel document, forge expulsion routes across borders, territories, and infrastructures. When particular destinations are not well served by regular commercial routes, or when the threat of disruption or escape during transit is high, states often resort to group deportations aboard the kinds of charter flights we noted earlier (Corporate Watch 2015). Often such flights entail an escalation of force as well as a corresponding decrease in public visibility. If consideration of all these and other elements suggests that the aerial geography of deportation is not smooth but fractured, multilayered, dynamic, and conflictual, then this impression is only strengthened when we consider that certain laws and frameworks make such fragmentation of deportation a structural feature as well. This is especially true with the EU's Dublin III regulation, which governs how member states are supposed to determine responsibility for handling an asylum claim. Dublin III has multiplied intra-European movements as a formal component of the deportation apparatus. There are now charter flights dedicated to Dublin transfers, which, if the inspection reports (Pirjola 2015) are a reliable guide, feature some of the most intensive deployments of force and violence. All of this is to suggest that it is high time migration scholars accorded a certain symmetry to the study of deportation. The journeys of migrants across oceans and deserts, along routes, and across transit territories have a high profile among publics and scholars, as do the complex temporalities, multiple agencies, and directionalities at stake (chapters 6 and 7, this volume). Here we stress that, contrary to the single-line image of expulsion, much the same could be said of deportation. Indeed, once we change the temporal focus, once we recognize that for many migrants a given deportation is not an end to their migration story so much as one more hurdle, and only one episode, the case for better integrating the study of migration and deportation is only strengthened.

Bamako 2007–2016: Mahamadou Keita, the Man at the Airport

Initially he had to put in a furtive appearance at this airport where he had long been an outsider. Deported from France in 2006, Mahamadou Keita returned to the airport in an act of militancy. It was in fact by being the man at the airport, the one who went almost every evening to wait for any arrival of deportees on the Air France flight from Paris to Bamako, that he became an important part of the Association Malienne des Expulsés (AME), an association of expelled migrants of which he soon became secretary general. In going to meet the ones he called his expelled brothers, he reenacted his own story each evening, as he hurried in nervously and warily, but he was also a tangible embodiment of the principle of self-help that was the founding principle of the association when it was founded in Bamako in 1996: in such a moment of abandonment, only the presence of someone who had himself experienced the bitterness of return could be seen as a friendly gesture toward those who were being sent back exhausted, often in a state of shock, and without luggage (Keita 2009).

The legitimacy of his presence in the airport and of the association's political action drew strength from this desire to get rid of the taboo and disgrace that surrounded deportees, to confirm their political presence in the public arena and their role as shapers and practitioners of measures for the social care of expelled

FIGURE 10.2 · An intervention by Mahamadou Keita concerning the repression of a sit-in organized by the AME during a debate on freedom of expression, Bamako, February 2009. Source: Clara Lecadet.

migrants. Mahamadou Keita had long been confined to the arrivals area; nevertheless, he obtained information on the presence or otherwise of deportees on board flights from French partners such as Cimade, RESF (Réseau éducation sans-frontières), Droits Devant!, CGT (Confédération Générale du travail), and also the police commissioner at the airport, with whom he had some contact. Even though his access to airport space was restricted, he had, by virtue of his contacts and networks on either side of the border, acquired gradual recognition by the airport authorities to the extent that, after some time, they issued him a badge that allowed him to move relatively freely within the airport, sometimes to the extent of meeting deportees on the tarmac as they came off the airplane.

The legitimization of a former expelled migrant within the airport not only symbolized the important place held by AME in Malian political debate since 1996, it also marked a victory and a personal transformation. A man who, by his own account, had little education and who felt himself to be far from the world of intellectuals and politicians, frequently appeared in the Malian media to denounce the fate of deportees and had also achieved permission to travel to Europe again, to take part in meetings of activists and NGOs. The "abject presence" (Nyers 2003) of the deportee had been transformed into a gesture of social and political action; once held in contempt, he now had the right to be an air passenger like any other, one of the crowd of tourists and other travelers. His actions with AME and within the airport had such a hold on him that he no longer wanted to go back to live in France when his travels took him there.

The story of his personal resilience in greeting his compatriots at the airport, and his desire to be there at their side, made his end all the more tragic. In Paris for a meeting, he took the opportunity to have some medical tests for an illness that turned out to be serious. He was in the hospital for several months, and as he had been told by his doctors that he had little time left to live, he wanted more than anything to return to his native country. But as his death approached, he found himself imprisoned once again: his insurance company refused to pay for repatriation due to health reasons, on the grounds that he had a preexisting condition about which he had not informed them. It was a strange and tragic irony that a man who had rebuilt his life in Mali through his militancy as an expelled migrant, and who had every day obsessively, passionately, and with sadness gone to meet those who were returning home destitute, should in his final hour have been held in France. His whole life was a tense and harrowing struggle.

Various accounts of his life were written in French daily newspapers and there remain some pictures, taken by journalists, of him going out onto the tarmac to greet a deportee (Vincent 2010a, 2010b; Steinmetz 2015). The publicity given to his actions (whether through portraits, interviews, or interventions in public meetings) provided a rare opportunity to turn the hidden and shameful experience of deportation into something public and then sharable. Like the picture of Oskar Goldberg, the focus on individuals allows a singular experience to be turned into the cement for collective action and public awareness. Only the collection of individual experiences seems to have the power to lead to the recognition of deportation as a political experience in its own right and to distance these accounts from the institutional frame of migration control. Like Oskar Goldberg's picture, which offers a glimpse of what could be the early stages of air deportation, Mahamadou Keita figures the transformation of deportation into a site of self-help and collective action (Lecadet 2016, 2017a, 2017b).

These accounts make us question the arrival conditions for deportees, their treatment by airport authorities, and also more generally their social and political situation. Mahamadou Keita and others who came after him show that deportees can be visible in the airport of their home country, through an organized intervention that makes their collective status the terms of a struggle and a social and political issue in the countries that are dealing with this return. It is something of a coup that expelled migrants' associations can be allowed within the limited and demarcated space of an airport. That a place can be made for them like this, for welcoming and linking up with expelled and abandoned people, is a sign both of what is now the structural, political importance of deportation by air, and of the collective organizational abilities that this ordeal has managed to arouse. The presence of a member of AME at Bamako-Sénou airport and of a representative of the Network of Ex-Asylum Seekers in Sierra Leone in a small office in a restaurant at Freetown airport in Lunghi frees deportees from existing merely furtively and as objects of control or surveillance. These small measures, set up as a means of re-creating a social link among expelled migrants and of raising awareness among the people of their country about the ordeals and losses that they have suffered—the fundamental watchword of this network in Sierra Leone is to fight the stigma associated with expulsion within the country itself (Lecadet 2018)—are set against the background of the logistics of air transport, which in the case of deportation combines aviation power with that of the police. Their presence and their power may appear minimal, but they have great symbolic power nonetheless, and they pose many practical and urgent questions inherent in deportation: How to leave the airport and where to stay when you don't have any money? What route to take, how to move on?

Airports and Planes as Political Sites

A great deal of mobilization has taken place in the airports of various European countries since the 1990s, through the efforts of migrants' organizations or associations involved in the defense of undocumented foreigners. Activists and migrants have developed tactics that include alerting passengers that deportees are being carried on their flight, making appeals and protests to flight crew and pilots to have the deportee removed from the plane, and more generally generating public awareness about the involvement of airlines and airports in the deportation system (Stierl 2012; Monforte 2016). While published, censored, or secretly taken photographs are an issue both for countries and for the militants trying to prevent or demonstrate against deportation where this is practiced, there is little likelihood of there being any images of the journey itself or of deportees arriving on the tarmac of the country to which they have been returned.[4] There are almost no pictures of arrivals. Does this mean that once deportation is complete, there is no further issue for the authorities and nothing more against which to protest? The dissymmetry between the analysis of the issues at stake in relation to expelling countries and in relation to countries to which deportees are returned is no doubt partially explained by the methodological bias of nationalism and the covering up of the question of the treatment of deportees by the country receiving them.

Airports in countries to which people are returned are rarely considered to be part of control and surveillance measures. They are a blind spot in the deportation process. The increasing attention to postexpulsion consequences, however, is beginning to shine a glaring light on the risks that deportees face on their return (Alpes 2015; Alpes et al. 2017): ill-treatment on the part of the police in their country of origin, which can lead to death, detention, interrogation in police stations, extortion, imprisonment, and so on. The arrival airport is often a dangerous place, and in all cases the return of deportees is supervised and watched. This control of expellees on their arrival may take the form of a simple administrative registration by the police chief at the airport, as happens at Bamako, usually without any consequences. But they can also experience violent and/or secretive treatment at the hands of officials when they arrive, as documented in UK inspection reports on deportations to Nigeria and Sri Lanka (HM Chief Inspector of Prisons 2011, 2012). In all cases, expellees are the subject of procedure and specific treatment. The question of formalities at the airport remains terra incognita as far as research is concerned, and precise methods would need to be established in work carried out country by country and in a historical perspective.

But these checks and the sustained attention given to expellees can take on a meaning that subverts them from within. Indeed, the measures taken within airports to control the arrival of deportees can become a signal to expelling countries. In Sierra Leone, one of the essential requirements is to check both the nationality of the deportee, since only Sierra Leonean deportees are accepted, and the documents justifying the deportation, to guard against forgeries. Checks on deportees can thus become a trial of strength with the authorities in the expelling countries and, over and above individual cases, may take on political significance in relation to what the country of arrival is ready to accept or not in terms of deportation practice and policy. The role of embassies in issuing, or refusing to issue, travel documents enabling deportation has been highlighted as a factor in a possible balance of power between deporting and receiving countries. Airports may also play the same, though less central, role through symbolic action that can become the object of political communication. In Mali in 2009, at the end of a long campaign against the signing of readmission agreements between France and Mali, several Malians with a three-month residence permit were turned away from a flight at Bamako-Sénou airport. Unlike previous actions over which the Malian authorities took no official position, repeated incidents such as this were strongly condemned by the minister of transport, Ahmed Diane Séméga, who declared that "l'aéroport de Bamako, ne saurait en aucun cas, être un second consulat de France" (Bamako airport should never act as a second French consulate) (Secoolio 2009). At the end of December 2016, the Malian government stated that it had sent back two Malians with European travel documents on the flight on which they had arrived. This "return to sender" was the subject of a huge amount of political correspondence, intended to restate the Malian government's refusal of European travel documents, which short-circuited the traditional consular process (Lecadet 2017a).

These examples show that an airport can become not only a place of political protest for activists opposed to deportation, but also a strategic place for the restatement by a political power of the right to oversight and intervention in relation to the treatment of its nationals by airlines, and ultimately by countries that issue a residence permit. Airports were thereafter in the ambivalent position of being potentially dangerous places in countries to which deportees were returned or at least areas for control, interrogation, and administrative checks, while also being a lever in the balance of political power with the deporting country. In Sierra Leone, the airport set up an internal protocol on the readmission of deportees in order to check their nationality, given that the country refuses to readmit a deportee without Sierra Leonean nationality, just as it gives very great importance to the validity of travel documents and the deportation notice carried by the traveler.

Cases of expelled migrants sent back to their country of residence on the same plane by which they had arrived are certainly rare but symbolically important, as they then take on a wider significance than a simple refusal to readmit them.[5] These cases demonstrate the possibility of response, of a show of political strength against the backdrop of the airport. The fact that these responses happened to take place in Mali and Sierra Leone does not seem to be totally unconnected with work on the ground undertaken by deportees organized into collectives. The associations created by deportees, together with a political context that allows them to speak out and to protest, have certainly played a part in raising awareness among airport staff of the terrible experiences suffered by these expellees. The presence of representatives of these associations at airports not only creates a small measure of solidarity toward deportees, but also leads to the development of a better balance between the various actors within airports. To legitimize the presence of this kind of association within airports is to legitimize the cause they represent. We may speculate that this presence has a wider, global influence on the treatment by officials of deportees on their arrival. It is this dynamic, this interaction between the micropolitics of migrants, deportees, and militants and the decisions taken by airport and government authorities that could provide the basis for studies of airports as places of conflict, but also of the renewal of forms of political action.

Toward Aerial Geographies of Deportation

Air transport has in the last seventy years or so transformed experiences of human mobility. As countless advertisements have put it with not a little cosmopolitan cliché, civil aviation has brought people and places together, shrinking time and space. Historians have offered a counterimage and a corrective to this one-sided, happy image: the point that from its inception, aviation was not just a way to smooth space across borders but a means to assert national identity, national sovereignty, and/or imperial reach (Bhimull 2017; Kranakis 2010). In a similar vein, we insist one should not ignore the way that aviation has transformed practices and processes of forcible movement, including deportation. We should be mindful of the role it has played in underpinning projects to police national boundaries and control the movement and residence of people deemed alien, forging corridors of deportation that all too frequently entrench global and racial inequalities between north and south. Deportation is rarely discussed within histories of civil aviation and transport. We hope that this chapter contributes to a fuller accounting of the various functions performed by civil aviation.

But we hope this chapter also contributes to a deepening of understandings of deportation itself. We make three points here. First, we have sketched some elements of an aerial geography of deportation. There is a growing move on the part of scholars of deportation to reject the single event- or act-focused image of deportation and to craft instead an extensive, horizontal account that encompasses multiple sites, experiences, phases, authorities, and actors (Peutz 2006; Drotbohm and Hasselberg 2015; Khosravi 2017; chapters 1 and 5, this volume). The growing interest in postdeportation worlds is a very significant development in this respect. Our notion of an aerial geography of deportation should be read as a contribution toward this extension and broadening of deportation studies. What it brings in particular is a much more three-dimensional account of all the activities, places, persons, vehicles, and knowledges that underpin the forced movement of people. In much scholarship, deportation appears—often by default—as a rapid movement across a kind of flat, empty space, a line from A to B. With the figure of aerial geography, we seek to change the image of empty airspace to reveal hubs, corridors, passages, and connections but also no end of friction, breakage, and leakage. The point is not that inside/outside images are false but that they are not adequate for capturing the multiple times and spaces.

Second, if this aerial geography can be likened to a kind of infrastructure, as we have implied, this is not to say that that is all it is. We don't want to sound too logistical, as though deportation were merely an infrastructure that moved people around like parcels. For this aerial geography does not consist in the movement of planes and people alone. A part of its reality is the capture (a term we use in its full double sense), production, and circulation of images too. With the case of Oskar Goldberg, we see that from the very beginning air deportation was entangled in images. Just as the genre of landscape painting was, from the seventeenth century, not just a reflection on landscape, not a second-order phenomenon but a constitutive and immanent part of its reality, so too are images a part of our understanding of aerial geographies of deportation. These images, or the absence of them, are a stake in the practices of deportation and resistance to deportation. As we have seen, states play with visibility, but so do many other actors.

Finally, we have insisted that aerial geographies should be attentive to power struggles on multiple scales and sites. Whereas the focus has usually been on the times and places of expulsion and departure, we have drawn attention to other times and places. We have emphasized the time of transit, but especially the scene of the airport of arrival. There we saw a man whose struggle is to welcome the deportees, and the border officials who insist on carefully checking papers in an act that in its diligence expresses not so much a bureaucratic dedication, or a fight against illegal immigration, but a refusal to have one's country used as a dumping ground for the unwanted people of Europe. If we have drawn attention to these other times, places, and acts, it is not just because they have been otherwise missed and we want to give a fuller picture. It is also because a bigger picture is sometimes best grasped in the little details that are often microcosms of that wider scene.

Notes

We thank the Social Sciences and Humanities Research Council of Canada for the funding (#435-2017-1008) that supported our work for this chapter.

1 In Britain's public culture, Elgar's orchestral music is strongly associated with displays of patriotism, ceremony, and military prowess. This is especially the case with his "Pomp and Circumstance" marches (c. 1901–30). We wonder if these were values the Home Office had in mind when naming one deportation initiative Operation Elgar.

2 Zygmunt Bauman (2006) establishes an analogy between the rejection by Western countries of foreigners from poor countries as their unwanted share of humanity, and the question of waste.

3 Note that an unescorted deportee will have the international aviation code DEPU imprinted on their flight reservation, a designation that will alert the air crew to their presence and ensure they are carefully monitored.

4 Durand (2003) illustrates a case against two passengers who were arrested after attempting to take photographs of an expulsion inside the plane.

5 It is worth highlighting the fact that these turnarounds, these return to senders in a way mimic a far more routine process on the part of the EU states who regularly bounce people back, requiring that, under carrier law, the airlines take responsibility for people lacking the right papers or the right nationality.

References

Aaltola, Mika. 2005. "The International Airport: The Hub-and-Spoke Pedagogy of the American Empire." *Global Networks* 5: 261–78.

Adey, Peter. 2010. *Aerial Life: Spaces, Mobilities, Affects.* Malden, MA: Wiley-Blackwell.

Alpes, Jill. 2015. "Airport Casualties: Non-admission and Return Risks at Times of Internalized/Externalized Border Controls." *Social Sciences* 4 (3): 742–57.

Alpes, Jill, Charlotte Blondel, Nausicaa Preiss, and Meritxell Sayos Monras. 2017. "Post-deportation Risks for Failed Asylum Seekers." *Forced Migration Review* 54: 76–78.

Bauman, Zygmunt. 2006. *Vies perdues: La modernité et ses exclus.* Paris: Payot.

BBC News. 2018. "Swedish Activist Stops Deportation of Afghan Man." July 25. https://www.bbc.co.uk/news/world-europe-44948604.

Bhimull, Chandra. 2017. *Empire in the Air: Airline Travel and the African Diaspora.* New York: NYU Press.

Bridle, James. 2015. "Seamless Transitions." BookTwo, February 25. https://booktwo.org/notebook/seamless-transitions/.

Britton, Bianca. 2019. "They Saved Migrants from Deportation. Then They Faced Terror-Related Charges." CNN, February 8. https://www.cnn.com/2019/02/05/uk/stansted-15-deportation-charter-flights-uk-intl-gbr/index.html.

Caprotti, Frederico. 2011. "Visuality, Hybridity, and Colonialism: Imagining Ethiopia through Colonial Aviation, 1935–1940." *Annals of the Association of American Geographers* 101: 380–403.

CBC. 2014. "'No Man's Land: The Story of Saeed Jama's Deportation to Somalia.'" CBC Radio, November 4.

Corporate Watch. 2015. *Collective Expulsion: The Case against Britain's Mass Deportation Charter Flights.* London: Corporate Watch.

Council of the European Union. 2000. "Analysis of Replies to the Questionnaire Concerning the Practice of Member States, Including Iceland and Norway, with Regard to Transit for the Purpose of Expulsion by Air." May 4. 7941/00.

CPT. 2015. "Report to the Government of the Netherlands on the Visit to the Netherlands Carried Out by the European Committee for the Prevention of Torture and Inhuman or Degrading Treatment or Punishment (CPT) from 16 to 18 October, 2013." European Committee for the Prevention of Torture. CPT/Inf 14. Strasbourg: Council of Europe.

De Genova, Nicholas. 2010. "The Deportation Regime: Sovereignty, Space, and the Freedom of Movement." In *The Deportation Regime: Sovereignty, Space, and the Freedom of Movement,* edited by Nicholas De Genova and Nathalie Peutz, 33–65. Durham, NC: Duke University Press.

De Genova, Nicholas. 2013. "Spectacles of Migrant 'Illegality': The Scene of Exclusion, the Obscene of Inclusion." *Ethnic and Racial Studies* 36: 1180–98.

De Genova, Nicholas, and Nathalie Peutz, eds. 2010. *The Deportation Regime: Sovereignty, Space, and the Freedom of Movement.* Durham, NC: Duke University Press.

Deutsche Welle. 2017. "Things to Know about Deportations in Germany." June 5. https://www.dw.com/en/things-to-know-about-deportations-in-germany/a-39119049.

Didi-Huberman, Georges. 2002. *L'image survivante: Histoire de l'art et temps des fantômes selon Aby Warburg.* Paris: Editions de Minuit.

Drotbohm, Heike, and Ines Hasselberg. 2015. "Deportation, Anxiety, Justice: New Ethnographic Perspectives." *Journal of Ethnic and Migration Studies* 41 (4): 551–62.

Durand, Jacky. 2003. "Roissy-Bamako, avec escale au tribunal." *Libération,* June 10.

Englebert, Theo, Peter Aldhous, Jules Darmanin, and Ryan Broderick. 2017. "France Has Spent Millions of Dollars Renting Planes to Deport Migrants." *BuzzFeed News,* September 11. https://www.buzzfeednews.com/article/theoenglebert/investigation-on-the-millions-of-business-airplane-2td76.

Fekete, Liz. 2005. "The Deportation Machine: Europe, Asylum and Human Rights." *Race and Class* 47: 64–91.

Fekete, Liz. 2011. "Accelerated Removals: The Human Cost of EU Deportation Policies." *Race and Class* 52: 89–97.

Feys, Torsten. 2019. "Riding the Rails of Removal: The Impact of Railways on Border Controls and Expulsion Practices." *Journal of Transport History* 40 (2): 189–210.

Fischer, Nicholas. 2005. "Clandestins au secret: Contrôle et circulation de l'information dans les centres de rétention administrative français." *Cultures et Conflits* 57: 91–118.

Frankl, Michal. 2017. "Photographing Refugee Deportation: On Visual Representation of Refugees." *European Holocaust Research Infrastructure Document Blog*, January 1. https://blog.ehri-project.eu/2017/01/01/photographing-refugee-deportation/.

HM Chief Inspector of Prisons. 2011. "Detainees under Escort: Inspection of Escort and Removals to Nigeria." April 20–21. London: HM Inspectorate of Prisons.

HM Chief Inspector of Prisons. 2012. "Detainees under Escort: Inspection of Escort and Removals to Sri Lanka." December 6–7. London: HM Inspectorate of Prisons.

Kanstroom, Daniel. 2007. *Deportation Nation: Outsiders in American History.* Cambridge, MA: Harvard University Press.

Keita, Mahamadou. 2009. "Les gens reviennent choqués et sans rien" (interview). *Causes Communes*, no. 61.

Khosravi, Shahram, ed. 2017. *After Deportation: Ethnographic Perspectives.* London: Palgrave Macmillan.

Kranakis, Eda. 2010. "European Civil Aviation in an Era of Hegemonic Nationalism: Infrastructure, Air Mobility, and European Identity Formation, 1919–1933." In *Materializing Europe: Transnational Infrastructures and the Project of Europe*, edited by Alexander Badenhoch and Andreas Fickers, 290–326. New York: Palgrave Macmillan.

Lecadet, Clara. 2016. *Le manifeste des expulsés: Errance, survie et politique au Mali.* Tours : Presses Universitaires François Rabelais.

Lecadet, Clara. 2017a. "Accords de réadmission: Tensions et ripostes." *Plein Droit* 114 : 15–18.

Lecadet, Clara. 2017b. "Europe Confronted by Its Expelled Migrants." In *The Borders of "Europe": Autonomy of Migration, Tactics of Bordering*, edited by Nicholas De Genova, 141–64. Durham, NC: Duke University Press.

Lecadet, Clara. 2018. "Frères dans l'expulsion." *Vacarme* 83 (2): 67–71.

Lee, Dasom. 2011. "Deportation Reconstruction as Aid to Action." Institute of Race Relations, August 4. http://www.irr.org.uk/news/deportation-reconstruction-as-aid-to-action/.

Makaremi, Chowra. 2018. "Deportation and the Technification of Force: Violence in Democracy." *Technosphere Magazine*, January 15. https://technosphere

-magazine.hkw.de/p/Deportation-and-the-Technification-of-Force-Violence-in
-Democracy-ngjuok8Rb5q1U7ae54VHwp.

Monforte, Pierre. 2016. "The Border as a Space of Contention: The Spatial Strategies of
Protests against Border Controls in Europe." *Citizenship Studies* 20 (3–4): 411–26.

Nyers, Peter. 2003. "Abject Cosmopolitanism: The Politics of Protection in the Anti-
deportation Movement." *Third World Quarterly* 24 (6): 1069–93.

Parker, Noel, and Nick Vaughan-Williams. 2009. "Lines in the Sand? Towards an
Agenda for Critical Border Studies." *Geopolitics* 14: 582–87.

Peutz, Nathalie. 2006. "Embarking on an Anthropology of Removal." *Current
Anthropology* 47: 217–31.

Pirie, Gordon. 2017. *Air Empire: British Imperial Civil Aviation, 1919–39*. Manchester, UK: Manchester University Press.

Pirjola, Jari. 2015. "Flights of Shame or Dignified Return? Return Flights and Post-
return Monitoring." *European Journal of Law and Migration* 17: 305–28.

Salter, Mark B., ed. 2008. *Politics at the Airport*. Minneapolis: University of Minnesota Press.

Secoolio. 2009. "Mali l'ambassade de France jusitifie le refus d'embarquer des pas-
sagers." June 29. https://secoolio.over-blog.com/article-33254152.html.

Sniderman, Andrew Stobo. 2013. "Jama Warsame Is a Citizen of Nowhere."
Maclean's, December 10. https://www.macleans.ca/news/canada/jame
-warsame-is-a-citizen-of-nowhere/.

Steinmetz, Muriel. 2015. "A Bamako ils sont nombreux à vouloir partir à tout prix."
L'Humanité, June 16.

Stierl, Maurice. 2012. "'No One Is Illegal': Resistance and the Politics of Discomfort."
Globalizations 9 (3): 425–38.

Telegraph. 2009. "Asylum Airways—Your One-Way Flight to Deportation." May 23.
https://www.telegraph.co.uk/news/uknews/5374109/Asylum-airlines-your
-one-way-flight-to-deportation.html.

The Times (London). 2002. "Deportee 'Stunt' under Attack by Rights Groups."
September 21.

Tyler, Imogen. 2018. "Deportation Nation: Theresa May's Hostile Environment."
Journal for the Study of British Cultures 25 (1).

Vincent, Elise. 2010a. "Keita, le 'toubab' de l'aéroport." *Le Monde*, September 27.

Vincent, Elise. 2010b. "Le Mali manque de moyens pour accueillir les expulsés." *Le
Monde*, September 27.

Walters, William. 2002. "Deportation, Expulsion, and the International Police of
Aliens." *Citizenship Studies* 6 (3): 265–92.

Walters, William. 2016. "The Flight of the Deported: Aircraft, Deportation, and
Politics." *Geopolitics* 21: 435–58.

Walters, William. 2018. "Aviation as Deportation Infrastructure: Airports, Planes,
and Expulsion." *Journal of Ethnic and Migration Studies* 44 (16): 2796–2817.

Walters, William. 2019. "The Microphysics of Deportation: A Critical Reading of Return Flight Monitoring Reports." In *Proceedings of the 2018 ZiF Workshop "Studying Migration Policies at the Interface between Empirical Research and Normative Analysis,"* edited by M. Hoesch and L. Laube, 161–86. ULB Münster (miami.uni-muenster.de). https://repositorium.uni-muenster.de/document/miami/974edbb1-7a4f-438a-ae16-bc1bed153ace/artikel_hoesch-laube_2019a_Proceedings-complete.pdf.

Afterword: For the Migrant, the Way

Is the Life | Ranabir Samaddar

I

If you want to know the migrant, go out to be on the way. There you will meet
the migrant. The way is the congealed life of people whom we know as migrants. The way is the route, and you will see the modes of migrants moving—in
buses, trucks, vans, trains, on foot, walking, coming out of airports, or disembarking from ships, steamers, and boats. You will see them with infants and children
on mothers' backs, fathers' shoulders, or walking holding the kids' hands. Of
course, you will not always see them, for they may be the stowaways, hiding
from your eyes, the eyes of the police, the clutches of the guards, searchlights
in the ports, curious reporters, and kiosks of immigration clerks and officials.
Routes determine the roads; roads determine modes of escape and travel; also
at times modes obligate the migrants to opt for particular routes and roads, to
risk life and accept death. It is all a connected world made up of routes, roads,
living beings, and modes of flight and travel—what we call the migrant world.

Yet, it is very much like a fragmented geography of this world and the mind.
It is a scattered geography of trails and vehicles—through mountains, hills,
snowfields, deserts, narrow lanes, railway tracks, open fields under sprawling
sky, homes, prisons, camps, schools, narrow lanes and byways of a city, UN or
immigration offices, checkpoints, broken-up sections of walls and wires, and
also through families, workplaces, and time. The migrant world is thus like an
assemblage. Indeed, migratory paths are redrawn through the assemblages of

tactics involving migrant escapes, but, equally importantly, migrant hunts that turn migrant bodies into targets of capture. These cartographies, uneven and fragmented in nature, reorganize the network of events, sequences, associations, and agencies and enable the figure called the migrant to live in dual time—the real time of living, as well as the transmogrified time through which the sequence of events and persons goes like passing shots. Not without reason, some people say that only through the reconstruction of events of flight and mobility are our accounts of migration finally decolonized. If the real time belongs to the bourgeois management of human mobility—in Walter Benjamin's (1940) words "homogenous empty time," a time connected to the standardized global regime of control and discipline, the transmogrified time belongs to freedom and decolonization.

Alfred Hitchcock's *North by Northwest* (1959) was supposed to be the Hitchcock picture to end all Hitchcock pictures. Cinema lovers know it was not; rather, it became a new template to view the eternally intriguing story of crime, spaces, mistaken identities, accidents in life, incognito runs, wide-open fields, attacks by insidious agencies of life—therefore what else but an attack on the hero by a crop duster plane, and a narrative that could end only as consummation in a tunnel? The film became a commentary on flight and fantasy, discrete spaces and links, that could be bridged only by a narrative. The spatial invocations in the narratives of this collection on viapolitics at one level are, or at least seem to be, connected logically. But a closer examination suggests two complications: first, these different parts of the book may be considered as disparate, held tenuously only by a geopolitical logic but in their lifeworlds existing separately; second, as the geopolitical logic connects these discrete parts, these spaces make sense only when bridged. When bridged, however, there is a new game of spaces and movements. What are those unknown, insidious agencies of material life that link spaces in their destinies? What, then, is the larger story that produces these shifting spaces, gazes, identities, and perceptions? This collection of essays, analyses, and reportage presents a larger story of laws, surveillance, visions of flight and control, material and social infrastructural stories of human movement, and their interface with the neoliberal mode of governance. One will find here clues to how spaces are bridged and in the process acquire new identities, such as the Mediterranean or the Indian Ocean. This is how spatial identities are made. Though we have to remember, if there is any idea of a sovereign spatial identity, it will be quickly cut down by the cold sword of capital. Spaces are identified by geopolitical logic, which includes human movements; at the same time, the geopolitical logic by itself is being remade on a continuous basis by the calculations of capital. Thus, there may be areas and hence spaces excluded from the abovementioned logic; yet these will be the areas waiting for future logistical operation in the world of migration. It is a complex game.

As an instance of this complexity, let us consider the dynamics of return migration. Migrants may decide not to return even if they want to give up on their journey or the hard and unpredictable life they had chosen; when they have, as we say, a hard lesson there may be no welcome mat back home. Let us listen to one report, which describes the fate of a fisherman from a village in Senegal and his successive migratory attempts:

The fishing village has long sent its men to sea, but after foreign trawlers scraped the bottom clean, the men began coming back empty-handed. It has long sent its men abroad for work, too, but their luck is often no better. Last November, when El Hadji Macoura Diop, a thirty-seven-year-old fisherman, failed to reach Europe by boat, he could not bring himself to call his wife and tell her he was giving up. "I knew it would just destroy her," he said. Hard as it is to leave home for an unknown land and an uncertain future, coming back, migrants say can be even harder. . . . Thiaroye-sur-Mer has been a major source of migration for more than a decade. Hundreds of men have tried to reach Europe—mainly Spain. Everyone knows the migrant motto, "Barca ou barzakh," in English: "Barcelona or die." . . . To the outsider, Thiaroye-sur-Mer can seem like an idyllic place, not somewhere people would be eager to leave: Men sit on the beach, mending their nets, while children play in the surf. But when they do come back home, migrants often get a stark reminder of why they left in the first place. One recent day, Mr. Diop, the Thiaroye-sur-Mer fisherman who abandoned his attempt to reach Europe, and his five partners came back to shore with about 100 small silver fish called sardinella in their nets. Once the owner of the boat got his share, they would earn about a dollar each, he said. . . . More recently, the grapevine has advised them to go by air to Morocco, where Senegalese do not need visas, and then catch passage across the Mediterranean with a smuggler. From the roofs of the village houses, the view of the ocean goes on forever. It is easy to imagine that Europe might be just beyond the horizon. And it is possible to forget, if only for a moment, the many dangers of the journey. Often, it is the women who encourage the men to migrate. Mr. Diop's mother, Fatou Ndaw, fifty-five, chose him to go because he was the oldest of three brothers, and a fisherman. "He was the one who knows how to read the signs of the ocean," she said. . . .

Mr. Diop tried twice. On his first attempt, in 2006, he headed for the Canary Islands. Along the way, he watched as six people from his village died after bouts of vomiting and dehydration, their bodies tossed overboard with a prayer. Mr. Diop landed, but he was deported two days before an uncle living in Spain arrived to claim him, he said.

To pay for his second attempt, last fall, Mr. Diop's mother sold her jewelry; his wife, Mbayang Hanne, saved the money that she earned frying doughnuts under a tent on the beach and selling them with coffee. Mr. Diop bought a round-trip plane ticket to Casablanca, where he did not need a visa and could stay with a childhood friend. From there, he took a bus to Tangier and boarded a boat for Spain. This time, his boat was stopped before it reached international waters. Mr. Diop says he was fingerprinted and dropped at the Algerian border. He walked sixteen hours with other migrants until a car picked them up and took them to Casablanca. In Casablanca, the weather was bad and the boats were not running. He slept on the street in the rain. His round-trip ticket on Royal Air Maroc was expiring in two days. Homesick and miserable, Mr. Diop called his parents. They advised him to use the ticket to return home.

He spent some sleepless nights agonizing over whether to call his wife, and decided not to. At the airport back in Dakar, he did not even have enough money for a taxi. A stranger took pity on him and drove him home. To Mr. Diop's relief, his wife was out when he got there—but all that did was put off the inevitable. When she returned, she was shocked to find him in the house.... He and his family are saving for him to leave again. (Hartocollis 2019)

Roads and routes are chosen in this way. Or we may say they are not chosen. Routes and roads present themselves as fate before the migrants. Thus, like the preceding report, the following report of 2015 tells us of the broad forces that, almost like fate, ordain the routes and roads:

By now, the unceasing tides of migrants arriving at the ports of Sicily fall into loose national categories. The Syrians usually arrive with money, bearing broken lives in canvas bags, and are able to slip out of Italy, bound for affluent northern Europe. The Eritreans may be far less wealthy but they too are well organized, with networks that move them north as well. Then there are men like Agyemin Boateng and Prince Adawiah, who were scooped out of the Mediterranean this month by an Italian rescue ship. Both are from Ghana, and neither has a plan for a new life in Europe, nor, they say, did either of them ever plan to come to Italy. They were working as labourers in Libya, until life there became untenable and returning to Ghana became unfeasible.

"There are guns and bombs," said Mr. Adawiah, twenty-five, who worked in Tripoli for nearly three years. "Every day, there is shooting. I'm afraid. That is why I travelled to Italy." . . .

"We don't know anything," said one migrant, Shamsudeen Sawud, eighteen, who arrived in Italy more than a week ago. "No one is telling us anything." . . .

The authorities have not published figures for April yet, but humanitarian and migration groups confirm that a majority of the arriving migrants came originally from sub-Saharan African countries—some directly, with Italy as a destination, but many end up here less deliberately. . . .

Now, though . . . African migrants at the detention centre said there was rampant abuse in Libya. Some men said the construction bosses had stopped paying wages to labourers, and other men who did get their pay said they were preyed upon by criminal gangs, including marauding teenagers who robbed people at gunpoint. . . .

Several men said that sympathetic Libyans had put them in touch with smugglers as a means of saving their lives, even as the smugglers were actively seeking black labourers to make the trip. "They say, 'If you want to save your life, leave, and we will take you to Italy,'" Mr. Adawiah said of the smugglers.

The growing population of migrants in Italy is becoming a political controversy. A group of Italian mayors recently tried to block plans by the national government to distribute migrants to detention centers around the country. Italy has also been criticized for allowing many Syrians and Eritreans to pass through and apply for asylum in northern Europe, a violation of European Union policy. (Yardley 2015)

Establishing humanitarian bases, say at Lampedusa or at Idomeni, where the immigrants are herded by the hundreds to suffer, become sick, or in extreme cases die, or returning the detainees to homelands on the basis of a vigorous deportation policy, or declaring the policy of distributing the migrant population over the European continent—all these not only call for flexible reception modes and creation of what one of the coeditors of this volume, William Walters (2011), has called the "humanitarian border," they also impel the migrants to find and choose routes and roads. Walters reminds his readers that the "humanitarian is a complex domain possessing specific forms of governmental reason"

(2011, 143). As he says, it is thus not a second-order reality. It is the field where we can find the fault lines on the smooth space of globalization, where the terms *Global North* and *Global South* meet in a "concrete and abrasive way," where the humanitarian border and the "poverty frontier" meet, and where "gradients of wealth and poverty, citizenship and non-citizenship appear especially sharply" (146). The humanitarian border thus materializes only in a certain specific context and way. It not only brings back the old frontier strategy, it also accommodates the tearing lines of conflict within the process of globalization. In this postcolonial context, values play, as in colonial times, a big role in producing humanitarianism and protection policy. Frontier making then also banked on a humanitarian ethos. This time, too, plans are afoot to reduce the humanitarian load on the state. In this worldwide remaking of boundaries, one crucial fact is that migration is rekindling old divisions. Thus, besides the divisions between Europe and Asia and Europe and Africa, we have now a reemergence of supposed divisions between western Europe and eastern Europe, the United Kingdom and Europe, or between North Africans and southern Africans. Migratory movements produce these divisions inasmuch as these divisions produce migratory movements. This collection testifies to the dynamics of borders and frontiers, and the intriguing and dramatic process of frontier making.

II

Yet, reading the empirically rich accounts of this book, we cannot but sense that the book suggests something more concrete than general statements in terms of the economy of punishment that produces viapolitics. Deportation modes, their cost effectiveness, efficiency, and impact; resettlement plans including plans to set up camps and other detention centers; and various modes of curbing mobility and confining the migrants as far as possible—all these go into making the economy of punishment, which shapes in turn migration strategies of roads, routes, and vehicles. This is not new, for the massive colonial experience of controlling alien societies was essentially one of finding the most effective ways to control, punishment, and discipline. These modes made the colonial economy of punishment. In northeastern colonial India, indentured laborers used the telegraph poles as guides to figure out escape routes. Something similar is visible today. From rail routes and the location of big railway junctions to the dynamics of governmental relief and dole disbursement operations (as in Bihar) in flood-stricken areas from where migrants in their hundreds leave in search of work in distant parts of the country—punitive modes, governmental relief operations, and infrastructure operate as crucial cogs in the armature of human mobility. In his seminal work, *Late Victorian Holocausts*, Mike Davis (2002) has shown how one of the specters facing rulers in the time of famine in the colonies was escaping bands of starving population groups, creating anarchy in nearby towns or simply dying irresponsibly, dropping dead here and there, and making governance impossible. In India, the Famine Code was framed in this context. One historian (Chakraborty 2011) has concluded:

> Overall, the available data do not indicate the socio-economic groups from which the emigrants were drawn, but the observations of a number of district collectors suggest that many "disbanded sepoys," weavers, agricultural labourers, and others engaged in low-caste service occupations were among them. A majority of emigrants were from rural areas and from "overcrowded agricultural districts," where "crop failure could plunge sections of the village community into near-starvation." In fact, there was a strong correlation between emigration and harvest conditions. Acute scarcity during 1873–75 in Bihar, Oudh and NW Provinces provoked large-scale emigration through the port of Calcutta. The famine in south India during 1874–78 also resulted in heavy emigration. Conversely, in good agricultural years recruits were not easily available. It has been reported that road blocks were hastily established to stem the flood of "stick-thin country people" into Bombay and Pune while in Madras the police forcibly expelled some 25,000 famine escapees. There is little doubt about the correlation between scarcity and forced migration. Most of the emigrants probably left their villages for the first time in their lives, and they were not fully aware of the hardships involved in long voyages and in living abroad. Diseases—cholera, typhoid, dysentery—were often rampant in the depots. Mortality among the emigrants was consequently high. Mortality at sea was alarmingly high. Before 1870, about 17 to 20 per cent of the labourers deported from the port of Calcutta died before they reached their destination. The data for the years 1871–90 of voyages to British Guyana suggest that the death rate on board was about 15 per 1000. The overall impact of colonialism was negative. There was no increase in per capita income between 1757 and 1947; income probably declined in the second half of the nineteenth century. It is an abiding irony that the cash crop boom accompanied a decline in agrarian productivity and food security. The great export boom of cash crops benefited the money lenders, absentee landlords, urban merchants and a handful of Indian industrialists. During

what constituted, in the imagination of the likes of Kipling and Curzon, the "the glorious imperial half century" (1872–1921) life expectancy of ordinary Indians fell by a staggering twenty per cent. *Pax Britannica*, it would appear, had more victims than long centuries of war.[1]

Likewise, studies of the Indian Ocean tell us of the colonial histories of setting up prison islands, networks of superintendence and surveillance, and new ports, thus creating new maps of usage of the seas—both for the rulers and for the migrants and escapees. Imperial infrastructure (the proliferation of steamships, railways, telegraph, and networks of roads and streets established through the mode of town planning) was probably one of the biggest marks of the second half of the nineteenth century in colonial history. The land and oceanic histories of carriers and vehicles in colonial times tell us of the infrastructure of human movement and the interrelations between the infrastructure and the terrains of population movements and construction of borders. This was the moment, or at least one moment, in the birth of viapolitics. The tale of overlapping domains of control and escape, and punishment and freedom, forms one of the most insightful aspects of the politics of roads and routes. The invention and designing of controls and escapes went hand in hand—like the interlocked adversaries in mortal combat.

Travelers' trajectories, best demonstrated in their autobiographies, interviews, and other depositions, tell us of the complex notion of illegality. Illegality in turn complicates the idea of a route, and thus the Balkan route, Mediterranean or eastern Mediterranean route, or the Bay of Bengal route. It looks as if we are in the midst of a war, and the generals have to find routes. Yet if migrant routes remind us of war, should it surprise us? For is it not said, *inter arma enim silent leges*, in the time of war law falls silent? Punishment has to produce the illegal; otherwise, how can punishment be legal? Much of global migration has to be illegal, by which we mean that migration as an act will be on the border of legality, questionable in terms of law. Therefore it is important to study the illegalism of migration in the context of general illegalisms in society in a particular time—to understand both the illegalisms of lower classes who will vote with their feet on the issue of the morality of the ways they are ruled as well as the legalisms the rulers continuously manufacture. In the lecture series titled *The Punitive Society*, Michel Foucault (2015) cautioned us not to see the illegalism of any particular class or segment of population in isolation but to see them in the context of the general trajectory of illegalism in which rulers often participated until it was convenient for them to practice legality. The history of the routes of circulation of credit, capital, money, arms, information, and so on is marked by illegal practices. And only when the circulation stabilized did the law give its seal of approval. Banking practices, company practices, digital practices—to name only few—are all marked by illegal origins. Think of the ways of doing business by chartered companies in the early modern age, like the East India Company, or the illegal financing of various operations including military operations, or the ways of funding data companies like IBM in its initial days. We shall see the interplay of legality and illegality in the very idea of "operation" (Mezzadra and Neilson 2019).

We must persist with this point a little more. In *The Punitive Society*, Didier Fassin (2015) reminds us, the idea of "illegalism" is linked by Foucault with another great idea, that of the civil war. Reading through the essays of this book, we cannot fail to imagine a scenario of civil war. It is not a Hobbesian civil war—a war of everyone against the others, ending with a compact among all to create an authority for the protection of all, the protection of everyone from the marauding other. This civil war is fought by the rulers against the society of the dis-propertied, by one section of society against another; it is also a war over the place of law in making society, fought by those whom society will designate as the criminal. The stakes in the management of migration are thus high, because they involve claims and counterclaims over resources, urban land, budgetary funds, and social capital, and precisely because the fight will determine the fate of the modes of circulation on the basis of which the economy will be secured. These essays are the windows through which to make sense of the migrant as the lawbreaker, the criminal, whom law must punish. These accounts remind us of other accounts of geopower, maritime borders and frontiers, naval wars, naval histories, migrant ships, rescue ships, and guarding vessels. It is therefore important to historicize the notion of roads and routes. Migration appears in the historical glass as the companion of phenomena like sea power or air power. Institutional accounts of the modes of migration appear in the historical mirror of law as the battleground of a civil war over the very way in which modern capitalism wants to move ahead.

Limits of law should lead us to the importance of networks in our time. Of course this was true also of colonial times, when networks of legal and quasi-legal intelligibility developed and facilitated empire building in such distant lands as Kenya, Ireland, and India. Today, however, administrative and policy regimes have overwhelmed the legal dimension of migration management. Networks of roads, markets, institutions, transportation modes, transfer procedures of money, information, and credit, and administrative policies influence the ways migrants move. This is best illustrated in the lives of the urban migrants and refugees as the postcolonial city increasingly resembles a cluster of camps, and camps look like cities. Networks reflect the continuous reorganization of space in the forms of corridors, zones, and supply routes. They make reorganization of laws an imperative for states. For this imperative, no aspect of social governance is as relevant as that of migration management. The chapters of this book suggest that the world of migration is forever going to be one that borders legality and illegality, because networks of laws, administrative practices, and policy regimes, along with other networks of communications and social forms, guide the migrants' world.

In short, migration presents a different scenario of globalization where control of the migrant reality is not the concern of governments only. Employers, recruitment agents, labor brokers in sending and receiving countries, lawyers, courts, training institutes, moneylenders and other credit agencies, bureaucrats, municipal authorities, smugglers, and a wide variety of intermediaries seek to gain from the transnational flow of workers and shelter seekers. Migrant routes often follow crime routes and act as the underside of the official story of globalization. Networks grew up as the template of mobility, some of which were, in Charles Tilly's language, "transplanted networks." Tilly pointed out that by the early nineteenth century, evolving capitalist economic and property relations marked by the spread of wage labor, the separation of households from the means of production, and the rising productivity of commercial agriculture, had combined with diminishing land resources and an expanding demand for labor in urban areas to make long-distance migration a rational choice for many Europeans. Local conditions, including land tenure patterns, agricultural requirements, and resource management, profoundly influenced rates of migration and return. They also determined the kinds of people who emigrated, such as from certain parts of southern Italy, where land ownership was still possible, and where the emigrants therefore hoped to use their American wages to purchase land upon their return. The sons of Norwegian cattle farmers shut out of ownership also left Europe. In all these acts of emigration, awareness of networks became a critical factor (Tilly 1990, 79–95; 2007). On the other hand, workers also developed different means to cope with these control mechanisms, even if partially most of the time, and if possible to evade them. But vulnerability remained overwhelming.

This book, like all good books, throws up in the end more questions than it answers. We may ask: Why is it that migration studies, forced migration studies in particular, were for long caught up in the ideology of government, care, and protection—elements that complete the arc of humanitarianism? Such a question implies also asking why vulnerability has to be measured most of the time (for instance, by duration, such as protracted or short) and by the magnitude of the protection involved. Yet it is also true that these inquiries bear the unmistakable imprint of an age when the process of displacement appears to have overwhelmed societies to such an extent that the concepts and policies relating to displacement appear to be nature-imposed necessity. Hence, the given knowledge of forced migration studies appears to treat all nonofficial, nonlegal knowledge, particularly preexisting nonofficial and nonlegal knowledge on migration, as belonging to nature, which is prescientific and prepractical in this age. Therefore important is the historical intelligibility of a concept, also to see the history of migration in modes, infrastructures, institutions, and continuities and discontinuities, which will require interepoch comparisons, handling of large data series, and, referring to Charles Tilly (1994; see also Tilly 1980) again, making sense of what he called, more than two decades back, history through big data.

Much of the scientific work in migration studies will become possible when we look back at other historical phases of transition, for example, when landed property was brought under the regime of the contract. For precisely at the very moment when the principle of contract triumphed and the range of feudal rights disappeared, peasant masses began to flee in the face of a new system of juridical appropriation, which dispossessed and pauperized vast populations of day laborers, smallholders, and petty traders, who could now live only by practicing illegalisms. With escape began the first illegal act.[2] Then too they had to decide how to escape, when to escape, what route to choose to escape....

Perhaps the main question that this book throws out to readers is not much different from that time. We can hope that this book will succeed in contributing to the existing corpus of historical intelligibility of the migration processes of our time.

Notes

1 The sources Chakraborty drew from are Hunter (2004, 497), Visaria and Visaria (1984, 515), Davis (2002, 26–27, 311ff.), Tinker (1974, 161–66), Davis and Huttenback (1987, 73–118).

2 In colonial India this was called by the British administrators the "up-stick habit," when entire villages, in order to escape the landlords and the colonial rent officials,

used to vanish overnight, with the villagers taking their bamboo huts away with them, thus leaving no trace of the settlement in question.

References

Benjamin, Walter. 1940. "On the Concept of History." Marxist Internet Archive. https://www.marxists.org/reference/archive/benjamin/1940/history.htm.

Chakraborty, Subhas Ranjan. 2011. "Colonialism, Resource Crisis, and Forced Migration." CRG Research Paper Series, Policies and Practices, 42. Calcutta: Calcutta Research Group.

Davis, Lance, and Richard Huttenback. 1987. *Mammon and the Pursuit of Empire: The Political Economy of British Imperialism, 1860–1912.* Cambridge: Cambridge University Press.

Davis, Mike. 2002. *Late Victorian Holocausts: El Niño Famines and the Making of the Third World.* London: Verso.

Fassin, Didier. 2015. "Didier Fassin on *The Punitive Society.*" *13/13: Michel Foucault's Collège de France Lectures* (blog). http://blogs.law.columbia.edu/foucault1313 /2015/10/07/didier-fassin-on-the-punitive-society/.

Foucault, Michel. 2015. *The Punitive Society: Lectures at the Collège de France, 1972–73.* New York: Palgrave Macmillan.

Hartocollis, Anemona. 2019. "A Hard Lesson for Migrants Who Give Up: There May Be No Welcome Mat Back Home." *New York Times*, September 15. https://www.nytimes.com/2019/09/15/world/africa/africa-migrants-return -home.html.

Hunter, William Wilson. 2004. *India and the Indians.* Edited by Herbert Risley. New Delhi: Reprint.

Mezzadra, Sandro, and Brett Neilson. 2019. *The Politics of Operations: Excavating Contemporary Capitalism.* Durham, NC: Duke University Press.

Tilly, Charles. 1980. *The Old New Social History and the New Old Social History.* Centre for Research and Social Organization Working Paper 218. Ann Arbor: University of Michigan Press.

Tilly, Charles. 1990. "Transplanted Networks." In *Immigration Reconsidered: History, Sociology and Politics,* edited by Virginia Yans-McLaughlin. New York: Oxford University Press.

Tilly, Charles. 1994. *Big Structures, Large Processes, Huge Comparisons.* New York: Russell Sage.

Tilly, Charles. 2007. "Trust Networks in Transnational Migration." *Sociological Forum* 22 (1): 3–24.

Tinker, Hugh. 1974. *A New System of Slavery: The Export of Indian Labour Overseas, 1830–1920.* Oxford: Oxford University Press.

Visaria, Leela, and Pravin Visaria. 1984. "Population." In *Cambridge Economic History of India*, vol. 2, edited by Dharma Kumar. Cambridge: Cambridge University Press.

Walters, William. 2011. "Foucault and Frontiers: Notes on the Birth of the Humanitarian Border." In *Governmentality: Current Issues and Future Challenges*, edited by Ulrich Bröckling, Susanne Krasmann, and Thomas Lemke, 138–64. London: Routledge.

Yardley, Jim. 2015. "Displaced Again and Again: Some Migrants Had No Plan to Land in Italy." *New York Times*, May 1. https://www.nytimes.com/2015/05/02/world/europe/displaced-again-and-again-some-african-migrants-had-no-plan-to-land-in-italy.html.

CONTRIBUTORS

ETHAN BLUE, senior lecturer in history at the University of Western Australia, is the author of the forthcoming *The Deportation Express: A History of America through Forced Removal* (2021). His previous works include *Doing Time in the Depression: Everyday Life in Texas and California Prisons* (2012) and the coauthored *Engineering and War: Militarism, Ethics, Institutions, Alternatives* (2013). His work has appeared in *Pacific Historical Review, Journal of Social History, Radical History Review, National Identities,* and *Law, Culture and the Humanities,* among other venues. His research focuses on critical prison studies, broadly conceived, in settler-colonial societies.

MARIBEL CASAS-CORTES was recently awarded a *Ramon y Cajal* research fellowship from the European Union and Spain's Research Agency to conduct research in the Department of Sociology of the University of Zaragoza (Spain). She holds a PhD in cultural anthropology from the University of North Carolina at Chapel Hill. Her publications include articles in journals such as *Citizenship Studies, Rethinking Marxism, Cultural Studies* and *Anthropology Quarterly,* as well as book chapters in edited volumes such as *Insurgent Encounters: Transnational Activism, Ethnography and the Political* (Duke University Press, 2013), *The Handbook on Critical Geographies of Migration* (2019), and *Mapping Precariousness, Labour Insecurity and Uncertain Livelihoods: Subjectivities in Resistance* (2017).

JULIE Y. CHU is an anthropologist at the University of Chicago with interests in mobility and migration, economy and value, material culture, media and technology, and the state. She is the author of *Cosmologies of Credit: Transnational Mobility and the Politics of Destination in China* (Duke University Press, 2010). Her current project is titled *The Hinge of Time: Infrastructure and Chronopolitics at China's Global Edge*. Based on fieldwork in transit zones between southern China and the United States, this project analyzes the various infrastructures in place (legal-rational, cosmic, piratical) for managing the temporal intensities and rhythms of people and things on the move.

SEBASTIAN COBARRUBIAS currently works as a full-time ARAID researcher in the Geography Department at the University of Zaragoza (Spain). Previously he was an assistant professor in the Global Studies Department at the University of North Carolina–Charlotte. His research interests include border studies, social movements, and critical cartographic theory. He has a PhD in human geography from UNC–Chapel Hill and has published in journals such as *Antipode, Political Geography,* and *European and Urban Regional Studies.* He has also contributed to edited volumes including *Estados de Contención, Estados de Detención* (2017), *The Handbook on Critical Geographies of Migration* (2019), and *Anthropology of Scale: Struggles and Modalities of Modern Power* (2020).

GLENDA GARELLI is lecturer in critical human geography at the University of Leeds, where she also serves as the School of Geography widening participation officer. Her research on migration and refugee issues in the Mediterranean region has appeared in a range of peer-reviewed journals, a monograph, and several edited books. She also translated a volume on Italian critical thought. Her current research project, "GLiTCH" (funded by the Economic and Social Research Council), explores the use of digital technologies and connectivity platforms in the governance of refugees and local populations in Lebanon and Jordan. She is part of the Bauman Institute Management Network and the Leeds Migration Research Network.

CHARLES HELLER is a researcher and filmmaker whose work has a long-standing focus on the politics of migration. In 2015, he completed a PhD in research architecture at Goldsmiths, University of London, where he continues to be affiliated as a research fellow, focusing on migration and its control across the Mediterranean Sea. He is currently research associate at the Centre on Conflict, Development and Peacebuilding, Graduate Institute, Geneva. Together with Lorenzo Pezzani, in 2011 he cofounded Forensic Oceanography, a collaborative project that critically investigates the militarized border regime in the Mediterranean Sea, as well as the WatchTheMed platform. Together with a wide network of NGOs, scientists, journalists, and activist groups, he has produced maps, video animations, installations, and human rights reports that attempt to document and challenge the ongoing death of migrants at sea. His work has been used as evidence in courts of law, published across different media and academic outlets, and exhibited widely.

SABINE HESS has been a full professor of Cultural Anthropology/European Ethnology at the University of Göttingen, Germany, since 2011. She specializes in migration and border studies, focusing on forms of transnationalization and Europeanization, with a specific interest in the external border region in southeastern Europe. She is a founding member of the European interdisciplinary Network on Critical Migration and Border Studies (kritnet) and directs the interdisciplinary Laboratory on Migration and Border Regime Studies at the University of Göttingen, which provides space for regular discussions on theories and research for eighteen PhD and postdoctoral students in their respective fields. She is author and coauthor of several volumes and is founding member of the editorial board of *Movements: Journal on Critical Border and Migration Regime Studies*.

BERND KASPAREK is a mathematician and cultural anthropologist with a focus on migration and border studies. He worked at the University of Göttingen, Germany, in the HORIZON 2020 funded research project RESPOND: Multilevel Governance of Mass Migration in Europe and Beyond (2017–2020). He recently completed his PhD with an ethnographic thesis on the European border agency FRONTEX; his book is forthcoming in 2021. His further research interests are the government of migration, Europeanization, digital infrastructures, racism, and regime theory. He is a member of the Network for Critical Migration and Border Regime Studies (kritnet), a member of the board of the journal *Movements: Journal on Critical Migration and Border Regime Studies*, and on the board of the research association BorderMonitoring.eu.

CLARA LECADET is a researcher at the National Center for Scientific Research and a member of the Institut Interdisciplinaire d'Anthropologie du Contemporain in Paris, France. Her research focuses on the emergence of expelled migrants' protest movements in Africa, and on the various forms of organization used by expelled migrants during the postexpulsion period. She coedited with Michel Agier *Un monde de camps* (2014) and with Jean-Frédéric de Hasque *Après les camps: Traces, mémoires et mutations des camps de réfugiés* (2019). She is the author of *Le manifeste des expulsés* (2016). She is currently participating in the Air Deportation Project directed by William Walters.

JOHAN LINDQUIST is professor of social anthropology at Stockholm University in Sweden. He is a member of the editorial board of *Pacific Affairs*, has published articles in journals such as *Ethnos, Journal of the Royal Anthropological Institute, Mobilities, Public Culture, Pacific Affairs*, and *International Migration Review*, is the coeditor of *Figures of Southeast Asian Modernity* (2013), the author of *The Anxieties of Mobility: Development and Migration in the Indonesian Borderlands* (2009), and the director of B.A.T.A.M. (2005).

RENISA MAWANI is professor of sociology and recurring chair of the Law and Society Program at the University of British Columbia. Her first book, *Colonial Proximities* (2009), details a set of legal encounters between Indigenous peoples, Chinese migrants, mixed-race populations, and Europeans in late nineteenth- and early twentieth-century British Columbia. Her second book, *Across Oceans of Law* (Duke University Press, 2018), is a global and maritime legal history of the *S.S. Komagata Maru*. With Iza Hussin, she is coeditor of "The Travels of Law: Indian Ocean Itineraries," published in *Law and History Review* (2014).

LORENZO PEZZANI is an architect and researcher. He is currently lecturer at Goldsmiths, University of London, where he leads the MA studio in forensic architecture. His research deals with the spatial politics and visual cultures of migration, with a particular focus on the geography of the ocean. Together with Charles Heller, in 2011 he cofounded Forensic Oceanography, a collaborative project that critically investigates the militarized border regime in the Mediterranean Sea, as well as the WatchTheMed platform. Together with a wide network of NGOs, scientists, journalists, and activist groups, he has produced maps, video animations, installations, and human right reports that attempt to document and challenge the ongoing death of migrants at sea. His work has been used as evidence in courts of law, published across different media and academic outlets, and exhibited widely.

RANABIR SAMADDAR is currently Distinguished Chair in Migration and Forced Migration Studies, Calcutta Research Group, Kolkata, India. He belongs to the critical school of thinking and is considered as one of the foremost theorists in the field of migration and forced migration studies. His writings on migration, forms of labor, urbanization, and political struggles have signaled a new turn in postcolonial thinking. Among his influential works is *The Marginal Nation: Transborder Migration from Bangladesh to West Bengal* (1999). His recent works are *Karl Marx and the Postcolonial Age* (2018) and the *Postcolonial Age of Migration* (2020).

AMAHA SENU is a visiting research fellow at the Johannesburg Institute for Advanced Study at the University of Johannesburg. His research has a maritime focus with interests in migration and mobility, security and borders, maritime security and global governance, and globalization and crime. He is also an associate fellow with the Seafarers International Research Centre at Cardiff University, where he completed his doctoral research on the issue of maritime stowaways in global shipping.

MARTINA TAZZIOLI is lecturer in Politics and Technology at Goldsmiths. She is the author of *The Making of Migration: The Biopoltics of Mobility at Europe's Borders* (2020), *Spaces of Governmentality: Autonomous Migration and the Arab Uprisings* (2015), and *Tunisia as a Revolutionized Space of Migration* (2016). She is coeditor of *Foucault and the History of our Present* (2015) and *Foucault and the Making of Subjects* (2016). Martina is on the editorial board of the journal *Radical Philosophy*. Her new book project is titled *Border Abolitionism: Migration Containment and the Genealogies of Struggles and Rescue*, and she is coauthoring a book with W. Davies, S. Dutta and N. Taylor about the political-economic transformations triggered by COVID-19 in the UK.

WILLIAM WALTERS is a professor of political sociology in the Department of Political Science and the Department of Sociology and Anthropology at Carleton University, Canada. His main research interests are secrecy and security, borders and migration, mobility and politics, and infrastructure and power. His most recent book is *State Secrecy and Security: Refiguring the Covert Imaginary* (2021). Previous books include *Unemployment and Government: Genealogies of the Social* (2000), *Governing Europe* (2005, coauthored with Jens Henrik Haahr), *Governmentality: Critical Encounters* (2012), and the coedited collection *Global Governmentality* (2004). He is the principal investigator on the Air Deportation Project, a five-year investigation (funded by Canada's Social Sciences and Humanities Research Council) into the aerial geographies of forced removal and expulsion in and from Europe.

INDEX

Page numbers in italics indicate figures.

53n26; open-plan systems, 42–45, 47–48. *See also* prison vehicles; trains

deportees: risks to, 272–73; status of, 267, *269*, 270–71

Didi-Huberman, Georges, 260

Dietrich, Helmut, 196–97, 199–200

Diop, El Hadji Macoura, 283–84

Discipline and Punish (Foucault), 35, 51–52

Dublin regulation, 189, 204n1

E. coli, 116–17

economy of punishments, 286–87

Elden, Stuart, 20, 251

El-Shaarawi, Nadia, 190–91, 193

Emergency Trust Fund for Africa, 177n20

environmentality, 24n6

Eritrean migrants, 284

EU Borderlands: Mapping Changing Geographies of Jurisdictions and Sovereignties project, 154

EUNAVFOR MED, 229

"Euro-(con)centric geographical imaginary", 154–55, *156–57*, 158–63, 174

EU-Turkey agreement (2016), 191

Europe: integration of, 193; migrant crisis, 12, 176n8, 211, 244; and migrant imaginations, 241

European Union: and Action Plan Iraq, 196–98; Dublin III, 268; as fortress, 158, 196; internal borders, 177–78n21; migration policies of, 155, *156–57*, 158–64, 172–73, 194–95, 204, 217, 228–29, 245; and non-EU governments, 165–66, 172–74, 198–99; Return Directive, 260, 265; Schengen Zone, *156*, 188, 194–99; visa denials by, 217

Eurosur, 223

exclusion, by routes, 4, 7

expelled migrants, status of, 267, *269*, 270–71

Famine Code, 287

Fassin, Didier, 289

forced mobility, 245–46, 253n3, 287, 291

foreign policy, and migration policies, 155

Forensic Oceanography project, 216, 220–21

Forschungsgesellschaft Flucht und Migration (Germany), 196

fortress Europe, 158

Foucault, Michel, 7, 13, 24n4, 35, 37, 51–52, 88, 240

foul airs, 115–16, 118

Four Boats Stranded: Red and Yellow, Black and White (Lum), 23, 25n9

France, border operations by, 213, 215, 235

France-Italy border. *See* Italy-France border

freedom/unfreedom, 66, 108. *See also* contract labor systems; *Komagata Maru*; slavery

French prisoners, 35–36

Frontex: and deportations, 265; Hera operations, 160, 165, 171, 213, 223; Triton operations, 224, *225*, 228

frontier strategies, 286. *See also* United States

Garelli, Glenda, 20–21, 235–53

genocide, of Indigenous peoples, 40

geophysics of migration, 19, 22, 209

geopolitical logics, 282–83

geopower, 19, 289

Georgi, Fabian, 199–200

Germany, 189, 193, 261

Gilroy, Paul, 63

Global Approach to Migration and Mobility, 154, 158–59, 163, 198–99

Global South, visa denials to, 217

Goffman, Erving, 88

Goldberg, Oskar, 258, *259*, 260, 263, 270–71, 275

Golden Venture, 108, 112

Greece, 188

Grosz, Elisabeth, 19

Guattari, Felix, 24n3

Hameršak, Marijana, 190

Hanne, Mbayang, 284

Harper, Stephen, 1, *2*

Hartman, Saidiya, 62

Mediterranean, 177n17, 218. *See also* Action Plan Iraq; Balkan Route; trajectories

routes thinking, 153, 161–62, 164–65, 170–73, 198

"rule of colonial difference," 6

Russell, Leo, 45–47

Samaddar, Ranabir, 10, 281–92

Santer, Kiri, 190

Sassen, Saskia, 11, 219, 226

Sawud, Shamsudeen, 285

Scheffner, Philippe, 230n3

Schengen Agreement, 194, 217

Schengen Zone, *156*, 188, 194–99

Schot, Johan, 193

Seahorse operations, 160–61, 165, 176n10

Security, Territory, Population (Foucault), 240

Séméga, Ahmed Diane, 273

Senu, Amaha, 14, 84–101, 225

Serbia, 187–88, 202–3

settler colonialism, in the US, 21, 36–37, 41, 51

shared knowledge, 17; of the Italy-France border, 242, 247–50, 252; of stowaways, 86–88, 95–97, 99–100; and technology, 248–50

Shiozaki, Yokichi, 70, *71*, 75

shipping containers, and human cargo, 110, *111*, 116–17

ships, 7, 61, 92; authority systems, 14, 64, 89; and forced labor transport, 37–38; logbooks, 90; and the Middle Passage, 63; modern invisibility of, 85–86, 88; and power relations, 13; of refugees, 194, *195*; search processes, 90–91, 99; and stowaways, 95–96. *See also* slave ships; *specific vessels*; stowaways

Shiraishi, Saya, 131, 134, 139, 141

Sierra Leone, 272–74

Silverman, Stephanie, 4

Silvey, Rachel, 144, 149n4

Singh, Amar, 69

Singh, Bhan, 67–72, 75

Singh, Gurdit, 4, 58, 65–67, *71*, 72, 74–76

Singh, Indar, 58, 60, 62, 66, 77–78

Singh, Nanak, 75

Singh, Pal, 76

Singh, Sundar, 73

Singh, Udan, 67

slavery, scholarship surrounding, 62–63, 66, 73

slaves, 36–38, 52

slave ships, 38, 63–64, 115; captains' authority, 64; and contract labor, 40; migrant ships compared to, 106; revolts on, 73; and slavery scholarship, 66. *See also Brookes*

Slovenia, 203

Smallwood, Stephanie, 64, 66

Smith, Adam, 107

Smith, Arthur, 118

Somalia, deportations to, 266–67

"Some Tips for the Long-Distance Traveler" (Abdul-Ahad), 183–84, *185*

South Asian workers, 40

Southern Pacific trains, 41–42, 47–48

Spain, 159–61

spatial identities, 282

Spillers, Hortense, 63–64

Stanley, Leo, 47

Steinberg, Philip, 86

Steyerl, Hito, 211

Stilgoe, John, 44

stowaways, 14, 85–86; costs of, 87, 101n6; historiography, 89–90; identity as, 86–87; interrogating, 93–94; interviews with, 88; lack of scholarship about, 85, 99; managing, 91–95; and mobility control, 87; P&I clubs, 84–85, 91–95, 100, 101n6; repatriation of, 94–95; as security problems, 90; shared knowledge by, 86–88, 95–97, 99–100; ship searches, 90–91, 99; technological detection of, 116–17; victimization of, 96–100. *See also* human cargo

"Strategy Paper on Immigration and Asylum Policy" (1998), 155, *156–57*, 158–63, 175n4, 175–76nn4–6

www.ingramcontent.com/pod-product-compliance
Lightning Source LLC
Chambersburg PA
CBHW071731270326
41928CB00013B/2641